FRANK LLOYD WRIGHT
COLLECTED WRITINGS

FRANK LLOYD WRIGHT
COLLECTED WRITINGS

Volume **5**

1949–1959

Edited by
Bruce Brooks Pfeiffer

Introduction by Kenneth Frampton

ank Lloyd Wright Foundation

First published in the United States of America in 1995 by
Rizzoli International Publications, Inc.
300 Park Avenue South, New York, New York 10010
Copyright © The Frank Lloyd Wright Foundation 1995

Library of Congress Cataloging-in-Publication Data
(Revised for Vol. 5)

Wright, Frank Lloyd, 1867–1959.
    Frank Lloyd Wright collected writings.
        Includes indexes.
        Contents: v. 1. 1894–1930—v. 2. 1930–1932—
        v. 3. 1931–1939—v. 4. 1939–1949—v. 5. 1949–1959.
        1. Wright, Frank Lloyd, 1867–1959—Philosophy.
        I. Pfeiffer, Bruce Brooks, II. Wright Frank Lloyd, 1867–1959—
        Autobiography—1992. III. Title.
            NA737.W7A35 1992   720   91–40987

        ISBN 0-8478-1546-3 (HC : v. 1).—ISBN 0-8478-1547-1 (pbk. : v. 1).—
        ISBN 0-8478-1548-X (HC : v. 2).—ISBN 0-8478-1549-8 (pbk. : v. 2).—
        ISBN 0-8478-1699-0 (HC : v. 3).—ISBN 0-8478-1700-8 (pbk. : v. 3).—
        ISBN 0-8478-1803-9 (HC : v. 4).—ISBN 0-8478-1804-7 (pbk. : v. 4).—
        ISBN 0-8478-1854-3 (HC : v. 5).—ISBN 0-8478-1855-1 (pbk : v. 5).

Printed in Hong Kong

Designed by Sisco & Evans, New York

Frontispiece: Frank Lloyd Wright, Taliesin West, 1955.
Photograph by John Amarantides. Fdn FA#6007.0051

CONTENTS

Frank Lloyd Wright, Hillside drafting room, 1957. Photograph by John Amarantides. FLLW Fdn FA#6007.0028

INTRODUCTION

This last volume of Wright's collected writings begins in 1950 and continues uninterruptedly until his death, at the age of ninety-one, in 1959. As is invariably the case with one of mature years, Wright had long been in the habit of repeating himself, and this tendency becomes particularly apparent in *The Living City* (1958), which is largely a repetition of his earlier book *When Democracy Builds* (1945). Throughout the fifties he reworks much familiar ground, remonstrating in general with the failed promise of our civilization and reacting sharply from time to time to events of the day, whether minor incidents or major disasters. In *The Architectural Forum* of April 1951, he expresses his despair at the increasing mechanization of everyday life and at the onslaught of its ever escalating speed. In the face of this, he urges the youth of his time to strengthen themselves by embracing the Buddhist doctrine of tranquillity. Elsewhere he belabors the reader with his pet anathemas, from his total contempt for all forms of speculation to his unremitting repudiation of urban congestion.

In the early fifties, he returns to his enthusiasm for Eugène-Emmanuel Viollet-le-Duc and to his simultaneous condemnation of both the Renaissance and the International Style, seeing the latter as part of the same classicizing impulse running forward from the middle of the fifteenth century to the present. As he put it after Victor Hugo, "The Renaissance in Europe—a setting sun that all Europe mistook for a dawn." In this regard his critical position is close to that of A. W. N. Pugin or even, paradoxically, to that of his contemporary Auguste Perret, who in other respects could be disregarded as a classicist.

Also in the early fifties, he is honored both nationally and internationally with a large retrospective exhibition of his work that travels throughout Europe, displaying his unquestioned brilliance in one prestigious venue after another, beginning, ironically enough, with the Palazzo Strozzi in Florence and passing from there to the Kunsthaus in Zurich, one of the few modern buildings in Europe that he unequivocally admired. In numerous valedictory letters sent to distinguished architects all over the world at this time, one senses that Wright was only too aware that this was almost certainly his last public appearance as the architect of the century. In these letters he reaffirms, once again, his lifelong respect for both the German and Japanese cultures and his lasting debt to the Netherlands for having been one of the first countries to accord him public recognition. He also acknowledges in this context the sympathetic visit he received from Hendrik Petrus Berlage as early as 1911, to be followed by other distinguished Dutch architects, most notably the neoplasticist Robert van't Hoff and H. Th. Wijdeveld, editor of *Wendingen* magazine, which in 1925 would publish five special numbers dedicated solely to Wright's work.

Wright's retrospective, designed by Oscar Stonorov and entitled *Sixty Years of Living Architecture,* originated at Gimbels in Philadelphia and traveled to Italy, Switzerland, France, Germany, Holland, and Mexico. It was an international celebration of Wright's heroic career on a grand scale, and Wright was understandably gratified by all the attention he received as a result: citations, medals, and special issues published by five different magazines around the world.

In the occasional essays of his last decade Wright was often at his most interesting when dealing with unlikely themes, as in his review of Edwin Lutyen's Memorial Volumes edited by Christopher Hussey, wherein, understandably enough, he prefers the Arts and Crafts Lutyens to the "Wrenaissance" of his Viceroy's Palace in New Delhi. The early fifties see Wright again engaged in condemning American militarism, only this time the cause célèbre is the Korean War and the accompanying American paranoia about the threat of communist domination. In his short, journalistic piece "Wake Up, Wisconsin" he again chides the American public for their political immaturity: "Do they really know what Communism means? Ask them. Their answers will make you laugh. Do they know what democracy means? Ask them and weep." Wright's loathing of totalitarianism was answered by his vehement antipathy to demagogy. Thus his tolerant attitude toward the Soviet Union, aided no doubt by Olgivanna's empathy for all things Russian, was matched by his simultaneous detestation for the witch hunt that was then being so ardently pursued by Senator Joseph McCarthy, to which Wright was by no means immune.

Toward the end of his life Wright is even less tolerant of what he regarded as totalitarianism in architecture, namely the so-called International Style. Hence the endless diatribe against the orthogonal box that comes to the fore once again in 1952 in a piece entitled "Organic Architecture Looks at Modern Architecture." This critique is followed by an essay in which he comes out against proselytizers of all kinds, from the so-called Big Three of the Yalta Conference to the superimposition of Bauhaus values on American culture. It is strange to find Wright divided at this juncture between his lifelong admiration of Germany and the total disdain he felt for the emigré functionalists of the Weimar Republic, above all for Mies van der Rohe, with his scandalous "less is more" slogan, and Gropius, who while remaining unnamed, was clearly the director of a major East Coast "plan factory," as Wright disdainfully refers to all university schools of architecture. Condemning Mies for having reduced architecture to nothing more than a dematerialized skeleton, he enters into an attack on the curtain-walled, freestanding slab, particularly as this had appeared in 1952 with the United Nations building in New York—an institution Wright would blithely condemn out of hand for being more fascist than democratic. Although neither the Unité d'Habitation at Marseille nor Le Corbusier are ever mentioned by name, this is surely the double target of an odd essay entitled "Massacre on the Marseilles Waterfront." Elsewhere, while condemning their work in Chandigarh, he disdainfully refers to Le Corbusier and Pierre Jeanneret as "the Swiss brothers," conveniently ignoring the fact that they were not siblings.

The Future of Architecture (1953) leads him to redefine the term organic, testifying to a certain hesitation on his part as to whether he should abandon it altogether in favor of the word intrinsic. He attempts to clarify the meaning of organic in a nine-point manifesto, beginning with a broad definition of nature as the intrinsic structure of any given system. He goes on to replace Louis Sullivan's famous "Form follows Function" slogan with his own dictum that "form and function are one," simultaneously criticizing the abstract rationalism of the International Style to the effect that "until the mechanization of building is in the service of creative architecture and not creative architecture in the service of mechanization we will have no great architecture." Elsewhere he reasserts his view that ornament must be of the thing and not on it and that only through adhering to this precept can one enhance the character of a building through ornament.

In a further attack on the Museum of Modern Art for its internationalism, Wright argues that if an intrinsic architecture failed to emerge in the United States, the country would never have a culture of its own. For Wright, only individual creativity could guarantee, as it were, the emergence of an independent native American culture as opposed to what he saw as left-wing standardization in the work of Mies van der Rohe. This unremitting critique of the Bauhaus movement is to be pursued by Wright throughout the fifties in one text after another.

The Natural House (1954) is also largely a reworking of Wright's previous writings. The initial chapter treating organic architecture first appeared in 1936 in the British *The Architect's Journal,* and the chapters "Building the New House" and "In the Nature of Materials" were taken straight from his autobiography. Only a lengthy essay at the end, entitled "Concerning the Usonian House," had in fact been expressly written for the occasion. All in all, Wright is at his nonrhetorical best on the theme of the elegant paradigm, which in the last analysis was perhaps his most "democratic" invention. Despite the fact that it was never as widely adopted as he would have liked, the Usonian House, in all its guises, remains even now the last serious attempt on the part of an American architect to render the suburb as a place of cultivation. In *The Natural House* Wright's intelligence reveals itself with refreshing directness. Once he abandons the repetitive, recalcitrant tone that characterizes so much of his writing, Wright is able to convey to the reader the raison d'être of the Usonian prototype in an extremely persuasive way. However, in advising his Broadacre clients to build as far from the city as possible, he overlooked the fact that there was little to support his contention that "We have all the means to live free and independent, far apart—as we choose—(while) still retaining all the social relationships and advantages we ever had, even to have them multiplied." Apart from such inevitable grandiose assertions, *The Natural House* is leavened throughout by pragmatic advice, from instructing the reader as to the advantages of drywall footings to maintaining that artificial light should be provided in much the same way as natural light so as to avoid the unpleasant glare of spotlighting. Wright even defends the lack of sufficient insulation in the Usonian three-ply timber wall on the grounds that the most important thing is to keep one's feet warm, thereby simultaneously justifying both the thinness of the walls and his use of radiant floor heating. He goes so far as to suggest that if it becomes very cold one must simply put on more clothes. To his credit he remained skeptical regarding the virtues of central air conditioning, particularly in private homes. He saw this as further evidence of the excesses of mechanization, which was both unhealthy and uneconomical.

Published in 1958, a year before his death, *The Living City* returns to the themes of *The Disappearing City* (1932). As in *The Natural House,* Wright cannibalizes an earlier text—in this case the interim version of the Broadacre thesis *When Democracy Builds* (1945). In many instances he does little more than change a word or subtitle here and there or rearrange the syntax. Reacting to earlier reviews in which he had been "accused," as he put it, with preposterous irony, of being unduly "Capitalistic," Wright responds by decapitalizing the 1945 text throughout. All these rearrangements seem to have been employed simply to eliminate any grounds for legal action between the two publishers, who had become, as it were, ensnared in Wright's compulsive reiterations.

Between 1953 and his death in 1959 Wright produced a seemingly endless stream of books and articles, including *The Future of Architecture* (1953); *An American Architecture* (1955), edited by Edgar Kaufman; *The Natural House* (1954); *The Story of the Tower* (1956); *A Testament* (1957); and *The Living City* (1958). Along with this rather self-serving output came two texts that were calm in tone and somehow fresh: the brief but lively gloss written for the beautiful photographic record of the building of the Price Tower in Bartlesville, Oklahoma, entitled *The Story of the Tower,* and the relaxed flow of somewhat distant but lucid reflections on his long and exceedingly rich life, simply entitled *A Testament.*

The Story of the Tower is compelling because it is so specific. It is a text written with the full enthusiasm of someone who has finally realized a work that he has dreamed of building for more than thirty years—certain aspects of the Price Tower date back, in tectonic terms, to his National Life Insurance building, projected for Chicago in 1924. Here we read a description that could be applied word for word to the Chicago project:

> The steel textile, embedded in concrete, a machine age product of great value and beauty, here clothes interior space inside the glass and allows more light or less light, more or less privacy as desired under changing conditions. All exposed surfaces of the building except the central mass and floors, the supporting structure itself, are of copper. Partitions and furniture are designed as one and fabricated in the shop. . . . see the spider—steel—spinning its web to enmesh glass—glass clear—glass translucent—glass in relief—glass in color. Iridescent surfaces of this light-fabric rising high against the blue out of the whole city, the city now seen as a park, the metal fabrication of the shafts themselves turquoise or gold, silver, bronze; the glass surfaces between the threads of fabric shimmering with light reflected, light refracted—sparkling light broken into imaginative patterns.

As the text proceeds, his mind runs back to the use of long-span, structural steel in the Robie House and forward to his vision of Broadacre City:

> This skyscraper, planned to stand free in an open park and thus be more fit for human occupancy . . . here doing for the tall building what Lidgerwood made steel do for the long ship. The ship had its steel keel: this concrete building has its steel core. A composite shaft of concrete rises through the floors, each slab engaging the floors at nineteen levels. Each floor proceeds outward from the shaft as a cantilever slab extended from the shaft, similar to the branch of a tree from its trunk. The slab, thick at the shaft, grows thinner as it goes outward in an overlapping scale pattern in concrete until at the final outer leap to the screen wall it is no more than 3 inches thick. The outer enclosing screens of glass and copper are pendent from the edge of these cantilever slabs. The inner partitions rest upon the slabs. . . . But the building is so placed that the sun shines on only one wall at a time and narrow upright blades, or mullions,

project 9 inches so that as the sun moves, shadows fall on the glass surfaces and afford the protection necessary for comfort.

    The building increases substantially in area from floor to floor as the structure rises, in order that the glass frontage of each story may drip clear of the one below, the building thus cleaning itself.

Elsewhere, challenged no doubt by the technocratic theories of Richard Buckminster Fuller, Wright goes so far as to proclaim proudly that his building weighs six-tenths as much as a steel-framed Art Deco skyscraper clad in masonry.

All in all, the reminiscent writing in *A Testament* is too mellow to hold one's attention for long. Only now and then does he really bring us up short, as in the following unmitigated attack upon the totally corrupt state of American culture:

> Meantime we boast the highest standard of living in the world, when it is only the biggest. Society finds itself helplessly committed to these excesses and pressures. Ugliness is inevitable to this inorganic, therefore senseless, waste motion of the precious life of our time become a form of involuntary homicide. So mesmerized are we by the "payoff" that any public participation in culture becomes likewise wasted. So little are we enlisted in the potential new life that belongs to America.
>
>   Thus cheated by ourselves of general culture we have little genuine architecture. Official authority being by nature more and more merely numerical is already helpless even to recognize this fact, basic as it is.

He writes elsewhere in the same text,

> To what extent is the bureaucrat to determine the culture of our civilization? The "insolence of office" thrives upon conformity. See now the distortion of our intrinsic social purpose by experts and specialists and the encouragement of mediocrity by mass-education. With the inspiration of great art unheeded, where is the check to deterioration? Are architecture and art simply to fade out with religion?

Despite this pessimism, *A Testament* ends on a positive note with a resumé of Wright's Usonian precepts and a documentation of his astounding mile-high skyscraper, otherwise known as The Illinois-Sky City, designed for Chicago. However we need only to read the science-fiction description of its atomic powered, mega-elevator system, rising for 528 floors, complemented by 150 helicopter landing pads cantilevering out from its progressively diminishing shaft, to realize how the proposal entailed levels of supra-mechanization that Wright himself would have totally abhorred in other circumstances.

Wright produced eight more occasional essays before his death on 9 April 1959. Although he wrote to the very end, among his final pieces only one short essay, celebrating the imminent realization of the Guggenheim Museum, manifests his usual aplomb. It is just possible that this self-serving, eccentric polemic in favor of liberating painting from the tyranny of the rectilinear wall was in fact some kind of veiled instruction to the recalcitrant first director of the Guggenheim, James Johnson Sweeney, despite his hostility toward him, as to how he might intelligently exploit the full potential of the building. The remaining essays are written in a minor key and, despite relieving flashes of irony and wit, the overall tone is mordant. Living long enough to realize finally the full implications of mass "motopian" expansion, Wright had cause to regret the buoyancy of his casual observation in part four of *The Living City* to the effect that "America needs no help to Broadacre City; it will haphazardly build itself. Why not plan it?" But planning, of course, was the one thing that consumerism could hardly bring itself to do, and so Wright lived to witness the first haphazard encroachments of the megalopolis upon the panorama of his beloved Taliesin West.

The Wrights at Taliesin West, 1955. FLLW Fdn FA#6204.0003

FRANK LLOYD WRIGHT
A BIOGRAPHICAL SKETCH:
1949–1959

In the final decade of his life Wright's architectural productivity was nothing short of astounding. In addition to the prolific work in the studio, there was also a steady increase in writing, lecturing, and exhibitions. Honors and citations came to him from universities and governments worldwide. Despite his age he traveled extensively around the country during these years, as well as abroad, making four trips to Europe, one to Central America, and one to the Middle East and Africa. He had planned a voyage to Japan, in connection with an exhibition, but the Korean war intervened, and he was hesitant to take his work to the Far East at that time.

For Wright, the years 1949 to 1959 were not as turbulent, as far as his personal life, as those of the 1920s, as financially desperate as the early 1930s, nor as frustrated by government building restrictions as the war years of the 1940s.

This is not to suggest that this final decade was tranquil for him. Tranquility was not in his makeup, nor was it a condition the architect enjoyed. He was beset with hardships and tribulations for most of his life, and his wife Olgivanna once remarked that he seemed to thrive on hardships rather than be defeated by them.

In the spring of 1949 he was awarded the Gold Medal for Architecture by the American Institute of Architects. This was followed by awards from the National Institute of Arts and Letters, the Philadelphia chapter of the A.I.A., and an honorary degree: The Peter Cooper Award for the Advancement of Art. Three prominent commissions for large buildings came his way: the New Theater for Hartford, Connecticut; a bridge for the second bay crossing in San Francisco Bay, California; and the self-service garage for Kaufmann's department store in Pittsburgh, Pennsylvania. However, none of these was built. But several residential designs were commissioned and executed, and construction of a new cabaret theater for his own home and studio, Taliesin West, was begun.

The following year he was invited to London to deliver an address and to present the prizes at the annual ceremonies of the Architectural Association School on July 14.[1] His host was the principal of the school, Robert Furneaux Jordan, who met Wright, his wife, and his daughter, at the boat at Southampton and took them by car to London. This was the first time Wright really saw the English countryside. His other voyages to Great Britain had been confined to London exclusively, where he arrived either from the airport or via rail. Jordan later wrote, "From the moment of his arrival in this country there was nothing about people or agriculture or the economic system about what he did not want to know the answer . . . his critical eye missed nothing. On the road from Southampton he noted the material of every cottage, the species of every cow and every piece of woodland, and then—at the end of a long day—he pushed all the furniture around to his better liking."[2]

During the winter of 1949 and through all of 1950 Wright and the members of the Taliesin Fellowship were at work preparing an exhibition of his work, *Sixty Years of Living Architecture*. Models were overhauled; drawings were selected; photomurals of his buildings were prepared. The exhibition was scheduled

The Wrights at Easter breakfast, Taliesin West, 1956. Photograph by Bruce Brooks Pfeiffer. FLLW Fdn FA#6204.0023

to open in the Palazzo Strozzi in Florence, Italy, with a preview at Gimbel's Department Store before its overseas venue. First sponsored by Arthur Kaufmann of Gimbel's, the exhibition traveled widely throughout Europe and Central America under the auspices of the United States government.

A most rewarding event in Wright's life was his 1951 trip with Olgivanna and his daughter, Iovanna, to Italy for the June opening of his exhibition in Florence. The Wrights were welcomed and escorted royally along their voyage from Rome to Florence via Assisi. In Assisi, he visited the church of St. Francis, where he saw the murals of Giotto. He had long admired the early Italian Renaissance painters, such as Giotto, Mantegna, and Piero della Francesca. The Italian landscape itself was a pleasure for him. (He delighted in the farms and fields, as they awoke memories of his own childhood spent on his Uncle James's farm in Wisconsin. On his return he told us, "There is not one of our buildings that would not look right at home in the Tuscany landscape.") He received the De Medici Medal conferred by the City of Florence in full ceremony at the Palazzo Vecchio. In Venice, escorted by the young architect Carlo Scarpa, he received further honors. In the doge's palace, with a ceremony of medieval splendor, he was awarded the Star of Solidarity, one of Europe's most coveted and rarely conferred medals.

Out of his trip to Italy came the commission for the Masieri Memorial, an architectural students' pension and library to be built on the Grand Canal in Venice. Unfortunately, opposition to a "modern" building being built in historic Venice defeated the project. At the time, Ernest Hemingway quipped that if Wright's design was built, Venice deserved to be burnt. When asked his reaction to Hemingway's remark, Wright simply replied, "A voice from the jungle."[3]

Back at home, twenty more commissions came into the studio at Taliesin, and the cabaret theater at Taliesin West was finally completed and opened for use. Here dinner was served, followed by a film or a concert. Wright had a passion for motion pictures, along with a great optimism. If a film was dragging its heels and appearing rather dull, Olgivanna would whisper to her husband, "Frank, this film is going nowhere. Why do we stay and watch it?" To which he would invariably reply, "But wait, Mother, it might get better."

Traveling from his winter home at Taliesin West, in Arizona, with his family and a handful of apprentices, Wright went north to Wisconsin early in the spring of 1952, leaving the bulk of the fellowship to follow in a few weeks. This migration between the two Taliesins had been a perennial event each spring and fall since 1938. This particular spring was cold and dry, and the first order of business was opening the Taliesin and Hillside buildings. Wright was sweeping and raking leaves around the theater, creating piles and setting them on fire. A sudden gust of wind swept the flames up along the side of the theater and into the overhanging roof. The small stream nearby, which might have provided water to fight the fire, was dry. The fire spread rapidly throughout the roof structure, and in a matter of minutes the theater, dining room, weaving gallery, and nine apprentice rooms had become a raging inferno. The small crew, along with Wright, managed to cut the building where it joined the living room, saving the nearby drafting room and two galleries that contained not only the drawings on the boards at the time, but also the entire collection of his architectural work since 1892. A good portion of Wright's time during that summer was spent in planning and beginning to rebuild the sections that were lost. What grieved Wright most about the fire was not the loss of the buildings—those could be reconstructed—but the loss of his extensive collection of artworks from China and Japan that were consumed in the flames. "Fire," Olgivanna later remarked, "is our Karma."[4]

During that summer he received a commission for a skyscraper in Bartlesville, Oklahoma, the Price Tower. With this work, he saw, finally, his St. Mark's Tower of 1929 realized in a new and revised version.[5]

In 1953 he negotiated for a new publisher, leaving Duell, Sloan, and Pearce for Horizon Press of New York, and began a publication program that would see one book a year published from 1953 to 1959.

By the fall of 1953 *Sixty Years of Living Architecture* had completed its European and Central American tour and was installed in a pavilion of Wright's design between 88th and 89th streets, on New York's Fifth Avenue, the site of the future Guggenheim Museum.

The next year, construction of the Guggenheim Museum seemed imminent, and Wright needed a New York office as a base of operations out of which he could monitor the ongoing work. For this, he rented an apartment in the Plaza Hotel, which he remodeled in a mixture of nineteenth-century elegance and modern simplicity. He claimed that because the apartment had once belonged to Diamond Jim Brady, he would come up with a solution that would be "Diamond Jim Brady Modern." The result was a suite complete with plum-colored velvet draperies, a plush wool peach-colored carpet, gilded mirrors and—conversely—simple black lacquered furniture of his own design made by the apprentices at Taliesin West.

Wright had long been interested in theater design, beginning with his work in 1915 for Aline Barnsdall in Los Angeles. He then designed the New Theater for New York in 1931 and one for Hartford, Connecticut, in 1949. In 1955 another theater project came alive again, at the urging of John Rosenfield, drama critic of the *Dallas Morning News* and longtime friend of Wright's, and Paul Baker, director of the Dallas Theatre Center. Eventually the project was realized as the Kalita Humphreys Theater.[6] Later in the year Wright received a commission for the headquarters of the Lenkurt Electric Company, a massive industrial plant to be built in San Carlos, California. As with the Johnson Wax Building (1936) and the Larkin Building (1903), he created a work environment dedicated to the worker, surrounding him with elements of beautiful design and a healthy, harmonious atmosphere.

The years 1956 and 1957 were especially productive for Wright, and included two important overseas trips for him: to Wales and to Baghdad, Iraq. The trip to Wales, in August, was sponsored by the University of Wales at Bangor, which offered him an honorary degree. This was the first time he had visited the land where his mother and his grandfather came from. Although the strong and powerful Lloyd-Jones clan figured so prominently in Wright's early life, he had never visited Wales. He was hosted by the architect Clough Williams-Ellis,[7] who wrote of the occasion,

> Perhaps one of the most striking things about his brief reconnaissance was his forthcoming, open-armed and zestful appreciation of all things authentically and characteristically Welsh, whether mountains and valleys, rivers, waterfalls and coastlines, or old stone buildings and trees, especially trees. With these he seemed to feel a particular affinity, saying that he rejoiced in their stalwart grace as much as in good building, insisting that American trees had no such

vigorous individuality. . . . Accompanied by Mrs. Wright and his daughter, the mileage covered in two or three days was immense, the sight-seeing gargantuan. Castles of course, the "Welsh scene" generally, including Lloyd George's tomb, which, being all boulder built amongst old trees and poised above a rushing river, gave him special satisfaction.[8]

During this same summer, back at Taliesin, Wright designed the Mile High Skyscraper (Chicago, Illinois), the Greek Orthodox Church (Wauwatosa, Wisconsin), the New Sports Pavilion (Belmont Park, New York), the Golden Beacon apartment tower (Chicago, Illinois), and the Bramlett Motor Hotel (Memphis, Tennessee). In his designs for the Mile High, the sports pavilion, and the Greek church Wright once again demonstrated his skill as an engineer, with designs that contained far-reaching solutions for modern life yet remained appropriate and feasible, using twentieth-century materials and technology.

In 1957 Wright produced even more innovative designs: the Arizona State Capital, the various Baghdad projects, and the Marin County civic center. In May, accompanied by Olgivanna and his son-in-law William Wesley Peters, he flew to Baghdad, Iraq. As with his trip to Wales the preceding year, Wright fulfilled a lifelong wish to see a culture he deeply revered. Since childhood, when he had read and loved the *Arabian Nights,* he had had enormous respect for Islamic culture. He was called to Baghdad by the Iraq Development Board, who wished him to participate in a mammoth building program. The specific project assigned to him was the opera house. The commission also involved other architects: Le Corbusier, Alvar Aalto, and Gio Ponti among them. But Wright not only designed the opera, he also submitted drawings for two museums, a university complex, a monument to Haroun-al-Rashid,[9] and a grand bazaar.

On his return from Baghdad he stopped in London and negotiated with Rathbone Press to write a book on the history of architecture, to be called *The Wonderful World of Architecture,* specifically targeted for children. Other, more pressing work in the studio forced him to delay work on this project, and it remained incomplete at the time of his death.

As the result of a mild stroke, Wright was inactive during part of the summer of 1958. But once he recovered he plunged into work with designs for Mike Todd's Todd A-O theaters, the Trinity Chapel (Norman, Oklahoma), the Pilgrim Congregational Church (Redding, California), and the Juvenile Cultural Center (Wichita, Kansas). Also in construction were the Beth Sholom Synagogue and the Guggenheim Museum. As the museum completion drew closer, tension and controversy continued over whether the building was appropriate for exhibiting works of art. The director, James Johnson Sweeney, took a distinct dislike to both building and architect, and had it not been for Guggenheim's nephew, Harry Guggenheim, the building may not have been completed in accordance with Wright's design.

In January 1959, Wright made his last trip to New York to work on the Guggenheim Museum. This commission, more than any other, consumed his strength and tested his patience. The struggles seemed endless, but he counted on Harry Guggenheim's support, and wrote on 12 February 1959:

Dear Harry: Thanks for your note. I am grateful. I cannot tell you how much your reassurance means in this late day of the supreme effort involved in the museum. That you are prepared to stand by the philosophy that gave the building its present form. It is there in good shape and working against the odds you yourself have stood against and are experiencing—the transition from the carpenter and his square to the more liberal and universal atmosphere of Nature. Affection, Frank Lloyd Wright.

Of Wright's total output of architectural work, almost one-third was done in this last decade, between 1949 and 1959. Many factors made this possible: following the war, building picked up across the nation; and with the assistance and support of the Taliesin Fellowship he had a "production team" that produced working drawings, supervised buildings, and guaranteed that his architectural ideas were translated, first into construction documents and second, into actual buildings.

It seemed that the fruits of his labors—so long denied him—were being realized at last during these years. Olgivanna noted that this was the first time in their life together that they were not so plagued with debt that they did not know where their next dollar was coming from. There was a special peace and contentment in Wright's personal life and a sense of great fulfillment in the life he led at Taliesin. He was supported by a wife who watched carefully over him, inspired him, and safeguarded his health; he was surrounded by apprentices whose youth and vitality were sources of energy for him as well. "If you are not an inspiration to me as I am an inspiration to you, this place is not going to work," he told his apprentices. In 1959 it appeared as though he were going to plunge into yet another decade. This momentum kept up until 4 April 1959, when he was taken to the hospital complaining of severe abdominal pains. He died five days later.

Toward the end of his life, Wright's eyesight had become impaired by cataracts. But although his eyesight became clouded, his vision was astoundingly clear. Following the stroke in 1958, his handwriting had become less steady, but armed with a T-square and triangle, sitting at his drafting board, he was able to project architecture into the future.

His life was cut short in the midst of enormous activity and the prospect of many new projects. He was nearing ninety-two, with little sign of letting up. He carried his age with magnificent grace and virility; his posture was erect, his walk a brisk stride, his mind sharp and perceptive. We can not help but contemplate: where would architecture be today had he been granted just one more decade of life?

1. *Architectural Association Journal*, August–September 1950, p. 32.
2. *Frank Lloyd Wright: The Crowning Decade 1949–1959* (Fresno: The Press at California State University, 1989), p. 24.
3. Brandoch Peters to Bruce Brooks Pfeiffer.
4. Olgivanna Wright to Bruce Brooks Pfeiffer, 1964.
5. See "The Story of the Tower," in this volume.
6. Completed in late 1959 and featured in *Architectural Forum* in March 1960.
7. 1883–1978.
8. *The Crowning Decade*, p. 28, 31.
9. Haroun-al-Rashid, c.786–809, fifth caliph of Baghdad, and a great patron of the arts and letters. Under him caliphate Baghdad rose to great heights. Wright dedicated his Baghdad projects to him.

Lloyd Lewis. Photograph courtesy Newberry Library, Chicago, Illinois.
FLLW Fdn FA#6701.0009

TRIBUTE TO LLOYD LEWIS

Lloyd Lewis, drama critic for the Chicago Daily News, was a longtime friend of Frank Lloyd Wright's. In 1940 Lewis requested that Wright design a home inspired by the architect's own home, Taliesin, and provide the same feeling of repose that he experienced each time he visited Taliesin. In a letter to Wright, the writer Alexander Woollcott expressed his own reactions after he made a second visit to Lewis's house:

> I was there last Sunday and want to confirm, by a second visit, the impression it made upon me. On the strength of that house alone I think I could go forth and preach afresh the gospel of Frank Lloyd Wright. I see now more fully than ever before what effect the right house can have upon the person inside it. I told Lloyd that this one makes even a group of his friends look distinguished.[1] Lloyd, whom I admire and enjoy, never did anything wiser in his life. Just to be in that house uplifts the heart and refreshes the spirit. Most houses confine their occupants. Now I understand, where before I only dimly apprehended, that such a house as this can liberate the person who lives in it. God bless you. A. Woollcott.[2]

Lewis was preparing an article about Wright's design for the New Theater in Hartford, Connecticut, when he died suddenly. Wright rarely qualified anything or anyone as "the best" or "the dearest." But in reference to Lloyd Lewis he wrote, "He was my dearest friend through thick and thin of the better part of my lifetime and his, and I am yet unable to realize that I have lost him." When Wright received the news about Lewis's death, he turned to his apprentices in the studio at the time and said, "There goes the last person to call me 'Frank.'" [Theatre Arts, July 1949]

PROOFS OF THIS LLOYD LEWIS ARTICLE ON THE NEW Theatre reached me as word came from his wife Kathryn telling me I should not see Lloyd again. He was my dearest friend through the thick and thin of the better part of my lifetime and his, and I am yet unable to realize that I have lost him. While we were building Lloyd's home at Libertyville we often talked of the theatre in which we both had so vital an interest. *Vital* was the word for Lloyd's interest in anything—the best word to describe his feeling for his friends, of whom he had more than anyone I ever knew. As I grew richer in building experience he grew richer in human experience. No man had more or truer friends than he, and I who knew so few could envy him his riches—but didn't. I enjoyed him when he was with them almost as much as I did when I had him to myself. Those clear seeing eyes of his that seemed alight with wit—the crack of his whip when the Quaker in him rose indignant. He insisted always I was a Puritan. My friend Lloyd Lewis never "let anyone down." This article of his on The New Theatre (the last thing he wrote) came to me as many a tribute had come from him who never failed to help whenever and wherever he *believed*. Lloyd had great capacity for *belief*— so I know he persists and we shall meet again.

1. Lewis's friends included Carl Sandburg, Marc Connelly, Charles MacArthur, Helen Hayes, and many other artists and writers. Woollcott is being somewhat "tongue in cheek" with this remark.

2. Letter to Frank Lloyd Wright, 19 April 1941.

BEAUTY

One Sunday morning in June 1950, Frank Lloyd Wright joined the members of his Taliesin Fellowship for breakfast, as was his custom each Sunday morning. In lieu of his usual discursive talk, he drew out of his pocket some notes he had jotted down the previous night on the subject of beauty. After Wright read them to the fellowship, apprentice Ling Po offered to transcribe them in his own inimitably beautiful lettering. To Ling, a student from China, calligraphy is a great tradition and a great art, which he has painstakingly practiced all his life. [Unpublished]

I

BEAUTY CONSISTS IN A CERTAIN NATURALNESS—IN exuberance—is a being in itself.

Beauty of form is always from within outward—the imitative of its outward countenance cannot live as the original lives because the light of the idea is within shines afresh only from the original.

Creative is a word not to be used for invention or composition but only for manifest entity hitherto unknown—subsequently eternal.

Beauty is a state of being wherein all *is* of never *on* and proceeds as the inevitable from general to particulars—there is no confusion—its simplicity is not merely plain but is often as delicately and completely from within as any wild flower or noble tree.

Beauty may gleam but seldom glitters.

Beauty may not be evident at a glance but imposes a second look and finally the love that recognizes itself afresh in unexpected ways recognizes its own.

To imitate Nature is to insult Beauty.

II

By no contrivances can the inspiration be had that reveals Beauty at its source. Only by being can being be perceived.

Only by feeling can knowledge of it be made to appear.

Only by way of Love can either of these happen.

Contrary to the old adage "Beauty is but skin deep" true Beauty is always profound because it is integral. Beauty is ever individual because it is of the Soul. Beauty is never superficial—but is a joy that always satisfies the heart, the head, and hands, needing no argument, suffering no apologies: An appeal not to reason but from Soul to Soul.

How then can Beauty be confined to formula, be a Style, or become a Fashion.

That can only happen outside its real being: an abuse of Nature no true use of its quality: a shallow illusion.

Beauty is always qualitative never quantitative.

Its mathematics are not calculatable—because all Sciences are no higher than analysis whereas the essence of Beauty is being far above or beyond all analysis.

Beauty can never be destroyed—only hidden by enormities or deformities.

It is eternal. All passes. Beauty endures alone.

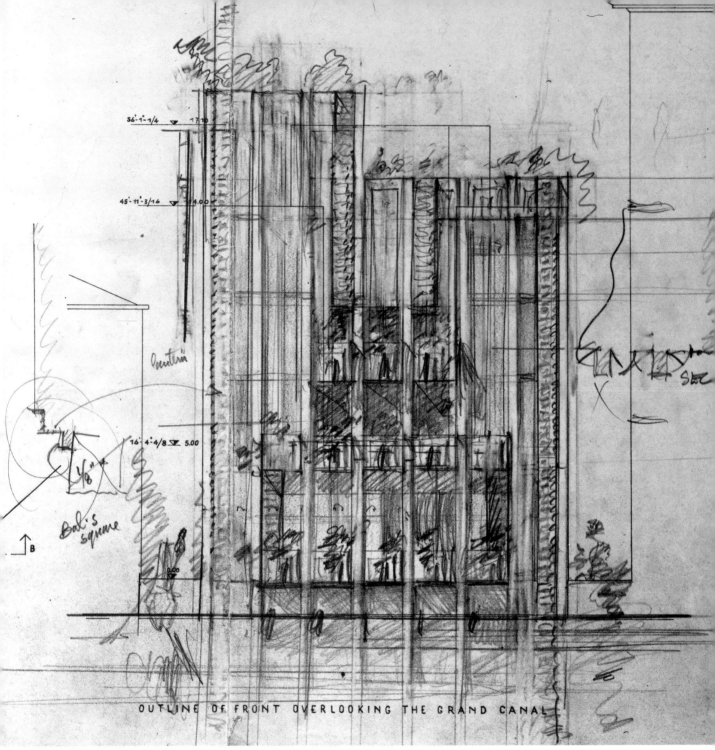

OUTLINE OF FRONT OVERLOOKING THE GRAND CANAL

Angelo Masieri Memorial Student Pension and Library (Project), Venice, Italy. 1953. Pencil on paper, 33 x 12". FLLW Fdn#5306.008

WHATEVER HIS AGE . . . TO THE YOUNG MAN IN ARCHITECTURE

The Architectural Forum published a third monograph issue on Wright in January 1951. The magazine had previously featured his work in January 1938 and January 1948. But for the first time in Wright's publication history, this issue contained full color illustrations of many of his newer buildings. Most of the text described the buildings illustrated. The editors, however, posed certain questions to Wright and those responses are recorded here.

He was asked about the realities of the machine civilization, why other architects found it so difficult to understand his methods of building, what effect the International Style had had on the nation, and about the origin and development of his own working methods.

The issue concluded with an essay entitled "A Dialogue." The dialogue is between the Son of the West (Frank Lloyd Wright) and the Buddha, whom Wright calls "The Studio Buddha" after one of the most beautiful works in his collection of Far Eastern art. This is a cast-iron head of Buddha that Wright placed high on an oak shelf, next to the fireplace, in the Hillside drafting room in Wisconsin. It was in this room that Wright performed all his architectural work. He comments in the article, "The expression of this ancient cast-iron head of the Studio Buddha, changing with the sun, sometimes pervades our thoughts. Sometimes in his expression there seems evidence of the deep, beneficent inner quiet our Art so needs and that Taliesin covets. Complete repose (especially in action) is in man the quality of Being we see recorded in this benign countenance." [Architectural Forum, *January 1951*]

I HOPE BY THIS CONTINUED, CONCENTRATED PUBLICATION in *Architectural Forum*, the Magazine of Building to rekindle enthusiasm for creative indigenous Architecture as against any cliché whatsoever. I am convinced, notwithstanding widespread imitation of effects only, that these works will eventually prove of lasting value to the younger architects of our modern times because of their integrity.

Like earlier publications of my work in this magazine in 1938 and again in 1948, I hope the buildings shown on the following pages, and selected from among many as worthy, will serve again to illustrate basic principles which give to them all such vitality, integrity and magic as they have. I still hope to see these basic principles more comprehended, therefore the effects imitated less. No man's work need resemble mine. If he understands the working of the principles behind the effects he sees here, with similiar integrity he will have his own way of building.

Meantime preserve us from all istics, all ites,

and any ism, especially naturalism. By way of style, preserve us above all, from a Style. Democracy deserves a free Architecture—at least Architecture free.

Taliesin West, December 15, 1950
Frank Lloyd Wright

Science alone beyond furnishing tools in the toolbox can never lead us to a culture of our own. Without the practice of Architecture as the great art of environment—the basic art of Architecture is still sadly lacking in our midst. Architecture in this sense is still our national blind-spot. Not until we understand this will we ever arrive at sanity in building not to say the culture of Beauty. It is no exaggeration to say that we have had little or no organic character in our Democracy.

Without this way of building how can a true culture grow among us? We've, so far, cheated ourselves in Architecture. We came over in buckled shoes, knee breeches, lace around our wrists and around our necks, Colonials with a nostalgia for things left behind. So Democracy has remained largely our empty boast. There is striking resemblance between our own situation and that of the people we fear most: the Russians. Although not in the same way, they are making the same mistakes we made.

Well, we have become famous as the nation of the Substitute. A nation wherein individual creation is good but only if it is good for any number of substitutes. Already we are more comfortable with mediocrity than any form of true originality. So our educational system now champions mediocrity. Only mediocrity is safe for the mediocre.

I often wonder why a true original has become so dangerous a thing? An idea is a sword. Any sword taken by the blade can destroy the one who thus mistakes it. Only when taken by the hilt and wielded as intended can it be used to achieve what culture alone can give—a great realization of the beauty of Life itself.

Here again by way of the author of the Helio house (the hemicycle) comes the Helio laboratory.[1] Both are sun-worshippers. Here in the laboratory is at least one industrial building we have salvaged from the vast industrial scrap heap—a structure proudly deficient in any fear at all.

We know (we architects) that there is nothing on this earth so timid as a million dollars . . . unless it is more millions. There will not be many such voluntary contributions to our national culture for some time. Our big industrial boys come and they go and our lack of culture seems to go on forever.

Nevertheless in spite of such waste there remains the inner glimmer of light that will thrust by way of the individual true to himself and his light upon the daily life of frightened, war-threatened human beings. There is something deeper than we know in this dangerous, beautiful thing we so carelessly call Democracy.

You have been called a "romanticist" in architecture. Since you were the first (1903) to point out some of the realities of our machine civilization, how do you account for this charge?

Well—there stands Romeo and Juliet, the wooden windmill triumphant over steel.[2] A structure built like a barrel, there it's been standing on top of its hill for 46 years. All the doubting Thomases who came regularly to their doors after every big storm to see if the windmill was wrecked have themselves all disappeared beneath the sod. Romantic?

But the name ("Romeo and Juliet") must have introduced me to the architectural world as a Romanticist. I am a Romanticist, but not of the favorite variety. I've been the kind of romanticist in search of Reality—Reality being new in Architecture and in Being—for me the fascinating quest of all quests. Eventually it will become the greatest of all paths of human discovery.

No, you cannot see the Machine in Romeo and Juliet but it is there. The Machine can be nowhere a Creator except as it may be a good tool in the creative artist's tool box. It is only when you try to make a living thing of the Machine itself that you begin to betray your human birthright. The Machine can do great work—yes—but only when well in hand of one who does not overestimate its resources, one who knows how to put it to suitable work for the human being.

The proper use of the Machine should be to make life more beautiful, more livable. No, not necessarily easier and quicker just to feed this American voracity which we call speed. If speed and destruction plus sanitation are to be the function of machinery among us, the machine will destroy us and its present idolatry will eventually defeat our attempt at a culture.

These buildings, this Architecture I myself have created, is simply a lifelong, fully conscious, unremitting effort to render the Machine—this tool of modern times—so useful that a great indigenous culture we could honestly call American might occur. A living expression of the greatness of the human spirit of our nation might be ours. So what quality you perceive in these buildings must be the reflection of a truly religious endeavor to make Beauty of environment come alive again for our own people; to make them aware of the richness of a life they now almost wholly miss. This innate richness of life can be theirs only when they learn how to command, restrain, and use the machine properly, that is to say as a mere tool instead of falling into the worship of it as a money maker. The Machine has yet nowhere given to America the flower of indigenous Culture. The Machine has so far produced for us only the weeds of a Civilization.

Why has it been so hard for other architects to understand the inner nature of your methods of building?

When the structure of an idea has once been frozen into an "effect" it can be too easily transferred. Now there can be nothing frozen or static about either the methods or effects of Organic architecture. All must be the spontaneous reaction of the creative mind to a specific problem in the nature of materials. A new esthetic is looking for its principles in Nature with a capital N.

You see, by way of concentrated thought, the idea is likely to spring into life all at once and be completed eventually with the unity of a living organism. In architecture each new plan will have its own grammar and law of growth. An inner module of space measured by a unit system in plan as well as elevation makes each detail proportionate in any plan we make, each part an inevitable and well-pro-portioned portion of the whole. Thus we arrive at entity and "atmosphere." Only entity lives.

This inner thing is what disciples (or imitators) have not fully grasped. How could they? Here is no secret of an "American Style"—in which any architect might find a "safe" grammar to carry from one job to the next. What most of the now world-wide followers of the organic effects fail to understand is that there is no possible transfer of the same grammar from one genuine building to the other. The law of growth for the Johnson Helio-lab, for instance, is as different from that of Taliesin West, say, as the oak tree differs from the cactus. But both are alike in their inner concept and consistency of grammar. Each is true to itself.

What then can I tell contemporary architects except to seek that inner freedom—a sense of being—which will enable each to grasp for himself the freedom of his own idea? He will then find that the inner nature of his problem always carries right there, within itself, its own solution.

Because of this inner sureness of "ways and means" in architecture as a part of myself I am often termed "arrogant." Now I submit that what seems "arrogance" is only a surface irritation caused by the hypocritical humility of a profession now become no higher than a labor union, by self-seeking "publicity" and by the natural enemies of all integrity bent on tearing our culture down. I would be glad to drop it, and do so occasionally.

What effect do you think the "International Style" has had on American architecture?

The internationalists say that they have an architecture of "restraint." What have they to restrain? All they have done seems to me just "strained."

If the motive of their work is examined for truth, it will seem to mean elimination of the individual—per se—as such. His God-given qualities as a creative being are left out in order to mass produce something fit only for mass consumption.

The great Art of Architecture is thus made a mere cliché, a pattern that could be cut from cardboard with a pair of scissors by the novitiate. Again they have robbed Organic architecture, the natural architecture of a Democracy, of all that it could give to an indigenous culture. The Internationalist (so called) seems to care little about freedom, freedom not for personality merely but for the individuality without which Democracy dies. Our little provincials in Architecture are quite eager to give our own American heritage away. So it seems. They do not know even now that they would give our American heritage away if they could. The philosophy of an Organic architecture is new to them. A grammar they are unable to read as the center line of our Democratic faith which really it is. This philosophy is old but is a new thing under the sun in this era. Organic architecture is the center line of Democratic philosophy not only where buildings are concerned but in the politics of government as well.

Can you give us some insight as to the origin and development of your own way of work?

I can only tell you that lifelong endeavor of mine began as an early—probably the first—effort to demolish the box seen as Architecture. I began as a young architect-engineer. When I looked at the hideous efflorescent boxing in of humanity upon the Chicago prairies of the '90's, I soon realized that the corners of the box were not the economical or vital bearing points of structure. The main load of the usual building I saw was on the walls and so best supported at points some distance back from the corner. The spans were then reduced by cantileverage. So I took the corners out, put in glass instead: the corner window. I gave here a real blow to all boxing up or boxing in. With the bearing points thus drawn in and clearly established aside from the corners another result was that box walls themselves became individual screens for interior space. Space could now be handled freely for either bringing in or shutting out the out-of-doors at will. This much was for the ground plan.

Later, say when the Johnson Administration Building evolved and coming from this earlier pursuit of the demolition of architecture as a box, I came upon the elimination of the horizontal corner, the corner between walls and ceiling.[3] Before this all building was more or less the inexorable box in both plan and elevation. Architecture (until then) was finally closed off at the upper angle by the heavy artillery called a cornice. This time (the Johnson Administration Building), I took off the cornice at the ceiling, took out the wall beneath it and so in this sacrosanct region I put in glass. Thus light was let into the interior space where light had never been seen before.

Making away with the box both in plan and elevation now became fundamental to my work. That opened the way for feeling the space within as the Reality of all true modern building, building not merely monumental. I have sought this liberation in some form or other in almost every building I have built. Here in this simple act may be found a "reason"—answering your question. These structures now bear the message of this liberation of space to space. It might be—must be—the basis for a new world concept, not only of Architecture but as a way of life which must eventually belong to a people loving freedom above license and practicing it in the name of Democracy.

NOTE: Architecture, to us at Taliesin, is the great Mother Art. We feel and see Architecture not only as the basic structure of what we call our environment, now so uncultured, but also its integrity. Only our own creative ability can give us Beauty as native evidence of ourselves: a quality of peace. We mean this quality when we use the word repose.

In Oriental Art the great Buddha taught his prophets other words to use than "repose." Some of these are familiar in the drafting room at Taliesin. Some of them we do not yet understand. But the expression of this ancient cast-iron head of the Studio Buddha, changing with the sun, sometimes pervades our thought. Sometimes in his expression there seems evidence of the deep, beneficent inner quiet our Art so needs and that Taliesin covets. Complete repose (especially in action) is in man the quality of Being we see recorded in this benign countenance.

A DIALOGUE

Buddha: "Why, Son of the West, has your great nation never realized that Creative Art is implicit in faith in one's own Ideal. His Ideal is all any man will ever see of God! We Orientals believe FORCE in your nation is now becoming your substitute for Soul: *substitute* for the creative power of poetic science. That sense of force is false. Its vast mechanical apparatus is too busy among you raising a vast crop of weeds. Regardless of true flowers the policy of the West seems to drive this weed crop ahead to a dead end.

"Innate justice is lost to you. What you call 'technique' is a dead thing. Good 'technique' never precedes but must follow inspiration. You neglect any knowledge of your own true Nature. Because of this basic neglect you attempt to use the substitutes invented by your genius for machinery. This neglect—Son of the West—will make yours the shortest lived civilization among so many that have tried and are still trying to live as ancient Rome lived. Your civilization too will die as Rome died."

"Reverend Buddha, that prophecy does apply to our 'higher education' and the 'capitalist success-ideal' driving youth to gregarious life in our cities, and to war. To these comprehensive mistakes we owe the FEAR so imposed upon us by our 'politics.' Dishonest expediency there and where we must live is only natural to such 'success.' Nevertheless see in the little green valleys between the long ranges of wooded hills of our country, love and reverence for Beauty. This humane growth you may find there where the hill slopes are dotted with cattle or are alive with crops as little streams fed by flowing springs are running to the great rivers. Here and there, still native to their share of Earth you will find what, for lack of a special name of our own, we call America. Culture no longer lives in our cities. Cities now are only market places in which to sell fish. There are no fish in the streams."

Buddha: "If so, why do your people flock from your countrysides to your big cities? Driven by some animal-instinct are they foregathering only to perish like flies crawling on a window pane? Your people will soon be victims of their own slaughter-machines. No. Son of the West . . . our ancient wisdom cannot respect such division of Will and Conscience in Man. We see in your ramping cities no vision. We see there only the trampling of self-seeking merciless herds. Your premiums are placed upon Mediocrity. The authority of the *average* is

imposing and imposed upon until a fiction—'the common man'—has become a national fetish. Does that not surely make of your pretended Democracy a failure? Seldom does authority among your millions know the difference between Freedom, a sacred inner thing, and the license that is only of animal-origin and dies like any animal."

"You speak Truth, great Buddha, for my people do yet realize no other or better choice. From creatures-of-habit they came. How can you expect much more from them than the habitual raised to extremes by machinery? Artificially powered they now are by their own Machines and are becoming themselves more and more like machines.

"But in this little green valley, as in others elsewhere, a message is being prepared: a message you have helped make clear to us. We aim to reach our people with the living message we call Architecture. One day we may look back and see Truth we can touch and feel because we live in it. Our nation will some day realize the great source of true power is Spirit and find Truth coming to them from a source where they have looked for it least and last: the buildings they build to live in. You have the right to speak of Spirit as more Oriental than Western. But the Occident has known it too. Some day East and West as one will waken to the honest practice of what we call a natural or organic Architecture. Today—on Earth everywhere youth is waking and working, loving this old, yet new, integrity."

Buddha: "Then you may not die as all civilizations preceding yours have died! Sharing our ancient Wisdom, you may live . . . not forever, no Forever, too, is finite. We will know eternal Life together. This meeting of East and West in thought will become a mighty feeling only when this vicarious Force you call the Machine becomes, instead of your master, your expedient servant. Then only will you know Freedom."

1. The Johnson Wax Research Tower, Racine, Wisconsin, 1944.

2. Windmill built for Wright's aunts Nell and Jane Lloyd Jones for the Hillside Home School in 1896. It was rebuilt in 1992.

3. Johnson Wax Administration Building, Racine, Wisconsin, 1936.

SIXTY YEARS OF LIVING ARCHITECTURE

By the autumn of 1949 Wright was actively involved in the preparation of an exhibition of his work that would premier in Philadelphia in January 1951 and move on to Florence, Italy, that June. The exhibition was conceived in, of all places, the United States embassy in Rome, in the office of the ambassador, Clare Booth Luce. Arthur Kaufmann, of Gimbel Brothers department store in Pittsburgh, Pennsylvania, had been visiting her. They were discussing the political situation in Italy, where communism was gaining influence, spurred on by Soviet propaganda maintaining that the culture of the United States was represented by degenerate artists who worshipped the almighty dollar. To counteract this line, Luce and Kaufmann thought it would be expedient to mount an exhibition in Italy, namely in Florence, showing the finest examples of American creative life. Several Italian architects, artists, and writers were asked whom they would select to be exhibited in Italy. The reply that invariably came back was "Frank Lloyd Wright."

Between January 1951 and July 1954 the exhibition, entitled Frank Lloyd Wright: Sixty Years of Living Architecture, traveled to three major cities in the United States, six in Europe, and Mexico City. Composed of models, large photographic murals, decorative objects, and over seven hundred original drawings, it was the largest exhibition ever mounted of Wright's work, and the largest to date of any single architect in history.

As the opening date of the exhibition grew near, Wright received a letter from C. Leslie Cushman, associate superintendent of the Philadelphia school district, Board of Public Education: "Dear Mr. Wright: I have just learned from my good friend Oscar Stonorov, the story of the exhibit of your work which has been prepared under his direction. We are delighted that this exhibition is to be shown first in Philadelphia. We shall arrange for large numbers of children of the public schools to see it." He went on to request that Wright write a brief statement to be included in a leaflet describing the exhibit, and addressed to American schoolchildren.

In the catalog Wright wrote an introductory preface for each of the nations the show toured: Italy, Switzerland, France, Germany, Holland, and Mexico. The introduction for the premier showing, at Gimbel Brothers Gallery on 25 January 1951, was actually that from his book When Democracy Builds, first published in 1945.

FLLW and the Davis children, Charlotte and Brian. Photograph by Dr. Richard Davis. FLLW Fdn FA#6855.0007

After its tour of Europe and Mexico, in the fall of 1953 the exhibition was set up in a pavilion designed by Wright and erected on the vacant lot in New York on Fifth Avenue between 88th and 89th streets on the site where the Guggenheim Museum would eventually be built. A full-scale Usonian house complete with furniture designed by Wright was built adjacent to the exhibition and decorated with works of art from his collection of Far Eastern art: Japanese and Chinese screens, textiles and sculpture. By the following summer it was installed in another Wright-designed pavilion connected to Aline Barnsdall's Hollyhock House in Los Angeles, California, and then finally dismantled and returned to Taliesin.

When the exhibition premiered, opening in Philadelphia on 25 January 1951, Wright added the following text to his original foreword from When Democracy Builds:

I ask you to see this exhibition before you now as being faithfully on the firing-line of this new frontier of all frontiers. You will see here the life-long struggle in the now prevailing fight for Faith: Faith in ourselves, Faith in Democracy. Faith which lies inevitably at the center of our life as a nation in which true individuality may thrive. Faith in Beauty as the natural efflorescence of the great Living Tree we call humanity. Why call our Nation a Democracy and not dare to live it? A great Architecture can rise only out of a Faith in Life as good to live for itself with no other reward necessary. Our integrity as human beings is what we must work for on the new Frontier.

DEAR CHILDREN

ALMOST ALL OF US LOVE TO DRAW—PAINT AND BUILD WITH blocks. I think building-blocks the best of all fun for boys. Why not girls? I used to build with them and learned a lot when I did so about the buildings I now build. You see, unless you do know something about the kind of building we call Architecture you can't really know very much about anything else worth knowing. Knowing what is good or bad about a building is knowing about the life you live and how you live and also *why*. So try to understand *why* the buildings are the way they are. There is always some reason in and behind every front you see or if there is none, then what you see is bad. I have myself been actively building these buildings for some 58 years. Some 557 works are on record as the result. I have tried to put them all on this basis of rhyme and reason I want you to see here. To see all there is to see takes long study and much cultivation.

Now, if you do ask "why" whenever you see what you like or like what you see you will start right along the path of comprehension. That will be good because there can be no great life for any peo- ple without that great culture which we call Architecture. Knowledge of the "why" in Architecture should be the true basis of our own Culture just now as it has ever been the basis of all great cultures. All we best know about great civilizations now dead is what we may learn from their Architecture.

If our civilization were to be destroyed now what would future civilizations have to think of us as a people?

What would they see—do you think were they to someday look back upon what we have done and are so busy doing?

So in this work you are to see for yourselves in this architecture, try to understand what they are all about—what they mean to you. What they mean today and tomorrow is important to you all because buildings last a long time. Most of these will stand 300 years at least, if they are not torn down.

So here in this exhibition you may see something of your own *today* that is your own *tomorrow*. And maybe the day after that. Please ask your teacher "why" when you don't understand. If they can't answer—be patient and wait.

TO YOUNG ITALY
May 1951

Here in your time-stained romantic historical country I now feel the sympathy of a gratified son honoring the great artists who faced sunset in the West—the Italian Renaissance—believing it sunrise. Out of ensuing night comes this work of mine about which in the Vilino Belvedere at Fiesole I wrote, June 1910.

The essential Italian spirit all creative artists love will yet salvage the great good in the Old to live as the New: live not as "Renaissance" but as Naissance: a dawn that need know no night.

Italian art may again grow great closer to the ground, though "the harvest shall not be yet." St. Augustine is with you to guide his awakening sons to the everlasting principles which I hope and believe young Italy is eager to know: a glory founded upon the eternal course of a sun that may fade but will never set because of light organic, ever risen in the human heart: a heart knowing Beauty to be Truth.

To all of you my best hope and thought.[1]

TO SWITZERLAND
January 28, 1952

Zurich is Switzerland to me and The United States of Switzerland is the perfect pattern for The United States of Europe.

May the honor of Switzerland's heroism, amidst the most brutal family brawl in all history, never diminish. From its premier in the Strozzi Palace at Florence this adequate collection of my work comes to Zurich for exhibition. Italy is still the beating heart of the creative-art world. Astonished, I saw that not one modern work included in the exhibition but would have graced Medieval Italy as against the Renaissance. I am glad this event takes place in Zurich in the museum built by Professor Karl Moser, one of that distinguished group of European architects to which Berlage and Otto Wagner belonged and brought the architectural thought of Europe abreast that of Louis Sullivan in my own country. Your Congress House is worthy continuation of that early devotion to a great ideal.

The Wrights arrive in Rome on way to exhibition in Florence, June 1951. FLLW Fdn FA#6203.0004

I have twice experienced the loveliness, love and hospitality of Zurich. With gratitude by this exhibition I hope for the third time to help point the path of progress toward a free architecture fit for the youth of your country. A free architecture for a free people is only free so long as maintained on a basis of principle. This is the message this exhibition brings with love and hope from the United States of America to the young architects of the United States of Switzerland.

MESSAGE TO FRANCE

April 1952

In a frightened world lost to soul by way of Force, O France, you have had a substitute for soul. Your substitute is delicacy. Do not lose the grace of your touch. Do not be misled by a frightened people that count on its fingers freedoms up to four because they do not know Freedom.

Freedom's secret is within the Spirit and, notwithstanding Napoleon, the lustre of France does not lie in the harsh glare of militarism but lives in her own genius—the love of reason in her philosophers and the love of beauty in her poets. France really lived when she lined up on the side of Freedom, Equality, and Fraternity: a lesson learned from the forefathers of the United States of America but which those States now seem to be in danger of forgetting.

O France, put your trust in your native genius. Internationalism is good only when and where preserving what is French in France, Italian in Italy, British in Britain, Russian in Russia and it consists in appreciation by each and every Nation of what constitutes the soul of the other and insists upon uniting for the protection of that Individuality.

I bring to France Architecture Free—free because based upon organic Principles. Free because of infinite variety found in the truth that Form and Function are one. Organic Architecture free of academic Tradition, free of all Tradition except Principle, is the greatest discipline as well as the greatest inspiration on earth. Because it is voluntary and interior Organic Architecture is the sovereign Architecture of Democracy.

"Free" means unafraid, self confident because sure of its ground and its star—fully aware of the fact that the soul of one race has not the color or precise form of any other but all have the love of truth in common and Truth is found by knowing Principle, knowing that Form and Function are one, that Beauty either of character, Form or Facade must be wooed and won by love alone.

Unity in variety is in the mind of the Creator. When one species becomes too dominant it is destroyed. Beauty can never yield to Force.

TO GERMANY

May 1, 1952

To two great but various cultures I owe most in that strange occurrence we call our education: to Old Germany and Old Japan. Both are no more except as they are alive and working in the soul of all humanity today.

I am happy to say they are living in mine. Both were working in what you will see of this exhibition of a large portion of my life-work as an architect.

Goethe, Beethoven and Nietzsche, their inspiration has lasted me lifelong, I knew so many other great Germans. With me also were the great Japanese, Rikyu, Sesshu and "moderns" like Korin, Sotatsu, Hiroshige and Hokusai. A multitude of great artist craftsmen I learned to know when working upon the Imperial Hotel in Japan from 1913 to 1919. Their inspiration is mine to this day. They went to school to Germany but went the wrong way.

German culture was more nearly ready for Organic-architecture in my early life as an architect than my own people in our United States. Kuno Francke, exchange professor of aesthetics at Harvard came to Oak Park, Chicago, to see my buildings in the Spring of 1909. Delighted by what he saw, he then and there tried to persuade me to come to Germany because he said my people were not ready for me but the German people were. Returning to Germany, soon afterward, he instigated the publication of my work by Wasmuth, 1910, Berlin: the *Ausgeführte Bauten und Entwürfe.*

Also, (but later) the Japanese sent a commission around the world to find an architect for the new Imperial Hotel. They first heard of me in Germany, and came straight to see my buildings. They said: "Nothing Japanese about these buildings, but would look well in Japan." They employed me to come and build the Emperor's new clearing-house for the foreign social obligations incurred by official Japan.

Somehow the two cultures—German and Japanese—came together in my life to enable me to further the education I had begun with both.

Gratitude is mine. I hope to see Germany, the great outpost of Western Culture, divested of the old

FLLW at construction site of exhibition pavilion, Fifth Avenue, New York, 1953. Photograph by P. E. Guerrero. FLLW Fdn FA#6007.0036

militarist complex which somehow I had never realized was so German as it seemed to become. What was profound in great German culture is inevitably now in the life-blood of the Western World for great good; probably the most valuable strain in it. What would Western Culture be without it?

The profound in Old German Culture must come back to us all again. I have never doubted but it would come strengthened and purified by the agony of defeat. No physical destruction can destroy the indomitable German love of beauty in the Song that is Life.

She will build her love into a great Architecture, greatest of Arts—now the blind-spot of the world and take her rightful leadership where she belongs—in the growing realm of Democratic Nations.

Old Germany has been and is still my love, never faltering and a great hope. She will suffer, but will never be destroyed.

MESSAGE TO FRANCE
May 15, 1952

It is my distinguished privilege to thank you and your officials one and all for the remarkable manifestation of hospitality extended to my work and to me in the recent exhibition in the great halls of the Ecole in Paris.

It has been my wish—always—that the friendship between our nations hitherto so close in politics, should continue and grow in our culture.

I have been assured by many in both France and the United States that this affair at the Beaux Arts has contributed greatly to that much desired end.

Therefore, my dear sir, I assure you of my satisfaction in this display of friendship, so far as I could see, on the part of everyone concerned.

May the Cause of a free architecture continue to grow and look back with gratitude upon this auspicious occasion.

Faithfully, my dear sir, with a wish to be kindly remembered to all of you who had a share in establishing the event—

I am most truly yours,

TO HOLLAND
June 1, 1952

Long ago this work owed appreciation to Holland when understanding of the nature of the work was not only new but rare.

Visiting America, the eminent Dutch Architect Berlage raised his voice in praise. Said he, "The two things which impressed me most in the United States were Niagara Falls and the Larkin Building." Architect Oud wrote in: "De Styl" an article which reached and encouraged me while I was unfortunate. Then Widjeveld and Wendingen came through with one of the most splendid of the many publications devoted to my effort in the direction of a native creative-culture. This publication reached me at a time when I was walking the streets of New York getting a worm's eye view of society.

Exhibitions of this work have known Holland before.

One, I remember, under Widjeveld at Amsterdam 1930. The American Ambassador, asked by Widjeveld to open the show, said, "Who is this man Wright anyway." The Ambassador came, waved the American flag. But Widjeveld made the Ambassador's speech.

As an architect I have had occasion to admire the work of Architects Oud, Dudock, Widjeveld and other Dutchmen. A young Dutch patriot Van't Hoff made his appearance in Chicago very early in my day and took home something of what he then saw there on the Chicago prairie.

At that same trying time in my life my first academic honor came to me from the Academic Royale D'Anvers, no doubt influenced by my Dutch friends, nearby. So I felt at home in Holland when again it was so happening in this world that a native culture dawning in a new nation was not recognized by its own provincials before that dawning had been noticed and approved in Europe where most of the people of the new nation came from.

So Holland will always have a warm place in my heart and due respect from my head.

My greatest admiration for her cultural achievements.

They establish Holland as one of the fundamental assets in world-culture by which what is vital in Art today stands up nobly under the test of time.

One of the truly independent Democracies on earth, she has suffered and shared much that is to be the soul of the new world-order. Someday common to us all.

I cannot imagine her contribution in any and every cultural field left out of the eventual reckoning.

Architecture is basic to that field.

More and more comes the recognition that the principles of Organic Architecture lie in the core of the freedom that we call Democracy.

So how glad I am to again know that there on exhibition in Holland is what I have for a lifetime done in that direction, sure that there is the kind of home-coming I would wish I might myself see and talk with you Hollanders about the great cause nearest our hearts today: world-peace. Organic peace can only come when the great Principles of the Art of Architecture organic are really understood. If they were they would soon be established as basic to the society and politics of this world.

So to you—mighty little nation—so right and so strong in the continuity that is the Future, this "The Italian Exhibition" is a friendly visitor already known to you. Of your welcome I feel assured because your feeling for truth and beauty has never yet failed you as a nation nor will ever fail humanity.

TO MEXICO

October 1, 1952

Saludos Amigos

This comprehensive exposition of my work is routed from Europe by way of Mexico City instead of London because our companion-nation of the South seems to me, just now, to be more in need of inspiration. This work may have something to offer Mexico in the new direction of Architecture Free in Mexico to be itself Mexican, eventually—say in a quarter of a century—a true expression of the individual humanity that is Mexico, the great Primitive, instead of the standardized typewriter Architecture evolved from European modern now so much in

evidence there. Much of it is the expression of a mental-confusion and spiritual poverty. Mexico deserves a richer share in the struggle to advance the great culture that is Organic in Architecture.

To most North Americans Mexico has become the great Nation of contradictions. She is the great Primitive struggling now to resolve these contradictions. This greatly favored and most beautiful land of magnificent historical Romance is worthy of a great Architecture. So the gospel of an Organic Architecture is the true basis as well as the heart of appropriate culture for the beauty-loving Mexicans. Thus it seems to me that what I have done is needed here while my confreres are concentrated at the eighth Pan American Conference.

I hope this conclusion will meet with approval and the characteristic enthusiasm of the Mexican nature. Should my confreres, whom I greatly esteem, approve I shall be happy and consider the show, as well as myself, well spent.

My best to my Mexican comrades—in true friendship.

TO U.S.A.

This Work Dedicated

To my Mother, Anna Lloyd Wright,

Friedrich Froebel, 1876

Dankmar Adler and Louis H. Sullivan, 1893

My Wife, Olgivanna

This exhibition of native architecture was first officially requested by Italy and consequently splendidly shown at the Strozzi Palace, Florence, June 1951. The generosity of Arthur Kaufmann enabled Oscar Stonorov to volunteer to get the material together and arrange a preview in Philadelphia in January 1951. It was there displayed much as it was later seen, as a guest at first in Italy, then Switzerland, France, Germany, Holland and Mexico exhibitions, also supervised by Oscar Stonorov. Each of the events was received in the various countries by official dignitaries and accorded high academic honors by citations and gold medals. There were illustrious celebrations, receptions, banquets-in-honor. Especial numbers of five architectural magazines were published in these various nations. Wherever the exhibition went there were national sponsors, patrons and important social occasions.

But here at home the case is different. This exhibition itself is not a guest but is host. There have been generous offers of sponsorship but as its own patron and sponsor now this work should beckon and welcome you. Art in a Democracy ought to be its own patron; no sponsor should be necessary if our Declaration of Independence means what it says.

As the citizen rises to eminence from humble circumstances by his own merit, so the artist must arise in his own good time.

Therefore here in your own country you are to see a life's work, in its own way, for what it may be worth to you. If there are patrons they are you. If there are sponsors they are friends in the circumstances who have helped make this exhibition possible. If we as a free people are ever to arrive at a culture of our own we should not get one nor try to maintain it by illustrious sponsors or powerful patrons but by friends genuinely interested in developing and preserving the innate virtues of that work.

If our form of society is true to its own nature conscientious independence should prove a proper test of values. By that test alone should any work in the arts survive. Fine-art lives and must eventually stand upon its own. The highest humility. Why not now?

So my friends known or unknown, "Sixty Years of Living Architecture" welcomes you.

1. In an earlier version of "To Italy" Wright reminisced about the time he was there in 1910 with Mamah Borthwick Cheney: "With humble gratitude therefore I am here again. Once more I hope to walk the winding road from Firenze to Fiesole. I long to go along the poppy-covered fields over the hills to the Vale of Vallambrosa." But in the final version he chose to remove the reference to that painful memory of forty years earlier.

Sixty Years of Living Architecture, exhibition pavilion, Hollyhock House, Los Angeles, California, 1954. Photograph by John Geiger.
FLLW Fdn FA#5427.0016

SIR EDWIN LUTYENS

Early in the summer of 1950, while Wright and his wife were in London, he was asked by A.H.T. Johnson, editor of Builder *magazine, to write a review of a monograph devoted to the British architect Sir Edwin Lutyens.[1] The work was still in press at that time, but by the following February the handsome three-volume monograph, entitled "The Lutyens Memorial" arrived at Taliesin.[2] Wright responded, "Dear Mr. Johnson: The 'Lutyens' has just arrived. And I see [sic] what I can do. Sincerely yours, Frank Lloyd Wright."[3] Wright praised his British colleague: "I have much admired the way in which his passion for Tradition thus graciously fitted its place in his own country." Yet, on the other hand, he admonished against a culture that does not heed changing conditions: "In common with multitudes I liked Sir Edwin the man and I admire his work as a great English architect. We can follow his own great qualities, not his buildings." [Unpublished]*

TO APPRAISE THE WORK OF THIS GREAT ENGLISHMAN, I AM incompetent. Sir Edwin so thoroughly expressed the cultural feeling of the better English of his day that a new-world reaction like mine could not be trusted to do more than voice admiration of the love, loyalty and art with which this cultured Architect, in love with Architecture, shaped his buildings.

To him the English chimney, the Gable, the Gatepost monumentalized in good brick-work and cut-stone were motifs to be used with great skill. He was able to dramatize them with a success unequalled.

Nor can I think of anyone able to so characteristically and quietly dramatize the old English feeling for dignity and comfort in an interior, however or wherever that interior might be in England.

I have much admired the way in which his passion for Tradition thus graciously fitted its place in his own country.

But when his great talents were employed in India I do not feel this admiration. It seems to me the work in Delhi showed him as strange to the land as the land was strange to him.

The English Arts and Crafts owe Sir Edwin a great debt of gratitude. He insisted upon good craftsmanship at a time when it was dying: competent to get the best out of the workman for the English Tradition he lifted high—probably to its last resting place here on Earth.

Now all effort in Art of the quality of Sir Edwin's effort is precious as a natural heritage, and rare. I am glad to see it regarded with reverence. These splendid volumes treasuring it all will preserve it as a national monument. My own faith and desire would leave it there worthy as such and go on toward the expression of a life inevitably changed and changing but changing for the better only if we apply the lessons learned from the devotion to the ideal of men like him. The symbolism of the period Sir Edwin Lutyens represented is being superseded by practice of the principles of Organic-structure employing to the utmost the materials, machinery and men of the Machine Age—the era we now live in—as profoundly worthy, even now, of the love and interpretation of the Architects of the era inevitably ending with Sir Edwin.

However much we must regret the Old we cannot preserve its best without meeting the law of Change with courage and intelligence—at whatever cost to sentiment.

Sentimentality is Sentiment degenerate.

License is Freedom degenerate.

Architecture is Culture degenerate unless it is abreast of the changing conditions of the time of its creation.

We cannot afford to build for a sentimental taste in this—our Day and Time. Where we used to *feel* we now need to *know,* in order to be safe Architects for any future that is now. In common with multitudes I liked Sir Edwin the man and I admire his work as a great English architect.

We can follow his own great qualities, not his buildings.

1. 1869–1944.

2. *The Lutyens Memorial: The Architecture of Sir Edwin Lutyens,* A.S.G. Butler, Charles Scribner's Sons, New York, 1950.

3. FLLW to A.H.T. Johnson, 23 February 1951.

WHAT THE AMERICAN GOVERNMENT SHOULD DO TO INSURE LASTING PEACE IN KOREA

From the moment of its founding in 1947, the United Nations seemed to Wright to be an organization of force rather than one of peace. His ideas about nations, politicians, militarism, statesmen, and the so-called Big Three clearly expressed in this unpublished article, seem even more pertinent today than they did some forty-three years ago. The infamous Big Three has certainly ceased to exist as a world force; and the United Nations' peace-making operations seem limited to invasions and airstrikes. Wright clearly foresaw this situation nearly half a century ago. [Unpublished]

NOT ONLY PEACE IN KOREA, THE PEACE OF THE WORLD, so it seems to me, would be best served if the United States of America would try to recover the lost art of minding its own business.

If Democracy has a genius it consists in the Democratic nation, in avoiding militarism as its citizens would avoid suicide.

The military mind has proved a dead mind. Only militarism thrives on it.

I should say the present situation calls for Statesmen. We have only politicians and soldiers. What has become of the idea that only units strong, that is to say independent within themselves, can ever live harmoniously together? Interdependence must mean unrest if not the perpetual bickering now going on. Is it not yet sufficiently evident that independence cannot be bought by either war or the dollar?

Where now are the smaller, more intelligent members of world-society like Switzerland, Sweden, Denmark, Holland, Finland, Belgium, Norway, Ireland, Italy, France, Germany, Yugoslavia, Canada, Spain, China, India, Mexico, Persia, the South American Republics, Japan and the various Island Republics? Where is their coalition?

Are they non-entities in the power-game because they are only smaller than big? They are still preponderant in humane realities! Of what moral value to this world in agony is a United Nations composed of a "big three" imposing their will upon the world and calling their will Freedom? Is gangsterism any better in the name of Freedom than it is in the name of Slavery?

Oh Lord, give us respite from "The Big Three." Subdivide all big power everywhere. Teach us how to learn this lesson so plainly taught the world by this deadly political fiasco in Korea!

Only by that lesson learned can the terrible loss of humanity there be justified—if ever.

FORCE IS A HERESY

It was a singular embarrassment to Frank Lloyd Wright that Joe McCarthy was a senator from Wisconsin, Wright's home state. At one point during the HUAC hearings McCarthy went after the architect on the grounds that his thoughts and activities were "un-American." But what infuriated Wright was the method of intimidation employed by McCarthy in his purge of American citizens in all walks of life. In this article, published in the Wisconsin Athenaean, *Wright queried, "When a McCarthy can exist in our country our politics cry out for revision . . . I ask my fellow citizens . . . which is most dangerous to our Democratic system of free men: a sociologic idiot like a Communist or a political pervert like a McCarthy?"* [Wisconsin Athenaean, *September 1951*]

OUR NATION WAS BORN IN BELIEF THAT FORCE SHOULD not govern. Force is what is governed. Force has never compelled obedience in the social order nor can do so today. All Force can compel is Death. This is known to men who think.

Yet the heretical system of force is returning to our Nation by degrees, trying to blackmark or herd all original thinkers into concentration camps. This Marxist theory of communism has now seriously injured our national intelligence.

Communism is a *theory* that can be stretched to mean "each according to his need." But, actually, communist production can never rise for long above a bare subsistence level. Marxist Communism is nonsensical because Capital and Labor can never make war on each other and either one survive. The potentiality of an Idea was entirely left out of the Marxist reckoning. A Communist has signed away his Sovereignty as an Individual. Therefore Communism is a make-shift for the Slave.

Our own Democratic system for the Sovereignty of the Individual as protected by our Constitution founded on Magna Carta is the *only method of organized government that leaves to the creative faculty of man and his capacity for production, the necessary freedom to grow.* Politics and Government—in a Democracy—(machines or no machine) are subordinate to this necessary freedom for individual *growth*.

This Freedom of the Individual now exists in the world because of America.

Observe that in the structure of our Government *all controls are corrective* not preventive. In a Society of Contract like ours framed by Statesmen who were inspired Architects of a social order—*all other controls must prove subversive if not destructive.* Government therefore may not initiate or lead. Government can only *execute* policy, correct or punish the Individual. Governmental leadership in a Democracy is poison.

The harm this communist harum-scarum by

government is doing to ourselves by ourselves is enormous. By perversion of our own Constitution we have put our own Faith in constant peril—not from without but *from within*. We have ourselves made our Nation ridiculous. Fear thus raised and exaggerated by politicians to scare and huddle the sheep is doom enough. What is it these rams (politicians) in the ram pasture (Washington) really want? Ask any citizen (the sheep) and mark the answer. Mine is on the record.

When a McCarthy can exist in our country our politics cry out for revision. Why not stand by the Constitution—speak up!

What a man thinks is his own.

What a man says is still his.

Only a man's acts concern Government.

Men in our free country should fear Fear more than all beside—but God. Of God a great French lover of liberty has said, "If God had not existed it would have been necessary for man to invent him." Well, if America had not existed it would be necessary, now, for man to invent America.

I ask my fellow citizens . . . which is most dangerous to our Democratic system of free men: a sociologic idiot like a Communist or a political pervert like a McCarthy?

As for perversion by this rapidly growing oppression of the military incubus we inherited from Roosevelt "leadership": why not ask the military to listen to Napoleon. He is still the supreme exponent of their craft.

Napoleon's last days on earth were spent in anguish trying to understand, he said, "why *force* could never organize anything."

Knowing he was dying, he said many things worth remembering. One of them: "A Nation taking men out of its fields to make soldiers of them is defeated before it starts to fight." Etc., etc.

Well, I wonder, what this supreme advocate of force would say of a Nation taking its children out of school on *suspicion* of aggression to make soldiers of them.

Aggression *actual* is one thing. Aggression *imaginary* is quite another. Especially if used to bolster a national economy or used by officious politicians to scare Free-men into war with the Serf. A Serf is a man who signs away his Sovereignty as an Individual.

Nothing can be so demoralizing to the Freeman—nothing so deadly—as the free-mind afraid of the servant-mind. Yes . . . again I say we, a free people, must fear Fear more than all beside—but God. Only the military octopus can thrive on fear. In a Society like ours Freedom dies with the death of the Sovereignty of the Individual.

ORGANIC ARCHITECTURE LOOKS AT MODERN ARCHITECTURE

Frank Lloyd Wright defined his term "organic architecture" in several different ways throughout his writings. But one basic principle remained the same—it was an architecture that grew outward from within, in which all the parts were related to the whole as the whole was related to the parts. He saw organic architecture as an integrated entity. In this respect, he saw architecture as following the principles that govern nature. For Wright the study of nature was never the looking at but rather, and far more profound, the looking in. It was a philosophic study, not a materialistic one.

In this article, published in The Architectural Record in May 1952, he brought to a fitting close a long association with that publication that had begun in 1908. In his early articles for the magazine he had explained the "new" architecture he was creating. In the 1920s, he wrote a series of articles that defined the essentials of his work in terms of materials and methods appropriate to twentieth-century technology. But in this latest article, he traced the origins of his work, its early publication in Europe, and its subsequent influence on a new generation of architects in Germany, Holland, and France. Such works as the Larkin Building (Buffalo, New York, 1903) and Unity Temple (Oak Park, Illinois, 1905) had a pronounced effect on European architects. Wright's work, especially these two buildings, demonstrated a negation of excessive ornamentation, and further demonstrated the application of the machine as a tool in the hand of the artist, or architect, in this instance. But what came back to the United States as a result of this early influence were machine-governed buildings that had absorbed the effects but not the principles of that early work. These were first evident in the early 1930s, but in the 1950s building after building was built in the so-called International Style. Wright saw it as no style whatsoever—and certainly not international—but instead merely a fashion. He wrote,

Thus Modern-architecture is Organic-architecture deprived of soul. Therefore architecture is now so easy to grasp that any boy of three months' experience can practice it and appear with a dose of it on the front page of the local newspaper next month, or within a year (or two) be heralded in color by the market-magazines of building-materials as the new "It." The "plan-factory" now has shows in Art-Museums.

Wright persistently believed that someday the concept would die on the vine from lack of any genuine, organic nourishment and that the respect for humanity evident in his work would eventually come to the fore and triumph: "Probably the humanly significant forms belonging to Organic-architecture now camouflaged or betrayed and called 'modern' will come back from the gutter of Fashion toward which they now seem headed: come back and—deepened by experience—start all over again . . . I hope. And I believe." [The Architectural Record, May 1952]

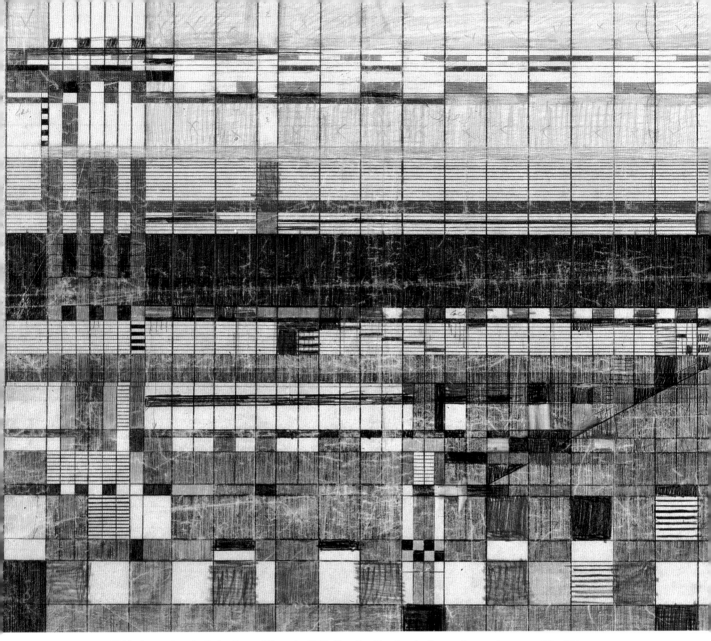

Hillside Theatre Curtain, Spring Green, Wisconsin. 1952. Elevation. Pencil and color pencil on tracing paper, 58 x 36".
FLLW Fdn#5223.002

MODERN-ARCHITECTURE IS THE OFFSPRING OF ORGANIC-architecture: an offspring, already emasculate and commercialized, in danger of becoming a Style. Having suffered many styles since Old Colonial washed up on eastern and Mission reappeared on western shores, this country takes over another one—this time the 58th variety—derived from its own exported Organic-architecture.

Organic-architecture was Middle West. Out of the "Cradle of Democracy" at the end of the nine-teenth and the beginning of the twentieth century, came this new sense of architecture. Gradually, over a fifty-year period, a period of ambiguous acceptance and university adversity, it planted and established fertile forms and new appropriate methods for the natural (machine) use of steel, glass, plastics (like concrete) and provided more ample freedom in shel-ter for the free new life of these United States than any "style" had ever provided or even promised. Organic-architecture thus came of America—a new

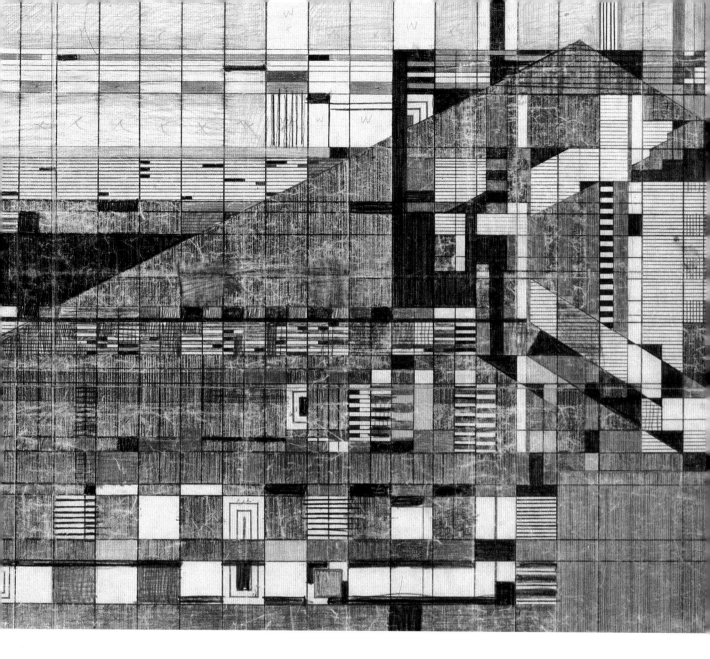

freedom for a mixed people living a new freedom under a democratic form of life. Susceptible of infinite variety, it changed the proportions of building throughout the world. The Machine was dedicated to it. Grandomania dead of it—or dying.

Organic-architecture was definitely a new sense of shelter for *humane* life. Shelter, broad and low. Roofs either flat or pitched, hipped or gabled but always comprehensive Shelter. Wide flat eaves were some-times perforated to let trellised light through upon characteristic ranges of windows below. Ornament was non-existent unless integral. Walls became screens, often glass screen, and the new open-plan spread space upon a concrete ground-mat: the whole structure intimate and wide upon and of the ground itself. This ground-mat floor eventually covered and contained the gravity-heating system (heat rises naturally as water falls) of the spaces to be lived in: forced circulation of hot water in pipes embedded in a broken stone bed beneath the floor slabs (soon misnamed "radiant-heat"). Other new techniques, new forms adapted to our inevitable machine-methods appeared in these new structures. The economics of continuity and cantilever-structure were realized. Even the walls played a new role or disappeared. Basements and attics disappeared altogether. A new sense of space in appropriate human scale pervaded not only the structure but the life itself lived in it was broadened, made more free because of sympathetic freedom of plan and structure. The interior space to be lived in became *the reality of the whole performance.* Building, as a box, was gone.

The integral character of the third dimension was born to architecture.

Here came to America by way of its own architecture a natural concept of cultural human growth as an integrity comparable to growth of trees or a plant to grace the already disgraced landscape and liberate the individual from the sham of classicism.

By way of the integral quality of depth due to the third dimension and new sense of space as contrived by the new formulas of continuity and cantilever in devising construction, a new countenance emerged. The clear countenance of principle. The old post-and-beam formula was now too wasteful. Hard and clumsy, it seemed like a rattling of the bones. The cut-slash-and-butt construction of the old camouflaged box of the Renaissance or otherwise seemed harsh or trivial. Ugly and false. Each organic building (an integument rather than a box) became as one with its site and occupancy. Nor could these buildings be imagined anywhere else nor for any other purpose whatever than where and for what they were built.

Thus by 1893–1900 a great negation transpired in America, entirely free of European influences. *But this sweeping negation was only the platform upon which to affirm* these new principles of life and economic building-construction. Naturally this negation had novel aesthetic aspects but wore the countenance of principle.

As a matter of course, these novel aspects of countenance were striking *effects:* startlingly clean, "stream-lined" "effects." Soon these effects were elsewhere seized upon, in Germany particularly, where years later they appeared at the Bauhaus.

Organic-architecture as built in America during the years 1893 to 1909 was first extensively published in Europe by Germany, 1910, owing to the insistence of Professor Kuno Francke, "Exchange Professor of Aesthetics" at Harvard.[1] (It had been published in England years before.) Reaching Paris soon, it there became, by way of journalistic ability and our own provincial museums, again the Box. But, the box nude! Duly dedicated to Machinery.

The original and elemental affirmative characteristics or the original negation made by Organic-architecture in three dimensional structure, *the Machine dedicated to it,* now reappeared as a bare two-dimensional facade *dedicated to the Machine!* The streamlined novelty of the original negation became thus a fit fad for Fascism. But our provincials began to import it because the culture-mongrel of our country and our museums believes, and will continue to believe, that American "culture" is a bastard. "Culture comes from Europe."

Well, this import was not an affair of construction at all but a mere "aesthetic," a painter's, not an architect's. Soon a cliché. The fruitful *affirmative negation* made by Organic-architecture in three dimensions now reappeared as a two-dimensional affair. *All* ornament was scraped off. A high box would be contrasted with a long low box or square boxes were placed together alongside very tall boxes. Or on came the nude box cut open or set up in the air on posts without pants. But always, nevertheless and notwithstanding—the BOX. Thus surfaced the box was invariably painted white to emphasize the fact that it did not intend being a becoming feature of the ground upon which it was put. By maintaining a white sepulture for unthinking mass-life, individuality was soon leeched from the performance. Otherwise no such cliché could have been made so useful to our American mass-education or serve our standard practice of quick commerce.

This sterilizing performance was duly dedicated to machinery, as any cliché should be, not *machinery dedicated to it* as in Organic-architecture. So, here came a kind of tapeworm into the entrails of Organic-architecture. Because of the novel effects of the original organic negation made for organic purposes this mixture of negation with negation is, as of today, what is called "Modern-architecture."

Any two-dimensional cliché is too easy to commercialize or teach. To educationists and the commercial capitalist it was providential—just what both wanted because so shallow an affair of surfaces. The Box now, sometimes of glass, say, but always a post-and-beam affair even if not rattling its bones, became more and more evident in standard education. Buildings began gradually to appear intermixed with the "effects" of Organic-architecture—to be now called "Modern-architecture."

The imported cliché was not only easy to teach. "Less is more" unless less, already little, becomes less than nothing at all and "much ado about nothing."

Now, because of a much too shallow aesthetic (a painter's), the original affirmative negation made by Organic-architecture (an architect's) seems too soon in danger of losing, under the name of Modern-architecture, its humane characteristics and original poetry. Confused with architecture superficially fashioned in two dimensions we have a superficial imitation of the original profound negation made by Organic-architecture itself.

Easy to practice, easier still upon the resources of human science and imagination, the Box, ornamental camouflage (the "Classic") scraped off—*but old thought unchanged*—again rises—educational and fashionable: The cliché of a new STYLE!

Regardless, the old box comes back. The crate now consecrate.

In it we see high and low purposes all packaged or banked alike.

Architectural careers thus become quick. The true amateur, sterilized owing to this revival of the box-facade by accredited schools—and names—is thus made "safe." Grateful for this sterilization, if for no other reason, our leading universities together with realtor "developers" and our swelling bureaucratic government are all ready to "take over" "Modern-architecture." It goes everywhere the educational institution and especially the Museum happens to be or to go. The Museum-as-Education and Education-as-the-Museum have found just what could easily be handled in the name of culture: culture must come from abroad! That is where the cliché came from.

Now, the moral nature of the Cuckoo (to be sure) characterized much if not most of the ambitious subscribers to this go-getter rush for the bandwagon. Any honest aspirant had small chance of recognition and none of genuine success. Any aspirant, tough or callow, could more easily exploit the Box bare than take time and pains to go deeper into the principles of Organic-architecture.

Organic-architecture based upon fundamental human and structural principles insisted upon *integral method and always significant form true to structure throughout. Or none.* It was profound—too slow for popular purposes. Therefore preparation for architectural practice would be not only slow but far too difficult. Also, a discerning client was needed rather than a fashionable one. There are still a few discerning ones developing in America.

Being truly individual, Organic-architecture lacked the journalist. America is nothing if not journalistic.

Writing as of 1952, the old Box—undressed—seems coming back again. The white-paint-men thrive on choice ways of setting it up on top of the ground. Regardless. They set it up tall, endwise; put it over there, down crosswise. Set it on the bias? Likely enough set it up on top of posts or anything else. Soon they will pivot it. Tyros slash and stripe its fascistic facades horizontally or vertically or checker-wise the fronts. Soon diagonally? They stamp it to look thick or stamp it to look thin: put lids on it—or none. Lids either square or askew, projecting or flush. The professors make a drum of it and beat it for dismal accord with the soulless character of an Era.

Thus Modern-architecture is Organic-architecture deprived of a soul. Therefore architecture is now so easy to grasp that any boy of three months' experience can practice it and appear with a dose of it on the front page of the local newspaper next month, or within a year (or two) be heralded in color by the market-magazines of building-materials as the new "It." The "plan-factory" now has shows in Art-Museums.

I fear the history of creative art down the ages thus repeats itself in our own modern times and again we have categories of names. Names! But now names all essentially *unlike* for performances as *alike* as any two peas.

So this is Modern-architecture! Well—if so—this affair, too, will pass as matter of intelligent choice. St. Augustine once observed, "The harvest shall not be yet." Perhaps what is left behind when we sicken of it all will be better (I so believe) than what came of similar betrayal of principles in times past. Better, because of what is left of the character of integral form and proportion—the plastic humanitarian space in building which Organic-architecture has already made. Probably the humanly significant forms belonging to Organic-architecture now camouflaged or betrayed and called "modern" will come back from the gutter of Fashion toward which they now seem headed: come back and—deepened by experience—start all over again.

The timeless war of Principle with Expediency will go on and on, in our country especially, because more than ever human nature here is habituate. Like vegetation. Or the parasite. To really change human habituation (even to the cigarette degree) would require more than one try in any one century. While nailing up a box in different ways is so easy, why should a Get-rich-quick Society like ours take time and the extreme pains necessary to make an organism of anything? A cultural organism (like any other true organism) must *grow*. Growth *is* slow. It cannot be had like a box nailed up by the tyro internationally. The answer is yet to come.

Any "international style" would probably be a cultural calamity fit for Fascism but intolerable to democracy. Meantime so-called "Modern-architecture" runs the gamut of the old Box stripped and trying to assume forms originated by Organic-architecture. As this pretentious shell, empty of true organic significance, goes rapidly toward the gutter of fashion—let us observe . . . "there goes to the gutter the architecture of this modern era from which succeeding generations will probably perceive what was missed and begin to build again on the basis of what was lacking when the gutter was reached."

I hope. And I believe.

---

1. Kuno Francke was actually a naturalized American and professor of History of German Culture at Harvard. See Anthony Alofsin, *Frank Lloyd Wright: The Lost Years, 1910–1922* (University of Chicago, 1993).

WAKE UP, WISCONSIN

Wright's reaction to the "smear-fear" tactics at the time of the Cold War is described from a more international perspective in the following article, "Missionaryism." But closer to home, in his native state of Wisconsin, he thrust his attack directly at the state's senator, Joseph McCarthy: "These fighters of Communism! Do they really know what Communism means? Ask them. Their answers will make you laugh. Do they know what Democracy means? Ask them and weep."

Wright prepared this article for his friend William T. Evjue, editor and publisher of The Capital Times, *Wisconsin's liberal newspaper. It was published on the front page of the newspaper on 22 September 1952.*

HOW THOSE WHO LOVE THIS GREAT STATE, JEALOUS OF ITS honor, can tolerate Wisconsin politics now is beyond a brain and heart like mine. Our public-enemy-number-one is no ISM. No, our worst enemy is the craven credulity of our citizenry. Fear is the real danger in any democracy. Our worst enemy now is this craven fear managed by conscienceless politicians.

Scare the mob! Huddle the timid voters at the polls and a politician gets what he wants by exploiting their fears. Look the credulity of this present stampede full in the face and see our public-enemy-number-one. Mobocracy, afraid, can always bid more votes than true democracy, unless aroused, can ever hope to counteract.

Not so long ago Wisconsin had the reputation of a great and noble State. Government by great individuals came from the aroused democratic heart of the State. It is now coming from demagoguery at the mobocratic level. Today, by the popular electoral record, Wisconsin is a stench in the nostrils of decency everywhere. Blame is not so much to the frightened mob knowing no better. Shame goes to those knowing better yet, to aid their own political fortunes, willing to play the ISMIC game to further exploit the multitude. Today the great name Wisconsin, well earned, stands more for damage to America by a deliberate, dishonest exaggeration of the significance, therefore the power, of communism than exists in any other State in the world.

These fighters of communism! Do they really know what communism means? Ask them. Their answers will make you laugh. Do they know what democracy means? Ask them and weep.

Fighters? Any rat will turn and fight. We are the victims of moral cowards putting up a sham fight.

Well—an ISM exploited for political purposes is great Wisconsin's shame now. This political scare huddles Wisconsin's timid voters at the polls like nothing else. A principle, violate, or inviolate, will move the mobocratic mass no longer. Low-level politicians knew this well enough to prostitute the nobility of a great State.

On what level are her citizens now represented?

But, after all, why blame anyone but ourselves for this degradation? We as citizens have only ourselves to blame for these losses politically, educationally, yes, and morally.

This huddle of timid voters at the primaries scared into voting for self-seeking rousers playing upon their timidity instead of for upright far-sighted statesmen telling unpleasant truths.

We are now marked not by great names of noble statesmen and famed as the home of great individuals, but by inciters of a sacred people.

As an architect, therefore, I submit a simple design for a suitable and perhaps salutary memorial to the chief demagogue in the prevalent ISMIC stampede.

Here it is: At all principal cross-roads of the State set up, on a solid concrete base, a large cast iron pot of simple but chaste design, say 6 feet in diameter. Pour into it a powerful charge of H2S or carbon dioxide. On the birthday of the chief demagogue of the prevalent ISM over the entire area of the State light a blaze under every pot and raise such a prodigious stink that the true character of such a "patriot" would be brought to the noses of the voters, there where they might actually realize the nature of his "patriotism" by their own nausea. This realistic celebration to continue for 24 hours or for long enough to bring to the voters realization of the character of such "patriotism."

What great State has not been eventually ruined by the "patriotism" of conscienceless public-servants? History has no conflict on this point. All have died of exploited FEAR.

MISSIONARYISM

The job of the missionary, to force one's creed, beliefs, or ideology upon another, regardless of ethnic or cultural background, was a reprehensible agenda to Wright. He witnessed the work of missionaries many times in Japan, when they sermonized against the traditional Shinto and Buddhist roots of the Japanese people, heralding Christianity as salvation, and Western culture and technology as the epitome of civilization and enlightenment.

"Missionaryism" on a much larger and more dangerous scale was occurring in a world where the Big Three could impose their will and beliefs on smaller, weaker nations. He saw no difference between the acts of the Soviet Politburo and the fear tactics used by the United States: "Nations, especially 'the big three'—America, England, Russia—were now big Missionaries. Each out with its own kind of 'Politburo' and bomb penetrating the other's Politburo even if—or especially—by FORCE. . . . *Fear! By way of the smear, fear is now officially fed to us, the huddled sheep."*

Just as the International Style proved a failure—as Wright predicted it would—this act of imposing "democracy" has likewise failed in underdeveloped and third world countries. To Wright, anything that was not organic, of the thing, intrinsically belonging to it, could prove only fruitless and harmful to it in the long run. Here he compares this type of political imposition to architectural situations as well. [Unpublished]

ALWAYS I HAVE DREADED MISSIONARIES. THEY ARE REALLY Salesmen. Myself the son of a Unitarian Minister's wife, I could not see it as essential to make others think as my father did. While in the Orient with the temblor constantly in mind, building the Imperial Hotel, I loved the Japanese people. There I had occasion to meet some of these missionaries pushing our Occidental civilization. I didn't like them. It seemed to me then—(now more so than ever)—that the very essence of Democracy lay in *the practical refutation of such gratuitous imposition by Missionary.* When Missionaryism reached the militant stage, as it seems to do sooner or later, it became murderous.

I first met Russian people in Tokyo during my long stay there. I loved these Russian people. They were aristocrats—refugees—1914. In my cozy quarters especially built next to the old German-built "Tei Koku" (Imperial Hotel) I had special hotel service, and the only grand piano in the world, so it seemed. The Russians were all cultivated, talented: true individuals. We had such high minded good times—music and theater—I shall never forget them. Sometimes they would put an arm around my shoulders and say—"but you are no American." My answer would be, "Oh, yes I am. Very American. You Russians don't know how American you are. You would love my people as I do."

Well, came 1937. Invited as honored guest of the Soviet Republic I, with my wife (though Montenegrin she speaks Russian) journeyed to attend the International Congress of Architects at Moscow. I wondered then if I would like the Russian proletariat as much as I liked the Russian aristocrat. I did. Even more. The same youthful, artist feeling. Warm, gay camaraderie. The same talent. Yes, I could take off my hat to Russian genius. Russians seemed to me fit stuff for Freedom. I could discern no damnable missionary spirit among them. They were as interested in the differences of people as in their sameness and were friendly to the point of selflessness. I saw among them no disposition nor any tendency whatever toward converting the world to their own way of life and thought. They were good to see and good to me although my thought was diametrically opposed to what, and how, they were then doing their planning and building in Moscow.

1945. I was shocked to learn that the dreaded "politburo" had so grown up among them that it was willing to convince them, FORCE preferred—that they must conquer the world if they wished to live their own lives. Hitlerism (conquer the world to make it safe for Kultur) was what the Russians most feared when we visited them 1937. But Communism, now by Politburo if necessary, had become "Conquer the world to make it safe for Marxism!" Great Russia now Missionary militant!

1950. I began to realize that in my own America the equivalent of the "Politburo" was growing up, similar thesis "Conquer the world to make it safe for Democracy." If not by guns, then *buy* it. A new ism: Dollarism!

Because I despised all isms whatsoever, openly, I was dubbed "suspect." "Isolationist" or "Nationalist." Both had become crimes. Expedient politics had become traitorous to the brave Declaration of Independence that made us a free nation. It was now

Interdependence. But the big Nation-missionaries had already clashed. As a matter of fact must inevitably crash. Which one would crash first? If one did crash could the others survive?

Now, just how this clash came to be or the crash must come about, I did not know. I do not know now except as the same old selfishness of soul and hatefulness of mind that marks the uninvited missionary had now become *national* and by blacking out all but ignoble fear politicians were making any free life for anybody quite unlikely while fear lasted. Missionaries (now Nations) were already "up and at it." International*ism* was now the slogan of the slugs. To be the fatal, final ISM on earth. Who knows.

Unity? Yes—One World? Not yet.

American *Internationalism!* I first heard it declared "the front line of our National-defense is the German Rhine": Roosevelt. A political obsession especially adapted to raising a world-wide crop of politburo. Soon the crop grew. It grew until America's front line of defense moved to the Balkan States, then on to Formosa. Missionary against missionary now all down the line.

Each Nation "all out" to maintain its own *"safety"*! America, England, Russia especially had come by way of a cold war over a mangled body to a shooting war in *Korea*. All we the people could do now, so many murdered and the rest utterly scared by official "Saviors," was pray. Or curse. Or *vote against* something. As a people we do not know how to vote *for* anything, yet.

Well, the Nation-missionaries, being what they now were with enlivened Politburos for "shepherds," were herding the poor sheep into huddles and shearing them all to burn their fleeces at the altar of Peace. Or else impounding them for slaughter. American Democracy—freedom of individual choice—now was to be had by FORCE! Ages old folly, rearing and rearming its ugly head again! The big Nations as militant Missionaries back at it now. And how? As "Saviors," of course. This perversion of Democracy by inversion with which the big Nations were now so obsessed that they were prattling about Democracy all meaning different things, must have come back to us by way of a new grouping of bell-wethers. But called by whatever name, here came the same murderous old Missionaryism, this time with a big stick—the atom bomb. It was now our *"Savior"*!

1950. World missionaryism extraordinary! All human life, especially if loving and liberal, become expendable. We, the mere peoples of this world again in a huddle, afraid. Politics, now no less than in ancient Rome under Caesar, become the extreme of human folly, hate and cruelty headed for conquest and or extinction.

Nations, especially "the big three"—America, England, Russia—were now big Missionaries. Each out with its own kind of "Politburo" and bomb penetrating the others' Politburo even if—or especially—by FORCE. One politburo pledged to murder any other politburo no matter what the wholesale slaughter of defenseless bystanders, all meantime shearing away at the huddled sheep, flinging their fleeces to the flames of FEAR by way of jealous suspicion. Mass-murder multiplied by plane and bomb soon rampant.

1952. *Fear!* By way of the smear, fear is now officially fed to us, the huddled sheep.

How did the huddle—"we the people"— ever come by this overwhelming Politburo Smearism? Well, look carefully at this Slab-temple erected to "world unity" in America's greatest flesh-pot—New York City—by way of subsidy.

Instead of symbolizing the promotion of love and friendship between Nations, this great slab idealizes division: really is apotheosis of the New York "party-wall." To this inhuman idealization and identification by slab every graveyard in the land, if it could talk, would devoutedly say, Amen! This is the perfect anti-democratic symbol to mark the end of an era. How did it happen? From where did it come?

Does this apotheosis of the New York party-wall (the perfect symbol of *division)* repress or express the spirit of Nations united? Does not this proclamation by Slab, show everything that stands in the way of world-concord today because it was ideal in hearts that would build it that way?

As an Architect and Democratic citizen I apologize for my own people. They are themselves to blame for their mischievous Missionaryism. Communists are to blame for theirs.

Democracy must learn to despise such mental confusion and spiritual poverty or give up Democracy.

To these armed aggressive nations, professional missionaries, American, English, Russian, German, French, Oriental or Negroid let us say—"WAR IS HELL." You National *Missionaries* are its salesmen.

Fear is your rod.
Peace is only your bait.
If this be Civilization then, O Lord, give us back barbarism.

ON THE SUBJECT OF ARCHITECTURE

Wright wrote this article for the American Peoples Encyclopedia Yearbook *in 1951. All we know of the commission is that it was to be "on the subject of architecture." When* The Architectural Forum *reviewed the entry in its April 1952 issue, it reprinted the entire article because Wright's comments "are brief, provocative and dangerous to excerpt." Here Wright addressed not so much the profession as the American people at large, emphasizing the importance of organic architecture. He wrote, "When I speak of architecture as organic, I mean the great art of structure coming back to its early integrity: alive as a great reality." He stressed the need for a natural building wherein "construction again proceeds harmoniously from the nature of a planned or organized inside outward to a consistent whole."*

In his view, the architecture of the time had ceased to be considered as works of art and instead was reduced to a technical makeshift. The civilization had become enamored of the machine—push-button power and gadgetry. He believed it to be the role of the architect to turn the tide from the rush to mediocrity to seek the "richness of the color of imagination and integrity of spirit." [American Peoples Encyclopedia Yearbook, 1951]

THE RENAISSANCE IN EUROPE—"A SETTING SUN ALL Europe mistook for dawn"—was imported by free America to bring architecture up to the level of a democratic civilization dedicated to freedom.

But the *spirit* of Architecture was dead. Human thought had found the printed book. The other arts had fled. Printing was the Machine. In spite of sporadic attempts at "rebirth" by special kinds of abortion, the ancient forms of architecture could only be outraged by the Machine.

Meantime the Machine became the monstrous power that moves us now. By way of it, all-out timely materials, like glass and steel, came to hand as a great new means of building. But there were no architectural forms suited to their use. The practice of architecture was so far gone to the composer of the picture that we had no architects able to conceive the radical new forms needed to use the new tools and materials with nobility, inspiration, or even intelligence. So our own architects in this new world further falsified ancient symbols and again prostituted the new materials not only by a kind of mimicry but by mechanical outrage that made our architecture what it is today—servile, insignificant refuse or puerile nostalgia.

When I speak of architecture as organic I mean the great art of structure coming back to its early integrity: alive as a great reality.

What forms shall buildings now take if the glory of the great edifice is to come back to man again and he be blessed with the great beauty of truth in the way of his life we call his environment: so meretricious, so inappropriate now?

How is the sap of human life which we call culture—escaping from autocratic monarchy to democratic freedom—going to establish itself?

It was evident long ago that we must no longer picturize, compose, or in any way pretend. We must conceive and integrate. Beginning again at the beginning we must build the right kind of building in the right way in the right place for the right man. An affair of genius.

Organic building is natural building so organic architecture is the right answer. Construction again proceeds harmoniously from the nature of a planned or organized inside outward to a consistent outside.

The space to be lived in is now the core of any building and in terms of space we find the new forms we seek. Or lose them. The old order called "classic" is therefore reversed and, where so many of our basic materials are wholly new, we are searching again for the natural way to build appropriate to the unprecedented life now to be lived in them. Our modern advantages should not continue so disadvantageous as they are becoming.

That we be enamored of the negations brought by the Machine may be inevitable, for a time. But I like to imagine this novel negation to be, as I have used it,—only a platform underfoot to enable a great splendor of life to be ours than any known to Greek or Roman, Goth or Moor. We should know a life beside which the life they knew would seem not only limited in scale, narrow in range but pale in richness of the color of imagination and integrity of spirit.

As the matter stands, the pallor is ours and the shame. The giant leverage the Machine might be for human good may fail in its own weight from helpless, human hands, far short of our hope.

Spirit only can control it but Spirit is a science Mobocracy does not know and Democracy must motivate.

Our American architecture has become no work of art at all but, at best, a technical makeshift. Buildings more than ever are a mere piece of prop-

erty. As for kindred "production" our big industrialists are so busily "streamlining" standardizations that we have been not only compelled to see some egregious makeshift touted, passed along as creation, but also to see superficial effects instead of causes finally accepted as euthenics by the "higher education" and the officialdom it must please in order to live at all.

Restlessly, we as a tirelessly exploited—and in turn exploiting—people must find some kind of release.

Lacking refreshment for whatever native love of beauty the god of the creative impulse may have passed along to us by nature, we turn to Organic architecture. As preceding generations found symbolism and empty pretensions called monumentality, so we find refreshment in rejection of shoddy sensationalism and new-fangled invention or the novelty of superficial beautifications by the commercial "designer."

These are really no higher than those of the professional beauty parlor or a cigarette in nimble fingers. We think we find—and we try to find—beauty in urbanism's streamlined machination. But Organic architecture finds no satisfaction in push-button power, not much entertainment in gadgetry or gag-ism; no happiness in preoccupation with the so-called efficiencies of every kind that have come to have no more spiritual significance than gangsterism itself. We take no pride in our triumph as "The Great Nation of the Substitute."

Last—but not least—this important line between the curious and the beautiful now becomes so confused by so-called "modern-architecture" itself that the dividing line between the curious and the beautiful—the line that marks civilization itself from savagery or degeneracy—grows dim indeed.

Organic architecture is itself a recourse for the deeper more essential Usonian-self. That self has a soul. Should that soul now be tempted to search for great repose: a serene and blessed mood? Ay, Peace. Not only a political peace but organic peace. Were we to find peace *organic* a native culture true to democracy would be so sure as to emerge even from the rubbish heap into which we have built ourselves.

MASSACRE ON THE MARSEILLES WATERFRONT

The title "Massacre on the Marseilles Waterfront" refers directly to Le Corbusier's apartment building L'Unité d'habitation, built in Marseilles from 1947 to 1952. A similar apartment building of his was built in Berlin from 1956 to 1958. To Wright, the proportion, the cold, massive, vertical slab of drab concrete were grossly inhuman, only proving that this sort of architectural application resulted in an unfit, uninspiring dwelling space for human beings. "The slums of the body converted into the slums of the soul" was frequently the way he described this kind of performance. In this unpublished article he spoke of buildings in Russia, Mexico, and India that followed the same course as this "massacre" in France. Just as he believed in the "sovereignty of the individual," he cherished the intrinsic characteristics that made up each nation across the globe. To impose one style on all seemed a crime to him: "Modern resources should develop and enrich the individualities of human life—not obliterate and impoverish them." When he designed for Japan, he carefully respected Japanese traditions; the same respect held true for his designs for Baghdad and for Venice. [Unpublished]

1952—INVITED TO THE INTERNATIONAL CONFERENCE OF Architects at Moscow (modern architecture then on trial), I ran into a tall opus—walls were two thicknesses, each mostly glass—a space between them into which heat was injected (50% for Russia, 50% for the inhabitants of the building) which I recognized as European formula for a "modern" façade. "Futuristic" this derivation of my own work was then called. There stood a bare-faced building, irrelevant, insolent, no feeling—whatever—for Russia or the Russians. Being Russians themselves of course they hated it. After taking one good look, they said, "If this is it (Modern Architecture)—it is not for Russia." "No heart." "Take it away."

In spite of all we (moderns) of the Congress of 1952 could do, Russia turned reactionary. Her "modern" architecture is their old "Classic" now—a hangover of the Monarchy they rebelled against.

More recently invited to a similar Congress of Pan American architects in Mexico City, this time I was again shocked—not to say enraged—to see the same disregard for native culture in the new University buildings just being finished. This University is probably one of the most remarkable cultural endeavors of any nation in modern times. But there stood the same type façade—regardless as ever. Except for six or seven worthy structures by natives (several of them truly noble), the place looked more appropriate to Waco, Texas than to ancient America in modern Mexico, or vice versa.

There is something inevitably crass and commercial in this type of façade-making for culture-wrecking. The same whether in Russia, Marseilles, Johannesburg, Mexico or India, the type—truly commercial—really has no soul; is only facial—Hypocritical. Again—visiting Acapulco, pride of Mexico, a Mexican resort on the ocean, there I found the place completely littered, literally, with the same typewriter sort of thing in building—utterly inappropriate. Inappropriate to people, climate and site—regardless as ever—more so than ever.

Again, arrogant insult to native culture or culture as native growth from within. Here again was a mere cliché as invalid there as a bad poster for a circus.

Into the present-day life of a great cultural Past had come these outrages upon environment, arrogant insult to culture. Well—asked by the sensitive (over-sensitive) Mexican architects for an honest opinion—(pressed hard for one) I gave it. I am not yet forgiven.

In spite of this fiasco Old Mexico in the name of Modern Architecture—copied partly from Brazil, no longer novel—there was enough truly noble building to make me wonder why Mexican architects threw away one of the most beautiful sites in the world (four-hundred splendid acres) to do something they could not (nor could anyone) possibly understand as anything above a mere passing fashion—now a shallow commercial cliché—pursued only to be soon surpassed and eventually regretted.

Again, in the *Review* of London—last June—I saw what had happened to Johannesburg, Africa. Johannesburg, it is true, had nothing to lose except what native culture the Johannesburgers might have brought with them (like ourselves). So we may leave Johannesburg at that. The English, being old Colonialists, destroyers of cultures by necessity if not by nature, can be expected to colonize a style as they have done in Johannesburg.

But again—now in India—we have a more than ever tragic instance of the curse of this cultural assassination. The Swiss brothers are "building" a modern city there—also regardless—more haphazard than ever.

I confess to a feeling that the great mother-art of Architecture I have loved life-long has fallen by way of its helpless, mundane, wandering adolescents under an evil aegis. By ignorance of principle where the depths of architecture as the great mother-art are concerned, are neophytes now at the mercy of a little clique of publicists exploiting *á la journalese* their own arrogance. Do "they" regard a native culture as something to be turned into a rubbish heap, regardless, as at Marseilles on the water-front? This wanton act admired, also regardless, for public consumption—all in the name of "modern"! Well, is it then not time to look behind this pushing of this conscienceless façade-wrecking for what this empty novelty—already stale—really is?

Our English forbears may be expected to look with calmness, even favor, upon the murder of any native culture. But can we Americans? Certainly India cannot, with her profound superb traditions! Nor France. Nor Russia. Nor Mexico.

Perhaps so far as we are concerned this lack of feeling in favor of a shallow fashionable pattern for building may also itself be the most reactionary of reactions by a generation born bastard to generate bastards.

Perhaps this loss of a sense of the advantages and virtues of nativity—this barging in upon the soul of a people, regardless, is an inevitable part of the loss of all true spiritual values in this present chaos of materiality now masquerading as "modern" when it really is old as Nineveh. Brakes now upon this craven return to a style by those to whom no true sense of style exists?—Murder, rape and arson—"crime without passion" in the name of Art—where native culture is concerned? This is old. Too old to be suffered again! Oh—Lord of hosts—any proof of validity, soundness or innate flavor in this particular pudding lies, only, "in a chewing of the string." Novelty is not originality. Modern resources should develop and enrich the individualities of human life—not obliterate or impoverish them. Only for empty souls could "One-World" mean one level.

THE LANGUAGE OF AN ORGANIC ARCHITECTURE

The Future of Architecture was Wright's first book to be published by Horizon Press. In 1953 Ben Raeburn, the president of the press, had agreed to be his exclusive publisher and as a result published a book on or by Wright each year, until the architect's death in 1959. The Future of Architecture was not a new work, however, but a reprinting of lectures and essays that had been out of print for many years. The opening chapter of the book was a transcript of a televised interview between Wright and Hugh Downs, simply called "A Conversation." Following were excerpts from Architecture and Modern Life; *the complete Kahn lectures of 1930,* Modern Architecture; *the Chicago Art Institute lectures,* Two Lectures on Architecture; *and the London lectures of 1939,* An Organic Architecture. *However, the concluding chapter was new. In this essay, entitled* The Language of Organic Architecture, *Wright further amplified his description of the term "organic architecture": "To defend and explain whatever I have myself built and written on the subject I here append a nine-word lexicon needed, worldwide, at this moment of our time."* [The Future of Architecture, *Horizon Press, New York, 1953*]

ORGANIC (OR INTRINSIC) ARCHITECTURE IS THE FREE architecture of ideal democracy. To defend and explain whatever I have myself built and written on the subject I here append a nine-word lexicon needed, worldwide, at this moment of our time.

The words.

1. NATURE. Why? As in popular use this word is first among abuses to be corrected.

2. ORGANIC. Ignorant use or limitation of the word organic.

3. FORM FOLLOWS FUNCTION. Too many foolish stylistic constructions are placed upon the slogan.

4. ROMANCE. A universal change is taking place in the use of this word, a change to which organic architecture has itself given rise. No longer sentimental.

5. TRADITION. Confusion of all eclectics, especially critics, concerning the word.

6. ORNAMENT. The grace or perdition of architecture; for the past 500 years "appliqué."

7. SPIRIT. Any version or subversion of the word by the so-called international style or by any fashion promoted by experts.

8. THIRD DIMENSION. Where and why the term was original. What it now means in architecture.

9. SPACE. A new element contributed by organic architecture as style.

When the nine words I have listed here are added together (they often are) a degradation of original form and intent which no vitality can bear, is widespread. Due to much prevalent imposition the gutter seems the only visible destination of an original idea of architecture that is basic to democratic culture: an ideal that might become the greatest constructive creative philosophy of our day if only understood and well practiced. That philosophy is surely the center line of integral or democratic culture in these United States if and when we awaken to the true meaning and intent not only of organic architecture but also of the American democracy we are founded as a nation to maintain. So I shall try to explain these nine terms. All are on the center line of both architecture and democracy. Current trends of standardized education today tend to turn young lives more and more toward sterility. Elimination of creation in favor of any cliché that will best serve mechanization. Mediocrity serves it best because mechanization best serves the mediocre. Present tendencies toward the mediocre international style not only degrade organic American architecture but will eventually destroy the creative architect in America, as elsewhere.

DEFINITIONS

1. NATURE means not just the "out-of-doors," clouds, trees, storms, the terrain and animal life, but refers to their nature as to the nature of materials or the "nature" of a plan, a sentiment, or a tool. A man or anything concerning him, *from within*. Interior nature with capital N. Inherent PRINCIPLE.

2. The word ORGANIC denotes in architecture not merely what may hang in a butcher shop, get about on two feet or be cultivated in a field. The word organic refers to *entity,* perhaps integral or intrinsic would therefore be a better word to use. As originally used in architecture, organic means *part-to-whole-as-whole-is-to-part*. So *entity as integral* is what is really meant by the word organic. INTRINSIC.

3. FORM FOLLOWS FUNCTION. This is a much abused slogan. Naturally form does so. But on a

lower level and the term is useful only as indicating the platform upon which architectural form rests. As the skeleton is no finality of human form any more than grammar is the "form" of poetry, just so function is to architectural form. Rattling the bones is not architecture. Less is only more where more is no good. Form *is* predicated by function but, so far as poetic imagination can go with it without destruction, transcends it. "Form follows function" has become spiritually insignificant: a stock phrase. Only when we say or write *"form and function are one" is* the slogan significant. It is now the password for sterility. Internationally.

4. ROMANCE, like the word BEAUTY, refers to a *quality.* Reactionary use of this honorable but sentimentalized term by critics and current writers is confusing. Organic architecture sees actuality as the intrinsic romance of human creation or sees essential romance as actual in creation. *So romance is the new reality*. Creativity *divines* this. No teamwork can conceive it. A committee can only receive it as a gift from the inspired individual. In the realm of organic architecture human imagination must render the harsh language of structure into becomingly humane expressions of form instead of devising inanimate facades or rattling the bones of construction. Poetry of form is as necessary to great architecture as foliage is to the tree, blossoms to the plant or flesh to the body. Because sentimentality ran away with this human need and negation is now abusing it is no good reason for taking the abuse of the thing for the thing.

Until the mechanization of building is in the service of creative architecture and not creative architecture in the service of mechanization we will have no great architecture.

5. TRADITION may have many traditions just as TRUTH may have many truths. When we of organic architecture speak of truth we speak of generic principle. The genus "bird" may fly away as flocks of infinitely differing birds of almost unimaginable variety: all of them merely derivative. So in speaking of tradition we use the word as also a *generic* term. Flocks of traditions may proceed to fly from generic tradition into unimaginable many. Perhaps none have creative capacity because all are only derivative. Imitations of imitation destroy an original tradition.

TRUTH is a divinity in architecture.

6. ORNAMENT. Integral element of architecture, ornament is to architecture what efflorescence of a tree or plant is to its structure. *Of* the thing, not *on* it. Emotional in its nature, ornament is—if well conceived—not only the *poetry* but is *the character of structure revealed and enhanced.* If not well conceived, architecture is destroyed by ornament.

7. SPIRIT. What is spirit? In the language of organic architecture the "spiritual" is never something descending upon the thing from above as a kind of illumination *but exists within the thing itself as its very life. Spirit* grows upward from within and outward. Spirit does not come down from above to be suspended there by skyhooks or set up on posts.

There are two uses of nearly every word or term in usual language but in organic sense any term is used in reference to the inner not the outer substance. A word, such as "nature" for instance, may be used to denote a material or a physical means to an end. Or the same word may be used with spiritual significance but in this explanation of the use of terms in organic architecture the spiritual sense of the word is uppermost in use in every case.

8. The THIRD DIMENSION. Contrary to popular belief, the third dimension is not *thickness* but is *depth.* The term "third dimension" is used in organic architecture to indicate the sense of depth which issues as *of* the thing not *on* it. The third dimension, depth, exists as intrinsic to the building.

9. SPACE. The continual becoming: invisible fountain from which all rhythms flow to which they must pass. Beyond time or infinity.

The new reality which organic architecture serves to employ in building.
The breath of a work of art.

If what I have myself written upon the subject of architecture and any one of the 560 buildings I have built are studied with this nine-word lexicon in mind, I am sure we will have far less of the confusion and nonsensical criticism upon which inference, imitation, doubt and prejudice have flourished. Isms, ists and ites defeat the great hope we are still trying to keep alive in our hearts in face of prevalent expedients now sterilizing the work of young American architects and rendering our schools harmful to the great art of architecture although perhaps profitable to science commercialized. If organic (intrinsic) architecture is not to live, we of these United States of America will never live as a true culture. Architecture must first become basic to us as creative art, therefore beneficent the world over. Present tendencies in education are so far gone into reverse by way of museum factotums, various committees and university regents spending millions left behind by hard working millionaires that owing to fashions of internationalism promoted by the internationalite we will have seen the last of the architecture of great architects not only in our democracy but all over the world beside where there is danger of the machine becoming a pattern of life instead of life using the machine as a tool.

Because our Declaration of Independence saw democracy as the gospel of individuality and saw it as above polemics or politics, probably a definition of the word democracy should be added to this lexicon of nine words. Therefore a tenth:

Democracy is our national ideal . . . not yet well understood by ourselves so not yet realized. But we are a new republic professing this ideal of freedom for growth of the individual. Why not cherish it? Freedom is not to be conceived as numbered freedoms. If true, freedom is never to be conceived in parts. Freedom is of the man and is not accorded to him or ascribed to him except as he may require protection. For that purpose government—as protection—exists, not as a policy maker. Democracy is thus the highest form of aristocracy ever seen. Aristocracy intrinsic.

A gentleman? No longer chosen and privileged by autocratic power he must rise from the masses by inherent virtue. His qualities as a man will give him title and keep it for him. Individual conscience will rule his social acts. By love of quality as against quantity he will choose his way through life. He will learn to know the difference between the curious and the beautiful. Truth will be a divinity to him. As his gentlehood cannot be conferred, so it may not be inherited. This gentleman of democracy will be found in any honest occupation at any level of fortune, loving beauty, doing his best and being kind.

Anyone may see by our own absurd acts and equivocal policies how confused we are by our own ideal when we proceed to work it out. But the principles of organic architecture are the center line of our democracy in America when we do understand what both really mean.

Only by the growth and exercise of *individual conscience* does the man earn or deserve his "rights." Democracy is the opposite of totalitarianism, communism, fascism or mobocracy. But democracy is constantly in danger from mobocracy—the rising tide of as yet unqualified herd-instinct. Mechanized mediocrity. The *conditioned* mind instead of the *enlightened* mind.

THE NATIONAL VALUE OF ART

This article was submitted by Wright to Lester Markel, editor of the New York Times, *with the following note: "Frank Lloyd Wright to Lester Markel—Would this go in your magazine?" The reply from Daniel Schwartz, assistant Sunday editor on the paper, explained that Markel had gone to Florida for a few weeks of needed rest and the manuscript had been turned over to him. Schwartz wrote, "I find it an interesting statement, but I'm afraid there is no way in which we can use it. I hate to turn it back to you because we would value having a piece by you in our magazine section, but this, I'm afraid, can't fill the bill."[1]*

Wright's terming the architecture of the United Nations building "a Fascist countenance," along with his accusation that "leading knowledge-factories in our nation today actively inculcate collectivism in our young architects," must have seemed to the rather conservative New York editors too strong a dose of liberal thought. But he is clearly pointing to where the art of architecture stood at this particular time, as well as the education of architectural students in collaboration and teamwork. Wright does not rule out teamwork, per se, but qualifies it by asking if its proper place is in the dominion of the creative act. [Unpublished]

ARCHITECTURE IS THE MOTHER-ART. ITS *NATIONAL VALUE* lies in its natural value. No architectonic construction can exist outside the realm of significance whether so intended or not. Significance may be haphazard or conceived with vision but whatever it implies is always there to be read by human intelligence. The significance of certain buildings would, therefore, be either communist, fascist, democratic or purely decorative.

There would be no escape from the consequences of significance though the builder himself might be unsure or unaware of what he was doing and, as the Art of building is now in our nation be merely executing a taste or trend without being aware of the nature of his act. On this basis the collectivism preached at certain of our colleges must be seen as the ideal collectivism of Communism. The U.N. opus is a Fascist countenance. Fascism and communism are at the poles of world dominion. Where then is the countenance of Democracy? That inward vision of the relation and truth of things—an eye quick to note and distinguish, sensitive to design and to over-all harmony?

No formal or quantitative method whatever is useful for the spread of Democracy. Democracy cannot standardize, proselytize and convert. It can be no missionary without betraying the principles of its very life.

Left-wing modern-architecture now tends to betray Democracy. Leading knowledge-factories in our nation actively inculcate collectivist doctrine in our young architects. In respect to any national value the great art of building might render our people in their tardy struggle for a culture of their own, universities spread the communist doctrine so completely that the "witch-hunt" by F.B.I. in the State Department for victims is ridiculous. A young builder remarked to one such professor that "the work of all his students looked like his nor could anyone tell the work of one student from that of another." The professor replied, "That is just what I want." So it is that Communism spreads into Architecture by collectivist exponents and shepherds.

Quantity vanquishes quality. If Doctors can thus indoctrinate the builders of a free democracy with what cannot be said in our midst, is this emasculation of the individual less harmful because higher up?

The weakness of the Collectivist philosophy of Communism lies in the quantitative denial of the virtues of the qualities of individuality. No one denies the virtues of "teamwork" (or of "the committee")—in proper place. But is this proper place conception? Are Shakespeare's, Blake's, Wordworth's, Goethe's, Dante's, Emerson's, Whitman's, Thoreau's, Melville's equivalents in the Art of Architecture to be rewritten Soviet-wise according to exponents of modern-architecture safely sitting in the arm-chairs of our own Universities? Not yet.

In any struggle for indigenous culture (what other culture is there), no matter how gentle and tactful they may be imports are always hazardous. I suggest that we, in these United States at least, continue, with honest arrogance, to *grow our own.*

MORAL: No Scientist should be allowed to teach ART.

L'ENVOI: Taint of the "Classic," Palladian or Greco-Roman in our Architecture has been pretty well purged from the "Modern." But now it would seem that the spirit of Democracy—(our Organic-architecture)—true basis of the "Modern," must be defended. Inspiration by the directness of vision of the free-mind must be recovered and maintained in our midst by our young architects if our native culture is to be lifted to the high level—(beyond ancient culture)—to which Organic Architecture aspired.

1. Letter from Daniel Schwartz to Frank Lloyd Wright, 15 January 1953.

FRANK LLOYD WRIGHT SPEAKS UP

Wright repeatedly spoke out about the hazards of the United States embracing the International Style. But in this article, published in House Beautiful *in July 1953, he elaborated—perhaps more clearly and more fully than ever before—the serious threat to any hope for a national culture if that wish for culture continued to be based upon the import of a style inimical to the very concepts of life in a democracy. The result, he prophesied, would be disastrous, not only for the art of architecture, but for the attainment of a homegrown culture of our own: "And what do we get now?" he asked, referring to the glass-clad buildings along the lines of the UN building. "The same old box, only now you really look inside and through the box and see that it is more of a box than ever. Thereby the tenant, as well as the poverty-stricken imagination of the architect, is mercilessly exposed."* [House Beautiful, *July 1953*]

THE "INTERNATIONAL STYLE" IS NEITHER INTERNATIONAL nor a style. Essentially it is totalitarianism, an old totalitarian cult made new by organized publicity.

The "International Style" is nothing but the old architecture of the box with its face lifted.

Any box is more a coffin for the human spirit than an inspiration. The box dominates, constricts, and constrains the individual into something made fit only for collectivism. Its champions now declare dictatorially that the old box is *it*. This is their great gift to the world—their "style."

So many university professors, museum authorities, magazine editors, feature writers, and critics seem to be trying hard to give notoriety to a group of architects imported, by a curious twist of fate, from the German Bauhaus to the New York Museum of Modern Art.

The Bauhaus architects ran from political totalitarianism in Germany to what is now made by specious promotion to seem their own totalitarianism in art here in America.

It is being more accidental than creative to mistake a disciplined sterility for austerity, mistake the plainness of bones or a barn door for simplicity (knowing nothing of *real* simplicity—the innate grace and significance of a wild flower). This is the mistake their promoters seem to make.

In their dubious champions, there is no sense of the depth called the third dimension. They operate on only two. Among these puppets of promotion, façades again become of uppermost importance. These façades all add up to the same thing—a cliché for tyros, teachers, and sycophants who crook the little finger and talk esthetics. Or by duped educators grasping something easy to teach, and approved as a foreign cult.

Sterilization is again mistaken for refinement. Provincial apostles of refinement name it "Classic," stupidly comparing it to frozen Greek classicism as though the ancient sterilization were a high virtue. But the cause of great architecture, the great truth of building beautiful buildings beautifully according to the nature of architecture, is travestied by this superficial mimicry, that always seems to follow in the wake of great ideas.

The classic or camouflaged old post-and-lintel box is still practiced in the passed-in cage or the glass-walled dwelling, both approved by these publicists and this latest procession of callow-professionals, now baptized (by whom?) "International." But this latest form of glassification is no true revolt, no actual dissidence. This affection is for free Americans no more than the petty pretenses of small men.

Old Man Box merely *looks* different when glassified, that's all. The more the box is glassed, the more it becomes evident as the box. No new ideas whatever are involved as might easily be demonstrated by intelligent reference to the origin of their drawing-board façades. The old sham front has had its face lifted; the only change is merely one of outward appearance. It is a change of face, not of heart.

There are fresh ideas to be brought to life, if you learn to labor for them and are willing to work for them and wait. You must tire, as I do, of seeing these original forms merely renamed. All we have received from "internationalism," aside from the dropped coping, is merely: "Make the walls *all* glass, boys."

And what do we get now? The same old box, only you now really look inside and through the box and see that it is more of a box than ever. Thereby the tenant, as well as the poverty-stricken imagination of the architect, is mercilessly exposed.

The nature of the freedom prophesied by the Declaration of Independence originally made by our nation is antipathetic to an international level either of style or of life. That "style" would be the communistic shadow descending over our own tradition, disgracing the great individualities that gave us our traditions in all their bewildering and wonderful fascination, color, and variety. Individuality is still beloved and prophesied by our nation. Never would we consent to be embalmed alive—to become prisoners of a style!

Organic or truly American architecture emerged from the confusion of the sudden awakening of architecture as a new idea 60 years ago. The *strength* of the *philosophy* of a free, intrinsic or *organic* architecture is that it loves and cherishes these infinitely individual, human traditions of the great Tradition.

Because of our increased techniques, organic architecture could easily afford *all* nations new means of realization, on their own soil, along lines of character and development already peculiar to themselves. Whatever is really modern in architecture should, in this new view of reality, intensify the individualities of all nations, not strip them of the charm of their innate distinctions.

Only when art is indigenous, the work of a particular time, according to the nature and character of the people of that time, is it for all time. Our American civilization is only a way of life. Our culture would consist of means of making that way of life beautiful. Either we die without a culture of our own or we live by moving forward into a more beautiful concordant life than we now have.

We are not going to die sterilized by this "International Style," a mere externality imposed by tyros upon American civilization as "culture." America was born to *destroy the façade* in all things, governmental or personal, that do not express the inner spirit. If, instead of our own inspired idea of architecture, we are to be reduced by organized expediency—commercial, educational, esthetic, or all together—to an "International Style" by petty factotums; if a fashion is all we merit as a civilization, let's go back to barbarism. It is far more richly humane.

Why do I distrust and defy such "internationalism" as I do communism? Because both must by their nature do this very leveling in the name of civilization. If communism (the factual religion of collectivism) is once established, the sun of creation, which is the sun of the individual, goes down and life has agreed to be embalmed alive.

I see collectivism in all its forms—especially in this cliché architecture—already becoming far too expedient in our midst. The drift away from quality toward quantity, toward all forms of standardization, can only mean the eventual success of the communist or of the totalitarian. All collectivism, such as the so-called "International Style," tends to diminish the human soul, because it relieves the individual of a developed conscience and takes from him the reward of being *true to himself as himself,* which is the essential spirit of Democracy.

This reward of individuality has been the Star of Creation since time began. That star will set if America accepts anything less than true style: not *A* style, but "style all the while." There is no sense in imprisoning the spirit of what should now constitute the free architecture of a democracy—organic architecture.

The "International Style," an architectural *ism,* at first no more than a "chic" notion, is becoming, by the efforts of its gulled concerts, an evil crusade. A fashion is always the passing show of imitation—in this case the imitation of a bad imitation by a bad imitator.

Unfortunately, this invading fashion is serviceable to the commerce of professional publicists whose latest propaganda, "Post-war Architecture," is being exhibited and sold over the counter at New York's Museum of Modern Art. I see in it propaganda for the rising tide of mediocrity. If you intelligently examine it, you will find that it betrays the term "organic architecture," feeding on it as a parasite.

Unfortunately for the cause of architecture, such unbecoming totalitarianism, offering the shortcut, has become proliferous. It is now on the march in a procession miscalled "Modern Architecture." Have its parading Knights-of-the-Cliché ever really studied architecture?

No—nor do they really practice it.

They are sometimes painters, sometimes sculptors—always enthusiasts, but never builders. They are the slaves, not the masters, of construction. They know nothing of the nature of materials and have contempt for the nature of human beings. They are not a wholesome people.

Yet, they are selling an architecture absolute, ready-made, to trusting people over the counters of American museums and in schools and periodicals.

Those who do know architecture are not affected. They are well aware that any "International Style" is the degeneration of a good idea. Regarded by whatever creative architectural intelligence is left

in our world, this substitution of façade for substance is shamefully wasteful—therefore demoralizing.

Let's face it, the main point of vantage for "internationalism" in any form lies in "collectivism." Collectivism is taught in architecture by too many of our schools, themselves representing an eclecticism just above the general level of universal imitation.

Collectivism will serve either totalitarian or communist, but can never serve the democrat, because it is merely a *conditioning* of the herd, not an *enlightening* of the individual. It could destroy democracy by playing on its great weakness—mobocracy. By this collectivist conditioning of the mind, *the machine becomes a dominating pattern instead of a tool.* We then have the "machine for living," the theory that "less is more" and other concepts that become, more and more, less.

If as a nation we are to have our own richly humane culture, we must work for it. Unless we waken soon to the nature of the nation we designed, we will see no more of the creative architecture of creative architects.

Our "plan factories" and the factory-produced young architect emerging from our colleges (now hanging by eyebrows from skyhooks or playing "jack-in-the-box" up on bare sticks) seem to have found in this negation just what is needed to make the long labor of becoming an architect less long and arduous. Such architects are appearing only to disappear.

Organic, or intrinsic architecture, on the other hand, offers rational hope for the future. It abolishes the old post-and-lintel box as unscientific, resents and rejects such "slabs" as the UN Building.

Organic architecture *is a new idea of what constitutes a building.* It introduces wholly new values into building. An entirely new ethic—and esthetic—comes to life when the building is so conceived as intrinsic, as the result of the nature of materials, tools, situations, and the human beings it shelters. Wherever it is honestly built, you may see a new countenance, the countenance of truth emerging.

Architecture is primarily interior; *of* the thing, not *on* it. It is not a dead aspect of style but *style* itself, bearing ever fresh form, like all living things in nature.

About 20 years ago, in the shadow cast upon modern organic architecture by the then new Museum of Modern Art, the "International Style" was named.

To the museums, then the morgues of art, it seemed to offer expedient resurrection. But this confluence of equivocal minds and circumstances now is identifiable as a sinister attempt to repeat the betrayal of American organic architecture in the way the Chicago World's Fair of '93 did it to the modern movement then led by Louis Sullivan. (The fair offered "classic" style and the American people seeing it on a huge scale for the first time were awed and sold, and the pioneer work in clarity and dissidence by Architects Sullivan, Richardson, and Root was set back by 50 years.)

Can the hucksters of this ready-made cliché of "internationalism" for our half-baked, snatch-and-run system of professional success recognize fundamental truth? No.

They can exist only by means of controlled publicity—more publicity—some more publicity—and salesmanship. In this activity publicists are the enemies of our culture.

What now is the educational policy of the "international-schoolism" of architecture?

Publicity—more publicity—some more publicity.

Publicity is becoming the great substitute for art, philosophy, and—yes, *being*.

Must the shameful, servile, provincial past of our national culture repeat itself *ad nauseam ad libitum?*

The servile recourse to a machine-style parallels the rise of mediocrity now flooding what should be high places. The world we share is not smaller than it used to be because of airships, atom bombs, and electrification. The world is larger because more comprehensive, though less comprehended by us. As human beings, our view, both personal and national, comprises so much we never dreamed of before and do not understand now. What merely existed for us, before mechanization set in and "International Style" appeared as the ideal expedient, is a growing problem for us to solve.

This does not mean *one* world, but many. Too many perhaps, because we are not yet ready with our own.

If ever international co-operation is to come true, the need for solidarity of the independent nation and individual grows immensely in importance, with easy intercommunication. The strength of our native spirit is more necessary than ever for the freedom not only of ourselves but the entire world.

INFLUENCE OR RESEMBLANCE

In April 1953 Dimitri Tselos published an article in Magazine of Art entitled "Exotic Influences in the Architecture of Frank Lloyd Wright." With impressive detail, Tselos matched, image by image, the works of Wright and historic works that he believed influenced the architect. Wright's Midway Gardens sprite (Chicago, 1913), for example, cast in concrete as a tall, narrow female figure, arms crossed over her breasts, gazing down from a high pedestal, is illustrated above a corresponding image of a vertical Japanese print by the eighteenth-century artist Shunsho, depicting a tall, robed woman, also looking down. A front view of the Ward Willits house (Highland Park, 1902) is carefully matched to a temple in Japan and the temple in the Japanese tea garden at the Columbian Exposition (Chicago, 1893); the A.D. German warehouse (Richland Center, 1915) to the Temple of Three Lintels in Chichén Itzá, Yucatan; Wright's own Oak Park home and studio to the east end of the Nunnery, also at Chichén Itzá, and so forth. Fortunately, Wright was alive at the time, read the article, and set the record straight with the article "Influence or Resemblance." Contradicting Tselos's theories, Wright maintained, "I did not see the preColumbian art at the Chicago World's Fair (1893) nor the Japanese building. I despised the fair, went there but one afternoon, came away angry and bewildered." (Along with Louis Sullivan, Wright regarded the Columbian World's Fair as a severe blow to the rise of an architecture expressive of the United States in the twentieth century. Instead, they felt the fair heralded the classics as the path and direction architecture should take in the United States, as indeed it did.) He explained:

> But I had seen preColumbian architecture illustrated in magazines and books in my youth—loved it profoundly and some day when riches came my way I wanted to go and continue excavations. . . . Nothing seen in my work by anyone is taken from anything, anywhere. So as they say in the movies "all resemblances to buildings living or dead is purely coincidental and not intended by me." I find the Tselos article so plausible I would myself have been convinced had I not known better.

> There can be do doubt that Wright was indeed influenced by sources around him, whether consciously or not. But to suggest that he would take a detail from a Mayan temple and apply it, line for line, onto one of his own buildings is nothing short of absurd. [Unpublished]

HAD I NOT LOVED AND COMPREHENDED PRECOLUMBIAN architecture as the primitive basis of world-architecture, I could not now build as I build with understanding of all architecture. Only with that understanding could I have shaped my buildings as they are. Yet, of all ancient buildings, wherever they may stand or whatever their time, is there one of them suitable to stand here and now in the midst of our time, our America, our machine-age techniques? Not one.

In the very center of my thought and feeling for Architecture from the first (the very first) has been the *growth* of the human-being.

So the time came, sixty years ago, 1893, when a whole reconsideration and restatement of all architectonics seemed necessary. There must come a readjustment of the whole nature of the science and art of Architecture for the sake of Democratic America. We must "grow our own" as we grow up or pass as all derivations have passed.

I know well that my buildings see clearly not only the color, drift and inclination of my own day but feed its spirit. All of them seek to provide forms adequate to integrate and harmonize our new materials, tools and shapes with the democratic life-ideal of my own day and time. Thus do I know work that is for all time. For the new evolutionary traits in the more and more standardized centralizations of our day—seemingly alone—I have not only perceived the necessity of *decentralization* but have modeled remedies (Broadacre City).

The wonders of past civilizations, their concentrations now can do no more than curse the opportunities of today and limit our enjoyment of life by confusing true comprehension of our real advantages. If we do not change the forms with new ones, more adequate, more appropriate, more honest, our ideal of Democracy is bound to fail.

A firmer, vastly broader new era has begun to exist in all the Americas and demands its prophets. A new challenge comes uppermost especially in the life of our own nation—the challenge of the modern Spirit. I have accepted the challenge but have not left the moorings of the morning of my own awakening. Organic Architecture sixty years ago began this needed readjustment toward the objective universe. The quite changed attitudes of the individual human-soul towards life—towards himself and toward his fellowmen everywhere surround us. This challenge to us all, especially to our Architects, is pressing hard upon us today.

None living may escape it as Cram (for instance) tried to do; as the so-called international style is trying to do; as so many contemporary architects, and the schools themselves, are trying to do by conceding and catering to our weaknesses instead of aiding us by abetting the strengths of our own National Spirit.

I know (poets have always known) that our strength today is spiritual and heroic though all that transpires of late seems determined to tear this modern epic down by force.

The main purpose of our government is not so-called "good" government but to establish so far as lies in its power the *self-regulation* of the individual growing up in the masses. No Democratic citizen can be regulated from without.

Democracy craves and was founded to grow the great individual citizen because he now must rise from the masses. To encourage that growth to greatness by the individual, this must be the true motive of our Nation, these United States of America. I like to call my country USONIA.

I see the nature of decentralization as *inevitable to our aspiration*. I have studied it as the most likely way of work and life for love of the life we call free. However the overwhelming, overlapping tides of the Past may sweep over us in our weakness, we must take that course.

As a people—a Nation—we resist these pervasive tides or we relinquish our destiny. To account for our failure our Nation will be called back in disgrace to whence or where we made the declaration that astonished and delighted the world.

And now some little attention to the amusing resemblances mistaken for influences by Dimitri Tselos, *Magazine of Art,* April 1953.

Having now (for sixty years past) seen my own history in the making I conclude with Henry Ford that "History is the bunk." The only valid conclusion reached by the Tselos painstaking research concerns what the Japanese print encouraged me to see.

Hokusai and Hiroshige are two of the greatest names in all art whatsoever. The Japanese did not design any sense of shelter nor the roofs that came out of it. The Japanese and I went to the same source—*Nature*. I did not see preColumbian art at the Chicago World's Fair nor the Japanese building. I despised the fair, went there but one afternoon, came away angry and bewildered. But I had seen preColumbian architecture illustrated in magazines and books in my youth—loved it profoundly and some day when riches came my way I wanted to go and continue excavations. I went to the same school they attended—Nature. Years later I did see some of the actual sculptures. But many of those in a Tselos article in the *Magazine of Art* I see for the first time, especially figure 14, figure 20, figure 12, figure 16, and most amusing figure 7 with the protruding serpents' tongues from which I might have derived the brackets for the flagpoles at the corners of the German Warehouse. But I did not.

No, I guess my imagination's digestion is too good for that sort of eclecticism. Besides it is too much trouble—too severe limitation—if one has been to the same school. My kind of eclecticism goes deeper, has its roots in a school more profound than selective admiration—more rooted in *sources* than to features.

Nothing seen in my work by anyone is taken from anything, anywhere. So as they say in the movies "all resemblances to buildings living or dead is purely coincidental and not intended by me."

I find the Tselos article so plausible I would myself have been convinced had I not known better.

FOR A DEMOCRATIC ARCHITECTURE

When this was published in House Beautiful *in October 1953, the article was prefaced by an editor's statement, "Written in response to a joint letter from 30 architects and designers of the San Francisco Bay area to Elizabeth Gordon, the editor of* House Beautiful, *disagreeing that architecture has no social or political significance." Clearly this idea blatantly contradicted all Wright ever believed about architecture and its significance for the life of man, especially—in his own work—for the life of man in a democracy. As he had written in the article itself:*

> *Beyond all other arts the basic art of architecture is either pro-social or anti-social . . . so an aesthetic not based on sound philosophy (the truth of the nature of the thing) is like a rudder without a ship. Any such aesthete, as architect, would be and is a greater menace to society than any gangster, boodler, or gunman could ever be.*

[House Beautiful, *October 1953*]

IN ANY (AND EVERY) WORK OF ART MAN MOLDS OR BUILDS himself into our view. The architect's building is a mirror of the man, but also a mirror of the value of the society he lives in.

You know the man by his building. Every building built in some measure partakes of the innate grace or disgraces of the character of the man who caused it to be as it is.

Almost all modern architecture as well as modern art is at this moment of time, eloquently deficient in this appreciation. Modern art and architecture, because they have become negative, are not only barren and undemocratic but are in consequence, to some degree, degenerate when our facilities and riches require regeneration.

Vacuity is being made an esthetic ritual. Divorcement from common sense is being glorified. "Uncomfortism" is being made virtue. The cult of the façade is being sold by a small group of esthetic fanciers. But we the people are awakening to see that something is left out. The people are left out who want no cults, no authorities, no divinity beyond truth.

Building without mastery over construction is sheer nonsense.

Rhyme without reason is not poetry.

Any so-called Style which is a mere formula is without the grace of individual quality; therefore soon, or already stale. As a style for democracy—a calamity!

Has our country not seen enough of stale styles?

"Internationalism" is necessarily mass. Massology's characteristic style could not know individuality. Any such style could only be one for the mass-man. Any set style would be only a mass-style for the mass-man. It could only betray the ideal of democracy.

There is no true social unit of any faith without characteristic building as the basis of its culture. Therefore a building for democracy (faith in the individual) can never be the same as for massology—the "mass-man."

Massology is anarchy, monarchy, fascism, or communism. All forms of totalitarianism. So the practice of building in a democracy could never be that of building for totalitarianism.

Each ideology does (or should have) its own natural architecture, expressing its own character in appropriate terms. Consciously or unconsciously each ideology will eventually do so, although, meantime, the people who do the choosing may not be aware of the significance of their choice. Left to taste without knowledge, it is amusing to witness the one ideology take the architecture natural to the other. Communism, for instance, now prefers the decadent architecture of monarchy. Democracy is attracted to the architecture of fascism, etc., etc. And we have seen an old town's civilization reduced to a rubbish heap by a conscienceless architect.

Beyond all other arts the basic art of architecture is either pro-social or anti-social. Every building erected is either anti-social or pro-social by way of sponsor or author.

So any esthetic not based upon a sound philosophy (the truth of the nature of the thing) is like a rudder without a ship. Any such esthete, as architect, would be and is a greater menace to society than any gangster, boodler, or gunman could ever be. Flesh and blood can be wiped out. The building seldom may be. Unfortunately it becomes sacrosanct as "property." The building outlives its executioner.

A warning! Without *individuality* architecture too soon hardens into static, frozen forms and becomes a Style. When our way of life thus hardens into a frozen thing, there is the end of democracy.

Therefore a free architecture, one not classic or primarily aiming at monumentality or determined to be "international," but one remaining as individual as may be, is the true architecture for us in America. Dangerous as this freedom may seem, its value to our structure as a democracy so far outweighs any evil consequences that it must be encouraged and protected by our society, if not by our government.

Quality is always a hazard in the making. But no sure thing on any other level can take the place of true architecture in the culture of a free society.

MAN

Issued on Christmas morning of 1953, this "Taliesin Tract" was printed privately and sent out by Wright to family, friends, apprentices, associates, and clients. Here he wrote not so much of architecture—although life and architecture were, to him, irrevocably linked—as of man as the enlightened being: "The herd disappears and reappears but the sovereignty of the individual persists." [Taliesin Tract, December 1953]

LITERATURE TELLS ABOUT MAN. ARCHITECTURE PRESENTS him. The Architecture that our man of Democracy needs and prophecies is bound to be different from that of the common or conditioned man of any other socialized system of belief. As never before this new free-man's Architecture will present him by being true to his own nature in all such expressions. This aim becomes natural to him in his Art as it once was in his Religion.

With renewed vision, the modern man will use the new tools Science lavishes upon him (even before he is ready for them) to enlarge his field of action by reducing his fetters to exterior controls, especially those of organized Authority, publicity, or political expediency. He will use his new tools to develop his own Art and Religion as the means to keep him free, as himself. Therefore this democratic man's environment like his mind, will never be stylized. When and wherever he builds he will not consent to be boxed. He will himself have his style.

The Democratic man demands conscientious liberty for himself no more nor less than he demands liberty for his neighbor. The way of life he calls Civilization will expand according to his inner vision to develop the integral beauty derived only from self-culture. This man's own conscience will be his constant concern and aim to correct his social standards in all acts that proceed from him. This constant vigilance constitutes his only guarantee of Freedom. The true democrat will seek and find "safety" in knowledge and courageous practice of the organic, or interior, laws of Nature, suspicious of all exterior interference or preparation for the use of Force.

Whenever organic justice is denied him he will not believe he can get it by murder but must obtain it by continuing fair dealing and enlightenment at whatever cost. He will never force upon others his own beliefs nor his own ways. He will display his social methods to others to best advantage as critic or missionary only when sought by them.

His neighbor will be to him (as he is to himself) free to choose his own way according to his own light, their common cause being the vision of the uncommon-man wherein every man is free to grow to the stature his freedom in America under the Constitution of these United States grants him.

Exterior compulsion absent in him, no man need be inimical to him. Conscience, thus indispensable to his own freedom, becomes more normal to every man.

As this vision of Democracy thus clears, man's powers would naturally increase. The soul of his society—Art and Religion—would gain dignity and range by constant performance until his life became that of a whole man: a wholesome one instead of the fraction the common man is: under-nourished or over-built by exterior controls, especially by those of Education. Peace would become normal but reform of the World so far as that reform was his concern could only begin with his own reform and proceed from there.

Remember the men who gave us our Nation. We have "the Declaration" and our Constitution because they were individualist. Great Art is still living for us only because of Individualists like Beethoven. We have creative men on earth today only as they are free to continually arise as individuals from obscurity to demonstrate their dignity and worth above the confusion raised by the herding of the common-man by aid of the scribes and Pharisees of his time—quantity ignoring or overwhelming quality. The herd disappears and reappears but the sovereignty of the individual persists.

Observe the buildings of the world. Uniqueness to Time, Place and Man constitutes the great universality we call the Art of Architecture. It is this appropriation to circumstance—not what buildings possess in common—that is the great virtue of all great Art.

RESUMÉ
Winds blow, fires burn, water falls and the law of gravitation holds but not what all have in common interests us most. Universality is no virtue in itself. It may only be weakness or default. To the individual we must look for that quality in life we call creative.

In the depth of a man's Faith would lie his true humility, that of the IDEAL MAN. His prayer would be humble only to ever-changing never-ending LIFE.

THE NATURAL HOUSE

Frank Lloyd Wright and his publisher, Ben Raeburn of Horizon Press, concurred that the press's second book should be devoted to house design. (The first had been The Future of Architecture, 1953.) Wright had begun his career as an architect for private residences, and for the next six decades the greater part, by far, of his architectural work was for residential designs. As early as 1893 he wrote that the house for the American citizen must belong to American soil and reflect a democratic way of living. Imported styles could never be at home in the United States, regardless of the prevalence of poor taste that abounded at the turn of the century: "What was the matter with the typical American house? Well, just for an honest beginning, it lied about everything. It had no sense of unity at all nor any such sense of space as should belong to a free people." At the same time that he began implementing his new concepts into residential design, he was lecturing and writing about them as well, for example: "Freedom of floor space and elimination of useless heights worked a miracle in the new dwelling place. A sense of appropriate freedom had changed its whole aspect. The dwelling became more fit for human habitation on modern terms and far more natural to its site. An entirely new sense of space values in architecture began to come home."

In the first edition of An Autobiography (1932), he had devoted much space to this subject; in the revised and expanded edition in 1943, he further amplified it. Then, working with Raeburn in 1953, he brought together and supplemented many of these earlier writings and published it the following year as The Natural House.

In assembling the new materials, he was asked a number of specific questions by his apprentices.[1] The answers found their way into the book, where he explained step by step the process of the design and construction of the Usonian home, in an unusually practical text, which drew on his earlier writings on specific materials. He also outlined his philosophy of the Usonian home: "Living within a house wherein everything is genuine and harmonious, a new sense of freedom gives one a new sense of life. . . . The Usonian house, then, aims to be a natural performance, one that is integral to site; integral to environment; integral to the life of the inhabitants."

By 1954 the Usonian Automatic, a type of new concrete block construction he had begun working on five years earlier, was already in effect in some houses that had been constructed. One chapter was devoted to the explanation of that system and its significance in trying to solve the problem of moderate-cost housing in the United States, for example:

We are often asked how a young couple, with a limited budget, can afford to build a house designed on these basic principles of organic architecture. What couple does not have a limited budget? . . . This problem will probably always exist in one direction or another. But we have gone far in solving this generic problem by the natural concrete block house we call the "Usonian Automatic." This Usonian house incorporates innovations which reduce most of the heavier costs, labor in particular.

In the final chapter, Wright returned to his sojourn in Japan while designing and building the Imperial Hotel. He concluded the book by answering a question frequently asked of him: "Many people have wondered about an Oriental quality they see in my work. I suppose it is true that when we speak of organic architecture, we are speaking of something that is more Oriental than Western. The answer is: my work is, in that deeper philosophic sense, Oriental." [The Natural House, *Horizon Press, New York, 1954*]

BOOK ONE: 1936–1953
ORGANIC ARCHITECTURE

THE TYPICAL AMERICAN DWELLING OF 1893 WAS CROWDING in upon itself all over the Chicago prairies as I used to go home from my work with Adler and Sullivan in Chicago to Oak Park, a Chicago suburb. That dwelling had somehow become typical American architecture but by any faith in nature implicit or explicit it did not belong anywhere. I was in my sixth year with Adler and Sullivan then, and they had completed the Wainwright Building in St. Louis, the first expression of the skyscraper as a *tall* building. But after building the great Auditorium the firm did not build residences because they got in the way of larger, more important work. I had taken over dwellings, Mr. Sullivan's own house among them, whenever a client came to them for a house. The Charnley house was done in this way.[2] I longed for a chance to build a sensible house, and (1893), soon free to build one, I furnished an office in the Schiller Building and began my own practice of architecture. The first real chance came by way of Herman Winslow for client.[3] I was not the only one then sick of hypocrisy and hungry for reality. Winslow was something of an artist himself, sick of it all.

What was the matter with the typical American house? Well, just for an honest beginning, it lied about everything. It had no sense of unity at all nor any such sense of space as should belong to a free people. It was stuck up in thoughtless fashion. It had no more sense of earth than a "modernistic" house.

And it was stuck up on wherever it happened to be. To take any one of these so-called "homes" away would have improved the landscape and helped to clear the atmosphere. The thing was more a hive than a home just as "modernistic" houses are more boxes than houses. But these "homes" were very like the homes Americans were making for themselves elsewhere, all over their new country.

Nor, where the human being was concerned, had this *typical* dwelling any appropriate sense of proportion whatever. It began somewhere way down in the wet and ended as high up as it could get in the high and narrow. All materials looked alike to it or to anything or anybody in it. Essentially, whether of brick or wood or stone, this "house" was a bedeviled box with a fussy lid; a complex box that had to be cut up by all kinds of holes made in it to let in light and air, with an especially ugly hole to go in and come out of. The holes were all "trimmed"; the doors and windows themselves trimmed; the roofs trimmed; the walls trimmed. Architecture seemed to consist in what was done to these holes. "Joinery" everywhere reigned supreme in the pattern and as the soul of it all. Floors were the only part of the house left plain after "Queen Anne" had swept past. The "joiner" recommended "parquetry" but usually the housewife and the fashionable decorator covered these surfaces down underfoot with a tangled rug collection because otherwise the floors would be "bare." They were "bare" only because one could not very well walk on jigsawing or turned spindles or plaster ornament. This last limitation must have seemed somehow unkind.

It is not too much to say that as a young architect, by inheritance and training a radical, my lot was cast with an inebriate lot of criminals called builders; sinners hardened by habit against every human significance except one, vulgarity. The one touch of nature that makes the whole world kin. And I will venture to say, too, that the aggregation was at the lowest aesthetic level in all history. Steam heat, plumbing, and electric light were the only redeeming features and these new features were hard put to it to function in the circumstances. Bowels, circulation, and nerves were new in buildings. But they had come to stay and a building could not longer remain a mere shell in which life was somehow to make shift as it might.

When I was 11 years old I was sent to a Wisconsin farm to learn how to really work. So all this I saw around me seemed affectation, nonsense, or profane. The first feeling was hunger for reality, for sincerity. A desire for simplicity that would yield a broader, deeper comfort was natural, too, to this first feeling. A growing idea of simplicity as organic, as I had been born into it and trained in it, was new as a quality of thought, able to strengthen and refresh the spirit in any circumstances. Organic simplicity might everywhere be seen producing significant character in the ruthless but harmonious order I was taught to call nature. I was more than familiar with it on the farm. All around me, I, or anyone for that matter, might see beauty in growing things and, by a little painstaking, learn how they grew to be "beautiful." None was ever insignificant. I loved the prairie by instinct as itself a great simplicity; the trees, flowers, and sky were thrilling by contrast. And I saw that a little of height on the prairie was enough to look like much more. Notice how every detail as to height becomes intensely significant and how breadths all fall short. Here was a tremendous spaciousness needlessly sacrificed, all cut up crosswise or lengthwise into 50-foot lots, or would you have 25 feet? Reduced to a money-matter, salesmanship kept on parceling out the ground, selling it with no restrictions. Everywhere, in a great new, free country, I could see only this mean tendency to

tip everything in the way of human occupation or habitation up edgewise instead of letting it lie comfortably flatwise with the ground where spaciousness was a virtue. Nor has this changed much since automobilization has made it no genuine economic issue at all but has made it a social crime to crowd in upon one another.

By now I had committed the indiscretion that was eventually to leave me no peace and keep me from ever finding satisfaction in anything superficial. That indiscretion was a determination to search for the *qualities* in all things.

I had an idea (it still seems to be my own) that the planes parallel to the earth in buildings identify themselves with the ground, do most to make the buildings belong to the ground. (Unluckily they defy the photographer.) At any rate, independently I perceived this fact and put it to work. I had an idea that every house in that low region should begin *on* the ground, not *in* it as they then began, with damp cellars. This feeling became an idea also; eliminated the "basement." I devised one at ground level. And the feeling that the house should *look* as though it began there *at* the ground put a projecting base course as a visible edge to this foundation where, as a platform, it was evident preparation for the building itself and welded the structure to the ground.

An idea (probably rooted deep in racial instinct) that *shelter* should be the essential look of any dwelling, put the low spreading roof, flat or hipped or low gabled, with generously projecting eaves over the whole. I began to see a building primarily not as a cave but as broad shelter in the open, related to vista; vista without and vista within. You may see in these various feelings all taking the same direction that I was born an American child of the ground and of space, welcoming spaciousness as a modern human need as well as learning to see it as the natural human opportunity. The farm had no negligible share in developing this sense of things in me, I am sure.

Before this, by way of innate sense of comfort, had come the idea that the size of the human figure should fix every proportion of a dwelling or of anything in it. Human scale was true building scale. Why not, then, the scale fixing the proportions of all buildings whatsoever? What other scale could I use? This was not a canon taught me by anyone. So I accommodated heights in the new buildings to no exaggerated established order nor to impress the beholder (I hated grandomania then as much as I hate it now) but only to comfort the human being. I knew the house dweller could seldom afford enough freedom to move about in built-in or built-over space, so, perceiving the horizontal line as the earth line of human life (the line of repose), this, as an individual sense of the thing, began to bear fruit. I first extended horizontal spacing without enlarging the building by cutting out all the room partitions that did not serve the kitchen or give needed privacy for sleeping apartments or (as in the day of the parlor) serve to prevent some formal intrusion into the intimacy of the family circle. The small social office I set aside as a necessary evil to receive "callers," for instance. Even this one concession soon disappeared as a relic of the barbarism called "fashion"; the "parlor."

To get the house down to the horizontal in appropriate proportion and into quiet relationship with the ground and as a more humane consideration anyway, the servants had to come down out of the complicated attic and go into a separate unit of their own attached to the kitchen on the ground floor. They liked this compulsion, though the housewife worried. Closets disappeared as unsanitary boxes wasteful of room and airy wardrobes in the rooms served instead.

Freedom of floor space and elimination of useless heights worked a miracle in the new dwelling place. A sense of appropriate freedom had changed its whole aspect. The dwelling became more fit for human habitation on modern terms and far more natural to its site. An entirely new sense of space values in architecture began to come home. It now appears that, self-conscious of architectural implications, they first came into the architecture of the modern world. This was about 1893. Certainly something of the kind was due.

A new sense of repose in flat planes and quiet "streamline" effects had thereby and then found its way into building, as we can now see it admirably in steamships, airplanes and motorcars. The age came into its own and the "age" did not know its own. There had been nothing at all from overseas to help in getting this new architecture planted on American soil. From 1893 to 1910 these prairie houses had planted it there. No, my dear "Mrs. Gablemore," "Mrs. Plasterbilt," and especially, no, "Miss Flat-top," nothing from "Japan" had helped at all, except the marvel of Japanese color prints. They were a lesson in elimination of the insignificant and in the beauty of the natural use of materials.

But more important than all, rising to greater dignity as idea, the ideal of plasticity was now to be developed and emphasized in the treatment of the building as a whole. Plasticity was a familiar term but something I had seen in no buildings whatsoever. I had seen it in Lieber Meister's ornament only.[4] It had not found its way into his buildings otherwise. It might now be seen creeping into the expressive lines and surfaces of the *buildings* I was building. You may see the appearance of the thing in the surface of your hand as contrasted with the articulation of the bony skeleton itself. This ideal, profound in its architectural implications, soon took another conscious stride forward in the form of a new aesthetic. I called it *continuity*. (It is easy to see it in the "folded plane.") Continuity in this aesthetic sense appeared to me as the natural means to achieve truly organic architecture by machine technique or by any other natural technique. Here was direct means, the only means I could then see or can now see to express, objectify and again bring natural form to architecture. Here by instinct at first (all ideas germinate) principle had entered into building as the new aesthetic, "continuity." It went abroad as "plasticity." They began to call it, as I myself often did then, "the third dimension." It was only a single phase of "continuity" but a phase that has come back home again to go to work on the surface and upon the novice. It will do him no harm as it is. But were the full import of continuity in architecture to be grasped, aesthetic and structure become completely one, it would continue to revolutionize the use and wont of our machine age architecture, making it superior in harmony and beauty to any architecture, Gothic or Greek. This ideal at work upon materials by nature of the process or tools used means a living architecture in a new age, organic architecture, the only architecture that can live and let live because it never can become a mere style. Nor can it ever become a formula for the tyro. Where principle is put to work, not as recipe or as formula, there will always be *style* and no need to bury it as "a style."

Although the wrap-around window, originally a minor outward expression of the interior folded plane in my own buildings, and various other minor features of the work of this period intended to simplify and eliminate "parts" are now scattered around the world and have become the rather senseless features of various attempts at formula, such as the sporadic "international" and other attempts characterized by plain surfaces cut into patterns by simple large openings, nevertheless the ideas behind these earlier appearances, the fundamental ideas that made them genuine expressions of architecture, have been altogether missed. The nature of materials is ignored in these imitations to get block mass outlines. The reverse of the period wherein mass material outlines tried to ignore the materials. But it is the same mistake.

The word "plastic" was a word Louis Sullivan himself was fond of using in reference to his scheme of ornamentation as distinguished from all other or any *applied* ornament. But now, and not merely as "form following function," came a larger application of the element called plasticity. "Form follows function" is mere dogma until you realize the higher truth that form and function are one.

Why any principle working in the part if not working in the whole?

I promoted plasticity as conceived by Lieber Meister to *continuity* in the concept of the building as a whole. If the dictum, "form follows function," had any bearing at all on building it could take form in architecture only by means of plasticity when seen at work as complete *continuity*. So why not throw away entirely all implications of post and beam construction? Have no posts, no columns, no pilasters, cornices or moldings or ornament; no divisions of the sort nor allow any fixtures whatever to enter as something added to the structure. Any

building should be complete, including all within itself. Instead of many things, *one* thing.

The folded plane enters here with the merging lines, walls and ceilings made one. Let walls, ceilings, floors now become not only party to each other but *part of each other,* reacting upon and within one another; continuity in all, eliminating any merely constructed features as such, or any fixture or appliance whatsoever as such.

When Louis Sullivan had eliminated background in his system of ornament in favor of an integral sense of the whole he had implied this larger sense of the thing. I now began to achieve it.

Conceive that here came a new sense of building on American soil that could *grow* building forms not only true to function but expressive far beyond mere function in the realm of the human spirit. Our new country might now have a true architecture hitherto unknown. Yes, architectural forms by this interior means might now grow up to express a deeper sense of human life values than any existing before. Architecture might extend the bounds of human individuality indefinitely by way of safe interior discipline. Not only had space come upon a new technique of its own but every material and every method might now speak for itself in objective terms of human life. Architects were no longer tied to Greek space but were free to enter into the space of Einstein.

Architectural forms might *grow* up? Yes, but grow up in what image? Here came concentrated appeal to pure imagination. Gradually proceeding from generals to particulars in the field of work with materials and machines, "plasticity" (become "continuity") began to grip me and work its own will in architecture. I would watch sequences fascinated, seeing other sequences in those consequences already in evidence. I occasionally look through such early studies as I made at this period (a number of them still remain), fascinated by implications. They seem, even now, generic. The old architecture, always dead for me so far as its grammar went, began literally to disappear. As if by magic new effects

Following pages: Sidney Bazett House, Hillsborough, California, living room, 1939. FLLW Fdn FA#4002.0001

came to life as though by themselves and I could draw inspiration from nature herself. I was beholden to no man for the look of anything. Textbook for me? "The book of creation." No longer need any more to be a wanderer among the objects and traditions of the past, picking and choosing his way by the personal idiosyncrasy of taste, guided only by personal predilection. From this hell I had been saved. The world lost an eclectic and gained an interpreter. If I did not like the Gods now I could make better ones.

Visions of simplicities so broad and far reaching would open to me and such building harmonies appear that I was tireless in search of new ones. In various form researches, with all my energy I concentrated upon the principle of plasticity working as continuity. Soon a practical working technique evolved and a new scale within the buildings I was building in the endeavor to more sensibly and sensitively accomplish this thing we call architecture. Here at work was something that would change and deepen the thinking and culture of the modern world. So I believed. . . .

From some laboratory experiments at Princeton by Professor Beggs which I saw while there delivering the Kahn Lectures in 1930,[5] it appears that aesthetic "continuity" at work in the practice of physical structure is concrete proof of the practical usefulness of the aesthetic ideal in designing architectural forms and, I hope, may soon be available as structural formula in some handbook. Welding instead of riveting steel is one new means to this new end and other plastic methods are constantly coming into use. But that and other possibilities (they will, I hope and believe, never need) are ahead of our story.

There were then no symbols at all for these ideas. But I have already objectified most of them. Were architecture bricks, my hands were in the mud of which bricks were made.

An idea soon came from this stimulating simplifying ideal (ideas breed, especially in actually making them work) that in order to be consistent, or indeed if all were to be put to work as architecture successfully, this new element of plasticity should have a new *sense* as well as a new *science* of materials.

It may interest you to know (it surprised me) that there is nothing in the literature of the civilized world upon that subject. Nothing I could find as *interpretation* in this sense of the nature of materials. Here was another great field for concrete endeavor, neglected. So I began, in my fashion, to study the nature of materials. Life is short. Lieber Meister had not reached this study. All materials alike were to receive the impress of his imagination. I began to learn to see brick as brick. I learned to see wood as wood and learned to see concrete or glass or metal each for itself and all as themselves. Strange to say this required uncommon sustained concentration of uncommon imagination (we call it vision), demanded not only a new conscious approach to building but opened a new world of thought that would certainly tear down the old world completely. Each different material required a different handling, and each different handling as well as the material itself had new possibilities of use peculiar to the nature of each. Appropriate designs for one material would not be at all appropriate for any other material. In the light of this ideal of building form as an organic simplicity almost all architecture fell to the ground. That is to say, ancient buildings were obsolete in the light of the idea of space determining form from within, all materials modifying if indeed they did not create the "form" when used with understanding according to the limitations of process and purpose.

Architecture might, and did, begin life anew.

Had steel, concrete, and glass existed in the ancient order we could have had nothing like our ponderous, senseless "classic" architecture. No, nothing even at Washington. Such betrayal of new life and new opportunities as ours has been would have been impossible to the ancients, the Greeks excepted, and we should have had a practice of architecture by the eclectic wherein tradition was not a parasite nor an enemy but a friend because the ancestors would have done the necessary work for us that we seem unable to do for ourselves. We would then have been able to copy the antique with sense and safety. Myself with the others.

Now there can be no organic architecture where the nature of synthetic materials or the nature of nature materials either is ignored or misunderstood. How can there be? Perfect correlation, integration, is life. It is the first principle of any growth that the thing grown be no mere aggregation. Integration as entity is first essential. And integration means that no part of anything is of any great value in itself except as it be integrate part of the harmonious whole. Even my great old master designed for materials all alike. All were grist for his rich imagination and he lived completely as artist, all to the contrary notwithstanding, only with his sentient ornament. Contrary to the ideas formed of him by wordwise but superficial critics, in this he created out of himself a world of his own, not yet appreciated at its true worth. How could it be yet? In this expression he went beyond the capacities of any individual before him. But all materials were only one material to him in which to weave the stuff of his dreams. Terra cotta was that one material. Terra cotta was *his* material, the one he loved most and served best. There he was master. But I honored him when I carried his work and thought further along by acting upon this new train of ideas, and the acts soon brought work sharply and immediately up against the tools that could be found to get these ideas put into new forms of building.

What a man does—*that* he has. You may find other things on him but they are not his.

What were the tools in use in the building trades everywhere? *Machines* and the automatic process, all too many of them. Stone or wood planers, stone and wood molding shapers, various lathes, presses, and power saws, the casting of metals and glass; all in commercially organized mills. The kiln; sheet-metal breakers; presses; shears; cutting, molding, and stamping machines in foundries and rolling mills; commercialized machine "shops"; concrete mixers; clay breakers; casters; glassmakers themselves; and the trade-unions versus capital; all laborers' or employers' units in a more or less highly commercialized greater union in which craftsmanship had no place except as survival for burial by standardization. Quantity production or standardization was already inflexible necessity either as enemy or friend. You might choose. And as you chose you became master and useful, or a luxury and

eventually the more or less elegant parasite we call an "eclectic"; a man guided only by instinct of choice called "taste."

By now I did not choose by instinct. I felt, yes, but I *knew* now what it was I felt concerning architecture.

Already, when I began to build, commercial machine standardization had taken the life of handicraft. But outworn handicraft had never troubled me. To make the new forms living expression of the new order of the machine and continue what was noble in tradition did trouble me. I wanted to realize genuine new forms true to the spirit of great tradition and found I should have to make them; not only make forms appropriate to the old (natural) and to new (synthetic) materials, but I should have to so design them that the machine (or process) that must make them could and would make them better than anything could possibly be made by hand. But now with this sense of integral order in architecture supreme in my mind I could have done nothing less unless I could have commanded armies of craftsmen as later I did command them in the building of the Imperial Hotel: a building in no sense a product of machine method. By now, safe inner discipline had come to me: the interior discipline of a great ideal. There is none so severe. But no other discipline yields such rich rewards in work, nor is there any man so safe and sure of results as the man disciplined from within by this ideal of the integration that is organic. Experience is this man's "school." It is yet his only school.

As I put these ideas to work in materials, lesser ideas took flight from this exacting ideal. But always in the same direction. They went farther on each occasion for flight, which was each new building I built, until great goals were in sight. Some few of the goals have been partially realized. You may see the "signs and portents" gathered together in various exhibition galleries if you can read drawings and models. The photographs are poor because the depth planes cannot be rendered by photography. But a number of the buildings are scattered or mutilated and unfortunately most of the best drawings are gone. The best buildings, too, were never built and may only be studied by the record. But later designs and models all exemplify in some material or grouping of materials, or idea of arrangement, these early objectives. Lieber Meister had been searching for "the rule so broad as to admit of no exception." For the life of me I could not help being most interested in the exception that proved the rule. This may explain "inconsistency" in performance and apparent departure from original objectives.

A group of young Chicago architects were gathered about me as disciples and friends in the early days, about 1893. They were my contemporaries and all learned from me to speak the new language. I wrote a little and later I tried to stem the tide of imitation. An instance was the paper read at Hull House in 1904 on "The Art and Craft of the Machine."[6] Occasionally, then an indifferent lecturer, I lectured. But talking isn't building, as I soon saw where any "school" as they called it (and later had names for the branches) had actually *to build*. Among these contemporaries the more ambitious began to call the new dwellings that appeared upon the prairies from 1893 to 1910 "the prairie school." I suppose this was modern architecture's first gallery. None knew much of Louis Sullivan, then, except by such work as he had done. And to a certain extent they imitated him too; imitating his individual ornamentation as the feature most in view. Some years later C. R. Ashbee came over to the United States and Kuno Francke of Harvard came to Oak Park. Both, in turn, saw the new work on the prairies and carried the tale of it to Europe in 1908. Some 15 or 20 years later a Swiss (in France) was to rediscover a familiar preliminary aesthetic; the affirmative negation declared by the Larkin Building, widely published at the time when it was built and recorded by an article in the *Architectural Record,* March 1908. But already (1910) in my own work the ideal of an organic architecture as affirmation had gone far beyond that belated negation that was at work in Europe itself.

Before trying to put down more in detail concerning goals now in sight, popular reaction to this new endeavor might be interesting. After the first "prairie house" was built, the Winslow house in 1893, which only in the matter of ornamentation bore resemblance in respect to the master (in the Charnley house I had stated, for the first time so far as I know, the thesis of the plain wall given the nature of decoration by a well-placed single opening which is also a feature of the Winslow house), my next client said he did not want a house "so different that he would have to go down the back way to his morning train to avoid being laughed at." That was one popular consequence. There were many others; bankers at first refused to loan money on the "queer" houses, so friends had to be found to finance the early buildings. Millmen would soon look for the name on the plans when the plans were presented for estimates, read the name of the architect and roll up the drawings again, handing them back with the remark that "they were not hunting for trouble"; contractors more often than not failed to read the plans correctly, so much had to be left off the buildings. The buildings were already off the main track. The clients themselves usually stood by interested and excited, often way beyond their means. So, when they moved into their new house, quite frequently they had no money left, had borrowed all they could and had to drag their old furniture into their new world. Seldom could I complete an interior because the ideal of "organic simplicity" seen as the countenance of perfect integration (as you have already read) naturally abolished all fixtures, rejected the old furniture, all carpets and most hangings, declaring them to be irrelevant or superficial decoration. The new practice made all furnishings so far as possible (certainly the electric lighting and heating systems) integral parts of the architecture. So far as possible all furniture was to be designed in place as part of the building. Hangings, rugs, carpets, were they to be used (as they might be if properly designed), all came into the same category. But the money matter generally crippled this particular feature of the original scheme, as I have said, and made trouble in this process of elimination and integration.

Nor, theoretically, was any planting to be done about the houses without cooperating with the architect. But, of course, it was done more often than not. But no sculpture, no painting was let in

Jorgine Boomer House, Phoenix, Arizona, 1953. FLLW Fdn FA#5305.0007

unless cooperating with the architect, although more often than not pictures were "hung." This made trouble. For no decoration, as such, was to be seen anywhere. Sculpture and painting were to be likewise *of* the building itself. In the Midway Gardens built in Chicago in 1913 I tried to complete the synthesis: planting, furnishings, music, painting, and sculpture, all to be one. But I found musicians, painters, and sculptors were unable to rise at that time to any such synthesis. Only in a grudging and dim way did most of them even understand it as an idea. So I made the designs for all to harmonize with the architecture; crude as any sketch is crude, incomplete as to execution, but in effect sufficiently complete to show the immense importance of any such attempt on any architect's part and show, indeed, that only so does architecture completely live. A new ideal of ornamentation had by now arrived that wiped out all ornament unless it, too, was an integral feature of the whole. True ornament became more desirable than ever but it had to "mean something"; in other words *be* something organic in character. Decorators hunting a job would visit the owners and, learning the name of the architect, lift their hats, turn on their heels, leaving with the curt and sarcastic "good day!" meaning really what the slang "good night!" of the period meant. This mat-

ter of integral ornament is the rock upon which a later generation of young architects splits and wisely decides to let it alone for the time being.

The owners of the early houses were, of course, all subjected to curiosity, sometimes to admiration, but were submitted most often to the ridicule of the "middle of the road egotist." To that ubiquitous egotist there was something about the owner too, now, when he had a house like that, "the rope tie around the monkey's neck."

Well, I soon had to face the fact that a different choice of materials would mean a different building altogether. Concrete was just coming into use and Unity Temple became the first concrete monolith in the world, that is to say, the first building complete as monolithic architecture when the wooden forms in which it was cast were taken away. No critic has yet seen it as it is for what it is except to realize that here, at least, was *something*. They might not like the temple but they were "impressed" by it. Meanwhile, the Larkin Building at Buffalo had just been built, a consciously important challenge to the empty ornamentality of the old order. The phrases I myself used concerning it in the issue of the *Architectural Record* in 1908 devoted to my work, put it on record as such. "Here again most of the critic's architecture has been left out. Therefore, the work may have the same claim to consideration as a work of art, as an ocean liner, a locomotive, or a battleship." The words may have escaped the Swiss "discoverer"; he was young at the time.

Plastered houses were then new. Casement windows were new. So many things were new. Nearly everything was new but the law of gravity and the idiosyncrasy of the client.

And simple as the buildings seemed and seem to be to this day because all had character and the countenance of principle, only the outward countenance of their simplicity has ever taken effect and that countenance is now being variously exaggerated by confirmed eclectics for the sake of the effect of a style. The innate simplicity that enabled them and enables them to multiply in infinite variety has not been practiced. I had built 187 buildings, planned and detailed about 37 more that had not been built, and all together they did not classify as a style. Nevertheless, all had "style."

As reward for independent thinking put into action as building and first plainly shown in the constitution and profiles of the prairie houses of Oak Park, Riverside, and other suburbs and Chicago and other cities, Unity Temple at Oak Park and the Larkin Administration Building in Buffalo, an entirely new sense of architecture for anyone who could read architecture had emerged. A higher concept of architecture. Architecture not alone as "form following function" in Lieber Meister's sense but architecture for the spirit of man, for life as life must be lived today; architecture spiritually (virtually) conceived as appropriate enclosure of interior space to be lived in. Form and function made one. The enclosed space within them is the *reality* of the building. The enclosed space comes through as architecture and may be seen in these exteriors I have built as the *reality* of the building I wanted to build and did build and am still building in spite of all opposition and the supreme obstacle, pretentious ignorance. This sense of the "within" or the room itself (or the rooms themselves) I see as the great thing to be realized and that may take the new forms we need as architecture. Such a source would never stultify itself as a mere style. This sense of interior space made *exterior*

as architecture, working out by way of the nature of materials and tools, transcends, as a fertilizing motive, all that has ever gone before in architecture. This clarifying motive of the whole makes previous ideas useful only as a means to the realization of this far greater concept of architecture. But if the buildings I have conceived upon this basis still seem enigmatical, most of all they must seem so to those who profess the "modernistic." A chasm exists between the usual profession and performance, because growth, where the quality we now call organic is concerned, must be slow growth. Eclecticism may take place overnight but organic architecture must come from the ground up into the light by gradual growth. It will itself be the ground of a better way of life; it is not only the beautifier of the building; it is, as a circumstance in itself, becoming the blessing of the occupants. All building construction naturally becomes lighter and stronger as fibrous "integument" takes the place of "solid mass." Our arboreal ancestors in their trees seem more likely precedent for us at the present time than savage animals who "hole in" for protection. But to properly put it on a human level, a higher *order* of the spirit has dawned for modern life in this interior concept of lived-in space playing with light, taking organic form as the reality of building; a building now an entity by way of native materials and natural methods of structure; forms becoming more naturally significant of ideal and purpose, ultimate in economy and strength. We have, now coming clear, an ideal the core of which must soon pervade the whole realm of creative man and one that, I know now, dates back to Laotse 500 B.C., and, later, to Jesus himself. The building era that Louis Sullivan ushered in is developing beyond the limitations that marked it, aside from his splendid elemental fluorescence, into the higher realm where as a human creative ideal throughout all culture it will make all form and function one.

Not much yet exists in our country—no, nor in any country outside plans and models—to exemplify steel and glass at its best in the light of this new sense of building. But a new countenance—it is the countenance of principle—has already appeared around the world. A new architectural language is being brokenly, variously, and often falsely spoken by youths, with perspicacity and some breadth of view but with too little depth of knowledge that can only come from continued experience. Unfortunately, academic training and current criticism have no penetration to this inner world. The old academic order is bulging with its own important impotence. Society is cracking under the strain of a sterility education imposes far beyond capacity; exaggerated capitalism has left all this as academic heritage to its own youth. General cultural sterility, the cause of the unrest of this uncreative moment that now stalls the world, might be saved and fructified by this ideal of an organic architecture: led from shallow troubled muddy water into deeper clearer pools of thought. Life needs these deeper fresher pools into which youth may plunge to come out refreshed.

More and more, so it seems to me, light is the beautifier of the building. Light always was the beautifier of the building in the matter of shadows but now especially needs these deeper satisfactions; needs a more worthy human ego for that tomorrow that is always today because of yesterday.

Inevitably this deeper sense of building as integral produce of the spirit of man is to construct the physical body of our machine age. But that in itself will not be enough. Unless this construction were to enable a broader, finer sense of life as something to be lived in to the full, all resources of time, place, and man in place to give us an architecture that is inspiring environment at the same time that it is a true expression of that life itself, the ideal will again have failed.

These gestures being lightly called "modernistic," what then is this new lip service, in shops, studios and schoolrooms? What are these pretentious gestures, this superficial association of ideas or this attempted academic rationalizing of this new work of mine? Why is the true content or motivating inner thought of this new architecture as organic architecture so confused in their hypocritical manifestations? Why is there so little modest, earnest effort to profit honestly by cooperation in these researches and, understanding such proofs as we have, honestly use

them, such as they are? Why not go ahead with them for growth instead of continuing to exploit them for a living or for a passing name? This self-seeking of some transient fame? "Publicity" is the only fame such shallow ambition may know, and like all such ambitions only the "advertising" that will be dead with yesterday's newspaper.

BUILDING THE NEW HOUSE

First thing in building the new house, get rid of the attic, therefore the dormer. Get rid of the useless false heights below it. Next, get rid of the unwholesome basement, yes absolutely—in any house built on the prairie. Instead of lean, brick chimneys bristling up everywhere to hint at Judgment, I could see necessity for one chimney only. A broad generous one, or at most two. These kept low down on gently sloping roofs or perhaps flat roofs. The big fireplace in the house below became now a place for a real fire. A real fireplace at that time was extraordinary. There were mantels instead. A mantel was a marble frame for a few coals in a grate. Or it was a piece of wooden furniture with tile stuck in it around the grate, the whole set slam up against the plastered, papered wall. Insult to comfort. So the *integral* fireplace became an important part of the building itself in the houses I was allowed to build out there on the prairie.

It comforted me to see the fire burning deep in the solid masonry of the house itself. A feeling that came to stay.

Taking a human being for my scale, I brought the whole house down in height to fit a normal one—ergo, 5' 8½" tall, say. This is my own height. Believing in no other scale than the human being I broadened the mass out all I possibly could to bring it down into spaciousness. It has been said that were I three inches taller than 5' 8½" all my houses would have been quite different in proportion. Probably.

House walls were now started at the ground on a cement or stone water table that looked like a low platform under the building, and usually was. But the house walls were stopped at the second-story windowsill level to let the bedrooms come through above in a continuous window series below the broad eaves of a gently sloping, overhanging roof. In this new house the wall was beginning to go as an impediment to outside light and air and beauty. Walls had been the great fact about the box in which holes had to be punched. It was still this conception of a wall-building which was with me when I designed the Winslow house. But after that my conception began to change.

My sense of "wall" was no longer the side of a box. It was enclosure of space affording protection against storm or heat only when needed. But it was also to bring the outside world into the house and let the inside of the house go outside. In this sense I was working away at the wall as a wall and bringing it towards the function of a screen, a means of opening up space which, as control of building-materials improved, would finally permit the free use of the whole space without affecting the soundness of the structure.

The climate being what it was, violent in extremes of heat and cold, damp and dry, dark and bright, I gave broad protecting roof-shelter to the whole, getting back to the purpose for which the cornice was originally designed. The underside of roof-projections was flat and usually light in color to create a glow of reflected light that softly brightened the upper rooms. Overhangs had double value: shelter and preservation for the walls of the house, as well as this diffusion of reflected light for the upper story through the "light screens" that took the place of the walls and were now often the windows in long series.

And at this time I saw a house, primarily, as livable interior space under ample shelter. I liked the *sense of shelter* in the look of the building. I still like it.

The house began to associate with the ground and become natural to its prairie site.

And would the young man in Architecture believe that this was all "new" then? Yes—not only new, but destructive heresy—ridiculous eccentricity. All somewhat so today. Stranger still, but then it was *all* so *new* that what prospect I had of ever earning a livelihood by making houses was nearly wrecked. At first, "they" called the houses "dress reform" houses because Society was just then excited about that particular reform. This simplification

looked like some kind of reform to the provincials.

What I have just described was on the *outside* of the house. But it was all there, chiefly because of what had happened *inside*.

Dwellings of that period were cut up, advisedly and completely, with the grim determination that should go with any cutting process. The interiors consisted of boxes beside boxes or inside boxes, called *rooms*. All boxes were inside a complicated outside boxing. Each domestic function was properly box to box.

I could see little sense in this inhibition, this cellular sequestration that implied ancestors familiar with penal institutions, except for the privacy of bedrooms on the upper floor. They were perhaps all right as sleeping boxes. So I declared the whole lower floor as one room, cutting off the kitchen as a laboratory, putting the servants' sleeping and living quarters next to the kitchen but semidetached, on the ground floor. Then I screened various portions of the big room for certain domestic purposes like dining and reading.

There were no plans in existence like these at the time. But my clients were all pushed toward these ideas as helpful to a solution of the vexed servant problem. Scores of unnecessary doors disappeared and no end of partition. Both clients and servants liked the new freedom. The house became more free as space and more livable too. Interior spaciousness began to dawn.

Thus came an end to the cluttered house. Fewer doors; fewer window holes though much greater window area; windows and doors lowered to convenient human heights. These changes once made, the ceilings of the rooms could be brought down over on to the walls by way of the horizontal broad bands of plaster on the walls themselves above the windows and colored the same as the room-ceilings. This would bring ceiling-surface and color down to the very window tops. Ceilings thus expanded by way of the wall band above the windows gave generous overhead even to small rooms. The sense of the whole broadened, made plastic by this means.

Here entered the important new element of plasticity—as I saw it. And I saw it as indispensable element to the successful use of the machine. The windows would sometimes be wrapped around the building corners as inside emphasis of plasticity and to increase the sense of interior space. I fought for outswinging windows because the casement window associated house with the out-of-doors, gave free openings outward. In other words, the so-called casement was not only simple but more human in use and effect. So more natural. If it had not existed I should have invented it. But it was not used at that time in the United States so I lost many clients because I insisted upon it. The client usually wanted the double-hung (the guillotine window) in use then, although it was neither simple nor human. It was only expedient. I used it once, in the Winslow house, and rejected it forever thereafter. Nor at that time did I entirely eliminate the wooden trim. I did make the "trim" plastic, that is to say, light and continuously flowing instead of the prevailing heavy "cut and butt" carpenter work. No longer did trim, so-called, look like carpenter work. The machine could do it all perfectly well as I laid it out, in this search for quiet. This plastic trim enabled poor workmanship to be concealed. There was need of that much trim then to conceal much in the way of craftsmanship because the battle between the machines and the union had already begun to demoralize workmen.

Machine resources of this period were so little understood that extensive drawings had to be made merely to show the mill-man what to leave off. Not alone in the trim but in numerous ways too tedious to describe in words, this revolutionary sense of the *plastic* whole began to work more and more intelligently and have fascinating unforeseen consequences. Nearly everyone had endured the house of the period as long as possible, judging by the appreciation of the change. Here was an ideal of organic simplicity put to work, with historical consequences not only in this country but especially in the thought of the civilized world.

SIMPLICITY

Organic Simplicity—in this early constructive effort—I soon found depended upon the sympathy with which such co-ordination as I have described might be effected. Plainness was not necessarily simplicity. That was evident. Crude furniture of the Roycroft-Stickley-Mission style, which came along later, was offensively plain, plain as a barn door—but was never simple in any true sense. Nor, I found, were merely machine-made things in themselves necessarily simple. "To think," as the Master used to say, "is to deal in simples." And that means with an eye single to the altogether.

This is, I believe, the single secret of simplicity: that we may truly regard nothing at all as simple in itself. I believe that no one thing in itself is ever so, but must achieve simplicity—as an artist should use the term—as a perfectly realized part of some organic whole. Only as a feature or any part becomes harmonious element in the harmonious whole does it arrive at the state of simplicity. Any wild flower is truly simple but double the same wild flower by cultivation and it ceases to be so. The scheme of the original is no longer clear. Clarity of design and perfect significance both are first essentials of the spontaneous born simplicity of the lilies of the field. "They toil not, neither do they spin." Jesus wrote the supreme essay on simplicity in this, "Consider the lilies of the field."

Five lines where three are enough is always stupidity. Nine pounds where three are sufficient is obesity. But to eliminate expressive words in speaking or writing—words that intensify or vivify meaning—is not simplicity. Nor is similar elimination in architecture simplicity. It may be, and usually is, stupidity.

In architecture, expressive changes of surface, emphasis of line and especially textures of material or imaginative pattern, may go to make facts more eloquent—forms more significant. Elimination, therefore, may be just as meaningless as elaboration, perhaps more often is so. To know what to leave out and what to put in; just where and just how, ah, *that* is to have been educated in knowledge of simplicity—toward ultimate freedom of expression.

As for objects of art in the house, even in that early day they were bêtes noires of the new simplicity. If well chosen, all right. But only if each were properly digested by the whole. Antique or modern sculpture, paintings, pottery, might well enough become objectives in the architectural scheme. And I accepted them, aimed at them often but assimilated them. Such precious things may often take their places as elements in the design of any house, be gracious and good to live with. But such assimilation is extraordinarily difficult. Better in general to design all as integral features.

I tried to make my clients see that furniture and furnishings that were not built in as integral features of the building should be designed as attributes of whatever furniture *was* built in and should be seen as a minor part of the building itself even if detached or kept aside to be employed only on occasion.

But when the building itself was finished the old furniture they already possessed usually went in with the clients to await the time when the interior might be completed in this sense. Very few of the houses, therefore, were anything but painful to me after the clients brought in their belongings.

Soon I found it difficult, anyway, to make some of the furniture in the abstract. That is, to design it as architecture and make it human at the same time—fit for human use. I have been black and blue in some spot, somewhere, almost all my life from too intimate contact with my own early furniture.

Human beings must group, sit or recline, confound them, and they must dine—but dining is much easier to manage and always a great artistic opportunity. Arrangements for the informality of sitting in comfort singly or in groups still belonging in disarray to the scheme as a whole: *that* is a matter difficult to accomplish. But it can be done now and should be done, because only those attributes of human comfort and convenience should be in order which belong to the whole in this modern integrated sense.

Human use and comfort should not be taxed to pay dividends on any designer's idiosyncrasy. Human use and comfort should have intimate possession of every interior—should be felt in every exterior. Decoration is intended to make use more charming and comfort more appropriate, or else a privilege has been abused.

As these ideals worked away from house to house, finally freedom of floor space and elimination of useless heights worked a miracle in the new dwelling place. A sense of appropriate freedom had changed its whole aspect. The whole became different but more fit for human habitation and more natural on its site. It was impossible to imagine a house once built on these principles somewhere else. An entirely new sense of space-values in architecture came home. It now appears these new values came into the architecture of the world. New sense of repose in quiet streamline effects had arrived. The streamline and the plain surface seen as the flat plane had then and there, some thirty-seven years ago, found their way into buildings as we see them in steamships, aeroplanes and motorcars, although they were intimately related to building materials, environment and the human being.

But, more important than all beside, still rising to greater dignity as an idea as it goes on working, was the ideal of plasticity. That ideal now began to emerge as a means to achieve an organic architecture.

PLASTICITY

Plasticity may be seen in the expressive flesh-covering of the skeleton as contrasted with the articulation of the skeleton itself. If form really "followed function"—as the Master declared—here was the direct means of expression of the more spiritual idea that form and function are one: the only true means I could see then or can see now to eliminate the separation and complication of cut-and-butt joinery in favor of the expressive flow of continuous surface. Here, by instinct at first—all ideas germinate—a principle entered into building that has since gone on developing. In my work the idea of plasticity may now be seen as the element of continuity.

In architecture, plasticity is only the modern expression of an ancient thought. But the thought taken into structure and throughout human affairs will recreate in a badly "disjointed," distracted world the entire fabric of human society. This magic word "plastic" was a word Louis Sullivan himself was fond of using in reference to his idea of ornamentation as distinguished from all other or applied ornament. But now, why not the larger application in the structure of the building itself in this sense?

Why a principle working in the part if not living in the whole?

If form really followed function—it did in a material sense by means of this ideal of plasticity, the spiritual concept of *form and function as one*— why not throw away the implications of post or upright and beam or horizontal entirely? Have no beams or columns piling up as "joinery." Nor any cornices. Nor any "features" as *fixtures*. No. Have no appliances of any kind at all, such as pilasters, entablatures and cornices. Nor put into the building any fixtures whatsoever as "fixtures." Eliminate the separations and separate joints. Classic architecture was all fixation-of-the-fixture. Yes, entirely so. Now why not let walls, ceilings, floors become *seen* as component parts of each other, their surfaces flowing into each other. To get continuity in the whole, eliminating all constructed features just as Louis Sullivan had eliminated background in his ornament in favor of an integral sense of the whole. Here the promotion of an idea from the material to the spiritual plane began to have consequences. Conceive now that an entire building might grow up out of conditions as a plant grows up out of soil and yet be free to be itself, to "live its own life according to Man's Nature." Dignified as a tree in the midst of nature but a child of the spirit of man.

I now propose an ideal for the architecture of the machine age, for the ideal American building. Let it grow up in that image. The tree.

But I do not mean to suggest the imitation of the tree.

Proceeding, then, step by step from generals to particulars, plasticity as a large means in architecture began to grip me and to work its own will. Fascinated I would watch its sequences, seeing other sequences in those consequences already in evidence: as in the Heurtley, Martin, Heath, Thomas, Tomek, Coonley and dozens of other houses.

The old architecture, so far as its grammar went, for me began, literally, to disappear. As if by magic new architectural effects came to life—effects genuinely new in the whole cycle of architecture owing simply to the working of this spiritual principle. Vistas of inevitable simplicity and ineffable harmonies would open, so beautiful to me that I was not only delighted, but often startled. Yes, sometimes amazed.

I have since concentrated on plasticity as physical continuity, using it as a practical working principle within the very nature of the building itself in the effort to accomplish this great thing called architecture. Every true esthetic is an implication of nature, so it was inevitable that this esthetic ideal should be found to enter into the actual building of the building itself as a principle of construction.

But later on I found that in the effort to actually eliminate the post and beam in favor of structural continuity, that is to say, making the two things one thing instead of two separate things, I could get no help at all from regular engineers. By habit, the engineer reduced everything in the field of calculation to the post and the beam resting upon it before he could calculate and tell you where and just how much for either. He had no other data. Walls made one with floors and ceilings, merging together yet reacting upon each other, the engineer had never met. And the engineer has not yet enough scientific formulae to enable him to calculate for continuity. Floor slabs stiffened and extended as cantilevers over centered supports, as a waiter's tray rests upon his upturned fingers, such as I now began to use in order to get planes parallel to the earth to emphasize the third dimension, were new, as I used them, especially in the Imperial Hotel. But the engineer soon mastered the element of continuity in floor slabs, with such formulae as he had. The cantilever thus became a new feature of design in architecture. As used in the Imperial Hotel at Tokyo it was the most important of the features of construction that insured the life of that building in the terrific temblor of 1922. So, not only a new esthetic but proving the esthetic as scientifically sound, a great new economic "stability," derived from steel in tension, was able now to enter into building construction.

IN THE NATURE OF MATERIALS: A PHILOSOPHY

Our vast resources are yet new; new only because architecture as "rebirth" (perennial Renaissance) has, after five centuries of decline, culminated in the imitation of imitations, seen in our Mrs. Plaster-built, Mrs. Gablemore, and Miss Flat-top American architecture. In general, and especially officially, our architecture is at long last completely significant of insignificance only. We do not longer have architecture. At least no buildings with integrity. We have only economic crimes in its name. No, our greatest buildings are not qualified as great art, my dear Mrs. Davies, although you do admire Washington.

If you will yet be patient for a little while—a scientist, Einstein, asked for three days to explain the far less pressing and practical matter of "Relativity"—we will take each of the five new resources in order, as with the five fingers of the hand. All are new integrities to be used if we will to make living easier and better today.

The first great integrity is a deeper, more intimate sense of reality in building than was ever pagan—that is to say, than was ever "Classic." More human than was any building ever realized in the Christian Middle Ages. This is true although the thought that may ennoble it now has been living in civilization for more than twenty centuries back. Later it was innate in the simplicities of Jesus as it was organic 500 years earlier in the natural philosophy, Tao (The Way), of the Chinese philosopher Laotse. But not only is the new architecture sound philosophy. It is poetry.

Said Ong Giao Ki, Chinese sage, "Poetry is the sound of the heart."

Well, like poetry, this sense of architecture is the sound of the "within." We might call that "within," the heart.

Architecture now becomes integral, the expression of a new-old reality: the livable interior space of the room itself. In integral architecture the *room-space itself must come through*. The *room* must be seen as architecture, or we have no architecture. We have no longer an outside as outside. We have no longer an outside and an inside as two separate things. Now the outside may come inside, and the inside may and does go outside. They are *of* each other. Form and function thus become one in design and execution if the nature of materials and method and purpose are all in unison.

This interior-space concept, the first broad integrity, is the first great resource. It is also true basis for general significance of form. Add to this for the

sake of clarity that (although the general integration is implied in the first integrity) it is in the nature of any organic building to grow from its site, come out of the ground into the light—the ground itself held always as a component basic part of the building itself. And then we have primarily the new ideal of building as organic. A building dignified as a tree in the midst of nature.

This new ideal for architecture is, as well, an adequate ideal for our general culture. In any final result there can be no separation between our architecture and our culture. Nor any separation of either from our happiness. Nor any separation from our work.

Thus in this rise of organic integration you see the means to end the petty agglomerations miscalled civilization. By way of this old yet new and deeper sense of reality we may have a civilization. In this sense we now recognize and may declare by way of plan and building—the *natural*. Faith in the *natural* is the faith we now need to grow up on in this coming age of our culturally confused, backward twentieth century. But instead of "organic" we might well say "natural" building. Or we might say integral building.

So let us now consider the second of the five new resources: glass. This second resource is new and a "super-material" only because it holds such amazing means in modern life for awakened sensibilities. It amounts to a new qualification of life in itself. If known in ancient times glass would then and there have abolished the ancient architecture we know, and completely. This super-material GLASS as we now use it is a miracle. Air in air to keep air out or keep it in. Light itself in light, to diffuse or reflect, or refract light itself.

By means of glass, then, the first great integrity may find prime means of realization. Open reaches of the ground may enter as the building and the building interior may reach out and associate with these vistas of the ground. Ground and building will thus become more and more obvious as directly related to each other in openness and intimacy; not only as environment but also as a good pattern for the good life lived in the building. Realizing the benefits to human life of the far-reaching implications and effects of the first great integrity, let us call it the interior-space concept. This interior-space realization is possible and it is desirable in all the vast variety of characteristic buildings needed by civilized life in our complex age.

By means of glass something of the freedom of our arboreal ancestors living in their trees becomes a more likely precedent for freedom in twentieth-century life, than the cave.

Savage animals "holing in" for protection were more characteristic of life based upon the might of feudal times or based upon the so-called "classical" in architecture, which were in turn based upon the labor of the chattel slave. In a free country, were we ourselves free by way of organic thought, buildings might come out into the light without more animal fear; come entirely away from the pagan ideals of form we dote upon as "Classic." Or what Freedom have we?

Perhaps more important than all beside, it is by way of glass that the sunlit space as a reality becomes the most useful servant of a higher order of the human spirit. It is first aid to the sense of cleanliness of form and idea when directly related to free living in air and sunlight. It is this that is coming in the new architecture. And with the integral character of extended vistas gained by marrying buildings with ground levels, or blending them with slopes and gardens; yes, it is in this new sense of earth as a great human *good* that we will move forward in the building of our new homes and great public buildings.

I am certain we will desire the sun, spaciousness and integrity of means-to-ends more year by year as we become aware of the possibilities I have outlined. The more we desire the sun, the more we will desire the freedom of the good ground and the sooner we will learn to understand it. The more we value integrity, the more securely we will find and keep a worthwhile civilization to set against prevalent abuse and ruin.

Congestion will no longer encourage the "space-makers for rent." The "space-maker for rent" will himself be "for rent" or let us hope "vacant." Give him ten years.

These new space values are entering into our ideas of life. All are appropriate to the ideal that is our own, the ideal we call Democracy.

A NEW REALITY: GLASS

A resource to liberate this new sense of interior space as reality is this new qualification called glass: a super-material qualified to qualify us; qualify us not only to escape from the prettified cavern of our present domestic life as also from the cave of our past, but competent actually to awaken in us the desire for such far-reaching simplicities of life as we may see in the clear countenance of nature. Good building must ever be seen as in the nature of good construction, but a higher development of this "seeing" will be construction seen as nature-pattern. *That* seeing, only, is inspired architecture.

This dawning sense of the *Within* as *reality* when it is clearly seen as *Nature* will by way of glass make the garden be the building as much as the building will be the garden: the sky as treasured a feature of daily indoor life as the ground itself.

You may see that walls are vanishing. The cave for human dwelling purposes is at last disappearing.

Walls themselves because of glass will become windows and windows as we used to know them as holes in walls will be seen no more. Ceilings will often become as window-walls, too. The textile may soon be used as a beautiful overhead for space, the textile an attribute of genuine architecture instead of decoration by way of hangings and upholstery. The usual camouflage of the old order. Modern integral floor heating will follow integral lighting and standardized unitary sanitation. All this makes it reasonable and good economy to abolish building as either a hyper-boxment or a super-borough.

Haven't senseless elaboration and false mass become sufficiently insulting and oppressive to our intelligence as a people? And yet, senseless elaboration and false mass were tyrannical as "conspicuous waste" in all of our nineteenth-century architecture either public or private! Wherever the American architect, as scholar, went he "succeeded" to that extent.

ANOTHER REALITY: CONTINUITY

But now, as third resource, the resource essential to modern architecture destined to cut down this outrageous mass-waste and mass-lying, is the principle of continuity. I have called it tenuity. Steel is its prophet and master. You must come with me for a moment into "engineering" so called. This is to be an un-avoidable strain upon your kind attention. Because, unfortunately, gentle reader, you cannot understand architecture as *modern* unless you do come, and— paradox—you can't come if you are too well educat-ed as an engineer or as an architect either. So your common sense is needed more than your erudition.

However, to begin this argument for steel: classic architecture knew only the post as an *upright.* Call it a column. The classics knew only the beam as a *horizontal.* Call it a beam. The beam resting upon the upright, or column, was structure throughout, to them. Two things, you see, one thing set on top of another thing in various materials and put there in various ways. Ancient, and nineteenth-century building science too, even building *à la mode,* con-sisted simply in reducing the various stresses of all materials and their uses to these two things: post and beam. Really, construction used to be just sticking up something in wood or stone and putting some-thing else in wood or stone (maybe iron) on top of it: simple super-imposition, you see? You should know that all "Classic" architecture was and still is some such form of direct super-imposition. The arch is a little less so, but even that must be so "figured" by the structural engineer if you ask him to "figure" it.

Now the Greeks developed this simple act of super-imposition pretty far by way of innate tasteful refinement. The Greeks were true estheticians. Ro-man builders too, when they forgot the Greeks and brought the beam over as a curve by way of the arch, did something somewhat new but with conse-quences still of the same sort. But observe, all archi-tectural features made by such "Classic" agglomera-tion were killed for us by cold steel. And though millions of classic corpses yet encumber American ground unburied, they are ready now for burial.

Of course this primitive post-and-beam con-struction will always be valid, but both support and supported may now by means of inserted and weld-ed steel strands or especially woven filaments of steel and modern concrete casting be plaited and united as one physical body: ceilings and walls made one with floors and reinforcing each other by making them continue into one another. This Continuity is made possible by the tenuity of steel.

So the new order wherever steel or plastics en-ter construction says: weld these two things, post and beam (wall and ceiling) together by means of steel strands buried and stressed within the mass material itself, the steel strands electric-welded where steel meets steel within the mass. In other words the up-right and horizontal may now be made to work to-gether as one. A new world of form opens inevitably.

Where the beam leaves off and the post begins is no longer important nor need it be seen at all be-cause it no longer actually *is.* Steel in tension enables the support to slide into the supported, or the sup-ported to grow into the support somewhat as a tree-branch glides out of its tree trunk. Therefrom arises the new series of interior physical reactions I am call-ing "Continuity." As natural consequence the new esthetic or appearance we call *Plasticity* (and plastici-ty is peculiarly "modern") is no longer a mere ap-pearance. Plasticity actually becomes the normal *countenance,* the *true esthetic* of genuine structural real-ity. These interwoven steel strands may so lie in so many directions in any extended member that the extensions may all be economical of material and though much lighter, be safer construction than ever before. There as in the branch of the tree you may see the cantilever. The cantilever is the simplest one of the important phases of this third new structural resource now demanding new significance. It has yet had little attention in architecture. It can do remark-able things to liberate space.

But plasticity was modest new countenance in our American architecture at least thirty-five years ago in my own work, but then denied such simple means as welding and the mesh. It had already elim-inated all the separate identities of post and beam in architecture. Steel in tension enters now by way of mesh and welding to arrive at actual, total plasticity if and when desired by the architect. And to prove the philosophy of organic architecture, form and function are one, it now enters architecture as the *esthetic* countenance of *physical reality.*

To further illustrate this magic simplifier we call "plasticity": see it as *flexibility* similar to that of your own hand. What makes your hand expressive? Flowing continuous line and continuous surfaces seen continually mobile of the articulate articulated structure of the hand as a whole. The line is seen as "hand" line. The varying planes seen as "hand" surface. Strip the hand to the separate structural identities of joined bones (post and beam) and plasticity as an expression of the hand would disappear. We would be then getting back to the joinings, breaks, jolts, and joints of ancient, or "Classic," architecture: thing to thing; feature to feature. But plasticity is the reverse of that ancient agglomeration and is the ideal means behind these simplified free new effects of straight line and flat plane.

I have just said that plasticity in this sense for thirty-five years or more has been the recognized esthetic ideal for such simplification as was required by the machine to do organic work. And it is true of my own work.

As significant outline and expressive surface, this new esthetic of plasticity (physical continuity) is now a useful means to form the supreme physical body of an organic, or integral, American Architecture.

Of course, it is just as easy to cheat by simplicity as it is to cheat with "classical" structure. So, unluckily, here again is the "modernistic" architectural picture-maker's deadly facility for imitation at ease and again too happy with fresh opportunity to "fake effects." Probably another Renaissance is here imminent.

Architecture is now integral architecture only when Plasticity is a genuine expression of actual construction just as the articulate line and surface of the hand is articulate of the structure of the hand. Arriving at steel, I first used Continuity as actual stabilizing principle in concrete slabs, and in the concrete ferro-block system I devised in Los Angeles.

In the form of the cantilever or as horizontal continuity this new economy by means of tenuity is what saved the Imperial Hotel from destruction, but it did not appear in the grammar of the building for various reasons, chiefly because the building was to look somewhat as though it belonged to Tokyo.

Later, in the new design for St. Mark's Tower, New York City, this new working principle economized material, labor, and liberated or liberalized space in a more developed sense. It gave to the structure the significant outlines of remarkable stability and instead of false masonry-mass significant outlines came out. The abstract pattern of the structure as a complete structural-integrity of Form and Idea may be seen fused as in any tree but with nothing imitating a tree.

Continuity invariably realized remarkable economy of labor and building materials as well as space. Unfortunately there is yet little or no data to use as tabulation. Tests will have to be made continually for many years to make the record available to slide-rule engineers.

In the ancient order there was little thought of economy of materials. The more massive the whole structure looked, the better it looked to the ancients. But seen in the light of these new economic interior forces conserved by the tensile strength of a sheet of plastic or any interweaving of strands of steel in this machine age, the old order was as sick with weight as the Buonarotti dome. Weak . . . because there could be no co-interrelation between the two elements of support and supported to reinforce each other as a whole under stress or elemental disturbance.

So this tremendous new resource of *tenuity*—a quality of steel—this quality of *pull* in a building (you may see it ushering in a new era in John Roebling's Brooklyn Bridge) was definitely lacking in all ancient architecture because steel had not been born into building.

The tenuous strand or slab as a common means of strength had yet to come. Here today this element of continuity may cut structural substance nearly in two. It may cut the one half in two again by elimination of needless features, such elimination being entirely due to the simplification I have been calling "plasticity."

It is by utilizing mass production in the factory in this connection that some idea of the remarkable new economics possible to modern architecture may be seen approaching those realized in any well-built machine. If standardization can be humanized and made flexible in design and the economics brought to the home owner, the greatest service will be rendered to our modern way of life. It may be really born—this democracy, I mean.

Involved as a matter of design in this mass production, however, are the involute, all but involuntary reactions to which I have just referred: the ipso facto building code and the fact that the building

Gerald Sussman "Usonian Automatic" House (Project), Rye, New York. 1955. Perspective. Pencil and color pencil on tracing paper, 36 x 25". FLLW Fdn#5524.001

engineer as now trained knows so little about them. However, the engineer is learning to calculate by model-making in some instances—notably Professor Beggs at Princeton.

The codes so far as I can see will have to die on the vine with the men who made them.

MATERIALS FOR THEIR OWN SAKE

As the first integrity and the two first new resources appeared out of the interior nature of the kind of building, called Architecture—so now, naturally, interior to the true nature of any good building, comes the fourth new resource. This is found by recognizing the nature of the materials used in construction.

Just as many fascinating different properties as there are different materials that may be used to build a building will continually and naturally qualify, modify and utterly change all architectural form whatsoever.

A stone building will no more *be* nor will it *look* like a steel building. A pottery, or terra cotta building, will not be nor should it look like a stone building. A wood building will look like none other, for it will glorify the stick. A steel and glass building could not possibly look like anything but itself. It will glorify steel and glass. And so on all the way down the long list of available riches in materials: Stone, Wood, Concrete, Metals, Glass, Textiles, Pulp and Plastics; riches so great to our hand today that no comparison with Ancient Architecture is at all sensible or anything but obstruction to our Modern Architecture.

In this particular, as you may see, architecture is going back to learn from the natural source of all natural things.

In order to get Organic Architecture born, intelligent architects will be forced to turn their backs on antique rubbish heaps with which Classic eclecticism has encumbered our new ground. So far as architecture has gone in my own thought it is first of all a character and quality of *mind* that may enter also into human conduct with social implications that might, at first, confound or astound you. But the only basis for any fear of them lies in the fact that they are all sanely and thoroughly *constructive*.

Instinctively all forms of pretense fear and hate reality. THE HYPOCRITE MUST ALWAYS HATE THE RADICAL.

This potent fourth new resource—the Nature of Materials—gets at the common center of every material in relation to the work it is required to do. This means that the architect must again begin at the very beginning. Proceeding according to Nature now he must sensibly go through with whatever material may be in hand for his purpose according to the methods and sensibilities of a man in this age. And when I say Nature, I mean inherent *structure* seen always by the architect as a matter of complete design. It is in itself, always, *nature-pattern*. It is this profound internal sense of materials that enters in as Architecture now. It is this, the fifth new resource, that must captivate and hold the mind of the modern architect to creative work. The fifth will give new life to his imagination if it has not been already killed at school.

And, inevitable implication! New machine-age resources require that all buildings do *not* resemble each other. The new ideal does *not* require that all buildings be of steel, concrete or glass. Often that might be idiotic waste.

Nor do the resources even *imply* that mass is no longer a beautiful attribute of masonry materials when they are genuinely used. We are entitled to a vast variety of form in our complex age so long as the form be genuine—serves Architecture and Architecture serves life.

But in this land of ours, richest on earth of all in old and new materials, architects must exercise well-trained imagination to see in each material, either natural or compounded plastics, their own *inherent style*. All materials may be beautiful, their beauty much or entirely depending upon how well they are used by the Architect.

In our modern building we have the Stick. Stone. Steel. Pottery. Concrete. Glass. Yes, Pulp, too, as well as plastics. And since this dawning sense of the "within" is the new reality, these will all give the main *motif* for any real building made from them. The materials of which the building is built will go far to determine its appropriate mass, its outline and, especially, proportion. *Character* is criterion in the form of any and every building or industrial product we can call Architecture in the light of this new ideal of the new order.

THE NEW INTEGRITY

Strange! At this late date, it is modern architecture that wants life to learn to see life as life, because architecture must learn to see brick as brick, learn to see steel as steel, see glass as glass. So modern thought urges all of life to demand that a bank look like a bank (bad thought though a bank might become) and not depend upon false columns for credit. The new architecture urges all of life to demand that an office building look like an office building, even if it should resemble the cross section of a beehive. Life itself should sensibly insist in self-defense that a hotel look and conduct itself like a hotel and not like some office building. Life should declare,

too, that the railroad station look like a railroad station and not try so hard to look like an ancient temple or some monarchic palazzo. And while we are on this subject, why not a place for opera that would look something like a place for opera—if we must have opera, and not look so much like a gilded, crimsoned bagnio. Life declares that a filling station should stick to its work as a filling station: look the part becomingly. Why try to look like some Colonial diminutive or remain just a pump on the street. Although "just a pump" on the street is better than the Colonial imitation. The good Life itself demands that the school be as generously spaced and a thought-built good-time place for happy children: a building no more than one story high—with some light overhead, the school building should regard the children as a garden in sun. Life itself demands of Modern Architecture that the house of a man who knows what home is should have his own home his own way if we have any man left in that connection after F.H.A. is done trying to put them, all of them it can, into the case of a man who builds a home only to sell it. Our Government forces the home-maker into the real-estate business if he wants a home at all.

Well, after all, this line of thought was all new-type common sense in architecture in Chicago only thirty years ago. It began to grow up in my own work as it is continuing to grow up more and more widely in the work of all the world. But, insulting as it may seem to say so, nor is it merely arrogant to say that the actual thinking in that connection is still a novelty, only a little less strange today than it was then, although the appearances do rapidly increase.

INTEGRAL ORNAMENT AT LAST!

At last, is this fifth resource, so old yet now demanding fresh significance. We have arrived at integral ornament—the nature-pattern of actual construction. Here, confessed as the spiritual demand for true significance, comes this subjective element in modern architecture. An element so hard to understand that modern architects themselves seem to understand it least well of all and most of them have turned against it with such fury as is born only of impotence.

And it *is* true that this vast, intensely human significance is really no matter at all for any but the most imaginative mind not without some development in artistry and the *gift* of a sense of proportion. Certainly we must go higher in the realm of imagination when we presume to enter here, because we go into Poetry.

Now, very many write good prose who cannot write poetry at all. And although staccato specification is the present fashion, just as "functionalist" happens to be the present style in writing—poetic prose will never be undesirable. But who condones prosaic poetry? None. Not even those fatuously condemned to write it.

So, I say this fourth new resource and the fifth demand for new significance and integrity is ornament *integral to building as itself poetry*. Rash use of a dangerous word. The word "Poetry" *is* a dangerous word.

Heretofore, I have used the word "pattern" instead of the word ornament to avoid confusion or to escape the passing prejudice. But here now ornament is in its place. Ornament meaning not only *surface qualified by human imagination* but imagination giving *natural pattern* to structure. Perhaps this phrase says it all without further explanation. This resource—integral ornament—is new in the architecture of the world, at least insofar not only as imagination qualifying a surface—a valuable resource—but as a greater means than that: *imagination giving natural pattern to structure itself*. Here we have new significance, indeed! Long ago this significance was lost to the scholarly architect. A man of taste. He, too soon, became content with symbols.

Evidently then, this expression of structure as a pattern true to the nature of the materials out of which it was made, may be taken much further along than physical need alone would dictate? "If you have a loaf of bread break the loaf in two and give the half of it for some flowers of the Narcissus, for the bread feeds the body indeed but the flowers feed the soul."

Into these higher realms of imagination associated in the popular mind as sculpture and painting, buildings may be as fully taken by modern means today as they ever were by craftsmen of the antique order.

It is by this last and poetic resource that we may give greater structural entity and greater human significance to the whole building than could ever be done otherwise. This statement is heresy at this left-wing moment, so—we ask, "taken how and when taken?" I confess you may well ask by whom? The answer is, taken by the true *poet*. And where is this Poet today? Time will answer.

Yet again in this connection let us remember Ong's Chinese observation, "Poetry is the sound of the heart." So, in the same uncommon sense integral ornament is the developed sense of the building as a whole, or the manifest *abstract pattern of structure itself*. Interpreted. Integral ornament is simply *structure-pattern made visibly articulate* and seen in the building as it is seen articulate in the structure of the trees or a lily of the fields. It is the expression of inner rhythm of Form. Are we talking about Style? Pretty nearly. At any rate, we are talking about the qualities that make *essential architecture* as distinguished from any mere act of building whatsoever.

What I am here calling integral ornament is founded upon the same organic simplicities as Beethoven's Fifth Symphony, that amazing revolution in tumult and splendor of sound built on four tones based upon a rhythm a child could play on the piano with one finger. Supreme imagination reared the four repeated tones, simple rhythms, into a great symphonic poem that is probably the noblest thought-built edifice in our world. And Architecture is like Music in this capacity for the symphony.

But concerning higher development of building to more completely express its life principle as significant and beautiful, let us say at once by way of warning: it is better to die by the wayside of left-wing Ornaphobia than it is to build any more merely ornamented buildings, as such; or to see right-wing architects die any more ignoble deaths of *Ornamentia*. All period and pseudo-classic buildings whatever, and (although their authors do not seem to know it) most protestant buildings, they call themselves internationalist, are really ornamental in definitely objectionable sense. A plain flat surface cut to shape for its own sake, however large or plain the shape, is, the moment it is sophisticatedly so cut, no less ornamental than egg-and-dart. All such buildings are objectionably "ornamental," because like any buildings of the old classical order both wholly ignore the *nature* of the *first* integrity. Both also ignore the four resources and both neglect the nature of machines at work on materials. Incidentally and as a matter of course both misjudge the nature of time, place and the modern life of man.

Here in this new leftish emulation as we now have it, is only the "istic," ignoring principle merely to get the "look" of the machine or something that looks "new." The province of the "ite."

In most so-called "internationalist" or "modernistic" building therefore we have no true approach to organic architecture: we have again merely a new, superficial esthetic trading upon that architecture because such education as most of our architects possess qualifies them for only some kind of eclecticism past, passing, or to pass.

Nevertheless I say, if we can't have buildings with integrity we would better have more imitation machines for buildings until we can have truly sentient architecture. "The machine for living in" is sterile, but therefore it is safer, I believe, than the festering mass of ancient styles.

GREAT POWER

A far greater power than slavery, even the intellectual slavery as in the school of the Greeks, is back of these five demands for machine-age significance and integrity. Stupendous and stupefying power. That power is the leverage of the machine itself. As now set up in all its powers the machine will confirm these new implicities and complicities in architecture at every point, but will destroy them soon if not checked by a new simplicity.

The proper use of these new resources demands that we use them all together with integrity for mankind if we are to realize the finer significances of life. The finer significance, prophesied if not realized by organic architecture. It *is* reasonable to believe that life in our country will be lived in full enjoyment of this new freedom of the extended horizontal line because the horizontal line now be-

comes the great architectural highway. The flat plane now becomes the regional field. And integral-pattern becomes "the sound of the Usonian heart."[7]

I see this extended horizontal line as the true earth-line of human life, indicative of freedom. Always.

The broad expanded plane is the horizontal plane infinitely extended. In that lies such freedom for man on this earth as he may call his.

This new sense of Architecture as integral-pattern of that type and kind may awaken these United States to fresh beauty, and the Usonian horizon of the individual will be immeasurably extended by enlightened use of this great lever, the machine. But only if it gets into creative hands loyal to humanity.

THE USONIAN HOUSE I

The house of moderate cost is not only America's major architectural problem but the problem most difficult for her major architects. As for me, I would rather solve it with satisfaction to myself and Usonia, than build anything I can think of at the moment except the modern theater now needed by the legitimate drama unless the stage is to be done to death by "the movies." In our country the chief obstacle to any real solution of the moderate-cost house problem is the fact that our people do not really know how to live. They imagine their idiosyncrasies to be their "tastes," their prejudices to be their predilections, and their ignorance to be virtue—where any beauty of living is concerned.

To be more specific, a small house on the side street might have charm if it didn't ape the big house on the Avenue, just as the Usonian village itself might have a great charm if it didn't ape the big town. Likewise, Marybud on the old farm, a jewel hanging from the tip of her pretty nose on a cold, cold day, might be charming in clothes befitting her state and her work, but is only silly in the Sears-Roebuck finery that imitates the clothes of her city sisters who imitate Hollywood stars: lipstick, rouge, high heels, silk stockings, bell skirt, cockeyed hat, and all. Exactly that kind of "monkey-fied" business is the obstacle to architectural achievement in our U.S.A. This provincial "culture-lag" in favor of the lag which does not allow the person, thing, or

Raymond Carlson House, Phoenix, Arizona, 1950. Photograph by John Amarantides. FLLW Fdn FA#5004.0054

thought to be simple and naturally itself. It is the real obstacle to a genuine Usonian culture.

I am certain that any approach to the new house needed by indigenous culture—why worry about the house wanted by provincial "tasteful" ignorance!—is fundamentally different. That house must be a pattern for more simplified and, at the same time, more gracious living: necessarily new, but suitable to living conditions as they might so well be in this country we live in today.

This need of a house of moderate cost must sometime face not only expedients but Reality. Why not face it now? The expedient houses built by the million, which journals propagate, and government builds, do no such thing.

To me such houses are stupid makeshifts, putting on some style or other, really having no integrity. Style *is* important. *A* style is not. There is all the difference when we work *with* style and not for *a* style.

I have insisted on that point for forty-five years.

Notwithstanding all efforts to improve the product, the American "small house" problem is still a pressing, needy, hungry, confused issue. But where is a better thing to come from while Authority has pitched into perpetuating the old stupidities? I do not believe the needed house can come from current education, or from big business. It isn't coming by way of smart advertising experts either. Or professional streamliners. It is only super-common-sense that can take us along the road to the better thing in building.

What would be really sensible in this matter of the modest dwelling for our time and place? Let's see how far the first Herbert Jacobs house at Madison, Wisconsin, is a sensible house. This house for a young journalist, his wife, and small daughter, was built in 1937. Cost: Fifty-five hundred dollars, including architect's fee of four hundred and fifty. Contract let to P. B. Grove.

To give the small Jacobs family the benefit of the advantages of the era in which they live, many simplifications must take place. Mr. and Mrs. Jacobs must themselves see life in somewhat simplified terms. What are essentials in their case, a typical case? It is not only necessary to get rid of all unnecessary complications in construction, necessary to use work in the mill to good advantage, necessary to eliminate, so far as possible, field labor which is always expensive: it is necessary to consolidate and simplify the three appurtenance systems—heating, lighting, and sanitation. At least this must be our economy if we are to achieve the sense of spaciousness and vista we desire in order to liberate the people living in the house. And it would be ideal to complete the building in one operation as it goes along. Inside and outside should be complete in one operation. The house finished inside as it is completed outside. There should be no complicated roofs.

Every time a hip or a valley or a dormer window is allowed to ruffle a roof the life of the building is threatened.

The way the windows are used is naturally a most useful resource to achieve the new characteristic sense of space. All this fenestration can be made ready at the factory and set up as the walls. But there is no longer sense in speaking of doors and windows. These walls are largely a system of fenestration having its own part in the building scheme—the system being as much a part of the design as eyes are part of the face.

Now what can be eliminated? These:

1. Visible roofs are expensive and unnecessary.

2. A garage is no longer necessary as cars are made. A carport will do, with liberal over-head shelter and walls on two sides. Detroit still has the livery-stable mind. It believes that the car is a horse and must be stabled.

3. The old-fashioned basement, except for a fuel and heater space, was always a plague spot. A steam-warmed concrete mat four inches thick laid directly on the ground over gravel filling, the walls set upon that, is better.

4. Interior "trim" is no longer necessary.

5. We need no radiators, no light fixtures. We will heat the house the "hypocaust" way—in or between the floors. We can make the wiring system itself be the light fixture, throwing light upon and down the ceiling. Light will thus be indirect, except for a few outlets for floor lamps.

6. Furniture, pictures and bric-a-brac are unnecessary because the walls can be made to include them or *be* them.

7. No painting at all. Wood best preserves itself. A coating of clear resinous oil would be enough. Only the floor mat of concrete squares needs waxing.

8. No plastering in the building.

9. No gutters, no downspouts.

To assist in general planning, what must or may we use in our new construction? In this case five materials: wood, brick, cement, paper, glass. To simplify fabrication we must use our horizontal-unit system in construction. We must also use a vertical-unit system which will be the widths of the boards and batten-bands themselves, interlocking with the brick courses. Although it is getting to be a luxury material, the walls will be wood board-walls the same inside as outside—three thicknesses of boards with paper placed between them, the boards fastened together with screws. These slab-walls of boards—a kind of plywood construction on a large scale can be high in insulating value, vermin-proof, and practically fireproof. These walls like the fenestration may be prefabricated on the floor, with any degree of insulation we can afford, and raised into place, or they may be made at the mill and shipped to the site in sections. The roof can be built first on props and these walls shoved into place under them.

The appurtenance systems, to avoid cutting and complications, must be an organic part of construction but independent of the walls. Yes, we must have polished plate glass. It is one of the things we have at hand to gratify the designer of the truly modern house and bless its occupants.

The roof framing in this instance is laminated of three 2 x 4's in depth easily making the three offsets seen outside in the eaves of the roof, and enabling the roof span of 2 x 12" to be sufficiently pitched without the expense of "building up" the pitches. The middle offset may be left open at the eaves and fitted with flaps used to ventilate the roof spaces in summer. These 2 x 4's sheathed and insulated, then covered with a good asphalt roof, are the top of the house, shelter gratifying to the sense of shelter because of the generous eaves.

All this is in hand—no, it is in mind, as we plan the disposition of the rooms.

What must we consider essential now? We have a

corner lot—say, an acre or two—with a south and west exposure? We will have a good garden. The house is planned to wrap around two sides of this garden.

1. We must have as big a living room with as much vista and garden coming in as we can afford, with a fireplace in it, and open bookshelves, a dining table in the alcove, benches, and living-room tables built in; a quiet rug on the floor.

2. Convenient cooking and dining space adjacent to if not a part of the living room. This space may be set away from the outside walls within the living area to make work easy. This is the new thought concerning a kitchen—to take it away from outside walls and let it turn up into overhead space within the chimney; thus connection to dining space is made immediate without unpleasant features and no outside wall space lost to the principal rooms. A natural current of air is thus set up toward the kitchen as toward a chimney, no cooking odors escaping back into the house. There are steps leading down from this space to a small cellar below for heater, fuel, and laundry, although no basement at all is necessary if the plan should be so made. The bathroom is usually next so that plumbing features of heating kitchen and bath may be economically combined.

3. In this case (two bedrooms and a workshop which may become a future bedroom) the single bathroom for the sake of privacy is not immediately connected to any single bedroom. Bathrooms opening directly into a bedroom occupied by more than one person or two bedrooms opening into a single bathroom have been badly overdone. We will have as much garden and space in all these space appropriations as our money allows after we have simplified construction by way of the technique we have tried out.

A modest house, this Usonian house, a dwelling place that has no feeling at all for the "grand" except as the house extends itself in the flat parallel to the ground. It will be a companion to the horizon. With floor-heating that kind of extension on the ground can hardly go too far for comfort or beauty of proportion, provided it does not cost too much

in upkeep. As a matter of course a home like this is an architect's creation. It is not a builder's nor an amateur's effort. There is considerable risk in exposing the scheme to imitation or emulation.

This is true because a house of this type could not be well built and achieve its design except as an architect oversees the building.

And the building would fail of proper effect unless the furnishing and planting were all done by advice of the architect.

Thus briefly these few descriptive paragraphs together with the plan may help to indicate how stuffy and stifling the little colonial hot-boxes, hallowed by government or not, really are where Usonian family life is concerned. You might easily put two of them, each costing more, into the living space of this one and not go much outside the walls. Here is a moderate-cost brick-and-wood house that by our new technology has been greatly extended both in scale and comfort: a single house suited to prefabrication because the factory can go to the house.

Imagine how the costs would come down were the technique a familiar matter or if many houses were to be executed at one time—probably down to forty-five hundred dollars, according to number built and location.

There is a freedom of movement, and a privacy too, afforded by the general arrangement here that is unknown to the current "boxment." Let us say nothing about beauty. Beauty is an ambiguous term concerning an affair of taste in the provinces of which our big cities are the largest.

But I think a cultured American, we say Usonian, housewife will look well in it. The now inevitable car will seem a part of it.

Where does the garden leave off and the house begin? Where the garden begins and the house leaves off.

Withal, this Usonian dwelling seems a thing loving the ground with the new sense of space, light, and freedom—to which our U.S.A. is entitled.

THE USONIAN HOUSE II

We have built over a hundred of them now in nearly all our states. Building costs in general in the

Kathrine Winckler and Alma Goetsch House, Version #2 (Project). Okemos, Michigan. 1949. Perspective. Pencil and color pencil on tracing paper, 35 x 26". FLLW Fdn#5006.013

U.S.A. were rising and are rising still.[8] We find that twenty thousand dollars is about the sum needed to do what the Jacobs bought for fifty-five hundred. The Usonian house would have cost from twelve, and in some certain extensive programs, on up to seventy-five thousand dollars. We have built several extended in every way that cost more than one hundred thousand.

The houses cost a good deal more to build now than when we started to build them in 1938. But this holds true—any comparison with the "regular" houses around them shows that they are more for the money physically for the sums they cost than the "regulars" around about them. Their freedom, distinction, and individuality are not a feature of that cost except as it does, by elimination, put the expenditure where it liberates the occupant in a new spaciousness. A new freedom.

It is true however that no man can have the liberation one of these houses affords with liberal outside views on three sides becoming a part of the interior, without incurring extra fuel—say twenty per cent more. Double windows cut this down—but also cost money.

GRAVITY HEAT

Concerning floor heating. Heated air naturally rises. We call it gravity heat because the pipes filled with steam or hot water are all in a rock ballast bed beneath the concrete floor—we call the ballast with concrete top, the floor mat. If the floor is above the ground it is made of two-inch-square wood strips spaced 3' 8" apart. The heating pipes are in that case set between the floor joists.

It came to me in this way: In Japan to commence building the new Imperial Hotel, winter of 1914, we were invited to dine with Baron Okura, one of my patrons. It is desperately cold in Tokyo in winter—a damp clammy cold that almost never amounts to freezing or frost, but it is harder to keep warm there than anywhere else I have been, unless in Italy. The universal heater is the *hibachi*—a round vessel sitting on the floor filled with white ashes, several sticks of charcoal thrust down into the ashes all but a few inches. This projecting charcoal is lighted and glows—incandescent. Everyone sits around the *hibachi*, every now and then stretching out the hand over it for a moment—closing the hand as though grasping at something. The result is very unsatisfactory. To us. I marveled at Japanese fortitude until I caught sight of the typical underwear—heavy woolens, long sleeves, long legs, which they wear beneath the series of padded flowing kimono. But as they are acclimated and toughened to this native condition they suffer far less than we do.

Well, although we knew we should shiver, we accepted the invitation to dine at Baron Okura's Tokyo house—he had a number of houses scattered around the Empire. As expected, the dining room was so cold that I couldn't eat—pretending to eat only and for some nineteen courses. After dinner the Baron led the way below to the "Korean room," as it was called. This room was about eleven by fifteen, ceiling seven feet, I should say. A red-felt drugget covered the floor mats. The walls were severely plain, a soft pale yellow in color. We knelt there for conversation and Turkish coffee.

The climate seemed to have changed. No, it wasn't the coffee; it was Spring. We were soon warm and happy again—kneeling there on the floor, an indescribable warmth. No heating was visible nor was it felt directly as such. It was really a matter *not of heating at all* but an affair of *climate*.

The Harvard graduate who interpreted for the Baron explained: the Korean room meant a room heated under the floor. The heat of a fire outside at one corner of the floor drawn back and forth underneath the floor in and between tile ducts, the floor forming the top of the flues (or ducts) made by the partitions, the smoke and heat going up and out of a tall chimney at the corner opposite the corner where the fire was burning.

The indescribable comfort of being warmed from below was a discovery.

I immediately arranged for electric heating elements beneath the bathrooms in the Imperial Hotel—dropping the ceiling of the bathrooms to create a space beneath each in which to generate the heat. The tile floor and built-in tile baths were thus always warm. It was pleasant to go in one's bare feet into the bath. This experiment was a success. All ugly electric heat fixtures (dangerous too in a bathroom) were eliminated. I've always hated fixtures—radiators especially. Here was the complete opportunity to digest all that paraphernalia in the building—creating not a heated interior but creating climate—healthful, dustless, serene. And also, the presence of heat thus integral and beneath makes lower temperatures desirable. Sixty-five degrees seems for normal human beings sufficient. But neighbors coming in from super-heated houses would feel the cold at first. It is true that a natural climate is generated instead of an artificial forced condition—the natural condition much more healthful, as a matter of course.

I determined to try it out at home at the first opportunity. That opportunity seemed to be the Nakoma Country Club but that Indianesque affair stayed in the form of a beautiful plan.[9]

Then came the Johnson Administration Building. Just the thing for that and we proceeded with the installation, but all the professional heating contractors except one (Westerlin and Campbell) scoffed, refusing to have anything to do with the idea. But as chance had it, the little Jacobs House turned up meantime and was completed before that greater venture got into operation.

So the Jacobs House was the first installation to go into effect.[10] There was great excitement and curiosity on the part of the "profession." Crane Company officials came in, dove beneath the rugs, put their hands on the concrete in places remote from the heater, got up and looked at one another as though they had seen a ghost. My God! It works. Where were radiators now?

As usual.

Articles on "radiant heat" began to appear in testimonial journals. But it was in no sense "radiant heat" or panel heating or any of the things they called it that I was now interested in. It was simply *gravity heat*—heat coming up from beneath as naturally as heat rises.

Many of the Usonian buildings now have floor heating. We have had to learn to proportion the heat correctly for varying climates and conditions. We have accumulated some data that is useful.

There is no other "ideal" heat. Not even the heat of the sun.

CONCERNING THE USONIAN HOUSE

To say the house planted by myself on the good earth of the Chicago prairie as early as 1900, or earlier, was the first truly democratic expression of our democracy in Architecture would start a controversy with professional addicts who believe Architecture has no political (therefore no social) significance. So, let's say that the spirit of democracy—freedom of the individual as an individual—took hold of the house as it then was, took off the attic and the porch, pulled out the basement, and made a single spacious, harmonious unit of living room, dining room and kitchen, with appropriate entry conveniences. The sleeping rooms were convenient to baths approached in a segregated, separate extended wing and the whole place was flooded with sunlight from floor to ceiling with glass.

The materials of the outside walls came inside just as appropriately and freely as those of the inside walls went outside. Intimate harmony was thus established not only in the house but with its site. *Came the "Open Plan."* The housewife herself thus planned for became the central figure in her menage and her housewifery a more charming feature (according to her ability) of her domestic establishment.

She was now more hostess "officio," operating in gracious relation to her own home, instead of being a kitchen-mechanic behind closed doors.

Nobody need care now how this thing happened. It may not be important. But if not—what is?

In addition to this new freedom with its implication of fresh responsibility for the individual homester came a technical recognition of the new materials and means by which the house was to be built. Materials were now so used as to bring out their natural beauty of character. The construction was made suitable to the appropriate use of machinery—because the machine had already become the appropriate tool of our civilization. (See essays written by myself at that time.)

To use our new materials—concrete, steel and glass, and the old ones—stone and wood—in ways that were not only expedient but beautiful was Culture now. So many new forms of treating them were devised out of the working of a new principle of building. I called it "organic."

Moreover, the house itself was so proportioned that people looked well in it as a part of them and their friends looked better in it than when they were outside it.

Thus a basic change came about in this affair of a culture for the civilization of these United States. What then took place has since floundered, flourished and faded under different names by different architects in an endless procession of expedients.

Here the original comes back to say hello to you afresh and to see if you recognize it for what it was and still is—a home for our people in the spirit in which our Democracy was conceived: the individual integrate and free in an environment of his own, appropriate to his circumstances—a life beautiful as he can make it—with her, of course.

BOOK TWO: 1954
INTEGRITY: IN A HOUSE AS IN AN INDIVIDUAL

What is needed most in architecture today is the very thing that is most needed in life—Integrity. Just as it is in a human being, so integrity is the deepest quality in a building; but it is a quality not much demanded of any building since very ancient times when it was natural. It is no longer the first demand for a human being either, because "Success" is now so immediately necessary. If you are a success, people will not want to "look the gift horse in the mouth." No. But then if "success" should happen today something precious has been lost from life.

Somebody has described a man of this period as one through the memory of whom you could too easily pass your hand. Had there been true *quality* in the man the hand could not so easily pass. That quality in the memory of him would probably have been "Integrity."

In speaking of integrity in architecture, I mean much the same thing that you would mean were you speaking of an individual. Integrity is not something to be put on and taken off like a garment. Integrity is a quality *within* and *of* the man himself. So it is in a building. It cannot be changed by any other person either nor by the exterior pressures of any outward circumstances; integrity cannot change except from

W. B. Tracy "Usonian Automatic" House, Normandy Park, Washington. 1954. Construction.
Photograph by W. B. Tracy. FLLW Fdn FA#5512.0033

W. B. Tracy "Usonian Automatic" House, Normandy Park, Washington. 1954. Construction. Photograph by W. B. Tracy.
FLLW Fdn FA#5512.0035

within because it is that in you which *is you*—and due to which you will try to live your life (as you would build your building) in the best possible way. To build a man or building from within is always difficult to do because deeper is not so easy as shallow.

Naturally should you want to really live in a way and in a place which is true to this deeper thing in you, which you honor, the house you build to live in as a home should be (so far as it is possible to make it so) integral in every sense. Integral to site, to purpose, and to you. The house would then be a home in the best sense of that word. This we seem to have forgotten if ever we learned it. Houses have become a series of anonymous boxes that go into a row on row upon row of bigger boxes either merely negative or a mass nuisance. But now the house in this interior or deeper organic sense may come alive as organic architecture.

We are now trying to bring *integrity* into building. If we succeed, we will have done a great service to our moral nature—the psyche—of our democratic society. Integrity would become more natural. Stand up for *integrity* in your building and you stand for integrity not only in the life of those who did the building but socially a reciprocal relationship is inevitable. An irresponsible, flashy, pretentious or dishonest individual would never be happy in such a house as we now call organic because of this quality of integrity. The one who will live in it will be he who will grow with living in it. So it is the "job" of any true architect to envision and make this human relationship—so far as lies in his power—a reality.

Living within a house wherein everything is genuine and harmonious, a new sense of freedom gives one a new sense of life—as contrasted with the usual existence in the house indiscriminately planned and where Life is *contained* within a series of confining boxes, all put within the general box. Such life is bound to be inferior to life lived in this new integrity—the Usonian Home.

In designing the Usonian house, as I have said, I have always proportioned it to the human figure in point of scale; that is, to the scale of the human figure to occupy it. The old idea in most buildings was to make the human being feel rather insignificant—developing an inferiority complex in him if possible. The higher the ceilings were then the greater the building was. This empty grandeur was considered to be human luxury. Of course, great, high ceilings had a certain utility in those days, because of bad planning and awkward construction. (The volume of contained air was about all the air to be had without violence.)

The Usonian house, then, aims to be a *natural* performance, one that is integral to site; integral to environment; integral to the life of the inhabitants. A house integral with the nature of materials—wherein glass is used as glass, stone as stone, wood as wood—and all the elements of environment go into and throughout the house. Into this new integrity, once there, those who live in it will take root and grow. And most of all belonging by nature to the nature of its being.

Whether people are fully conscious of this or not, they actually derive countenance and sustenance from the "atmosphere" of the things they live in or with. They are rooted in them just as a plant is in the soil in which it is planted. For instance, we receive many letters from people who sing praises for what has happened to them as a consequence; telling us how their house has affected their lives. They now have a certain dignity and pride in their environment; they see it has a meaning or purpose which they share as a family or feel as individuals.

We all know the feeling we have when we are well-dressed and like the consciousness that results from it. It affects our conduct and you should have the same feeling regarding the home you live in. It has a salutary effect morally, to put it on a lower plane than it deserves, but there are higher results above that sure one. If you feel yourself becoming-

ly housed, know that you are living according to the higher demands of good society, and of your own conscience, then you are free from embarrassment and not poor in spirit but rich—in the right way. I have always believed in being careful about my clothes; getting well-dressed because I could then forget all about them. That is what should happen to you with a good house that is a *home*. When you are conscious that the house is right and is honestly becoming to you, and feel you are living in it beautifully, you need no longer be concerned about it. It is no tax upon your conduct, nor a nag upon your self-respect, because it is featuring you as you like to see yourself.

FROM THE GROUND UP
WHERE TO BUILD

When selecting a site for your house, there is always the question of how close to the city you should be and that depends on what kind of slave you are. The best thing to do is go as far out as you can get. Avoid the suburbs—dormitory towns—by all means. Go way out into the country—what you regard as "too far"—and when others follow, as they will (if procreation keeps up), move on.

Of course it all depends on how much time you have to get there and how much time you can afford to lose, going and coming. But Decentralization is under way. You may see it everywhere. Los Angeles is a conspicuous example of it. There the powers that be are trying to hold it downtown. Robert Moses is struggling to release New York to the country. He thinks he is doing the opposite. But he isn't. New York's Moses is another kind of Moses leading his people *out* from the congestion rather than into it—leading the people from the city.

So go out with these big ferry-boats gnashing their chromium teeth at you as they come around the corner. But don't buy the huge American car with protruding corners but buy the smaller one, such as Nash has produced, and go thirty or forty miles to the gallon. A gallon of gas is not so expensive that you cannot afford to pay for the gas it takes to get pretty far from the city. The cost of transportation has been greatly decreased by way of the smaller car. In this way, decentralization has found aid, and the easier the means of egress gets to be, the further you can go out from the city.

I tried to get a congregation out of the city when we built the Unitarian Church in Wisconsin, but before it was finished, a half dozen buildings had sprung up around it. Now it is merely suburban instead of in the country. In Arizona we went twenty-six miles from the center of town to build Taliesin West; and are now there where we will soon be suburban, too. Clients have asked me: "How far should we go out, Mr. Wright?" I say: "Just ten times as far as you think you ought to go." So my suggestion would be to go just as far as you can go—and go soon and go fast.

There is only one solution, one principle, one proceeding which can rid the city of its congestion—decentralization. Go out, un-divide the division, un-subdivide the division, and then subdivide the un-subdivision. The only answer to life today is to get back to the good ground, or rather I should say, to get forward to it, because now instead of going back, we can go forward to the ground: not the city going to the country but the country and city becoming one. We have the means to go, a means that is entirely adequate to human purposes where life is now most concerned. Because we have the automobile, we can go far and fast and when we get there, we have other machines to use—the tractor or whatever else you may want to use.

We have all the means to live free and independent, far apart—as we choose—still retaining all the social relationships and advantages we ever had, even to have them greatly multiplied. No matter if we do have houses a quarter of a mile apart. You would enjoy all that you used to enjoy when you were ten to a block, and think of the immense advantages for your children and for yourself: freedom to *use* the ground, relationship with all kinds of living growth.

There is no sense in herding any more. It went out when we got cheap and quick transportation. When we got a kind of building, too, that requires more space. The old building was a box—a fortification more or less. It was a box which could be put close to other boxes so that you could live as close together as possible—and you did. You lived so close together in houses of the Middle Ages because you had to walk to communicate. You were concentrated for safety also. So there was ground only for you to get into a huddle upon. Also, one town was liable to be attacked by townsfolk coming in from the North or from somewhere else to conquer you and take your ground away. You were forced to live compactly. Every little village in the old days was a fortress.

Today there is no such condition, nor is there ever going to be such again in our country or in any other country as far as I know. Today the threat is from the sky in the form of an atom bomb (or an even more destructive bomb), and the more you are divided and scattered, the less temptation to the bomb—the less harm the bomb could do. The more you herd now the more damage to you, as conditions now are.

Looking at it from any standpoint, decentralization is the order of this day. So go far from the city, much farther than you think you can afford. You will soon find you never can go quite far enough.

WHAT KIND OF LAND

With a small budget the best kind of land to build on is flat land. Of course, if you can get a gentle slope, the building will be more interesting, more satisfactory. But changes of ground surface make building much more expensive.

It is also cheaper to build in the South where no deep foundations or insulation are necessary, rather than in the North where summers are short and you have to prepare for them in air-conditioning a house, and for the long winters: piling up firewood, putting away food, etc., etc., etc.

But it is because of this need for resourcefulness that the man of the North has traditionally and actually conquered the man softened by the South; and then, these comforts thus won, the Northern man has himself grown soft only to be re-conquered. So it seems to go on ceaselessly.

A SUITABLE FOUNDATION

The sort of foundation that should be used for a house depends upon the place where you are going to build the house. If you are building in the desert, the best foundation is right *on* the desert. Don't dig into it and break it.

One of the best foundations I know of, suitable to many places (particularly to frost regions), was devised by the old Welsh stone-mason who put the foundations in for buildings now used by Taliesin North. Instead of digging down three and a half feet or four feet below the frost line, as was standard practice in Wisconsin, not only terribly expensive but rendering capillary attraction a threat to the upper wall, he dug shallow trenches about sixteen inches deep and slightly pitched them to a drain. These trenches he filled with broken stone about the size of your fist. Broken stone does not clog up, and provides the drainage beneath the wall that saves it from being lifted by the frost.

I have called it the "dry wall footing," because if the wall stayed dry the frost could not affect it. In a region of deep cold to keep a building from moving it is necessary to get all water (or moisture) from underneath it. If there is no water there to freeze, the foundation cannot be lifted.

All those footings at Taliesin have been perfectly static. Ever since I discovered the dry wall footing—about 1902—I have been building houses that way. Occasionally there has been trouble getting the system authorized by building commissions. A recent encounter was with the Lake Forest Building Department of Illinois. It refused to allow the building to be so built. The Madison, Wisconsin, experts also refused to let me use the system on the hillsides above the lake. When the experts do not accept it, they will not accept the idea of saving the builders of the house many thousands of dollars. But we have in all but eight or ten cases put it through now, thereby saving the client excess waste of money below ground for no good purpose.

That type of footing, however, is not applicable to treacherous sub-soils where the problem is entirely different. For example, the Imperial Hotel was built on soil about the consistency of cheese, some eight feet thick, and a foundation for that particular soil had to be devised to bear the load of any building we wanted to build. I remembered I had bored holes with an auger on the Oak Park prairie. So I had driven into the soil a tapered pile eight feet long which punched a hole. I made tests to determine how far apart each of these piles would have to be to carry the necessary load and found that centers, two feet apart, were far enough—had they been further apart, not all of the ground would have been utilized. We punched these holes and filled them with concrete. We had to do it quickly, because, since we were almost down to water level, the water might come right up. On these tapered concrete piles we spread a thin plate of concrete slab, or beam, which gathered all these little pins in the pin cushion together and added up to enough resistance to carry the walls.

No one foundation, then, is suitable for all soils; the type of foundation used must be applicable to the particular site.

ADVANTAGES OF THE BERM-TYPE

The berm-type house, with walls of earth, is practical—a nice form of building anywhere: north, south, east or west—depending upon the soil and climate as well as the nature of the site. If your site contains a lot of boulders or rock ledges it is impossible. In the berm-type house the bulldozer comes along, pushes the dirt up against the outsides of the building as high as you want it to go and you may carry the earth banking as far around the structure as you please. Here you have good insulation—great protection from the elements; a possible economy, too, because you do not have to finish any outside below the window level. You do not have to finish the inside walls either if not so inclined. I think it an excellent form for certain regions and conditions. An actual economy and preservation of the landscape.

HOW TO LIGHT THE HOUSE

The best way to light a house is God's way—the natural way, as nearly as possible in the daytime and at night as nearly like the day as may be, or better.

Cities are commonly laid out north, south, east and west. This was just to save the surveyor trouble, I imagine. Anyway that happened without much thought for the human beings compelled to build homes on those lines. This inevitably results in every house having a "dark side."

Surveyors do not seem to have learned that the south is the comforter of life, the south side of the house the "living" side. Ordinarily the house should be set 30–60 to the south, well back on its site so that every room in the house might have sunlight some time in the day. If, however, owing to the surveyor the house must face square north, we always place the clerestory (which serves as a lantern) to the south so that no house need lack sunlight. It is a somewhat expensive way to overcome the surveyor's ruse.

THE GREAT LUMINARY

Proper orientation of the house, then, is the first condition of the lighting of that house; and artificial lighting is nearly as important as daylight. Day lighting can be beautifully managed by the architect if he has a feeling for the course of the sun as it goes from east to west and at the inevitable angle to the south. The sun is the great luminary of all life. It should serve as such in the building of any house. There is, however, the danger of taking "light" too far and leaving you, "the inmate," defenseless in a glass cage—which is somewhat silly. You must control light in the planning of your home so that light most naturally serves your needs without too much artificial production and consequent control—putting light in only to block it out.

As for all artificial lighting, it too should be integral part of the house—be as near daylighting as possible. In 1893, I began to get rid of the bare light-bulb and have ever since been concealing it on interior decks or placing it in recesses in such a way that it comes from the building itself; the effect should be that it comes from the same source as natural light. Sometimes we light the grounds about the house putting outside light so that it lights the interior of the rooms.

Wiring for lights, as piping for plumbing and heating, should not show all over the house unless by special design—any more than you would have organs of your body on the outside of your skin. Lighting fixtures should (as should all others) be absorbed *in* the structure, so that their office is *of* the structure. All this after the building has been properly orientated.

STEEL AND GLASS

There is much new good in houses being built today and chiefly on account of the new freedoms afforded organic architecture by the uses of steel and glass; miraculous materials. As a result of these space is now freer, wider spans are easier; therefore more open spaces, made possible owing to steel in tension, and a closer relation to nature (environment) owing to the use of glass. These materials, everywhere to be seen now, are enabling building to go in varied directions with more ease; to go beyond the traditional constraint of the box with economy.

THE BASEMENT

A house should—ordinarily—not have a basement. In spite of everything you may do, a basement is a noisome, gaseous damp place. From it come damp atmospheres and unhealthful conditions. Because people rarely go there—and certainly not to live there—it is almost always sure to be an ugly place. The family tendency is to throw things into it, leave them there and forget them. It usually becomes—as it became when I began to build—a great, furtive underground for the house in order to enable the occupants to live in it disreputably. Also, so many good housewives, even their lords and masters, used to tumble downstairs into the basement and go on insurance for some time, if not make it all immediately collectible.

Another objection to the basement is that it is relatively expensive. It has to be some six to eight feet below grade and so you have to get big digging going. It is a great inhibition in any building because you must construct a floor over it and the space it provides you with is, as I have said, usually disreputably occupied.

Of course, a basement often is a certain convenience, but these conveniences can now be supplied otherwise. Mechanical equipment is now so compact and good-looking. So we decided to eliminate it wherever possible and provide for its equivalent up on the ground level with modern equipment.

INSULATION AND HEATING

In either a very cold or a very hot climate, the overhead is where insulation should occur in any building. There you can spend money for insulation with very good effect, whereas the insulation of the walls and the air space within the walls becomes less and less important. With modern systems of air conditioning and heating you can manage almost any condition.

But the best insulation for a roof and walls in a hot climate is nearly the same as the best insulation for a roof and walls in a cold region. Resistance to heat in a building is much the same as resistance to cold, although of course the exact specifications should vary according to circumstances. In a warm region it is important that the overhead not get overheated. You have to use a very tough cover for roof insulation or the sun will take the life out of it quickly. We have never found a roofing that lasts as long as we would like in a hot climate like the desert—but a white-top is economical partly because white, of course, reflects heat rather than absorbs it.

But in a cold climate like southern Wisconsin the real basis for purposeful insulation is floor heating. When you have the floor warm—heat by gravity—insulation of the walls becomes comparatively insignificant. You may open the windows in cold weather and still be comfortable, because, if your feet are warm and you sit warm, you are warm. In this case overhead insulation is extremely important: heat rises and if it finds a place overhead where it can be cooled off and dropped, you have to continuously supply a lot of heat. If, however, the overhead is reasonably defensive against cold, you can heat your house very economically, more so than by any other system.

On the other hand, snow is the best kind of insulation. You do not have to buy it. In northern climates you can see how well a house is insulated by noticing how quickly the snow melts off the roof. If the snow stays for some time, the roof is pretty well insulated. If you get insulation up to a certain point, snow will come and give you more. To hold snow on the roof is always a good, wise provision and a good argument for a flat roof. I have seen people shovelling snow off the roof and I never could understand why—unless the snow was creating a load that the roof could not bear or the roof was steep

and the snow load might slide down and injure someone or something.

THE KIND OF ROOF

Now the *shape* of roof—whether a shed roof, a hip roof or a flat roof—depends in part on expediency and in part on your personal taste or knowledge as to what is appropriate in the circumstances.

One of the advantages of the sloping roof is that it gives you a sense of spaciousness inside, a sense of overhead uplift which I often feel to be very good. The flat roof also has advantages in construction. It is easy to do, of course. But with the flat roof, you must devise ways and means of getting rid of the water. One way to do this is to build, on top of the flat, a slight pitch to the eaves. This may be done by "furring." There are various ways of getting water off a flat roof. But it must be done.

The cheapest roof, however, is the shed roof—the roof sloping one way, more or less. There you get more for your money than you can get from any other form of roof. There is no water problem with a shed roof because the water goes down to the lower side and drops away. With a hip roof the water runs two ways into a natural valley, so there is not much problem there either.

Suitable to flat roof construction in many locations is the flat roof covered with a body of good earth—what I call the "berm type" roof. On top of the building there will be—say—about sixteen inches of good fertile earth in which may be planted grass or whatever you please to plant. There is the most natural insulation that can be devised. Probably the cheapest. Always I like the feeling you have when beneath it. The house I will build for my son, Llewellyn, in Virginia has a flat roof with earth to be placed on top.

I have also sometimes pitched roofs from high on the sides to low in the center. You can do with a roof almost anything you like. But the type of roof you choose must not only deal with the elements in your region but be appropriate to the circumstances, according to your personal preference—perhaps.

THE ATTIC

Why waste good livable space with an attic any more than with a basement? And never plan waste space in a house with the idea of eventually converting it into rooms. A house that is planned for a lot of problematical space or space unused to be used some other day is not likely to be a well-planned house. In fact, if you deliberately planned waste space, the architect would be wasted, the people in the house would be wasted. Everything would probably go to waste.

If, however, in future you are going to need more room for more children and you wish to provide that room it need not be waste space if properly conceived. But the attic, now, should always come *into* the house to beautify it. Sunlight otherwise impossible may be got into the house through the attic by way of what we call a lantern or clerestory. And that should also give you the sense of lift and beauty that comes in so many of our plans at this time.

We *use* all "waste" space: make it part of the house; make it so beautiful that as waste space it is inconceivable. It is something like the little boy eating an apple, and another little boy ranges up alongside and wants to know if he can have the core, but the apple-eater says—"Sorry, there ain't gonna be no core."

SIZE OF KITCHEN

In the Usonian house the size of the kitchen depends largely on the home-maker's personal preference. Some homesters like to get a lot of exercise in the homestead—walking from place to place. Some women want things on ball bearings. Some don't want to bend over; they like to stand up when they work: for them we put everything high: ovens up in the wall, etc. Women who do not mind bending over like things more compact; they do not want to waste their substance going to and fro. For them we put things on ball bearings as you may easily do now that modern gadgetry is so well designed.

So we like to make kitchens small, and put things on ball bearings. We have more money to spend on spaciousness for the rest of the house. Sometimes we are caught making a kitchen too small, and then the woman of the house comes in and asks us to make it bigger; sometimes they get

this but sometimes they do not—it depends on the good proportions of the design as a whole.

But I believe in having a kitchen featured as the work space in the Usonian house and a becoming part of the living room—a welcome feature. Back in farm days there was but one big living room, a stove in it, and Ma was there cooking—looking after the children and talking to Pa—dogs and cats and tobacco smoke too—all gemütlich if all was orderly, but it seldom was; and the children were there playing around. It created a certain atmosphere of a domestic nature which had charm and which is not, I think, a good thing to lose altogether. Consequently, in the Usonian plan the kitchen was called "workspace" and identified largely with the living room. As a matter of fact, it became an alcove of the living room but higher for good ventilation and spaciousness.

The kitchen being one of the places where smells originated, we made that the ventilating flue of the whole house by carrying it up higher than the living room. All the air from the surrounding house was thus drawn up through the kitchen itself. You might have liver and onions for dinner and never know it in the living room, until it was served to you at the table. The same is true of other smells and conditions in the way the bathrooms were made. We were never by this means able to eliminate noise. So in a Usonian house a needlessly noisy kitchen is a bad thing.

Everything in the Usonian kitchen should be (as it may so easily be) modern and attractive as such. Because it is incorporated into the living room, the kitchen (workspace) should be just as charming to be in or look at as the living room—perhaps more so. When we built the Usonian house in the New York Exhibition (fall of 1953) the kitchen was a delightful little place to look at, no less so as a "work place."

THE CLIENT AND THE HOUSE

The needs and demands of the average client should affect every feature of a house but only insofar as the clients do manifest intelligence instead of exert mere personal idiosyncrasy. This manifestation of intelligence is not so rare. Yet when a man has "made his money"—is therefore a "success"—he then thinks, because of this "success," that he can tell you, or anybody else, all about things of which he really knows nothing at all—a house in particular. His success as a maker-of-money makes him a universal expert. So he begins to exercise his idiosyncrasies as this universal expert.

But I've really had little enough trouble with good businessmen or their wives. They *do* have what we call "common sense." A man does have to have common sense to make any sort of fortune in this country dedicated to ruthless competition—and you can usually explain the subtle inner nature of things to a man of good sense who has never thought about them—but must now go in for them.

But, the wife? Well, too often she is quite another matter, having made him what he is today. Although the wives we encounter are so often far wiser in this affair of home making than their husbands. The peripatetic marriage is the enemy of good architecture—as a matter of course.

EXPANDING FOR GROWING FAMILY

A Usonian house if built for a young couple, can, without deformity, be expanded, later, for the needs of a growing family. As you see from the plans, Usonian houses are shaped like polliwogs—a house with a shorter or longer tail. The body of the polliwog is the living room and the adjoining kitchen—or work space—and the whole Usonian concentration of conveniences. From there it starts out, with a tail: in the proper direction, say, one bedroom, two bedrooms, three, four, five, six bedrooms long; provision between each two rooms for a convenient bathroom. We sometimes separate this tail from the living room wing with a loggia—for quiet, etc.; especially grace.

The size of the polliwog's tail depends on the number of children and the size of the family budget. If the tail gets too long, it may curve like a centipede. Or you might break it, make it angular. The wing can go on for as many children as you can afford to put in it. A good Usonian house seems to be no less but more adapted to be an ideal breeding stable than the box.

CHILDREN'S ROOMS

People who have many children want to build a house usually, but do not have enough money to do justice to the children. As a rule, they do not have *any* on account of the children. But they keep on having children just the same no matter what else they may do or not do. So you see their architect has to tuck the extra children in somehow; and the idea seems to be to give them the smallest possible sleeping space with double deckers but to try also to give them a playroom. If possible this should be apart from sleeping quarters. Or build a separate section entirely for progeny.

For the children's bedrooms, then, we introduced the double-decker bed. We put two children in a small room next to a bath—two children high is the limit in most of our houses. But you could put in a third. The boys and girls still have to be separated, for some mysterious reason. So the compact three-bedroom house is about the minimum now.

The playroom is planned as part outdoors and part indoors and so gives children a little liberty for play, etc. Usually, of course, they now play in the living room and the house is a bedlam. Everything loose is likely to be turned inside out or upside down, and there is not much use trying to do anything about them at that. Building a house for the average family (children and their adults) is a pretty rough extravaganza. Either the children get left or must get spanked into place, else they have the whole house and the grown-ups do what they can do to make themselves as comfortable as they may be able.

It is more important for the child to live in an appropriate, well-considered home development than it is for the grown-ups, because the grown-ups are halfway through and consequently do not have so much to lose or gain from the home atmosphere. The child, however, is a beginning; he has the whole way to go and he may go a lot further in the course of time than Pa and Ma ever had a chance to go. But after forty—even thirty-five—the home is not so important for the parents as for the child, as the case may be, although they leave soon for homes of their own. The Catholics say, "Give me a child up to the age of seven, and who cares who takes the child after that." This is because it is in childhood that impressions become most indelible.

For these and many unmentioned reasons it is peculiarly important that a child should grow up in building conditions that are harmonious, live in an atmosphere that contributes to serenity and well-being and to the consciousness of those things which are more excellent, in childhood. What a pity that parents have children so fast, so inconsiderately, that their architect must put them into little cells, double-decker them, and shove them off into the tail of the house where life becomes one certain round of washing diapers.

FURNISHINGS

Rugs, draperies and furnishings that are suitable for a Usonian house are those, too, that are organic in character; that is, textures and patterns that sympathize in their own design and construction with the design and construction of the particular house they occupy and embellish (or befoul). A mobile, for instance, should be composed of the design elements of the room it hangs in.

Out of the nature of the materials used in building a house come these new effects. The "effect" is not all that the artist-architect gives you. He not only sees more or less clearly the nature of the materials but, in his own trained imagination and by virtue of his own feeling, he qualifies it all as a whole. You can only choose the result that is sympathetic to you.

The range of choice is growing wider now. But it is extraordinary still to see how the manufacturer is trying to burn the candle at both ends, still hanging on to the old William Morris era and old rococo fabrics. You may—at your own peril—get L'art Nouveaux, rococo, Morris, ancient and modern in the same store for the same purpose for the same price.

CHAIRS

My early approach to the chair was something between contempt and a desperation. Because I believe sitting to be in itself an unfortunate necessity

not quite elegant yet, I do not yet believe in any such thing as a "natural" chair for an unnatural posture. The only attractive posture of relaxation is that of reclining. So I think the ideal chair is one which would allow the would-be "sitter" to gracefully recline. Even the newest market chairs are the usual machines-for-sitting. Now I do not know if whatever God may be ever intended you or me to fold up on one of these—but, if so, let's say that fold-up or double-up ought to make you look more graceful. It ought to look as though it were intended for you to look and be just that.

We now build well-upholstered benches and seats in our houses, trying to make them all part of the building. But still you must bring in and pull up the casual chair. There are many kinds of "pull-up" chairs to perch upon—lightly. They're more easy. They're light. But the big chair wherein you may fold up and go to sleep reading a newspaper (all that kind of thing) is still difficult. I have done the best I could with this "living room chair" but, of course, you have to call for somebody to help you move it. All my life my legs have been banged up somewhere by the chairs I have designed. But we are accomplishing it now. Someday it will be well done. But it will not have metal spider-legs nor look the way most of the steel furniture these days looks to me. No—it will not be a case of "Little Miss Muffet sat on her tuffet, eating of curds and whey, when up beside her came a great black spider and frightened Miss Muffet away." I am for "Little Miss Muffet" frightened by the spider—away.

Yet every chair must eventually be designed for the building it is to be used in. Organic architecture calls for this chair which will not look like an apparatus but instead be seen as a gracious feature of its environment which can only be the building itself. So the stuffed-box-for-sitting-in is not much better than the machine-for-setting-it-in.

No doubt most practical sitters are troubled by these chairs, too. Finding a good comfortable chair in which to place one's trunk is never quite easy and so most sitting to date still lacks dignity and repose. But it is possible now to design a chair in which any sitter is compelled to look comfortable whether he is so or not. And there is no reason why he, or she, should not be comfortable in mind as well as body folded up or down.

When the house-interior absorbs the chair as in perfect harmony, then we will have achieved not so minor a symptom of a culture of our own.

PAINT

In organic architecture there is little or no room for appliqué of any kind. I have never been fond of paints or of wallpaper or anything which must be applied *to* other things as a surface. If you can put something by skill *on* the thing that becomes part *of* it and still have that thing retain its *original character* that may be good. But when you gloss it over, lose its nature—enamel it, and so change the character of its natural expression, you have committed a violation according to the ideals of organic architecture. We use nothing applied which tends to eliminate the true character of what is beneath, or which may become a substitute for whatever that may be. Wood is wood, concrete is concrete, stone is stone. We like to have whatever we choose to use demonstrate the beauty of its own character, as itself.

The only treatment we aim to give to any material is to preserve it pretty much as it *is*. A strange fallacy has developed that to paint wood preserves it. The reverse is true. Wood must breathe just as you must breathe. When you seal wood off from this innate need to breathe, you have not lengthened its life at all, you have done just the opposite. Merely staining wood is one thing; painting is quite another. When you coat anything in the way of a natural material you are likely to shorten its life, not preserve it.

AIR CONDITIONING?

To me air conditioning is a dangerous circumstance. The extreme changes in temperature that tear down a building also tear down the human body. Building is difficult in a temperate zone, where you have extreme heat and extreme cold. For instance—the boards in the ceiling over my bedroom at Taliesin West, overheated during the day, begin to pull and crack and miniature explosions occur at about three o'clock in the cool of the morning. Owing to

changes of temperature nothing in construction is ever completely still.

The human body, although more flexible, is framed and constructed upon much the same principles as a building. I can sit in my shirt sleeves at eighty degrees, or seventy-five, and be cool; then go outside to 118 degrees, take a guarded breath or two around and soon get accustomed to the change. The human body is able continually to adjust itself—to and fro. But if you carry these contrasts too far too often, when you are cooled the heat becomes more unendurable; it becomes hotter and hotter outside as you get cooler and cooler inside. Finally, Nature will give up. She will just say for you, "Well, what's the use?" Even Nature can't please everybody all the time.

So air conditioning has to be done with a good deal of intelligent care. The less the degree of temperature difference you live in, the better for your constitutional welfare. If one may have air and feel the current of air moving in on one's face and hands and feet one can take almost any degree of heat. But as for myself if I feel close *and* hot, I cannot well take it. Neither can anybody else, I believe.

So, in a very hot climate, the way to deal with air conditioning best would be to have a thorough protection overhead and the rest of the building as open to the breezes as it possibly can be made. On the desert slopes at Taliesin West there is always a breeze. But when we first went there, and spent a summer in town, I had to wrap myself in wet sheets to get to sleep. Being a man from the North, I was unaccustomed to such heat as came from living in a bake-oven. But if I lived there all year round—and could get air by breezes—I would soon get accustomed to it.

Another way of dealing with air conditioning in a humid, hot climate is the "fireplace" as I devised it for a house in tropical Acapulco, Mexico. In this "fireplace" the air came down the flue instead of going out, and the hearth was a pool of cool water as artificial rain poured down the chimney and the pool was cooled by one of the devices designed for air conditioning. You could sit around the "fireplace" and be especially cool but the rooms were each cooled. The chimney now did not stick up much above the roof—it was just rounded up to keep the water from running in—just a low little exuberance on the roof.

Even in cold climates air conditioning has now caught on because the aim now is to maintain the degree of humidity for comfort within, no matter what is going on outside. I do not much believe in that. I think it far better to go *with* the natural climate than try to fix a special artificial climate of your own. Climate means something to man. It means something in relation to one's life in it. Nature makes the body flexible and so the life of the individual invariably becomes adapted to environment and circumstance. The color and texture of the human skin, for an example—dark or bright—is a climatic adaptation—nothing else. Climate makes the human skin. The further north you go, the more bleached the hair and the whiter the skin, even the eyes; everything becomes pallid. The further south, the darker everything gets. It is climatic condition that does the protective coloring. I doubt that you can ignore climate completely, by reversal make a climate of your own and get away with it without harm to yourself.

THE CONTRACTOR

In choosing a contractor, the only way to judge him is to look carefully into his previous work. You should be able to tell fairly well from what he has done what he may do.

Dankmar Adler—the old Chief—used to say that he would rather give work to a crook who does know how to build than to an honest man who does not know how to build. He had this to say about that: "I can police a crook, but if a man doesn't know good work, how am I to get it out of him?" Remember also what Shakespeare said about one's not being able to make a silk purse out of a sow's ear?

GRAMMAR: THE HOUSE AS A WORK OF ART

Every house worth considering as a work of art must have a grammar of its own. "Grammar," in this sense, means the same thing in any construction—whether it be of words or of stone or wood. It is the shape-relationship between the various elements that enter into the constitution of the thing.

The "grammar" of the house is its manifest articulation of all its parts. This will be the "speech" it uses. To be achieved, construction must be grammatical.

Your limitations of feeling about what you are doing, your choice of materials for the doing (and your budget of course) determine largely what grammar your building will use. It is largely inhibited (or expanded) by the amount of money you have to spend, a feature only of the latitude you have. When the chosen grammar is finally adopted (you go almost indefinitely with it into everything you do) walls, ceilings, furniture, etc., become inspired by it. Everything has a related articulation in relation to the whole and all belongs together; looks well together because all together are speaking the same language. If one part of your house spoke Choctaw, another French, another English, and another some sort of gibberish, you would have what you mostly have now—not a very beautiful result. Thus, when you do adopt the "grammar" of your house—it will be the way the house is to be "spoken," "uttered." You must be consistently grammatical for it to be understood as a work of Art.

Consistency in grammar is therefore the property—solely—of a well-developed artist-architect. Without that property of the artist-architect not much can be done about your abode as a work of Art. Grammar is no property for the usual owner or the occupant of the house. But the man who designs the house must, inevitably, speak a consistent thought-language in his design. It properly may be and should be a language of his own if appropriate. If he has no language, so no grammar, of his own, he must adopt one; he will speak some language or other whether he so chooses or not. It will usually be some kind of argot.

THE ARCHITECT OF THE FUTURE

The first thing to do to get a Usonian house is to go to a Usonian architect! That is to say, go to some architect who has been trained from the ground up in consistent organic construction and has lived in it as a natural circumstance. He may have absorbed it only intellectually. But through the pores of his skin, his soul becomes awakened and aware of it (he will say instinctively) by his own experience.

Bernard Schwartz House, Two Rivers, Wisconsin, living room, 1939. FLLW Fdn FA#3904.0021

I doubt that this affair can be *taught* to anyone. It does not come from a university with some degree or other. You cannot get it from books alone and certainly no conditioned Harvard man would be likely to have it. Harvard seems degraded to believe in the work of the committee-meeting instead of the inspired individual. But I know you can never get it through any form of collectivism. A true work of art must be induced as inspiration and cannot be induced or inspired through "teamwork." So it will not come through communism or fascism or any ism—only as slow growth by way of Democracy.

I doubt if there is much hope for the present generation's ever learning to discriminate surely between what makes a building good or what it is that makes a bad one. Hope lies within the next generation now in high school.

It is necessary for the child to grow up in an atmosphere conducive to the absorption of true esthetic values. It is necessary to study building as a kind of doing called Architecture. Not merely is Architecture made at the drafting board, but Architecture in all of its aspects is to be studied as environment, as the nature of materials to be used, as the forms and proportions of Nature itself in all her forms—sequences and consequences. Nature is the great teacher—man can only receive and respond to her teaching.

IT IS VALIANT TO BE SIMPLE

One of the essential characteristics of organic architecture is a natural simplicity. I don't mean the side of a barn door. Plainness, although simple, is not what I mean by simplicity. Simplicity is a clean, direct expression of that essential quality of the thing which is in the nature of the thing itself. The innate or organic pattern of the form of anything is that form which is thus truly *simple*. Cultivation seems to go against simplicity in the flower, as it does much the same thing in human life with the human being.

As we live and as we are, Simplicity—with a capital "S"—is difficult to comprehend nowadays. We are no longer truly simple. We no longer live in simple terms, in simple times or places. Life is a more complex struggle now. It is now valiant to be simple; a courageous thing to even want to be simple. It is a spiritual thing to comprehend what simplicity means.

In attempting to arrive at definitions of these matters, we invariably get into the spirit. The head alone cannot do enough. We have overrated what the head can do, consequently we now are confused and in a dangerous situation where our future is concerned. We have given up those things that are leading lights to the spirit of man; they are unfortunately no longer sufficiently important to us for us to pay for them what they cost.

This architecture we call organic is an architecture upon which true American society will eventually be based if we survive at all. An architecture upon and within which the common man is given freedom to realize his potentialities as an individual—himself unique, creative, free.

THE "USONIAN AUTOMATIC"

We are often asked how a young couple, with a limited budget, can afford to build a house designed on these basic principles of organic architecture.

What couple does not have a limited budget? It is within limitations that we have to work in designing houses for the upper middle third of the democratic strata in our country. Our clients come from that strata. We are often asked: "Will you build a house for us for $15,000;" or "Will you build us a house for $25,000;" sometimes for $75,000 or even $200,000.

The other day someone came with $250,000. He embarrassed me. Very wealthy people usually go to some fashionable architect, not to a known radical who is never fashionable if he can help it.

REDUCING THE COSTS

How then, you may ask, can people with even more limited means experience the liberation, the sense of freedom that comes with true architecture? This problem will probably always exist in one direction or another. But we have gone far in solving this generic problem by the natural concrete block house we call the "Usonian Automatic." This Usonian house incorporates innovations which reduce most of the heavier building costs, labor in particular. The earlier versions of these concrete block houses built in Los Angeles about 1921-24 may also be seen in the Arizona-Biltmore cottages.[11] The Millard house in Pasadena was first; then the Storer and Freeman and last—the Ennis house in Los Angeles. Among recent examples are the Adelman cottage and Pieper cottage in Phoenix, Arizona.

With the limited budget of a G. I. you cannot pay a plasterer, mason, bricklayer, carpenter, etc., twenty-nine dollars a day (and at that never be sure whether the work is done well). To build a low cost house you must eliminate, so far as possible, the use of skilled labor, now so expensive. The Usonian Automatic house therefore is built of shells made up of pre-cast concrete blocks about 1' 0" x 2' 0" or larger and so designed that, grooved as they are on their edges, they can be made and also set up with small steel horizontal and vertical reinforcing rods in the joints, by the owners themselves, each course being grouted (poured) as it is laid upon the one beneath; the rods meantime projecting above for the next course.

HOW THE "USONIAN AUTOMATIC" IS BUILT

The Usonian Automatic system is capable of infinite modifications of form, pattern and application, and to any extent. The original blocks are made on the site by ramming concrete into wood or metal wrap-around forms, with one outside face (which may be patterned), and one rear or inside face, generally coffered, for lightness.

All edges of the blocks, having a semi-circular groove (vertically and horizontally), admit the steel rods. When blocks are placed, edges closely adjoining, cylindrical hollow spaces are formed between them in which the light steel "pencil" rods are set and into which semi-liquid Portland cement grout is poured.

Walls may be either *single* (one layer of blocks), the coffered back-face forming the interior wall surface, or *double* with two layers of blocks, with an interior insulating air space between.

Ordinarily the procedure of erection of walls is as follows:

a) Vertical reinforcing bars or dowels are set on unit intervals in slab or in footing which is to receive the block wall-construction.

b) The blocks are set between these rods so that one vertical rod falls in the round cylindrical groove between each two blocks.

c) Grout, formed of one part cement and two parts sand, is then poured into the vertical groove at joints, running into the horizontal groove at joints locking all into a solid mass.

d) Horizontal rods are laid in horizontal grooves as the courses are laid up.

e) If double walls are planned, galvanized U-shaped wall tie-rods are set at each joint to anchor outer and inner block-walls to each other.

f) Another course of blocks is set upon the one now already poured.

g) As each course is added, grout is again poured into vertical joints, automatically filling the previous horizontal joint at the same time. Etc. Etc.

The pattern, design and size of the blocks may vary greatly. In some cases blocks have been made with patterned holes into which glass (sometimes colored) is set. When these glazed perforated units are assembled they form a translucent grille or screen of concrete, glass and steel.

At corners special monolithic corner blocks are used; in the case of double walls inside and outside corner blocks are required. About nine various types of block are needed to complete the house, most of them made from the same mold. For ceilings the same block units have been employed to cast horizontal ceiling and roof slabs, the same reinforcing rods forming a reinforced slab on which to put built up roofing above.

In this "Usonian Automatic" we have eliminated the need for skilled labor by prefabricating all plumbing, heating and wiring, so each appurtenance system may come into the building in a factory-made package, easily installed by making several simple connections provided during block-construction.

Here then, within moderate means for the free man of our democracy, with some intelligence and by his own energy, comes a natural house designed in accordance with the principles of organic architecture. A house that may be put to work in our society and give us an architecture for "housing" which is becoming to a free society because, though standardized fully, it yet establishes the democratic ideal of variety—the sovereignty of the individual. A true architecture may evolve. As a consequence conformation does not mean stultification but with it imagination may devise and build freely for residential purposes an immensely flexible varied building in groups never lacking in grace or desirable distinction.

ORGANIC ARCHITECTURE AND THE ORIENT

When I built the Imperial Hotel in Tokyo, Japan, I tried to make a coherent link between what the Japanese then were on their knees and what they now wanted to be on their feet. Every civilization that had gone to Japan had looted their culture. Because it was the only such genuine culture, coming from their own ground as it did, I was determined as an American to take off my hat to that extraordinary culture. At the same time I was now faced with the problem of how to build a modern building earthquake-proof.

This was mainly the Mikado's building. So I had also to consider the Mikado's needs for a social clearing house for the official life that would inevitably now come to Japan. So the Impeho would have to be comfortable enough for foreigners, although primarily it would need to serve the needs of the Japanese.

That became quite a problem—in addition to the earthquake which we never lost sight of day or night. The seismograph in Japan is never still. At night you have the feeling that the bed is going down under you and you are lost. You never get rid of that nice feeling.

But across the moat just beyond, there was the Emperor's Palace, and since I was the Emperor's "Kenchikukaho" (High Builder) and he was really my client, I felt impelled to devise ways and means not too far removed from what would be becoming to that palace of his across the moat. I think I succeeded. It is all there so far as it could be done at the time.

Of course, when I wanted to use native materials for the building—the common stone that was underfoot in Tokyo, called *oya,* which is something like travertine with big, burned, brown spots in it—there was a terrific objection by the building committee. Too common. But I liked the material and finally won. We built with "oya." We could use it by the acre—which we proceeded to do. We bought whole quarries far up at Nikko, so we quarried it there and floated it down to the site—in great barges.

The problem was how to help the Japanese people up from their knees and onto their feet. That problem still remained. When the Japanese had selected foreign things to live with, they had taken our most obvious forms which are our worst. They were uncomfortable at awkward high tables, and when sitting on the high chairs suitable to us their short legs would dangle. The first thing to do then was to get everything down to their own human-scale so that they could sit on a chair with their feet on the floor, eat at tables that did not require them to sit with food just under their chins. Sleep in beds up off the floor. Thus, to start with, the whole scale of the building became Japanese.

The next problem was how to devise things that were in reasonable accord with their high state of civilization. Instead of making so many things that would simply stand around, the way we have

them, everything began to have its own place in its own way—to be put away out of sight when not wanted—the living areas kept clear. For example, the dressing table became just a mirror against the wall with a little movable cabinet against the wall beside it. It could be moved around and a chair belonging to the room could be brought up to sit there beside it. All such things I simplified in accordance with Japanese culture so far as possible, making them easy and natural for Japanese use. At the same time, everything must have true esthetic effect and be not too impractical for the foreigner.

The Japanese had never had interior bathrooms or toilets. They had what they called the "benjo," and the benjo had to be kept out of the "devil's corner." What was the devil's corner? It was only that corner from which the prevailing winds blew, bringing the scent from the benjo. But now in the Imperial Hotel these little detached toilet rooms became organic features of the building. And in these little bathrooms, floor heat was born. The tub was of tiles and sunk in the floor; the tile was a small vitreous mosaic and you would come out of the tub with a print of the mosaic designs on your backside. But that didn't matter.

Anyhow, it was all becoming one thing—the things within it in relation to each other—organic. The heating pipes ran across the wall above the tubs and so became a gleaming hot towel rack on which the towel would naturally dry very quickly. It was a very pretty thing to look at too, one of those bathrooms, modern but also quite in the Japanese way of doing things.

Their way of doing things was always more or less organic. The Japanese house is the closest thing to our organic house of anything ever built. They already had the instinct of adapting and *incorporating* everything, so that is one reason why I brought into the Imperial Hotel this incorporation of everything in it. The heating was in the center of the room in a little hand-wrought filigree copper tower, on top of which was a light fixture that spread light over the ceiling—indirect lighting. The beds were one this way and one that way, at right angles, and to one side in their center was a nest of small tables that could be decentralized and spread around the

CREDO:

I believe a house is more a home by being a work of Art.

I believe the man is more a man by being an individual rather than a committee-meeting.

For these two reasons, I believe Democracy (though difficult) is the highest known form of society.

I believe Democracy is the new innate aristocracy our humanity needs.

I believe success in any form consists in making these truths a reality according to ability.

I believe all agencies tending to confuse and frustrate these truths are now continuous and expedient — therefore to be exposed and rejected.

I believe truth to be our organic divinity.

FRANK LLOYD WRIGHT

Endpaper of *The Natural House*, Horizon Press, New York, 1954

room—all more or less organic in itself, again like their own arrangements at home.

Finally we used to go around to determine the impact of the building on "the foreign guest." We would see these fellows come in with their trunks and bags—accompanied by the timid little Japanese house-boy—the boy apologetic and bowing them in, trying to show them everything (how this should be, how they should do that). The "guest" would come up and perhaps kick the table nest in the center and say, "What the hell do you call this?" and "Where is the telephone?" and "Where do these things go?"

Well, the utility all went into appropriate closets provided for them. Everything was there but everything was absorbed, and so puzzled them. The little Japanese boy would be very kindly and apologetic for everything that existed. But the whole attitude of the American tourist was: "Well, what do you know? Now, what the hell do you call this?" Etc., etc., etc.

THE PHILOSOPHY AND THE DEED

Many people have wondered about an Oriental quality they see in my work. I suppose it is true that when we speak of organic architecture, we are speaking of something that is more Oriental than Western. The answer is: my work *is*, in that deeper philosophic sense, Oriental. These ideals have not been common to the whole people of the Orient; but there was Laotse, for instance. Our society has never known the deeper Taoist mind. The Orientals must have had the sense of it, whatever may have been their consideration for it, and they instinctively built that way. Their instinct was right. So this gospel of organic architecture still has more in sympathy and in common with Oriental thought than it has with any other thing the West has ever confessed.

The West as "the West" had never known or cared to know much about it. Ancient Greece came nearest—perhaps—but not very close, and since the later Western civilizations in Italy, France, England and the United States went heavily—stupidly— Greek in their architecture, the West could not easily have seen an indigenous organic architecture. The civilizations of India, Persia, China and Japan are all based on the same central source of cultural inspiration, chiefly Buddhist, stemming from the original inspiration of his faith. But it is not so much the principles of this faith which underlie organic architecture, as the faith of Laotse—the Chinese philosopher—his annals preserved in Tibet. But I became conscious of these only after I had found and built it for myself.

And yet the West cannot hope to have anything original unless by individual inspiration. Our culture is so far junior and so far outclassed in time by all that we call Oriental. You will surely find that nearly everything we stand for today, everything we think of as originated by us, is thus old. To make matters in our new nation worse, America has always assumed that culture, to be culture, had to come from European sources—be imported. The idea of an organic architecture, therefore, coming from the tall grass of the Midwestern American prairie, was regarded at home as unacceptable. So it went around the world to find recognition and then to be "imported" to its own home as a thing to be imitated everywhere, though the understanding of its principles has never yet really caught up with the penetration of the original deed at home.

It cannot truthfully be said, however, that organic architecture was derived from the Orient. We have our own way of putting these elemental (so ancient) ideals into practical effect. Although Laotse, as far as we know, first enunciated the philosophy, it probably preceded him but was never built by him or any Oriental. The idea of organic architecture that the reality of the building lies in the space within to be lived in, the feeling that we must not enclose ourselves in an envelope which is the building, is not alone Oriental. Democracy, proclaiming the integrity of the individual *per se,* had the feeling if not the words. Nothing else Western except the act of an organic architecture had ever happened to declare that Laotsian philosophic principle which was declared by him 500 years before our Jesus. It is true that the wiser, older civilizations of the world had a quiescent sense of this long before we of the West came to it.

For a long time, I thought I had "discovered" it, only to find after all that this idea of the interior space being the reality of the building was ancient and Oriental. It came to me quite naturally from my Unitarian ancestry and the Froebelian kindergarten training in the deeper primal sense of the form of the interior or heart of the appearance of "things." I was entitled to it by the way I happened to come up along the line—perhaps. I don't really know. Chesty with all this, I was in danger of thinking of myself as, more or less, a prophet. When building Unity Temple at Oak Park and the Larkin Building in Buffalo, I was making the first great protest I knew anything about against the building coming up on you from the outside as enclosure.[12] I reversed that old idiom in idea and in fact.

When pretty well puffed up by this I received a little book by Okakura Kakuzo, entitled *The Book of Tea,* sent to me by the ambassador from Japan to the United States. Reading it, I came across this sentence: "The reality of a room was to be found in the space enclosed by the roof and walls, not in the roof and walls themselves."

Well, there was I. Instead of being the cake I was not even dough. Closing the little book I went out to break stone on the road, trying to get my interior self together. I was like a sail coming down; I had thought of myself as an original, but was not. It took me days to swell up again. But I began to swell up again when I thought, "After all, who built it? Who put that thought into buildings? Laotse nor anyone had consciously *built* it." When I thought of that, naturally enough I thought, "Well then, everything is all right, we can still go along with head up." I have been going along—head up—ever since.

1. Olgivanna Wright prompted the questions. She gave each apprentice a specific question to ask one morning after Sunday breakfast. The transcribed answers were then handed over to Wright to edit.

2. The James Charnley residence, Chicago, Illinois, 1891.

3. William Herman Winslow residence, River Forest, Illinois, 1893.

4. FLLW footnote from original text: Louis Sullivan.

5. "Modern Architecture, Begin the Kahn Lectures, 1930." Reprinted in *FLW Collected Writings,* volume 2.

6. Wright delivered the paper "The Art and Craft of the Machine" at Hull House in 1901.

7. FLLW footnote from original text: Usonia was Samuel Butler's name for the United States.

8. Brought up to date by Frank Lloyd Wright, 1954.

9. Nakoma Country Club, golf course clubhouse, Madison Wisconsin, 1923. Unbuilt project.

10. Herbert Jacobs house, Madison, Wisconsin, 1936–1937.

11. Cottage apartments at the Arizona Biltmore Hotel, Phoenix, Arizona, 1929.

12. Unity temple, 1905. The Larkin Company Administration Building, 1903.

THE ETERNAL LAW

When the University of Wisconsin awarded Frank Lloyd Wright an honorary doctorate of fine arts in 1955, he felt "obliged" to submit a thesis after the occasion had taken place. Therefore, on April 29 he wrote to the president of the university:

> My dear President Fred:
> It has occurred to me that the old fashioned requirement of a thesis at graduation was never written and presented by me to my University (it was Class of '86). So here is the missing thesis—THE ETERNAL LAW—to be back-filed, perhaps, with those of my ancient class?
>
> May I hope this goes on record to repair my lost opportunity. If such requirement (in some form) should come under the rules of my subsequent "graduation," you are welcome to use it how you please—even in the wastebasket.
>
> Faithfully yours, Frank Lloyd Wright

The subject of "The Eternal Law" springs from Wright's admiration of the Greek philosopher Heraclitus (535–475 B.C.) and his wholehearted subscription to that philosopher's belief that permanence is an illusion, that the only real state is the transitional one of becoming. Wright felt the same impact from the Chinese philosopher Laotze, and he took Laotze's dictum that the reality of a vessel consisted not in the walls of the container but the space within and made it read, "The reality of a building does not consist in the walls and roof, but the space within to be lived in." Laotze was concerned with the intangible quality of space; Wright also was concerned with that same quality—not limiting space to a mere architectural "presence" but giving it a deeper meaning altogether, as in the following:

> Today, around the circumference of architectural thoughts, basic error still exists concerning the new concept I have stated of the good old third dimension—usually seen as thickness, weight, a solid. Sublimated by organic architecture, it is interpreted as depth. The "depth-dimension"—really a fourth now—the sense of space.[1]

He often emphasized that the intangibles of today become the tangibles of tomorrow.

These concepts—the intangible, the law of change, a sense of becoming, space as a new "fourth" dimension—are philosophic in essence and defy hard and fast scrutiny. But their application in his work certainly produced an atmosphere that could be sensed and experienced.

Wright spoke frequently to his apprentices on the subject of the law of change, often saying that Heraclitus was stoned in the streets of Athens for saying that the only immutable, unchangeable law was the law of change itself. Wright commented further:

The Law of Change, then, means that we are all in a state of becoming, that is to say, of growth, or decay: decay being but another form of growth. Death is but a becoming something else. If you observe this major tradition, you will wish to become aware of what might well be better tomorrow than today; and what it is that will keep you continually alive, alert, and conscious: let's say creative.

[Frank Lloyd Wright: The Crowning Decade 1949–1959, *California State University, Fresno, California, 1989*]

"ALL IS A STATE OF BECOMING"—HUMAN TRADITIONS should be made and maintained subject to the Law of Change. Other laws are minor laws—subject, not ultimate. Major, or minor, as growth may appear according to the eternal law—the Law of Change. Heraclitus, radical Greek. . . .

You may have heard it frequently said, concerning something or other, "it's a museum-piece." When you do visit a museum, you may be told that what you see there is "the accumulated riches of the human race." That is true but what you see is there in the museum, no longer living, because the civilizations represented finally failed to apprehend the Law of Change that applied to them. At least, what you *should* see if you *would see* is there according to this great law of Nature. You see in those vast accumulations the "debris" of the human race.

Unfortunately, most people going into museums do see this accumulation as though it was of today, not as living in its own time. Many of the things the visitor looks upon represent "monumental" achievements or are noble in themselves. But the beholder seldom has an idea of what that quality "monumental" meant in the time the things he now sees were in use. Education sometimes tries to enlighten him but seems to succeed only in conditioning him to whatever seems, now, the expedient view: fails to really enlighten him because the Law of Change has not been well interpreted.

For instance, teachers may ruin the majesty of a Shakespearean sonnet by having their students paraphrase it, as though such majesty could be recast in the idiom of a sophomore. Or I, as an architect, may ask why architects construct, in the middle of a twentieth century industrial city, buildings with poster-facades, no more appropriate to human life within them than Doric columns or Turkish minarets would be. Or, why continue to crowd more skyscrapers together to attract crowds to the death of all skyscrapers and all crowds? Or why build buildings where none ought to be and not build them where they do belong?

Yet these things are happening to us without comment right here all the time. They now stand as characteristic of the spiritual weakness and mental confusion of this time in which we live—where and while—and because the Law of Change is operating beyond our ken. Characteristic? Yes, because but few of us ever try to define what tradition is minor and which is major *in regard to the eternal Law of Change!* We live observing and obedient to scores of completely outdated minor traditions which we, a polyglot people, have inherited. They are now called "conservative" but, tugging and pulling in opposite directions, all of them are irrelevant to the splendid thing that America aims to be and that our national spirit should by now represent by virtue of the Law of Change, if well interpreted and accepted.

There are traditions right or wrong for our use now. We do not yet seem to want to know what they are, except that by the study of Nature, if intelligent and sincere, we should discover the principles which we need to know and firmly regard in order to understand what it is that has already happened to us—and is likely to happen. This, I take it, is the enlightenment our educational "conditioning" lacks. The two, education and culture, now seem scarcely on speaking terms. We have plenty of traditional limitations and many imitations of many limitations "by tradition." Some of us are struggling enormously to clarify what little knowledge we have to hasten perceptions we now need in order to meet and go with the law of laws. But most of us have not yet pinned this down to action. We dread to face the eternal, drastic changes that make or break us continually, according to our right or wrong interpretations.

It is clear enough by now that there is no great tradition that should dare ignore this great law of laws. The one law that is true: true of all men and of all things, at all times and in all places. This never-ceasing, tragic law is rooted in the principle of growth, elemental to Nature. The Law of Change, then, means that we are all in a state of becoming, that is to say, of growth, or decay: decay being but another form of growth. Death is but a becoming something else. If you observe this major tradition, you will wish to become aware of what might well be better tomorrow than today; and what it is that will keep you continually alive, alert, and conscious: let's say *creative*. You will cultivate a tremendous flexibility of mind and if you have true moral courage to face it, what you learn may make this courage useful not only to you but to others. What this Law of Change means in practical application is really Progress! The *organic* expression of Life itself.

1. *A Testament*, p. 155.

FAITH IN YOUR
OWN INDIVIDUALITY

Dr. *Benjamin Masselink and his wife, Gertrude, moved to Fort Lauderdale, Florida, from Michigan when he retired from dentistry. They were the parents of a Taliesin apprentice, Eugene Masselink, and came to Wisconsin for several weeks each summer to visit their son and partake in the life of the fellowship. One winter they sent to Taliesin a luxurious collection of sea shells garnered from the Florida coastline. Wright was enthralled by the shells' beauty and variety of form and color, and he laid them out on a Japanese lacquer tray set on the table next to his desk. On Sunday morning, 21 March 1953, while he was at breakfast with his family and apprentices, he asked that the tray of sea shells be brought into the dining room. One by one he picked up each shell, examined it, and described it in terms of architecture and housing:*

> *Look at this one! Probably called a "genius" by the tribe! Imagine all this as* housing. *These are homes. These are nature-buildings. Shall we call each a different* idea, *a different* principle*? No, they are not different. They are all the experience of but* one *idea. Out of that idea, which is generic, and so productive, comes infinite variety.*

> *As he described the sea shells, he returned continually to the concepts of mankind, architecture, and culture:* "Now, how about us, the highest form of life, we say? . . . What has become of us? When we can see what is done by forms of life on the plane of the sea shell, we may glimpse what we should be doing on our own plane."

> *The talk was transcribed and later edited by Wright for publication in* House Beautiful *in November 1955. The entire issue was devoted to his work, and the discussion of sea shells and housing was renamed "Faith in Your Own Individuality."* [House Beautiful, *November 1955*]

THIS MORNING, BOYS, I WANT TO GIVE YOU A LITTLE LESSON in housing. I will show you what housing amounts to in nature, and what a good place nature is to go to if you really want to study housing.

Look carefully at these hundreds of beautiful, infinitely various little houses *(Mr. Wright shows the apprentices a tray full of sea shells)*. Here you see housing on a lower level, it is true, but isn't this humble instance a marvelous manifestation of life? Now, where, in all this bewildering variety of form, is the *idea?* Is there not just one *idea* or *principle* here? But where is the limitation to variety? There is none.

Speaking of human housing, here is a good lesson that you young architects may now get. If the human mind is so limited that it can take in only some special one *(pointing to one shell),* what we now need to see is that we must inform ourselves, if we really want to develop a culture of our own, so that we can perform similar "miracles" *(pointing to them all)* in order that we do not have to submit to those impositions by code or formula, in the name of science or authority, which impose a living death on our performances.

Here, in these shells, we see the housing of the life of the sea. It is the housing of a lower order of life, but it is a housing with exactly what we lack: inspired form. In this collection of houses of hundreds of small beings, who themselves built these houses, we see a quality which we might call invention. The beauty of their variation is never finished. Creation here goes on forever. It is not a question of degree, but of principle of design. This multitudinous expression indicates what design can mean.

There is no reason why our buildings and the housing of human beings, which we so stupidly perpetrate all alike as two peas in a pod, shouldn't be quite as fertile in imaginative resource as these little sea shells. Why do we ever take to any one formula, carry it out to a dead end, and execute it as though that were all? Here in this collection of little houses is one of the best lessons you could possibly find. Study them.

There is but one generic principle here: All these little shell-houses are doing the same thing, but not in the same way. This one *(a clam shell)* is based on the opening and shutting of the house.

Two halves hinged together. These and many others without hinges—are they of a higher development, or, being less mechanical, are they inferior? Or the reverse? Can you see how all these lines and forms in all these colors and textures are tributary to the forces which are being exerted from within as the shell is being made, or, we might say, designed?

Every ornamentation, that is to say, every *pattern,* you see here, and the exquisite forms of the shells themselves, are tributary to the force that is being exerted by its like upon itself from within, as the growing shell is being made. Probably this one grew in coral beds, where the very shape and decoration of the thing was a feature of the preservation of its life, keeping its inhabitant from destruction by alien forces. That was true generally of these more exclusive cellular shells.

Look at this fantasy! *(Mr. Wright holds up a striking shell).* Here is an original! All these infinitely variable forms are saying exactly the same thing. No interior change in *idea,* yet here is another and another and another *individual.* Here you may see what individuality might mean in a democracy. If you want a lesson in organic structure and decoration, here it is. And what colorations, what beautiful, textured color! Always, in these forms, in these little poems, there is the ebb and the flow, the plasticity of the elements by way of which, and in which, they came to exist. They are natural, you see. These little things are all of them lovely in their own way. Beautiful. All of them. Some of them are still young, growing up perhaps, the species still a becoming.

Here, for instance, is a beautiful form of *principle at work.* Every single one comes to a different conclusion, wherever it may start or whatever the harmony may be. Yet, see the variety of *means to ends?* When you get the simple secret of this inner life of the thing, why that thing is what it is, and why a certain aim does persist in all these various shells of this or any other type of life, that means you have the secret of differences in a family, differences that mean various races—true dissidence, in other words.

See the great, seemingly utter difference between these two shells! What in common do they have? Here we see reinforced shells, evidently due to a scarcity of raw materials. Here we see the rein-forcing rib, instead of the heavier mass, the outer-wall-bearing pattern. The pattern here is seemingly predestined to purpose, since these shells are the children of movement—the movement of the sea and the sand. Why can't we be as fertile in our work? Where should we go to study the inner forces that have such wide consequence?

Look at this one! Probably called a "genius" by the tribe! Imagine all this as *housing*. These are homes. These are nature-buildings. Shall we call each a different *idea,* a different *principle?* No, they are not different. They are all the experience of but *one* idea. Out of that one idea, which is generic, and so productive, comes infinite variety. It can go on forever. Yes, it is infinite. That is why I show you these little manifestations of housing. Not only does this opportunity for individual expression develop form by way of changes of material, but it changes owing to the slightest influence of environment. All is recorded by changes in *form.*

That one *(pointing to a shell)* is a sober sister, isn't it, all gray and smooth and white inside. It makes you feel pretty stupid to see this infinite variety, doesn't it? And *we* sit down at our drafting boards and try to do something!

Well, what is this element in nature which produces such fascinating, rich, harmonious individualities? Is it the same element that produces different human races, differing individualities within the races? Yes, it is all the same. But what is the secret of the forming of it all? These are the major things you should study, as artists, in the great book of creation. Because here is where the artist finds light thrown on what he feels. This expression of inner life by appropriate form is really his field.

Now, is there a *mind,* would you say, producing these infinite changes of form in nature? Is it a matter of mind? What is doing this? Why is it done? Science can investigate it, but science comes against a barrier it can never pierce. What this inner life is, we do not know. But this innate source of expression is what should inspire you all—give you faith in your own divinity, if that is the word for it, in your own inspiration, if that is more understandable.

You see, there never is a limit. Nothing indi-cates that the infinite variety could end, so long as the principle is inviolate. Look at this little beauty. Such a sweet little individuality! Civilization comes in and says, "Oh, hell, let's get an easy pattern out of this, so we can stamp them out, all just the same." It becomes a cliché, a style. Then the divine element in it goes out. The quality that is divine disappears.

Housing has become a mere materiality of no great value to life whatsoever, except as little breeding stables entirely without any sense of God. There must have been a sense of God in these little forms to produce this infinite beauty of form. Just as there must be slumbering in all of us. There is in us, too, that interior sense of becoming, which we call God, working in us all, and which, you will see, has infinite capacity which no human mind can ever encompass and imprison.

There in these shells you have humble innate evidence. If we go into the human phases of what we call our divinity and consider the inherent element at work in us, as in all of life, you may find the same idea. Therein lies the value of these little things to us, if we study them as artists should. Here, in nature, is an architect's "school."

The coral family is another fascinating family, because the innate principle works in the coral branch in totally different schemes, and yet the same. Some of the branches will grow out in the water as great long spears and wave to and fro with the movement of the water, all on a little hinge, and then at times become detached and float away to find another attachment, and the whole thing goes on over and over again.

There is, in all of this, an element of becoming, determining the shape of these things. Form develops accordingly: its circumstances are always by way of its own life principle.

Now, this common tendency throughout them all unites them. In all of us there is exactly the same thing working all the time. What would our divinity be? Certainly divinity is manifest here in these shells, in their humble form of life.

Now, how about us, the highest form of life, we say? What has become of us? Are science and civilization killing our divinity, instead of developing it? What are we pursuing? What is it that we call civilization if it lacks the harmonious forms developed by inner principle, by true individuality?

Nature loves individuality, resists and punishes the loss of it in any field of creation. If our civilization goes contrary to this divinity within the nature of us all, if it does not learn these secrets of behavior, of character, of appropriate changes of form, then what is going to happen to us? Where shall we go? Now is the time for us to say wherein lies salvation for us as human beings.

Is the solution creativity? Yes, that is the element needed now. It alone can prevent us from becoming standardized, from losing our rich and potent sense of life, which we see here as the beauty of these shells in their housing.

When we can see what is done by forms of life on the plane of the sea shell, we may glimpse what we should be doing on our own plane. We are not now doing anything at all like it. Why aren't we? It is for *that* that architects are members of society: for the *preservation* of individuality, thus making beautiful, in various ways, the common necessity of living. That is our job. I do not think we could have a better instance of common generic principle at work as individuality than in these little shells.

What is our conclusion? This one: Once you understand the principle upon which this differentiation depends, you will astonish your kind by your own prolific capacity. To always turn out a different design from the one you did before will become inevitable. The secret of that variety is inherent in nature. She is jealous of it! If an architect does not have that secret, he will not be a great artist. He is missing essential quality. The key to creation is not in him.

THE FUTURE OF THE CITY

The plight of the city, especially those of the United States, never ceased to be a major concern to Wright. In books, articles, and lectures he constantly reiterated the desperate need for decentralization: "Our American cities are the most overgrown, yet definitely dated, form of centralization. . . . A true vision of tomorrow (modernity) sees that decentralization is the basic principle of the good life." The good life. *That was the quest in his lifelong battle against the overcrowding, against the fumes of the internal combustion engines poisoning the citizens, against the ruse of the landlord to incarcerate the citizen into a rent-debt situation, which were some of the more obvious problems of city life. Wright believed that "Soon relief must take a tangible cultural form. Planning a new and better scheme of life is fundamental to architecture—and surely wisdom now."* [Saturday Review, *May 1955*]

HERACLITUS OF ATHENS—A RADICAL GREEK—WAS STONED in the streets by his foolish fellow citizens for declaring that only one law is unchangeable—the law of change. "All is in a state of becoming," he wrote. Today we also know, of course, that the law of change is the law of growth.

At this time in our own fantastic century of change Americans must not deny the changes that already are operating on yesterday's changes with inscrutable force and increasing rapidity. Our own fearsome mechanization is meant to promote human comfort, but instead it has thrown into ugly confusion nearly everything our lives touch. Our responsible authorities are sunk in vested, static institutions. They *fear* change. We citizens ourselves actually lack the necessary perspective, vision, courage, and the common sense to face the inexorable law of change. We pass by great opportunities with a wisecrack, now and then; but we want the wit to see them as they are and plan accordingly.

American big cities are perhaps the most heretical violation of Heraclitus's law of organic change. But sponsors of the modern city, first founded by Cain (the murderer of his brother), refuse to consider fundamental and human alteration in the city's structure because of our gigantic "investment" in the city as it is. And so the Machine Age has not liberated us. We are imprisoned: witness the new buildings on our city streets. Isn't it true to say that—in these buildings—Novelty is mistaken for Progress? Of steel and glass we have aplenty; but what of the imaginative and creative powers which make of these glittering materials structures responsive to the needs of the Human Individual? What of Real Sun. Real Air, Real Leisure?

Now, the mind is not modern that is still conditioned by self-interest, or clings desperately to quantity instead of quality. It is folly to believe that, instead of a new and different city, our present ones—born in ancient times and captives of commerce—can yet be made over to survive, if not suit, modern man. The old sun itself may be one of those stars going their way to make room for greater ones. So our present cities must go to make way for the greater city we can now build: a plan for man liberated, freed from his own excesses by the integrity of his vision.

Since "science-in-uniform" has already dated and perhaps doomed the urbanites of our planet, and continues to date even itself, why should we continue to believe that science will make an exception of the city? Science, having—in the city—taken society all apart in human terms, cannot put it back together again. Integration and humanization of society must be, as they always have been, the work of the Creative Mind: of the architect, the artist, the poet, the prophet. Especially at this moment we need the architect, for so long absent or a prostitute. The creative mind must rehumanize the decentralized society that is coming when the city at last dies. Without such conscientious spiritual leadership, this nation of ours—so long ridden by fear and commercial selfishness—must accept cultural, and therefore political, mediocrity. That means inferiority—if our democracy endures at all.

Our American cities are the most overgrown, yet definitely dated, forms of centralization. Certain insects have gone further (and done better) with the act of centralization as a principle; but, anyway, centralization as a principle is always a dubious one, at best, where the concern is humanity. During the past half-century radical changes wrought in all our lives have settled the fate of centralized urbanization. A true vision of tomorrow (modernity) sees that decentralization is the basic principle of the good life. Any sensible man must see that further centralizations of any America city are only postponements of the city's end—if not its post-mortem. Can people be expected to live indefinitely in such prisons as our "new" metropolitan housing projects? What about Lever House—a very dangerous mirror used as a poster for soap.

(Too bad that indecent exposure can't be achieved by safer means than such an abuse of glass.) And now comes the whiskey-building [Editor's Note: *The Seagram Building going up on Park Avenue and 52nd Street in New York*], trying to trump the deck of façades in this rat-race for natural extermination.

The deadline for eventual decentralization and planned reintegration of our cities is being continually tightened by science itself. Art and Religion, already declining, have been forced either to sink with or abandon the city. The alphabetical bombs now dropped into our already overstuffed tool-box—wherein are so many other marvelous new tools we have not learned to use—are rendering the survival of our cities more hopeless than ever. Had we really learned to use our amazing new tools, unlearned for so many bad reasons (not the least of these the gregarious character of the animal nature we have inherited), the open city of tomorrow would be ours to inhabit today. But no! This trampling of the herd we now hear is the shrieking of brakes and the blasts of motor horns. Instead of dust rising from hooves we have invisible carbon monoxide rising from herds of internal combustion engines—not dust from hooves, but poison gas. And the trends of quadruple tires, rolling on upended streets, carrying men hanging on by slender steel strands. Modern man more and more precariously continues on his mission of delay, hazard, and congestion, a continuous excursion which, with all his great new instruments, now forms the American trend—toward equalitarianism, quantity before quality, more or less senseless commotion.

Politicians know this well. "Scare a man enough and you can get from him what you will." Democracy, founded upon individual self-improvement as the condition of freedom, cannot now survive even its own politics. Democracy is already sinking into dreadful equalitarianism, of which the city is the structural symbol! Man's timidity, a most salient feature of his character, compels him to remain in his present fix. When Cain devised the city he was defying, "fearing," the Lord. Ironically, fear will be uppermost in the minds of his urbanized descendants when they abandon the city. The alphabetical bomb may help somewhat to show this natural coward that now there is every good reason why the citizen should study and act in accordance with inexorable law—the law of change. He either gets out *of* the city or he blows up *with* the city. But contagious fear, and man's own shortsighted interests, conspire to keep him right there where he is, regardless not only of his own peril and discomfort, but even of continual pain and the constant waste of what is best in himself.

Progress, an undercurrent without program, has been the story we have to tell of life-changes, "advances" which are now leaving us helpless in the affairs of our own cities. Much as the falling away of the level of the ocean exposes the surface of the earth beneath, so are we exposed. A simple change in water level brings new topography into view and into uses hitherto hidden. Mountain tops become islands: lakes appear in the hollows of the new leveling; unwanted vegetation takes the place of depths of water. Erosion keeps on and sculptures again the nearly new contours. So are changes visible in the life of man. What is to come? Movements countering upon one another continually take new directions, as sea life eventually becomes animal life. So much that was living dies, and the dead fertilizes new life, as under inexorable influences it issues in forms hitherto predicate, but yet unknown. This radical change seems no less evident today in the life of man. Where are all the civilizations of yesterday? Are not the dead ones those unable to meet change?

Subject to ever-present radical or organic change, such is the social life of modern man on this—his earth; and though changes being wrought may sometimes be even slower in realization than changes of sea and earth, they are as inevitable. One customary form of society weakens and gradually disappears, or, growing stronger, awakens to growth by way of great impulses. But probably with infinite slowness. Eventually the dreaded change takes place in spite of the coward's quandary, and all he can do to prevent it helps it along. But if man awakens, all organic change is to his *immense* gain.

So, the medieval city was for centuries a cultural necessity. Much as we may wish for the intimate human richness of that medieval time, that city has mostly done its work. What we now have, in New York and Chicago, etc., is still the ancient city, only overloaded with gadgetry inside and out (only gadgets and the garages are new), with the citizen himself becoming more or less a gadget. Trucks the size of freight cars zoom and ruin the streets for human beings, while garbage cans stand patiently on the curbs for weeks. Meanwhile story is added on story is added on story, to squeeze out the last dime for enormously inflated ground-rents. The modern city is a modern wreck without the charm of an ancient ruin. What has it left for our time when civilization no longer needs it? When our own democratic culture arrives we will abhor its inhumane impositions. Our modern economy—when and if really modern—will have neither room nor time for such cities as we have, except as we are able to conceive the city in the terms of that today which we call tomorrow. Even while expecting the city's doom, mankind seems shamefully blind to its equivalent or to its superior—the city suited to man alive in our own good place in time. Our Today includes all we can see of Tomorrow. What can we see of tomorrow in this, the American city of today?

Organic architecture has already modeled a prophetic pattern of tomorrow's democratic city in the new scale and sense of space now desirable and possible for mankind by means of mobilization, electrification, and the Machine. This plan, called Broadacre City, was modeled and exhibited in Rockefeller Center in 1934.

Neither urban nor rural, this modern equivalent of the ancient medieval city, entirely new, is made possible by our great new facilities in ground-speed, the sky-port, electrical intercommunication, sanitation, medication, and gadgetry. These are all beneficial to us only when we learn to use them to proper advantage, planning to do so according to human nature. Planning, not as robots, but as human beings; learning to know what to ask of architecture, art, and religion in order to profit by a new use of all these new agencies in a harmony of Time, Place, and Man. Thus we arrived at the model of Broadacres, wherein we learned to use our new facilities for a better world: use them all as marvelous new tools—

Edgar J. Kaufmann House "Boulder House" (Project). Palm Springs, California. 1951. Perspective. Pencil and color pencil on tracing paper, 35 x 25". FLLW Fdn#5111.002

Previous pages: "The Living City" (Broadacre City, 1934) (Project). 1958. Perspective. Pencil on tracing paper, 42 x 32". FLLW Fdn#5825.006

not use the machine as "motif," but use it as a powerful *tool* for the enlargement of the human horizon of the life of democratic-man-awake in possession of his own ground, his natural inheritance as man.

Tomorrow's City? Yes, but its connections planned as a bunch of grapes or a vine with berries, not as a melon or an apple. These old hangovers of the medieval city that we have not outgrown will gradually disappear into the green spaciousness of Everywhere. What becomes of the drastic divisions now existing between town and country? As none will be needed all will cease to exist as such. City and Country will have happily married, and, agreeing to quality for all instead of quantity, one quality for all will enable all becomingly to settle down together, humanity the richer in every way. Richer in the humanities themselves, as well as in more productive, timely new conditions less time-serving, less servile.

Then will the civilization we are calling Democracy (the new aristocracy) become integral. Life itself will have new meaning, because what is really desirable in the present division of town and country will be born again under more favorable conditions in what comes of both together. This ideal of an integral aristocracy we are calling Democracy arrives only when the Arts, Architecture, and Religion together take up this neglected work of a culture of our own—quality for all as against the vagaries of quantity. This planned superintegration of both town and country is made possible not only by the new tools with which to work, which we have been given by science, but a new architecture: an awakening of man to his true place in nature. This new city is necessary because our sciences have unintentionally taken the old one apart and scientists cannot ever put it together again to live. The ancient city science has already destroyed; only the architecture of art and religion and the art and religions of architecture can give it appropriate new birth.

Multitudes of ancient traditions have automatically drifted into our civilization from ancient civilizations. These minor traditions will all be swept away under the stress of such multiple and rapid changes in social, political, structural economics as we see and suffer from day by day. New traditions will be born. The overgrown village (this dated city of today) is the chief burden now confusing and hindering our lives. For our modern life in America the only tradition we shall be able to keep in the city of tomorrow—Broadacre City—is the great Tradition under which all traditions hover—tradition with a capital "T"—*organic change* is the new wisdom. "From the ground up" is now our wisdom and our plan.

Uppercurrents and undercurrents of the new way—the undertow—are actually already having their way. We may not yet see them for ourselves. The gas station was the first minor manifestation. The factory going to the country was another; the department stores following were a symptom. Produce markets appear along roadsides. The congestion of the cities is already driving them out. Under the growing shadow of the H-bomb any concentrations are murder.

Soon relief must take a tangible cultural form. Planning a new and better scheme of life is fundamental to architecture—and surely wisdom now. It may be truthfully said that if the best people remain in the city it is probably in a penthouse for a limited part of the year. The "better element" has already left, or is about to leave or would leave if it could. The average citizen would go afield if possible. Oppressive, red prison towers for those doomed to remain loom everywhere in the overgrown village now—the new aspect of the slum, the slum transferred from the region of the body to the realm of the soul. People are not safe in them. These "authorized" towering slabs, soulless but sanitary—see in all these sterilized city structures, however novel or extensive, not greatness, but weakness—the final dirge of the era of urbanism. More important, see in these sterilized façades the degeneracy of this democracy of ours—the equalitarianism our forefathers dreaded. These sterilized human hives accommodate no qualifications or discriminations of the human spirit. They only reveal a sterilized conformity to commercial necessity, always quantity at expense to quality. What of those who must therefore

Beth Sholom Synagogue, Elkins Park, Pennsylvania, 1954. FLLW Fdn FA#5313.0020

remain in the hangover of the ancient city? For them this era will be called "The Sanitary Age."

So it is that all now lies in the lap of change. Our growing population continues to increase more and more rapidly. One consequence is that all urban accommodations are becoming less desirable for human life. Isn't our name for all that we see of such excess centralization "degeneracy"? Our forefathers would see just that in it—and call an emergency meeting to "deal" with such social conditions. As for Mother Nature, is she in stitches or in despair, firmly calm or merely indifferent?

THE STORY OF THE TOWER

Construction on the H.C. Price Tower in Bartlesville, Oklahoma, began in 1952. The client, Harold Price, was anxious to have a special publication on its completion in 1956. Horizon Press agreed to publish the book, and the Price family agreed to support its production with photographs taken by their younger son, Joe Price. Wright gathered material from his past writings on tall building construction and added a section devoted exclusively to the new Price Tower to create the book The Story of the Tower. *Released in a relatively limited edition, the book was soon out of print. Wright's original 1956 texts are published here in their entirety.* [The Story of the Tower, *Horizon Press, New York, 1956*]

PRINCIPLE IS THE ONLY SAFE TRADITION. ORGANIC ARCHI-tecture—natural architecture—is capable of infinite variety in concept and form but faithful always to principle. It is—in fact and in deed—itself principle. A natural architecture true to the nature of the problem, to the nature of the site, of the materials and of those for whom it is built—in short, of the Time and Place and Man. Building *of* these, not applied or imposed *on* them. Neither a mere facade nor a glass poster, set up or "put over," regardless of man or the elements in which he must live—and built regardless of the basic principles which are the blood and the sinews of architecture organic.

By way of illuminating this perennial—eternal—matter of principle inherent in the solution of any problem, principle which lives and refuses to compromise wherever compromise is death to the integrity of the concept, here is The Tower as "idea."

Not since I first began to think around it and work on aspects of the structure in 1891 with Lieber Meister, Louis Sullivan; but since this form first took shape for me in the design of St. Mark's-on-the-Bouwerie:

1929[1]

Here is a fresh development of "St. Mark's," the now realized design of individual modern building for centralization or decentralization that, as a type, fulfills modern requirements either way and utilizes machine age resources at work upon machine age materials in a characteristic machine age way! The straight line and flat plane architecture suited to the technique of the machine age is seen here in significant outline instead of monumental mass.

The *constitution* of the whole building emphasizing interior space in light, with a novel combination of offices and apartments.

National Life Insurance Company Office Building (Project). Chicago, Illinois. 1924. Perspective. Pencil on tracing paper, 18 x 24".
FLLW Fdn#2404.005

Crystal Heights Hotel, Apartments, Theater and Shops (Project). Washington, D.C. 1939. Perspective. Sepia ink on tracing paper, 34 x 31". FLLW Fdn#4016.001

Rogers Lacy Hotel (Project). Dallas, Texas. 1946. Perspective. Pencil and color pencil on tracing paper, 23 x 52". FLLW Fdn#4606.001

St. Mark's-in-the-Bouwerie Apartment Tower (Project). New York, New York.
Reproductive print, 8 x 11". FLLW Fdn#2905.020

The structure is the cantilever—steel in tension—light and strong as it looks: one third lighter yet three times stronger than the heavy masonry-encrusted box frame of steel. In the nineteen stories of this structure the equivalent of at least two floors are available to live in, instead of being thrown away to give place to useless destructive wall-weights. There is but ten percent more glass area as "exposure" than you may see in the average commercial building such as Gordon Strong's Republic Building down on State Street, corner of Adams, in Chicago.

The steel textile, embedded in concrete, a machine age product of great value and beauty, here clothes interior space inside the glass and allows more light or less light, more or less privacy as desired under changing conditions. All exposed surfaces of the building except the central mass and floors, the supporting structure itself, are of copper. Partitions and furniture are designed as one and fabricated in the shop. Conservation of much space is effected by this resilient construction and this also means that the equivalent of a five room apartment, cave style, may be had in two thirds of the usual space. Sunlight methods in arrangement are everywhere evident.

Economy is extraordinary here in every sense. In any operation on large scale such construction affords enormous economy. Astonishing release from the usual field waste is the result of this use of the skyscraper form.

Naturally somewhat strange at first sight, but the kind of beauty we see in the liner, the plane and the motor is here. Added to that in the interior you will find a graceful sense of harmony in the whole, an imaginative touch in all detail that makes the parts sing in unison with the form of the whole. (Now The Tower is an apartment-building within an office-building, both more useful than ever.)

Beautiful? Let time say.

What is beauty?—yours—and yours—yes, and yours, my sophisticated savant! I hear you, I imagine your answer. Yours would simmer down to a mere matter of "taste," if you spoke the truth. "Taste" is usually a matter of ignorance, or some personal id-iosyncrasy, trusted to overmuch in our culture.

Eclecticism must come to terms—to knowledge. None of the great architectures of the world ever grew up on such a flimsy basis as "taste." Even rare taste such as yours, my dear connoisseur! Nor is it yet calculated by aesthete philosopher or functionist. Great architecture grows as this building grew—true to nature, therefore to materials, method and men—aimed at greatest human benefits by way of least expenditure of money—spontaneous individual insight inspiring more individuals to ever increasing insight until a new technique of a new life is here and individuality is still free. So, this village "skyscraper" is not only the embodiment of human use and comfort; it is a true satisfaction to the *mind*. Not a satisfaction merely to the intellect for that would be as unsure as the satisfaction offered to the taste of this transitory-period. I mean a satisfaction to the mind that *is* a mind and includes a heart.

The fact is this tower-building gets fresh hold on the sense of beauty as a new sense of order, recognizing beauty as something that can never come by putting anything *on* anything at will. It comes as a *quality* (that must be found in the thing itself as reward for integrity of means to ends. Here is individual love of nature—in no "exterior" sense.

You see here an expression of the new city as it might be when decentralization proceeds—no further betrayal of machine increment to hold rents.

PREMISE: This type of tall building may enable you to imagine similar ones, though infinite in variety rising as gleaming shafts of light, tall as you please from every village in the country. Space in town, courting the sunbeams and the view—no masonry cavern standing on the streets—the areas thus thrown back into the village planted as green parks. Out of this varied mass of shade trees and flowering shrubs, see the spider—steel—spinning its web to enmesh glass—glass clear—glass translucent—glass in relief—glass in color. Iridescent surfaces of this light-fabric rising high against the blue out of the whole city, the city now seen as a park, the metal fabrication of the shafts themselves turquoise or gold, silver, bronze; the glass sur-

H. C. Price Company Office Tower ("Price Tower"). Bartlesville, Oklahoma, 1952. FLLW Fdn FA#5215.0005

H. C. Price Company Office Tower ("Price Tower"). Bartlesville, Oklahoma. 1952. Perspective. Pencil and color pencil on tracing paper, 34 x 44". FLLW Fdn#5215.004

faces between the threads of the fabric shimmering with light reflected, light refracted—sparkling light broken into imaginative patterns. Eventually all buildings will stand free of each other in natural greenery. The cost of all this devotion to the value of sunlit space would be, all told, one half the cost of the stuffy caverns it replaces. Imagine the savings thus made, put into ground to free the city of demoralizing congestion, to enable men to live and let live by spreading out into the country and up into the air!

Imagine all these human benefits of our new freedom to be coming alive again by *means of the Machine*. You will then have a glimpse of our forthcoming new machine age, where the man himself is more a man and happier because of his advantages, not allowing them to become disadvantages.

See art now as much nature as Nature is herself. We are developed enough as a people to desire such ultimate features as of "human nature."

We must ourselves *make* it. Artificers . . . all. But artificial only as humble means to a greater integrity of life with Nature. This is the great atonement . . . still possible to the human race in spite of expedient abuses. Without this atonement the race dies—should die. Usonia will never have been born.

1938[2]

This skyscraper, planned to stand free in an open park and thus be more fit for human occupancy, is as nearly organic as steel in tension and concrete in compression can make it; here doing for the tall building what Lidgerwood made steel do for the long ship. The ship had its steel keel: this concrete building has its steel core. A composite shaft of concrete rises through the floors, each slab engaging the floors at nineteen levels. Each floor proceeds outward from the shaft as a cantilever slab extended from the shaft, similar to the branch of a tree from its trunk. The slab, thick at the shaft, grows thinner as it goes outward in an overlapping scale pattern in concrete until at the final outer leap to the screen wall it is no more than 3 inches thick. The outer enclosing screens of glass and copper are pendent from the edge of these cantilever slabs. The inner partitions rest upon the slabs.

There are three offices to each floor and one double-decked apartment to every alternate floor; each apartment is unaware of the other or the offices, as all look outward. The structure throughout eliminates the weight and waste space of masonry walls. The supporting members stand inside, away from day-lighted space and carry elevators and the entrance hallways well within themselves. Two of the exterior walls of every apartment and office are entirely of glass set into metal framing. But the building is so placed that the sun shines on only one wall at a time and narrow upright blades, or mullions, project 9 inches so that as the sun moves, shadows fall on the glass surfaces and afford the protection necessary for comfort.

The building increases substantially in area from floor to floor as the structure rises, in order that the glass frontage of each story may drip clear of the one below, the building thus cleaning itself. Also, areas become more valuable the higher (within limits) the structure goes. The central steel-reinforced masonry shaft extending well into the ground may carry with safety a greatly extended top mass. This building is earthquake-, fire- and soundproof from within by economics inherent in its structure. The structure weighs less than half the usual tall masonry encased building and increases the area available for living by more than 20 percent.

This is a logical development of the idea of a tall building in this age of glass and steel; as logical engineering as the Brooklyn Bridge or an ocean liner. But the benefits of modernity such as this are not merely economic. There is greater privacy, safety, and beauty for human lives within it than is possible in any other type of building.

In plan a 1–2 triangle is here employed, because it allows flexibility of arrangement for human movement not afforded by the rectangle. The apparent irregular shapes of the various rooms would not appear irregular in reality; all would have great repose because all are not only properly in proportion to the human figure but to the figure made by the whole building.

Also the building has complete standardization for prefabrication; only the concrete core and slabs need be made in the field. Our shop-fabricating industrial system could function at its best here with substantial benefits. Owing to the unusual conformations the furniture would properly be a part of the building as the metal (copper) furniture is designed to be. Here again is the poise, balance, lightness and strength that may well characterize the creations of this machine age.

1953–1955[3]

The first expression of a tree-like, mast structure was designed in a project for St. Mark's-in-the-Bouwerie, New York, in 1929. The skyscraper is indeed the product of modern technology, but not suitable if it increases congestion. It inevitably would unless it could stand free in the country. This was the one planned as a feature of the model Broadacre City—so those from the city wouldn't feel lost in that vision of the country, and the Johnson Laboratory Tower is another such. But it was an idea that had to wait twenty-five years for full realization. It is actually built now by H. C. Price in Bartlesville, Okla. The total weight of the building is about ⁹⁄₁₀ of the conventional structure of the Rockefeller Center type, due to cantilever and continuity. Now the skyscraper comes into its own on the rolling plains of Oklahoma.

The urban skyscraper, unintentionally, has hastened the process of decentralization. But, to the rolling plains of Oklahoma it goes as a fresh realization of the advantages of modern architecture yet unknown to the great city. As a tree crowded in the forest has no chance to become a complete entity—standing free it may establish identity and preserve it. The "upended street" by nature gains more natural advantages from natural use of the technical triumphs of steel and glass in pre-fabrication.

Individuality should be no less appropriate to American business, be even more appropriate than to other facets of American life. The Hal Price Company intends to enjoy all there is to be had through complete use of preferred, convenient, compact space open to air and sky; the Price people will be thus surrounded and have access to roof gardens and fountains. Here in appropriate splendid proportion they will defy climatic discomfort, enjoy supremacy, winning dominance at no man's expense but their own.

This type of sheltered-glass tower-building was first designed by myself in 1924 for Chicago and in 1929 for St. Mark's-in-the-Bouwerie in New York. The idea has since been used, more or less, all over the world.

Has our country in the interval grown up to skyscraper status? No—the skyscraper takes a field trip of its own to the place where it belongs—in the country. I believe this type of structure, weighing but a fraction of Rockefeller Center structures, will become a "natural" everywhere in these United States for successful men, for aspiring commerce, for remarkable achievements in engineering such as the one this building tells us about and was built to serve.

Steel, the spider spinning, here serves the democratic principle well—the individual's healthy aspiration—with even more privacy and greater convenience than the lower structures or the ranch house type lower down in the dust in this region.

Freedom of use by interior and exterior occupation, also protection from excess light and air, are here. In this structure, shaded by copper blades and glazed with mellow tinted glass the air conditioning is less expensive and the occupant more comfortable while his "pump" is more likely to hold out where rash extremes of warm and cool now too frequently alternate to tear his human structure down. At his peril man divorces himself from his native climate.

The self-service elevator—now perfected—is part of that especial gadgetry to the advantages of which the American people are sufficiently awake. Someday they will waken to the "payoff" of good design in all their building projects—learning little by little to know good architecture when they see it.

Witness this release of the skyscraper from the slavery of commercial bondage to the human freedom prophesied by our Declaration of Independence.

Democracy builds . . .

1. The year in which Wright designed the St. Mark's Tower for New York. It was not built.

2. The year Wright designed Crystal Heights for Washington, D.C. It was not built.

3. The years of the Price Tower design and construction.

A TESTAMENT

Of all the books Frank Lloyd Wright wrote, A Testament had the broadest agenda. It dealt not only with his ideas, his beliefs, and his principles, but it also returned to the early years of his work to give a much more lucid account of his practice at the turn of the century. In many respects the book was autobiographical. Indeed, he divided the work into two parts, calling the first one, "Book One—Autobiographical."

The book opens with his clarification of the obligation of an architect, and then suddenly plunges into the years he spent with Adler and Sullivan in Chicago, from 1887 to 1893. He recounts how his architectural office was set up in 1893 and presents the friends and comrades (in architecture) with whom he associated at that time. Concurrently, as he explains the meaning of his work—architecture as something once again creative and awakened—he reflects on the early years of his life in Chicago and Oak Park and also on the education he received under the watchful eye of his mother. He candidly expresses the importance of early influences: the Froebel kindergarten training from his mother, the reading of Notre Dame by Victor Hugo, and his first exposure to pre-Columbian architecture in the monograph by Catherwood and Stevens. He reminisces, "I remember how as a boy, primitive American architecture—Toltec, Aztec, Mayan, Inca— stirred my wonder, excited my wishful admiration. I wished I might someday have money enough to go to Mexico, Guatemala and Peru to join in excavating those long, slumbering remains of lost cultures; mighty, primitive abstractions of man's nature—ancient arts of the Mayan, the Inca and the Toltec . . . Architecture intrinsic to Time, Place and Man." Although admiring this ancient source, he distinctly focuses the present: "But now the man, potent lever of primitive authority in architecture, has been given even more powerful means with which to build. The science of the Machine. . . . So many centuries later, American man begins to build again. Something has happened to his buildings. Notwithstanding his new sciences, nor due to them, a more powerful vision has come to him, the higher sense of his own soul."

"Book Two—The New Architecture" opens, "At last we come to the analysis of the principles that became so solidly basic to my sense and practice of architecture . . . the new buildings were rational: low, swift and clean, and were studiously adapted to machine methods. The quiet, intuitional, horizontal line (it will always be the line of human tenure on this earth) was thus humanly interpreted and suited to modern machine-performance. . . . The main object was gracious appropriation of the art of architecture itself to the Time, the Place, and Modern Man."

Step by step, feature by feature, he recapitulated the principles of architecture as he had been designing and building for the past sixty-four years:

There is no more precious element of immortality than mankind as thus humane. Heaven may be the symbol of this light of lights only insofar as heaven is thus a haven. Mankind has various names for this interior light, "the soul," for instance. To be truly humane *is divinity in the only sense conceivable. There can be no such thing as absolute death or utter evil—all being from light in some form. In any last analysis there is no evil because shadow itself is of the light."*

Thus, this second-to-last book—written when he was ninety—was permeated with a sense of finality, in the light of a testimonial, and a desire to "put the record straight once and for all." [A Testament, *Horizon Press, New York, 1957*]

BOOK ONE: AUTOBIOGRAPHICAL

PART ONE

PHILOSOPHY IS TO THE MIND OF THE ARCHITECT AS EYESIGHT to his steps. The term "genius" when applied to him simply means a man who understands what others only know about. A poet, artist or architect, necessarily "understands" in this sense and is likely, if not careful, to have the term "genius" applied to him; in which case he will no longer be thought human, trustworthy or companionable.

Whatever may be his medium of expression he utters truth with manifest beauty of thought. If he is an architect, his buildings are natural. In him, philosophy and genius live by each other, but the combination is subject to popular suspicion and the appellation "genius" likely to settle him—so far as the public is concerned.

Everyone engaged in creative work is subject to persecution by the odious comparison. Odious comparisons dog the footsteps of all creation wherever the poetic principle is involved because the inferior mind learns only by comparisons; comparisons, usually equivocal, made by selfish interests each for the other. But the superior mind learns by analyses: the study of Nature.

The collected evidence of my own active worktime is for my guidance, pride and pleasure as much as for any other reason half so good. Romanticist by nature—self-confessed—I am pleased by the thread of structural consistency I see inspiring the complete texture of the work revealed in my designs and plans, varied building for my American people over a long period of time: from the beginning—1893—to this time, 1957. This architecture is often called "engineering-architecture." I plead guilty to the tough impeachment.

So the poet in the engineer and the engineer in the poet and both in the architect may be seen here working together, lifelong. William Blake—poet—has said "exuberance is Beauty." It took me sometime to know just what the great Blake meant when he wrote that. For one thing, this lesson, now valuable to the creative architect, I would finally illustrate here; in this poetry-crushing, transitory era of the Machine wherein development of a national culture or even a personal culture of one's own has long been so recreant. Blake meant that Beauty always is the consequence of utter fullness of nature in expression: expression intrinsic. Excess never to be mistaken for exuberance; excess being always vulgar. He who knows the difference between excess

Frank Lloyd Wright at the Unitarian Church, Shorewood Hills, Wisconsin. FLLW Fdn FA#6007.0008

and exuberance is aware of the nature of the poetic principle, and not likely to impoverish, or be impoverished, by his work. The more a horse is Horse, a bird Bird, the more a man is Man, a woman Woman, the better? The more a design is creative revelation of intrinsic nature, whatever the medium or form of expression, the better.

"Creative," then, implies exuberance. It is not only true expression but true interpretation, as a whole, of the significance, truth and force of Nature, raised to the fullest power by the poet. That design revealing truth of inner being most abundantly is best design. Design that lasts longest; remembered by mankind with greatest profit and pride.

Art formalized, empty of this innate significance, is the cliché: cut and dried content no longer humanely significant. The so-called modern "classic" has become cliché and does not live under this definition of exuberance. Only the mind of one who has left the region of the soul and inhabits the region of the nervous system in our time mistakes florid or senseless elaboration for exuberance. The "efficient" mind that would put Pegasus to the plough never knows the difference between the Curious and the Beautiful or the difference between the prosaic and the poetic.

ARCHITECTURE IS ALWAYS HERE AND NOW

Victor Hugo, in the most illuminating essay on architecture yet written, declared European Renaissance "the setting sun all Europe mistook for dawn." During 500 years of elaborate reiteration of restatements by classic column, entablature and pediment—all finally became moribund. Victor Hugo, greatest modern of his time, went on to prophesy: the great mother-art, architecture, so long formalized, pictorialized by way of man's intellect could and would come spiritually alive again. In the latter days of the nineteenth or early in the twentieth century man would see architecture revive. The soul of man would by then, due to the changes wrought upon him, be awakened by his own critical necessity.

THE SEED

I was fourteen years old when this usually expurgated chapter in *Notre Dame* profoundly affected my sense of the art I was born to live with—lifelong; architecture. His story of the tragic decline of the great mother-art never left my mind.

The University of Wisconsin had no course in architecture. As civil-engineer, therefore, several months before I was to receive a degree, I ran away from school (1888) to go to work in some real architect's office in Chicago. I did not want to be an engineer. A visit to the pawnbroker's—"old man Perry"—made exodus possible. My father's Gibbon's *Rome* and Plutarch's *Lives* (see Alcibiades) and the mink cape collar my mother had sewed to my overcoat financed the enterprise.

There, in Chicago, so many years after Victor Hugo's remarkable prophecy, I found Naissance had already begun. The sun—architecture—was rising!

As premonition, then, the pre-Raphaelites had appeared in England but they seemed sentimentalist reformers. Beside the mark. Good William Morris and John Ruskin were much in evidence in Chicago intellectual circles at the time. The Mackintoshes of Scotland; restless European protestants also—Van de Velde of Belgium, Berlage of Holland, Adolph Loos and Otto Wagner of Vienna: all were genuine protestants, but then seen and heard only in Europe. Came Van de Velde with *Art Nouveau*, himself predecessor of the subsequent Bauhaus. Later, in 1910 when I went to Germany by instigation of Professor Kuno Francke, there I found only the rebellious "Secession" in full swing. I met no architects.

But more important than all, a great protestant, grey army engineer, Dankmar Adler, builder and philosopher, together with his young partner, a genius, rebel from the Beaux-Arts of Paris, Louis H. Sullivan, were practising architecture there in Chicago, about 1887.

After tramping the Chicago streets for some days I got in with Cecil Corwin, foreman for J. L. Silsbee, then Chicago's foremost resident architect. He was a minister's son—as I was—and so were Cecil and the other four draughtsmen there at the time. One year later I was accepted by Mr. Sullivan and went to work for "Adler and Sullivan" then the only moderns in architecture, and with whom, for that reason, I wanted to work. Adler and Sullivan were then building the Chicago Civic Auditorium, still the greatest room for opera in the world.

The tragedy befallen beloved architecture was still with me, Victor Hugo's prophecy often in mind. My sense of the tragedy had already bred in me hatred of the pilaster, the column for its own sake, the entablature, the cornice; in short all the architectural paraphernalia of the Renaissance. Only later did I come to know that Victor Hugo in the sweeping arc of his great thought had simply affirmed the truth: *Art can be no restatement.*

The great poet had foreseen that new uses of new materials by new inventions of new machine-methods would be devised and therefore great social changes become inevitable in the life of mankind. The poet saw that inherited styles and customs would undergo fundamental change in life and so in architecture: to make man ready to face reality anew in accord with "the great becoming." The inexorable Law of Change, by way of which the very flow of human life provides fresh inspiration, would compel new architecture, based upon Principle, to come alive.

The poet's message at heart, I wanted to go to work for the great moderns, Adler and Sullivan; and finally I went, warned by the prophecy and equipped, in fact armed, with the Froebel-kindergarten education I had received as a child from my mother. Early training which happened to be perfectly suited to the T-square and triangle technique now to become a characteristic, natural to the machine-age. Mother's intense interest in the Froebel system was awakened at the Philadelphia Centennial, 1876. In the Friedrich Froebel Kindergarten exhibit there, mother found the "Gifts." And "gifts" they were. Along with the gifts was the system, as a basis for design and the elementary geometry behind all natural birth of Form.

Mother was a teacher who loved teaching; Father a preacher who loved and taught music. He taught me to see great symphony as a master's *edifice of sound*. Mother learned that Friedrich Froebel taught that children should not be allowed to draw from casual appearances of Nature until they had first mastered the basic forms lying hidden behind appearances. Cosmic, geometric elements were what should first be made visible to the child-mind.

Taken East at the age of three to my father's pastorate near Boston, for several years I sat at the little kindergarten table-top ruled by lines about four inches apart each way making four-inch squares; and, among other things, played upon these "unit-lines" with the square (cube), the circle (sphere) and the triangle (tetrahedron or tripod)—these were smooth maple-wood blocks. Scarlet cardboard triangle (60°–30°) two inches on the short side, and one side white, were smooth triangular sections with which to come by pattern—design—by my own imagination. Eventually I was to construct designs in other mediums. But the smooth cardboard triangles and maple-wood blocks were most important. All are in my fingers to this day.

In outline the square was significant of integrity; the circle—infinity; the triangle—aspiration; all with which to "design" significant new forms. In the third dimension, the smooth maple blocks became the cube, the sphere and the tetrahedron; all mine to "play" with.

To reveal further subordinate, or encourage composite, forms these simple elemental blocks were suspended from a small gibbet by little wire inserts at the corners and whirled. On this simple unit-system ruled on the low table-top all these forms were combined by the child into imaginative pattern. Design was recreation!

Also German papers, glazed and matte, beautiful soft color qualities, were another one of the "gifts"—cut into sheets about twelve inches each way, these squares were slitted to be woven into gay colorful checkerings as fancy might dictate. Thus color sense awakened. There were also ingenious "constructions" to be made with straight, slender, pointed sticks like toothpicks or jack-straws, dried peas for the joinings, etc., etc. The virtue of all this lay in the awakening of the child-mind to rhythmic structure in Nature—giving the child a sense of innate cause-and-effect otherwise far beyond child-comprehension. I soon became susceptible to con-

Daniel Wieland Motor Hotel (Project). Hagerstown, Maryland. 1956. Perspective. Pencil and color pencil on tracing paper, 36 x 19".
FLLW Fdn#5521.001

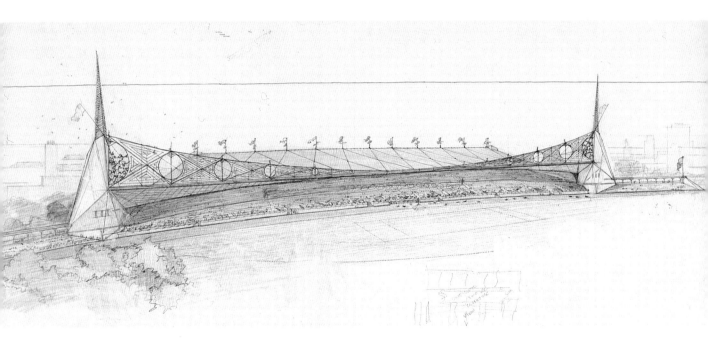

New Sports Pavilion (Project). Belmont Park, New York. 1956. Perspective. Pencil and color pencil on tracing paper, 58 x 26".
FLLW Fdn#5616.020

structive pattern *evolving in everything I saw*. I learned to "see" this way and when I did, I did not care to draw casual incidentals of Nature. I wanted to *design*.

Later, when I was put to work as a teen-ager on my Uncle James' farm in the valley where I now live, this early habit of *seeing into and seeing from within* outward went on and on way beyond until at the age of nineteen when I presented myself as a novice to Mr. Sullivan I was already, and naturally, a potential designer with a T-square and triangle technique on a unit-system; the technique that could grow intimate with and master the rapacious characteristics of the Machine in consistent straight-line, flat-plane effects natural to machine technology, which then, as now, confronted all who were to build anything for modern life in America.

THE CONFUSION

Among most of the architects I soon saw the great mother-art, architecture, completely confused when not demoralized. I saw their work as hackneyed or sentimentalized travesty of some kind; some old or limited eclecticism or the so-called "classic" of Beaux-Arts training encouraged by too many influential American Beaux-Arts graduates. The pilaster again!

But of the *Naissance* needed to replace moribund Renaissance I saw little or nothing outside the offices of Adler and Sullivan to take the place of the futility of restatement at least. Awakening was to come. Whoever then acknowledged the importance of art did not seem to know so well as we now know that art cannot be restatement. Against all this face-down servile perversion by education, encouraged by my early training at the kindergarten table and subsequent work on the farm in the valley, I came to feel that in the nature of Nature—if from within outward—I would come upon nothing not sacred. Nature had become my Bible.

Man the spiritual being, I now saw continually defeating himself—confusing his spiritual power with his mentality; his own beauty lost by his own stupidity or cupidity simply because he could not see from inside by his intellect alone: could not see the nature of his own intrinsic values: see his own genius, therefore. So during those days of early apprenticeship to Adler and Sullivan I found that

when I talked about Nature I was not talking about the same thing those around me meant when they used the term. I could not fail to see (nearby was the Chicago Art Institute) each noble branch of the fine-arts family driven to filch what might be from the great wreck of architecture—the head of the regal family of art—and trying to make a go of it.

To survive, our American art was cheating itself of life. This consequent spread of the tragic Renaissance, I saw largely due to outworn but desperate reliance upon a dated formal professionalism: the Classic. This not alone in architecture but in all the arts; partly, perhaps mostly, due to the fearfully efficient tools, invented by Science, so abusing artists and abused by them. These new tools I saw wrecking the "classic" imitation of ancient formalism, called modern art but founded upon a philosophy completely false to modern life.

Human life itself was being cheated.

All was the same dire artificiality. Nature thus denied was more than ever revenging itself upon human life! The very soul of man was endangered. The Machine thus uncontrolled enlarged, and was living upon, these abuses. Already machine systems had done deadly harm—and more harm, as things were then. Modern machine-masters were ruling man's fate in his manufactures as in his architecture and arts. His way of life was being sterilized by marvelous power-tools and even more powerful machine-systems, all replacing hand labor by multiplying—senselessly—his activity and infecting his spirit. Everywhere these inventions of science by ignorant misuse of a new technique were wiping out the artist. He was himself now becoming a slave. The new chattel. I saw in these new "masters" no great motive above the excess of necessity-for-profit; all likely themselves by way of their own assembly lines to become machines. The kind of slavery that now loomed was even more monstrous and more devastating to our culture now dedicated to senseless excess, so it seemed to me, than ever before. Slavery more deadly to human felicity than any yet devised. Unless in the competent artist's hand.

The pole-and-wire men in the name of social necessity had already forged a mortgage on the landscape of our beautiful American countryside while all our buildings, public and private, even churches, were senseless commitments to some kind of expediency instead of the new significances of freedom we so much needed. In the name of necessity, false fancy fronts hung with glaring signs as one trod along the miles of every urban sidewalk—instead of freedom, license—inextricable confusion. Trimmings and embellishments of trimmings pressed on the eye everywhere, made rampant by the casual taste of any ignoramus. These were all social liabilities forced upon American life by the misconception, or no conception at all, of the mother-art—architecture. Man, thus caricatured by himself—nature thus violated—invaded even the national forest-parks by a clumsy rusticity false to nature and so to architecture. The environment of civilized mankind was everywhere insulted by such willful stupidity.

But soon this saving virtue appeared to me in our disgraceful dilemma: Realization that any true cultural significance our American free society could know lay in the proper use of *the machine as a tool and used only as a tool*. But the creative-artist's use of mechanical systems, most beneficial miracles, was yet wholly missing.

AWAKENING

Steel and glass themselves seemed to have come to use only to be misunderstood and misused, put to shame by such abuses as might be seen anywhere because they were everywhere.

In the plans and designs here presented in much detail may be seen the appropriate uses of the properties of steel in tension in relation to concrete (concrete the new-old plastic). With glass and the growing sheet-metal industries, these were, it seemed to me, only awaiting creative interpretation to become the body of our new democratic world: the same being true of new uses of the old materials—wood, brick and stone.

Often I sat down to write about this as well as continue to design new forms for these new methods and materials. Occasionally, when invited, I went out to speak on the subject of the proper use of all these—always to say "we must know better the here and now of *our own* life in its Time and Place.

In all we must learn to see ourselves as we are, as *modern* man—and this be our true culture." As architects young and old we owed this to ourselves, and certainly to our people. In this country of ours we were free now to abandon outdated idiosyncrasy in the name of taste, or arbitrary academic formalisms without thought or feeling—and learn to show, by our own work, our love and consequent understanding of the principles of Nature. Life *indigenous* was now to be embodied in new forms and more significant uses; new forms of materials by the inevitable new machine-methods yet missing or misunderstood. A natural heretic, I declared these materials and methods to be in themselves a new potential needed in the culture of modern life. Because of the machine itself, architecture was now bound by its own nature to be prophetic. The architect's interpretations would show the way to the right use of these great new organic resources. Our new facilities were already capable of inspiring and enriching human life if provided with true forms, instead of perpetually inciting American life to folly and betrayal of its own nature by ignorant or silly eclecticism or any of the 57 fashionable Varieties of the day. Despite artificial limitations, a new beauty would be ours. Thus awakening to action, we architects had to become effective soon—or our civilization would destroy its chances for its own culture. Instead of by the handle, man had taken this dangerous new tool by the blade!

REALIZATION

In this sense I saw the architect as savior of the culture of modern American society; his services the mainspring of any future cultural life in America—savior now as for all civilizations heretofore. Architecture being inevitably the basis of an indigenous culture, American architects must become emancipators of senselessly conforming human beings imposed upon by mediocrity and imposing mediocrity upon others in this sanitary but soulless machine-age. Architecture, I believed, was bound to become more humanely significant because of these vast new facilities. Therefore not only special but social knowledge of the nature of architecture as presenting man himself, must be greatly expanded. Architecture was to be liberated from all formalistic stylizing by any elite, especially from that perpetuated by scholastic architects or by the criteria of insolent criticism. Architecture of the machine-age should become not only fundamental to our culture but natural to the happiness of our lives in it as well. All this was rank heresy at the time. We have made some progress since because it does not seem so heretical now.

Young heretic, then, I freely spoke but steadily planned all the time: hope of realization firmly at heart—pretty well in mind now, as poetry. I loved architecture as romantic and prophetic of a true way of life; life again coming beautifully alive today as before in the greatest ancient civilizations. We were free men now? The architect among us then should qualify as so inspired; be free leader of free human beings in our new free country. All buildings built should serve the liberation of mankind, liberating the lives of *individuals*. What amazing beauty would be ours if man's spirit, thus organic, should learn to characterize this new free life of ours in America as natural!

RETROGRESSION

But soon I saw the new resources not only shamefully wasted by machinesters but most shamefully wasted by our influential architects themselves; those with the best educations were most deadly. Our resources were being used to ruin the significance of any true architecture of the life of our own day by ancient ideas imposed upon modern building or ancient building ruined by so-called "modern" ideas. Thus played upon, some better architects, then called modern, were themselves desperately trying to reorganize American building and themselves as well. The A.I.A., then composed of architects who came down the hard way, was inclined to be sincere, but the plan-factory was already appearing as public enemy number one.

I had just opened my own office in the Schiller Building, 1893, when came disaster—Chicago's first World's Fair. The fair soon appeared to me more than ever tragic travesty: florid countenance of theoretical Beaux-Arts formalisms; perversion of what modern building we then had achieved by negation;

already a blight upon our progress. A senseless reversion. Nevertheless at that time—now more than sixty years ago—I was myself certain that awakening in our own architecture was just around the turn of the corner of the next year. That year I wrote *The Art and Craft of the Machine,* delivering the essay at Hull House by Jane Addams' invitation. Next day a Chicago Tribune editorial announced that an American artist had said the first word for the appropriate use of the machine as an artist's tool. I suspect that Jane Addams wrote the editorial herself.

By this time the American people had become sentimentally enamored of the old-lace, nervous artificiality of the "classic" grandomania endorsed by the A.I.A. at the fair. It was everywhere in evidence: excess—as usual—mistaken for exuberance. Owing to this first World's Fair, recognition of organic American architecture would have to wait at least another half-century.

"THE CHICAGO SCHOOL"

No school exists without something to teach; and until the phrase "Chicago School" appeared so many years later, I was not aware that anything like a "school" had existed. At the time, there was a small group composed of my own adherents and of contemporary dissenters by nature. The work of Adler and Sullivan was in constant contrast to the work of Richardson and Root; later, Shepley, Rutan and Coolidge (heirs of Richardson), but few of the architects, young or old, then admitted the Adler and Sullivan influence.

Because I was, so far as they were concerned, Sullivan's "alter ego," a small clique soon formed about me, myself naturally enough the leader. Friendships were formed in those early days, especially after the gold letters ARCHITECT were put upon the plate glass door of my office in the Schiller Building. The "followers" were not many: first among them Cecil Corwin and Robert C. Spencer, Jr. (Bob)—first converts to the new architecture. Bob was regarded by his "classic" comrades as apostate because his employers—Shepley, Rutan and Coolidge—had gone "classic" soon after the romantic Richardson's death. Bob and I were often seen together; later he took the office next mine in the Schiller. Chicago conformists working in other offices, seeing us arm in arm down the street, would say in derision, "There goes God-almighty with his Jesus Christ." Bob didn't mind. He stuck. Some others began to "come around": George Dean, Hugh Garden, Myron Hunt, Dwight Perkins, Dick Schmidt and Howard Shaw; all were friendly but not willing to cut their umbilical cord to the Colonial or the French château, the English manor house or the grandomania of Beaux-Arts days.

Before long a little luncheon club formed, comprised of myself, Bob Spencer, Gamble Rogers, Handy and Cady, Dick Schmidt, Hugh Garden, Dean, Perkins and Shaw, several others; eighteen in all. We called the group the "Eighteen."

The "Eighteen" often wanted to know how I convinced my clients that the new architecture was the right thing. "Do you hypnotize them?" was a common question. The idea of an American architecture fascinated them to a certain degree according to the nature of their understanding. Almost all admired what I was doing though they were not yet willing to say it was the right thing.

Gamble Rogers never left the Gothic; Howard Shaw never dared leave colonial English. But most of the others fell in with the idea of some sort of modern architecture. I became original advisory exemplar to the group.

The little luncheon round-table broke up after a year or two. I with those nearest me rented a vacant loft in Steinway Hall: a building Dwight Perkins had built. But Spencer, Perkins, Hunt and Birch Long (clever boy renderer) moved in with me. Together we subdivided the big attic into studio-like draughting rooms. We felt the big attic especially appropriate for our purpose. We each had a share in a receptionist and stenographer in common as "office force" on the floor below, trying to please us all. The entrance door panel was a single sheet of clear plate glass, the second one in existence, like the entrance door to the Schiller offices, with all our names thereon in the same kind of gold letters.

By this time an increasing number of young draughtsmen, like Max Dunning et al, began to come around. I got Lieber Meister to address the Chicago Architectural Sketch-Club, which he did with great effect. Dankmar Adler was dean of the A.I.A. at the time, and he also wrote valuable papers on the subject of skyscraper construction, and the effect of steel on modern life. Meantime, buildings were going up under "the Adler and Sullivan influence." A little of the new was worked in by others here and there. But all in all, from my impatient standpoint, weak if not impotent or cowardly. On occasion, I did say so, but patiently worked on their plans when I could be helpful. My most enthusiastic advocate, young Myron Hunt, was first among them to set up in Evanston, Illinois, as a "modern," with the building of the "White" house. That was a characteristic instance. I believed myself helpful to them all.

I remember an ebullient Italian, Boari by name, who won the competition to build the National Grand Opera House in Mexico City. He came into our attic space, temporarily, to make plans for that edifice. He was far from all of us but observing, curious and humorous. He would look at something I was doing and say with a good natured grunt, "Huh, temperance-architecture!" turn on his heel with another grunt and go back to his Italian Renaissance "gorge" as I called it in retaliation. What he was then doing is now there in Mexico City but badly affected by the universal settlements going on because of the lowering of the water-level beneath the city.

Other work went on in our studio-loft for several more years. But when I had left Adler and Sullivan to settle down in Oak Park, Bob had moved out to River Forest, the next suburb to the west. I— the amateur still with Adler and Sullivan—was able to build a little house on Chicago Avenue; and, on my own, built a studio adjoining my home, where the work I had then to do enabled me to take in several draughtsmen and a faithful secretary, Isabel Roberts, for whom I later built a dwelling in River Forest, now owned by and revised for the Scotts.

But by that time at Oak Park I had lost touch with most of the original group. Into the now flourishing Oak Park studio had come Walter Griffin, Marion Mahoney (later married to Walter), William Drummond, George Willis, Andrew Willatzen, Frank Byrne, Albert McArthur. Others came and went as time went along.

By that time, 1894–5, architecture so-called "modern" had made sporadic appearances here and there around Chicago; reminiscent of Lieber Meister's ornament or something I had myself done or was doing as a dwelling.

George Elmslie—I had brought George from Silsbee's as my understudy (lasting the seven years I remained with Adler and Sullivan and staying on for many more years)—would sometimes come out to lend us a hand in the Oak Park studio, putting in overtime when pressure of work would keep us all up all night, and the dawn would find the boys asleep on their draughting boards.

But, now independent, I didn't use the fascinating ornament, had struck out a new line in a field of my own—the American dwelling: the nature of materials and steel in tension. Of what was going on abroad at this time I had no knowledge nor any interest in. Nor was there any Japanese architectural influence, as may be seen in these illustrations.

DISASTER

Schools of thought, to and fro, soon arose in America—one of them misled by the dictum "Art is art precisely in that it is not nature"; misunderstanding the word "nature." This was really art for art's sake? "Form follows function" came along now also to become the new slogan (also misunderstood). But art was not as yet transferred to the region of the mere nervous system; the nervous system had not yet been mistaken for the soul. But little men were using little brains and little-finger sensibility to confect semblances that "tasted" to them like inspiration, confections mistaken for architecture. All but several architects seemed to be trying to annul the idea of architecture as noble organic expression of nature; the Form-Follows-Function group seeing it as a physical raw-materialism instead of the spiritual thing it really is: the idea of life itself—bodily and spiritually—intrinsic *organism*. Form and function as one.

Well—Daniel H. Burnham was right. The Chicago World's Fair became the occasion of modern architecture's grand relapse. The nature of man was there reduced to the level of a clever trained animal: Architecture contrived as a hackneyed ruse to cheat modern life of its divine due instead of serving to glorify it. Beaux-Arts intellectualism was the aesthetic that could only eventuate as some kind of menial to the monumental. Therefore "classic" misuse of the "Classic" slandered the noble idea of art as organic, and I was compelled to see that it would go on so long as man had no true sense of his own dignity as a free man. Only if his intellect, which had been stimulated but pauperized by education, again became subject to the inner laws of his own being, could he be a valid force in Architecture, Art or in Religion: only so could he ever rise creative above our inventive sciences in the grasp of the Expedient. Otherwise his life in America would remain helplessly afloat upon a sea of corrupted taste; no realization would be possible.

CONTRIBUTION

When man's pride in his own intellect was set up as an anti-nature-formalism in art, he became responsible for the dictum: "where every prospect pleases and only man is vile."

Different were the Orientals and different were Jesus, Shakespeare, Milton, Blake, Wordsworth, Coleridge, Keats, Shelley, Beethoven, Bach, Brunelleschi, Goethe, Rembrandt, Dante, Cervantes, Giotto, Mantegna, Leonardo, Bramante, Angelo. Different were the prophets of the human soul. All masters of the Nature of Man and the hosts they have inspired. No longer trying to lift himself by his boot-straps or busy cutting out the head of his drum to see whence comes the sound, man by nature still creative may grow.

MAN AND THE MACHINE

As Victor Hugo wrote also in *Notre Dame,* Gutenberg's invention of shifting-type was the beginning of the great triumph of the machine over all the fine-arts and crafts of architecture. By way of the machine came the soulless monstrosities now so far out of human scale as to be out of hand. Death came to handicraft and to any corresponding culture in the world, blindly inherited by us. As for America, cultural confusion had already come upon us in our new "house," almost before we were born. Buildings, business, education—all were becoming great enterprises stimulated by infatuations with science and sentimentality concerning the past. The inventive engineering of mechanization lacked the insight—creative poetic imagination, let's say—to recognize the power of interpretation by architecture of these vast new facilities. As they came fresh from science, they but stimulated the cupidity of commerce. As for the architects, they were either silent or huddled in the lap of overpowering change. Our capitalism was a kind of piracy, our profit-system tended to encourage low forms of avaricious expansion. American culture, such as it was, wore a false face, a hideous masquerade. Success was misunderstood as essential to progress. Really success was worse than failure. Wanton denials of humanity were made by machine-power, abetted by the impotence of artists and architects, themselves blind to the fresh opportunities, really their duties. Such failures as they were making of life, then as now, were a standardized slander upon the liberated individual rather than any true reflection of his innate power. Thus doomed to spiritual sterility, art and architecture were facing extinction in all the hell there was.

Well, nevertheless—rather more—I kept on planning, preaching, presenting the real social need for the creative artist-architect—the competent, conscientious interpreter of his kind and time! But where were such architects? Was the A.I.A. alive to the new ideals? The story by now might have been different if the A.I.A. had not been more interested in architects than in architecture. In such circumstances how could the architect's vision become effective action? Could action come to grips with selfish forces to humanize their excesses by rejecting their power, to evolve the new forms modern man needed to sustain the freedom he had declared, 1776? This was up to the greater architect we had neither inherited nor cultivated. Because of this default I kept trying to gather together the dangling, loose ends, so twisted by this confusion; gather them little by little into organic synthesis of means to ends, thus showing with all my might the idea and purpose of organic charac-

ter and proportions in building, if made appropriate to life under American Democracy.

New architecture was fundamental necessity. But it seemed impossible for architecture to rise without deeper knowledge of the poetic principle involved. The slide-rule of the engineer could not diminish, but only cherish and confirm, all this damnation—and did so.

The needed interpretation had arrived in my own mind as organic and, being true to nature would naturally, so I thought, be visible to my fellow architects. In spite of myself, because becoming more and more articulate, I became a kind of troublesome reminder—a reproach to my fellows. Naturally enough I would not join the profession to help make a harbor of refuge for the incompetent? So, deemed arrogant even by those who might have been expected to go a little deeper and go to work themselves, I had to go it pretty much alone— Lieber Meister gone.

THE FIELD

Among the architects practising in America when I entered Adler and Sullivan's offices, Richardson had the high honor of the field; Beaux-Arts graduate, Bostonian well-connected with the better elements of society, the Adamses, etc. But Richardson had robust appetite for romance. His Romanesque soon overthrew prevailing preferences for Renaissance. Eventually he became the most productive and successful of those men, the great eclectics of their time. Many of them fell in love with his love of the Romanesque. Yes, his Romanesque soon amounted to something wherever his fellow architects were concerned with a style.

Louis Sullivan himself kept an eye upon Richardson's superb use of stone in the arch. H. H. Richardson's use of the arch in early days, "but not his ornament," had a visible effect upon Lieber Meister. Richardson disciples were legion; his success was tremendous. Henry Hobson Richardson, though an artist and giving signs of emerging as modern, was just what America deserved most but should have had least—a powerful romantic eclectic. Gone now.

Anderton Court Shops. Beverly Hills, California. 1952. Perspective. Pencil and color pencil on tracing paper, 29 x 31".
FLLW Fdn#5032.001

McKim, Mead and White, Richardson's elite running competition, were also Beaux-Arts men. Their eclecticism was of another more elegant order, faithful to the more choice effects of early Italian (moyen-age or better-day) Renaissance. In their affected cultivated stride they took the ancient buildings verbatim. Whenever they found the buildings they admired, they copied them, enlarging the details by lantern slide. Used them straight. Their following was, of course, automatically more socially elite than Richardson's but extensive. Gone now.

Richard M. Hunt, darling of New York's four hundred, head of their procession on Fifth and other American avenues, was a good technician with a finished preference for the French-Gothic ensemble. He was fashionable, too, his eclecticisms immensely popular and profitable to him. But not to America. Gone now.

There was another much less idolized group, to which Adler and Sullivan, Major Jenney, John Root, Cass Gilbert, Van Brunt and Howe and several others, belonged. Of them the only men indicating genius above engineering ability and the capabilities of front-men were Louis Sullivan and John Root. Of Root it might be said that Sullivan was slightly envious because the two firms, Adler and Sullivan and Burnham and Root, were in direct competition, the latter firm having the best of it. Then Root's office building, the Monadnock of Chicago, might be put against Louis Sullivan's Wainwright of St. Louis. Although the Monadnock arose later, it was vital too, but an unsuitable forcing of the material: brick. See the unbricklike molded corners.

The strain of genius in Root was far less than the miracle of genius in Sullivan. Unfortunately Root barely survived the Chicago World's Fair, in the planning of which he had a major hand, supported as he was by the great master-manager, his partner Daniel H. Burnham, head architect of the Fair. He, "Uncle Dan" ("make no little plans") would have been equally great in the hat, cap or shoe business.

Of young aspirants at the time there were many, mostly head-draughtsmen like myself. There were also independents like S. S. Beman, J. L. Silsbee and many other talented men in the offices of the Middle West and of the East, such men as the Beaux-Arts Carrère and Hastings, etc., etc.

The Chicago World's Fair was a procession of this talent that brought these leaders of their profession out into the open. Their merits and defects might be there seen and appraised. Due largely to "Uncle Dan" Burnham's ("Frank, the Fair shows our people the beauty of the Classic—they will never go back")[1] ability to promote ideas of Charles McKim et al, the Fair reopened wide the case for European Renaissance, and America had a memorable field day à la Paris Beaux-Arts. The "Classic" easily won and the more pertinacious and influential among the more successful architects of the A.I.A. were for the time being almost totally in command. "The eye of the vox-populi" (as a popular Fourth of July orator once put it) opened wide in dreamy-eyed wonder at the Chicago World's Fair. The ambitious ignoramus in the architectural profession throughout America was captivated. The old, old story! By this overwhelming rise of grandomania I was confirmed in my fear that a native architecture would be set back at least fifty years.

But Louis Sullivan's Transportation Building was the only picture building at the Fair presented by the Paris Beaux-Arts itself with its distinguished gold medal; which must have astonished the Beaux-Arts society of America. A society of which the original French Beaux-Arts seemed not to think highly, as I learned long years later, 1940.

Such in broad outline was the rough contour of the A.I.A. during my apprenticeship with Adler and Sullivan. There in the Adler and Sullivan offices high in the Chicago Auditorium Tower I worked for nearly seven years—George Elmslie alongside—occasionally looking out through the romantic Richardsonian Romanesque arches over Lake Michigan or often, after dark, watching the glow of giant Bessemer Steel converters reddening the night sky down towards South Chicago. I looked from those high-up arches down upon the great, growing city of Chicago as the Illinois Central trains puffed along the lake front.

CIVILIZATION AS ABSTRACTION

This abstraction we are calling Civilization—how was it made and how is it misused or being lost now? By "abstraction" I mean taking the essence of a thing—anything—*the pattern of it,* as the substance of reality. Incidental effects aside, the *heart* of the matter would lie in the abstraction if well made, and nature truly interpreted—expressed in pattern by the true artist: Linear and spatial significance of the reality *within*—this is what is patterned forth. If thus intrinsic, this is the artist's contribution to his society: truly the *creative* artist's affair. Our customs, costumes, habits, habitations and manners, all are, or should be, such abstractions; and made, as such, true to the great abstraction we call civilization. That, genuine, would be our culture. If the abstraction is truly made well above the animal nature in man— his gregarious nature—it will keep the ancient rituals of his higher nature as long as possible. Human abstractions if true usually become rituals. Once made, although the ritual may become "obsolete," the original abstraction will be cherished by man because the rituals recorded what his kind once considered beautiful to see, to feel, to hear or to know. Sometimes all together.

This retention of the abstract as beautiful goes to the extent that few now living can distinguish in those abstractions (civilizations now dead) what differs essentially from those still alive. "Taste" still meanders about among them all— confused as it is in this vast forest of the ancient abstract. "Taste," waif or prostitute, lost in the interminable stretches of the abstract. We therefore need the prophet always to make new abstractions for life more in accord with the eternal Law of Change. This is largely the service the creative architect renders to his society, now no less than ever. The service he alone may render with conscience, justice and lustre.

What means more to the life of the individual in our own place in Time than this study of the nature of human nature, the search to discover pertinent traces of hidden impulses of life, to form continually new abstractions uplifting the life he lives? From such intensive introversion issues inestimable treasure for extroversion in interpreting his civilization. This, alone, justifies the trust that society must repose in the architect if creative. The true architect is a poet who will someday discover in himself the presence of the tomorrow in our today.

POET—"UNACKNOWLEDGED LEGISLATOR OF THE WORLD"

Then, as now, I knew that he alone could have the inspiring insight needed to give human society true answers—answers always related to philosophy continually new. Yes, I knew, even then, that the revelations American society needed to go with our new declaration of faith in man could not possibly come from science. Except for Louis Sullivan among the many poets I knew and have named, there were then none among all the architects of this world. The poet had been too long absent from architecture. So long indeed, architecture was no longer considered as a great creative art. But where might the soul of any humane culture we might ever know be found unless in architecture?

Thoreau, Emerson, were ours. Yes. And then, too, Walt Whitman came to view to give needed religious inspiration in the great change: our new Place for the new Man in our Time. Walt Whitman, seer of our Democracy! He uttered primitive truths lying at the base of our new life, the inspirations we needed to go on spiritually with the brave "sovereignty of the individual." Might not the *spirit* of creative art, desperately needed by man, lie in the proper use of the radical new technologies of our times, and so arise? Not from, nor by, any established authority whatsoever, nor any religious sectarianisms. This kind of inspiration was nothing to expect from the committee-mind or from any officialdom. I well knew it was not there. Sixty years ago I knew that until the needed inspiration could be found forthcoming in architecture—enlightened instead of conditioned in this realm we have been calling Education—we would probably look in vain for coherent interpretation of our time and our place in time.

Consider that the United States of America appeared 160 years ago with this unique, inspiring message that started a world revolution in government. Freedom for the human being to be his better self! Reflect that man thus became the unit of a civilization itself *individual*. See how inspired and brave were our founders. What courage then to declare *officially a nation* of people free! Consider too: Were American freemen conscious of being newborn to the mundane society of this world, how inevitable to America, then, was great art and so as its basis a genuine architecture. *Organic* to go with the nature of that Declaration! Organic architecture based upon this new faith, not only faith in mankind's manhood but faith in the man as himself *creative;* man always greater than any system he might ever devise! Therein fresh opportunity came to us. Modern man enabled to conceive and achieve a new harmony with life. New hope now for a man to improve himself— *as himself:* to serve with good conscience the new idea of State according to his ability. Men were now bound to *grow;* to become useful leaders in their own time, in their own country, because they were now free to use and be used by their fellows each to each preserving the integrity and beauty of life for each and so for all. This was what our new democracy, as a form of government, meant? Heresy when it was declared. A quandary even now?

CONFORMITY

Unfortunately conformity reaches far and wide into American life: to distort our democracy? This drift toward quantity instead of quality is largely distortion. Conformity is always too convenient? Quality means *individuality,* is therefore difficult. But unless we go deeper now, quantity at expense to quality will be our national tragedy—the rise of mediocrity into high places.

Servility increases—already a seemingly unguarded danger to democracy not only in art and architecture and religion but in all phases of life. Between the radical and the conformist lies all the difference between a lithe tendon and a length of gas-pipe.

Because of this all the more, it was for illustrious *sovereignty of the individual* that I wanted to build. Too little of the beautiful had ever been built for man's personal life on earth and nothing whatever by government with the depth of understanding essential to this new ideal of manhood. So, 1921, I wrote (badly) *The Disappearing City,* followed this later by *When Democracy Builds,* prophesying and promoting the inevitable American City of tomorrow—ours if democracy is to survive.[2] At least I did succeed in outlining what I thought would be the center-line in building democratic man into his environment according to his new ideals of government, by means of his amazing new scientific leverage: the machine. Planning the new city now became organic: organic building design and construction. This new city belonging to America also to accord with our political Declaration. Accordingly, Taliesin (1932) modeled Broadacre City. I saw it coming as an irresistible current to vindicate new uses of science and bring closer to reality the new vision of man's social integrity as an individual. I had learned to see the right use of machine-craft as a living element in the organism of our society—and therefore bound to come right side up in the American City. I saw this new city denying all enforced formalisms in any style whatsoever. I saw our big cities as the overgrown villages they are—over-invested, under-engineered, unclassified, the outmembered, over-numbered, over-gadgeted cliché of antiquity. European civilizations of the Middle Ages had left us our city and we had done nothing with it but cram it with gadgetry. We, the last word in progress, were still back there with Sodom and Gomorrah. See the chapter in Genesis where Cain, the murderer of his brother, went forth with his sons to found the city. The City still murdering his brother.

NEW THOUGHT

Other than the declaration of the master-poet of our world: "The Kingdom of God is within *you,*" it seemed to me that organic architecture was the only visible evidence of this in modern art. Old definitions were sadly lacking perspective anywhere; new definitions were now imperative all down the line: definitions long past due in religion as well as art. This new-old philosophy, too—and therefore—had to appear if we were ever to experience inspiring creation and—soon enough—find a basis for the free culture we might honestly call our own. We the American people would learn to develop a true humane joy in the environment of our daily life, and achieve beauty of life—the home as a work of art part of this vision. This, despite all confusions, I saw wrought by and for the self-hood of the individual. But confusions of the public "taste" were only increased by self-made, self-willed, self-styled critics, also an affliction by "taste." I then believed critics were by nature no less confused than confusing.

Were I as an architect to work thus for the Beautiful—I loved the idea of "romantic"—in the everyday American city and the country by myself, my first thought must be a valid social science, a conscious point of view in society: philosophic thought basic to democracy, organic planning no less basic to a new architecture fit for the machine-age. What necessarily then, would such organic planning be? Naturally true to our Declaration: thought free. Not only the artist's motive free but also the *political* basis of the democracy we love as an ideal made valid and try to believe we still desire, free.

ROMANCE—THE FREE PHILOSOPHY

Comes to our American view, then, the highest form of aristocracy yet known—the highest because *innate:* Aristocracy natural as the quality of the man himself, no longer *on* him but *of* him: aristocracy his, not by way of privilege nor inheritance, but truly his: a quality developed from within himself. Unique.

The ancient American architectures of the Inca, the Mayan and the Toltec are lying centuries deep buried in the earth where ages ago instead of the free soul of man, the cosmic-order of sun, moon and stars inspired primitive man to level mountains and erect great temples to his material power.

Again in America we erect temples but this time not so much to the mystery of great terrestrial or cosmic forces as to the interior or spirit-power of manhood as released by American democracy and its sciences. How much greater is this new expression of the soul of man! A new light may shine from every edifice built by the human mind.

JEFFERSON'S ARISTOI

Thomas Jefferson prophesied the democratic Aristoi. We his people must now not only meet the radical changes in our political and social systems but face no less these changes in the basis of our culture. If integrity of spirit inheres in man, its natural countenance will be found in his architecture: the countenance of principle. Because architecture presents man as he is, he will live anew in the free spirit of organic architecture of our own time.

New, but still natural, interpretations of man in a living architecture thus become our privilege. A new abstraction, as civilization, arises to express the new life-of-man as free. He is yet a changeling of tide and time. This I believed long ago even as I became an architect, trained at the kindergarten table. So nearly everything I saw standing outside myself—man-made—had to be *new*. How could buildings any longer be of past or future "schools" so-called? There could now never be schools! Schools could only be remade and so be makeshifts: old cultures that were originally in themselves eclecticisms.

But now for us must come an America neither modern cliché nor ancient classic. Nor any habitual repetitions, restatements, restorations, under which the spirit of man has so long languished to disintegrate. For 500 years at least, these pressures of temporal authority have prevailed. The old manipulations of mankind by authority, politics, fashions, academic pressures, prevailed but were not really authentic.

Fresh cultural life, now to issue from the "reality within," begins a new world!

INTEGRITY

Meantime many contumacious substitutes have arisen and more will arise. A natural or organic architecture, as modern, has already been misused. Much perversity has been extolled, admired as expedient. Worthless architectural façades in novel materials are now commercial posters—hailed by the "avant garde" as modern. Abuses are disastrously imposed as proper uses upon sincere but ill-advised efforts and the clever apostate is here and there front-paged and lionized, as usual in our country. The widely accepted prophet is rarely prophetic. Seen as heroic he is too often only the blind leading the blind. Thus the plausible expedient has become gospel and continues to be generally foisted upon those who seek better things; the conformities proclaimed by authority, however specious, temporarily mistaken for Godhead. But if they were seen for what they are worth in the realm of art as they would be seen in other realms, I am sure that the world of architecture would rise above the current abuse of the thing-mistaken-for-the-thing, to rebuke and reject these traces of simian ancestry now appearing as modern.

In every new expression of a fundamental Idea there will always be the substitutes, the imitations, dangling from it, as the soiled fringe from a good garment. It takes long years to learn that superficial commotion is habitually mistaken by our provincial society for emotion, and that motion itself—action—is dangerous: the danger ever precedent to the practice of any new essential truth. This weakness in our provincial society I have seen during the more than sixty years of my own practice of architecture: see it now none the less, perhaps exaggerated by television, radio and press. So any deeper desire for indigenous culture thus is impeded.

How, then, can it be eagerly sought by our people? A deeper hunger is needed spiritually than we seem to know. The popular desire for entertainment is exploited by the commodity merchant all down the line. In upper social brackets, as in lower, there does not seem to exist enough desire to fight exploitation by mediocrity for a more enlightened life in art but rather a disposition to succumb. Therefore beauty of thought and grace of entertainment as well as beauty of environment suffer. The culture of the spirit we so desperately need we will discover with a *new integrity*—the integrity actually necessary to preserve our civil liberties! We will learn to see what is consistent with the poetic principle in the way of daily living. If our lives are to be sacrificed let it be for a humane, more beauty-loving tomorrow: make this new age more lasting and beneficent than any lying back there in ruins ever was. We should not be looked back upon tomorrow as merely the Scientific or the Sanitary Age. This means that America must be wholeheartedly involved in the arts of town-plan-

Point View Residences Apartment Tower, Version #1 (Project). Pittsburgh, Pennsylvania. 1953. Perspective. Pencil and color pencil on tracing paper, 30 x 35". FLLW Fdn#5222.001

ning and living in homes that are true works of art. This new integrity is now possible to us: as a free people we must know how to use the new sciences for genuine culture; the only genuine culture is indigenous culture.

Beautiful buildings are more than scientific. They are true organisms, spiritually conceived; works of art, using the best technology by inspiration rather than the idiosyncracies of mere taste or any averaging by the committee mind.

NEW OR OLD

Almost all our so-called "modern" is not yet new. It is merely novel by imitation or indirection; or pretense by imported picture. Our fresh architecture will be based upon nature, reinforced by the genuine democratic sentiment already existing among us as a people—a people conscious of it as the proper basis of survival as a democracy. Whether we yet know it well or not, we of this Machine-Age are growing inevitably toward organic unity not only in our

Point View Residences Apartment Tower Version #2 (Project). Pittsburgh, Pennsylvania. 1953. Perspective. Pencil and color pencil on tracing paper, 29 x 34". FLLW Fdn#5310.001

architecture but in every feature of our national as well as of our private life: no *re-birth* in philosophy, art or religion for us now in any form. Birth itself.

All this as *new* is not clear enough yet, not naturally enough our social purpose. Did it so seem to our forefathers?

Why is this not more widely recognized as *natural* in the realm of education? Is it because civilization itself proceeds only by the authority of intellect and so soon becomes non-integral? Is false abstraction always the consequence of spiritual degeneration? Is decline of the spirit toward utter materialism the reason why it is so difficult for any ideal to survive? Is only the gas-pipe (materiality) safe and the lithe tendon (spirit) so difficult? Is the human nervous system now being groomed by the slaves of the expedient as a substitute for soul? If so, vital abstraction is unlikely now.

Creation is not only rare but always hazardous. Always was. But why is it growing so much more hazardous now? Is it owing to our "systems," educational and otherwise, that we seem to be capable always of less and less rather than more—less *vision* and less love essential to the understanding of exuberance? Comes to mind a triad from the old Welsh *Mabinogion* defining genius: A man who sees nature. Has a heart for nature. The courage to follow nature.

NAISSANCE

Renaissance no longer. Comes *Naissance:* Nature. Just as Naissance has always come to the brotherhood of man at the critical moment so it came to us as a nation in the brave Declaration of principle. 1776. It has come to our architecture as the dawn of a natural free American spirit in building ourselves "into" our country, and really began about 1890. This in but one American century of civilization is dawn indeed. Thus inspired, there can be no prolonged discouragement hereafter. Many new buildings, characteristic of our own place in Time and of modern Man, have already appeared East, West, North and South. First appearing on American prairie, Midwest, they aimed to be organic and appropriate and so refused to accept, accent, or in any way serve the old forms of either European or Ori-

ental architecture. From the start, confident, seminal, inspired by the love of architecture as well as the nature of man, notwithstanding the prevailing confusion, waste and slip by the abuse of machine-powers, the new architecture came gradually into view—in focus by 1893. A prophecy sustained.

REVERSION

Unhappily for this early development, old-world ideas of architecture revived at the Chicago World's Fair by the professional A.I.A. had already been so firmly fixed by official and educational America that reaction was reprompted and spread countrywide over the surface of our nation. The prophecy of "Uncle Dan" already quoted, "Frank, the American people are going 'classic'" came true. European or Beaux-Arts training—old ways in architecture—were indeed "going"! Became more than ever a stumbling block. The "classic" more than ever hindered organic architecture. Even now it is confirming the robbery of our proper use of scientific invention.

THE VIEW

Most critics of the time, as we then knew, were masters of or mastered by the odious comparison; or were inexperienced, teaching architecture by book. All were well-meaning enough but mostly made by academic armchair or managed publicity of some kind. Naturally all these agencies, though willing enough, were helpless, when deeper independent thought was urgent, especially in discriminating where architecture concerned the culture of our own society as distinguished from other societies. It has remained the blind spot of our nation. Architectural magazines were naturally more interested in architects than architecture. Architecture was not a subscriber. To them, as to the plan-factory magnate, the cliché proved a godsend. If they abandoned the one it was only to take up another. Whatever the likely cliché happened to be or wherever it came from, it was quickly salvaged by publicity and accepted, promoted and fed to the American people as the proper thing. To "the improper press" the cliché most useful in advertising and standardizing the vast fabric of our industrial and educational system was always the latest one; the names changing with stunning rapidity. But although organic architecture had already met the crushing blows of machine-age science with the right technique, not for another half-century was it to become at all operative in education. The struggle to and fro on the part of our own robust new thought, or any action based upon it, did not prevail then against the firmly established standard that "culture had to come from abroad." Suspicious always of change, established order was as usual hostile to enlightenment. So the art of building as an organism remained unfamiliar except to the more discerning, courageous, and already sentient American individual.

BETRAYAL

As one consequence (even as a cause) architects of that period did not love architecture enough to have it on their consciences—nor did their successors. Our so-called "modern architect" lived, then as now, a curious hybrid. Gadget-lover and servile auctioneer of novelty, he was prime merchant of the commonplace; speedster in all ways; quick to arrive first along the beaten path. Were he a shell-fish he would not hesitate to eat holes in his own shell. Could anything be made of *his* "housing" or *his* government's? But he has happened to us, to our country, and thrives under enormous bureaucratic expansion. Look at the seashell—and listen to the indictment of this hybrid.

FAITH IN MAN

Again: mainspring of any true architecture is sound philosophy of Nature. Wherever it appears unhampered, it is the basis of the only indigenous culture yet to appear in our modern American life. The new architecture is not yet "officially" understood at home because not imported. So if not imported, as culture, not "safe"? No. No matter how sane. As for our political esthetes if they had only a glimpse of the significance of the philosophy of the new architecture, they would know it to be native. But therefore inutile or controversial. Being controversial, government would shun it. To sponsor it would not be safe for a politician because there is always "the next election." Besides since "culture has always come from abroad anyhow—why not forget the whole native thing?"

Nevertheless original organic architecture, widely recognized abroad, is now being accepted here at home although the principles upon which it stands have had little comprehension. In government, good or bad, and in education, too little of it is yet established. Gradually growing, but still puzzling or offending "arty" or routine architects and critics educated far beyond their capacity. Only among the better citizens, able to function independently of the popular effects of managed publicity or mannered art do we find the practicing architect not servile to fashion nor influenced by academic authority. Is he rare because architects have to live or because they are not sufficiently alive—and so not fit to live as architects?

THE TROJAN HORSE—CONFIDENTIAL

Germany, 1910. After Kuno Francke's admonition at Oak Park, "Your life will be wasted here, do come to Germany," I remember Herr Dorn, majordomo of the world-famous Wasmuth Publishing House of Berlin once introduced me, when I first arrived, as "the Olbrich of America." Curiosity aroused, I went to Darmstadt to see Olbrich, only to find that the famous German architect had just passed away.

About fourteen years later, when several German architects of whom I had then not heard—Mies of the Barcelona Pavilion, Gropius of the Bauhaus, Curt Behrendt of Prussia and, later, Erich Mendelsohn of the Einstein Turm—came over to America—I welcomed them all as sincere advocates of the battle for freedom in the dynamics of a new architecture. They knew in 1910 that I was waging a one-man war. Some twenty years or more later, it appeared that Mies (owing to Hitler's closing of the Bauhaus) was available for the post of leader at Armour Institute. The motion was seconded by me with what influence I had. Mies first arrived at Taliesin, before taking up his post in Chicago. He stayed with us there for a fortnight, speaking no English. Soon to be inducted at Armour; a banquet was given in his honor by the A.I.A. in the ballroom of the Palmer House. Mies, feeling himself a stranger, did not want to go unless I went with him.

The banquet was standard as those things go but a fulsome affair, functioning chiefly through the A.I.A. M.I.T. President Emerson read an unctuous falsification of modern architecture. Speakers of welcome, all face down to modern architecture from abroad, followed suit. All this seemed false to me and false to Mies as well. But, Mies, of course, understood nothing, sat ready to read the twenty-minute paper he had written in German at Taliesin. I was sitting next to Emerson on the raised platform where the principal speakers were gathered to honor modern architecture from abroad. Next me sat Mies. By this time I was wondering: why not let Mies speak for himself and be properly translated? But when finally his turn came I put my arm around his shoulders, led him to the podium and said, "Ladies and Gentlemen—Mies van der Rohe! Treat him well. He will reward you. He will now himself address you. He is worthy of any support you can give him. Ladies and gentlemen, I give you Mies van der Rohe." Accent on the *I*. Then, displeased, turning the podium over to Mies, I left the room, not because I did not understand German but because the whole affair had made me feel the attitude toward both Mies and myself was false; just as false to itself; another proof that modern architecture for the A.I.A. had to come from abroad. A.I.A., in one way or another, was itself from abroad—mostly Beaux-Arts à la Paris. The fact that modern architecture had been originated by a contemporary in Chicago was simply not to be borne.

Well, the twenty-minute paper Mies had prepared in his own language he proceeded to read in full, all expecting a proper translation. My friend, Ferdinand Schevill (Chair of History at Chicago University) was present. He said that Mies' paper was to be translated by A.I.A. president Woltersdorf. Woltersdorf appeared, shuffled his feet, cleared his throat several times, looked toward President Emerson for help. Finally he said, "Ladies and gentlemen, Mr. van der Rohe says he is so sorry that Mr. Frank Lloyd Wright left so early." And that was all the assembly ever heard or will ever know of the van der Rohe acceptance speech on his American debut—unless they understood German or have since read a copy that may exist, somewhere.

Said Dr. Schevill later, "Frank, Mies van der Rohe's speech throughout was a splendid tribute to you. Obviously this was not what these A.I.A. sponsors wanted or expected. Thus—clumsily—when it appeared, they cut it out."

CONSEQUENCES

Nevertheless the straight-line, flat-plane effects, the new shapes of shelter I had published in Germany (1910) and France (1911) have, by stimulating world-wide imitation and some true emulation, scattered far. As one consequence, temporal novelty often appears upon our urban streets; and façades more quiet than usual. They not only loom upon our urban streets, but ride our housing in countless subdivisions. But as yet, *no deep satisfaction*. This "modern-architecture" we see as a negation in two dimensions. An improvement? Yes, but with too little evidence of the depths of the architecture conceived according to Principle, built from inside outward as organism. The essence of construction itself is yet haphazard or old-fashioned steel-framing of the box. Natural elegance, the true serenity (due to indigenous character) of an organic original seems likely to be lost: sterilized by studied stylizing or by careful elimination of all ornament and pretty much all but the box-frame with a flat lid. The tranquil emphasis on space as the reality of the building is mostly missing. Parasitic practices appear everywhere, credit given to this or that new name. Always new names. But no matter how many, such derivations from the outside in all run dry. Then there are the novelty-façades that have appeared in our big cities, usually façades glassified as steel-framed boxes, often great mirrors acting as commercial posters. Fair enough! But why call this manifest advertising in the abuse of new materials, architecture? Is it possible that the City is entitled only to such negation?

Angelo Masieri Memorial Student Pension and Library (Project). Venice, Italy. 1953. Perspective. Pencil and color pencil on tracing paper, 19 x 25". FLLW Fdn#5306.002

Nevertheless a conscientious architect learns to understand the nature of human nature so well that the character of his structural ability may eventually justify calling organic architecture man's love of life presenting man to Man. Democracy needs this inspiration to keep democracy alive and the American people free.

Meantime pseudo-scientific minds, like those of the scientist or the painter in love with the pictorial, both teaching as they were taught to become architects, practice a kind of building which is inevitably the result of *conditioning* of the mind instead of *enlightenment*. By this standard means also, the old conformities are appearing as new but only in another guise, more insidious because they are especially convenient to the standardizations of the modernist plan-factory and wholly ignorant of anything but public expediency. So in our big cities architecture like religion is helpless under the blows of science and the crushing weight of conformity—caused to gravitate to the masquerade in our streets in the name of "modernity." Fearfully concealing lack of initial courage or fundamental preparation or present merit: reactionary. Institutional public influences calling themselves conservative are really no more than the usual political stand-patters or social lid-sitters. As a feature of our cultural life architecture takes a backward direction, becomes less truly

Lenkurt Electric Company Factory (Project). San Carlos, California. 1955. Office interior. Pencil on tracing paper, 23 x 19".
FLLW Fdn#5520.014

radical as our life itself grows more sterile, more conformist. All this in order to be safe?

How soon will "we the people" awake to the fact that the philosophy of natural or intrinsic building we are here calling organic is at one with our freedom—as declared, 1776?

THE EXPEDIENT

Circumstances I have been describing indicate lack of spiritual insight inspired by love of our own nation.

The old-time "committee-mind" is the devil's advocate in education, being justified there by the teaching of "teamwork" as safer substitute for inspiration. This justification is admission of spiritual failure. As a people we remain comparative strangers to our own life in our own time in our own home: native culture waiting in vain on our door step. Our foreign relations—nationalities abroad—seem to have inherited better perspective. Having once enjoyed a culture of their own is it easier for them to recognize indigenous culture when they see it? The peripatetic cliché, shallow by nature, is their expedient too but it cannot, there as here, wake up the average business mind in commerce; although there too, whenever this mind says *practical,* only *expedient* is meant. They say that substitutes are everywhere preferred to originals in America because originals, having more character-value and strength, are not so easily controlled and exploited as the substitute. Nor can imitation ever do more than insult original inspiration. Imitation is always insult—not flattery.

THE SUBSTITUTE

The national recourse is the substitute, freely distributed in mutual byplay between the kind of journalese-architect, popular educator and museum-director—purveyors of the fashion—all more or less in the business of themselves—therefore all "busy" with such activity as I have described. For this, if for no other reason, degeneration of creative ability in America has had ample support, and what nobility our society might still have is in danger of being submerged in overwhelming tides of rising conformity. The artist-teacher too becomes only a conformist trader when he should by no means be either. Knowledge of principle as creative is still

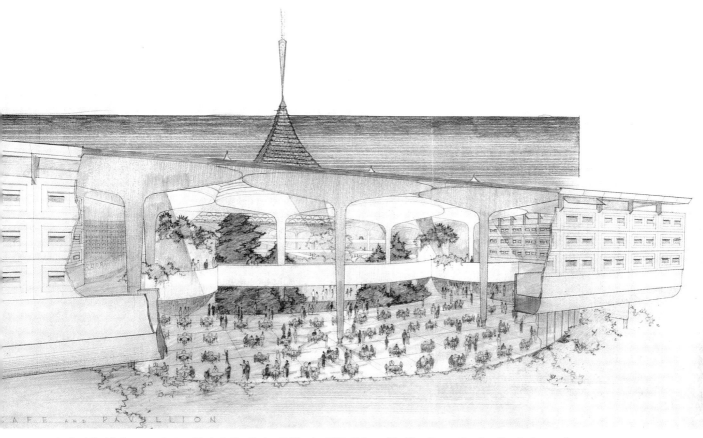

CAFE and PAVILLION

Lenkurt Electric Company Factory (Project). San Carlos, California. 1955. Cafe and Pavilion. Perspective. Pencil and color pencil on tracing paper, 63 x 36". FLLW Fdn#5520.004

behind us or under foot, the uncommon slandered on suspicion and left to be revived by the youth of the future.

Meantime the multitudinous substitutes for indigenous culture cannot grow. Having no roots, they can only age and decay. Studious, sincere youth retires, defeated. American youth, capable of becoming serious competent artists, under such pressure as this on every side, confused, try not to give up—or "fall in line." This is the nature of about all that can be called American education in the arts and architecture at this time. As for religion true to the teaching of the great redeemer who said "The Kingdom of God is within *you*"—that religion is yet to come: the concept true not only for the new reality of building but for the faith we call democracy. Nevertheless and notwithstanding, I have wanted to *build* this faith—life-long.

"THE COMMON MAN"

Our schools today, busy turning out "the common man," seem to be making conformity a law of his nature. The study of architecture is often relegated to the abandoned military shed or the basement of our educational institutions, and the old adage— "those who can, *do,* those who can't, *teach*"—was never more truly descriptive of purveyors of "the higher education" in architecture. Life-long I have been shocked by the human deficiency capitalized by American education.

Many of our young men are eager, groping; hopeful that our civilization, now over a century and a half old, may still wholeheartedly desire indigenous culture and enable the fundamental distinctions between art creative, science inventive and taste intuitive to be learned by schooling. But they are fed

Lenkurt Electric Company Factory (Project). San Carlos, California. 1955. Perspective (night rendering). Tempera on black illustration board, 65 x 31". FLLW Fdn#5520.016

prejudicial comparisons instead of the results of patient intelligent analyses or performance based upon nature-study encouraged. Forced to choose this or that personality, they must give up trying to find their direction within themselves, their powers of interior analysis weakened and confused by stock comparisons. Comparisons made by whom? By those who themselves have been bred upon similar comparisons—all odious. No wonder that persistent analysis based upon actual experience is so rare.

Also, "Truth told with bad intent beats all the lies man can invent."[3] Truth faces this travesty today.

This is no exaggerated indictment of our nationwide neglect of basic experience and principle as a qualification. Regents, curators, professors and critics, with too few exceptions seem paid to honor by comparison—still unable to go deeper into the vital nature of art. Should our life be either ready-made or made to the measure of this conformity, by casual journalese or the prophets of the profit system? Why should it be essentially influenced by such personal opinion as our critics and museums seek to inflict? The answer seems to be that education has not learned to draw with firm, courageous hand the dividing line between the merely Curious and the truly Beautiful; and knows culture only by rote or hearsay or taste. Science may easily mistake the curious for the beautiful and often does, instinctively preferring the curious. For evidence we need only go to the buildings in which scientific education unwittingly administers paralysis of the sense of beauty to the optic nerve. This fatal defect in "the higher learning" is tragic and can only beget servility to our "catch-as-catch-can" culture. Reform only means more conformity. It is form first that is needed. And it is not to be found in sporadic endeavors to remodel our lives by imported aesthetics—even if we import our own export. We will not be able to maintain faith in democracy merely by profit-system equipment, nor help it grow by the conditioning our youngsters receive in the name of education.

THE NEED FOR THE NEW AMERICAN

New enlightenment and courage is needed to help resist such influences. The soul of any civilization on earth has ever been and still is Art and Religion, but neither has ever been found in commerce, in government or the police. We cannot long console ourselves with the thought that we are at the mercy of a numerical materialism. Votes are counted. Yes—but vision can neither be counted nor discounted.

Our good hope lies in the hearts of men and women of vision rather than in the minds habituated by such education as we now provide. Democracy's best hope for survival lies in, let's say, the upper middle third of our American families—the better units of our present society. In the communications we at Taliesin receive daily from students in the high schools of the nation, I see teenage interest in architecture already evident there: Dynamic spiritual force, parallel to the spirit of our democracy itself—when not pushed too far scienceward or arrested by conformity; or when not too sentimentally inclined by parental sense of tradition or confused by the categorical-imperative in art—is now organic and therefore poetic. Art expression is by nature romantic; and this awakening interest cannot long survive without a sound philosophy to give it direction and true religion to give it emotion. Both Art and Religion are on the way. Both must go hand in hand as ever before. Both together illuminating our sciences will constitute the soul of this civilization.

MAN ABOVE LAW OR LAW ABOVE MAN

By attempts to keep man-made law alive when by nature it is dead, the spirit in which law was made is betrayed and so is law. My father taught me that a law is originally made to prevent or cure some timely, manifest evil; the law usually made by "experts." (An expert? Generally, a man who has stopped thinking because he knows!) So whenever court judgments continue to be based upon "the letter of the law," long after the good intended by the letter goes out of it, judges defy its sense and betray justice. The law, whenever (too often) put above man, ceases to shed the light of reason. Justice then becomes, not true servant of the humanities, but mere routine; and so we fail of democracy, robbed of our title to manhood. Again, the calamitous drift toward conformity. Again, fear instead of reverence for life as hoped by our forefathers. Again, "bigness" legally engendered—by standardizing human beings into "the common man."

Yes, and because the "common" man is a man who believes only in what he sees and sees only what he can put his hand on, he—the hero of "all men are created equal but some are more equal than others"—is by lack of vision made to become a caricature of himself.

Do not call this exploitation of massology—Democracy. Mobocracy is the more proper term: When any man is compelled to sign away his sovereignty as an individual to some form of legalized pressure by government or society or to some kind of authorized gangsterism democracy is in danger of sinking to communism. This shall not be our fate.

WALT WHITMAN—SEER OF DEMOCRACY

When Walt Whitman, asked for the cure for evils of Democracy, replied, "more Democracy," for us he touched a great truth. But patriotism can eventually become "the last refuge of the scoundrel." What did our poet of democracy mean by *democracy?*

The terms of democratic salvation may only be found deep within man himself by his comprehension of the basic principles of nature and of his own human nature. Then—without popular prejudice, sentimentality or fear—we will achieve the native culture we can *honestly call our own.* We will reach the expressions of our own democratic nature by probing the depths to discover our one-ness. More important than war or "segregation" is this original idea of "integration"? Integration that lies implicit in life as in art, architecture and natural religion.

BEGINNING

Back to the Froebel kindergarten-table. Presented by my teacher-mother with the Froebel "gifts," then actually as a child I began to be an architect; unless long before, when I chose my ancestors with the greatest care. So this son of a teacher-mother and a musician preacher-father grew up blissfully unaware of worldly conflicts in our brave experiment in human liberation, as here presented. Many years later when I had grown up and began to practice architecture it was in time to become keenly

aware, perhaps too zealous, where the social situation I have been trying to describe was a concern; thus earning the epithet "arrogant."

Looking backward now: When I put the gold letters "Frank Lloyd Wright Architect" on the plate-glass panel of my office door in "The Schiller," 1893, the causes of the cultural lag I encountered lay in the social bias created by growing eclecticisms in the practices of the A.I.A. Dead-sea fruit of inadequate architectural education. The true character of American life was being submerged.

Nevertheless—rather more—owing to this social confusion of ethics in our ways and means, there was growing up native strength enough to keep faith with this vision of the new birth in art and architecture, the awakening prophesied by the great French poet: first made imperative by the American Declaration and Constitution. We have come thus far to see the end, forever, of "restatement" as creative art. We know that the beginning of all true significance in great art must be not only appropriate but parallel in philosophy to our faith in man. The fundamental new freedom in architecture was on record about 1893; the new philosophy in architecture came to parallel in art what had been so bravely asserted by the original statesmanship of 1776. American architecture confirmed the prophecy of Victor Hugo by becoming action; beginning to feel sinews anew, take on vital flesh, lift its head high for new vision. New forms were born—forms natural to freedom! Shapes in building, unfamiliar but peculiar to the modern circumstances of machine-technique, were then evolving. Engineering advances by adventure in new machine-age materials and techniques began to be natural and many of these are to be seen in the illustrations herewith. For the first time, then, new straight-line, flat-plane, "streamlined" designs, adapted to machine uses, became more or less familiar as technique to architects (imitations of these effects you may buy today as a cliché from the plan factories). These new effects were born with a new sense of integrity. They were not unbecoming nor devoid of human grace. Call that grace: ornament. Even though a disgrace, machine-made, ornament stayed and still thrives.

John Gillin House "Alladin" (Project). Hollywood, California. 1956. Perspective. Pencil and color pencil on tracing paper, 44 x 30".
FLLW Fdn#5528.004

But no sincere help for "the new reality" was found in any authoritarian body, either Beaux-Arts or A.I.A. No jealousy is comparable to professional jealousy, so this trait was to be expected by the new architecture to say nothing of a new architect. So the New by sheer force of character was compelled to break through neglect and barriers continually arising and due to private and public indifference, animosity or fear—the dominant characteristics of "culturists," promoted and patronized by machine-masters, themselves becoming merchandisers of "the Past." Our tradition was the inexorable Past. As regents and leaders, these would-be bulwarks of tradition had and still have ownership in the realm of education. Worthless traditions were "safe." Ideas not utterly archaic but traditional were alone respectable. This graft upon the future still called

conservatism. As a matter of fact our social register itself was then not much above a market record. Family and especially official society, if unconsciously, made merchandise of itself. All purblind cultures were thus on sale, our "57 varieties" were made available by the A.I.A. itself to the elite who kept on buying by taste—and regardless.

Thus culture at the time I was entering the practice of architecture seemed to be hopelessly involved with making a living. It was this mongrelized affair which had never learned the values of native beauty or even realized the virtues of original beauty. The meretricious substitute everywhere: the elite, enthusiastically all looting "from abroad," were scavengers in the name of "refinement." William Randolph Hearst was perhaps ideal exemplar in this class

though he had powerful competition. American wealth quite generally founded "modern" museums, and art institutes were dedicated as educational enterprises to this or that; town libraries all over the country were thrown in. An amazing mass of perfectly good material was to be found there, all wrong in the right places or right in the wrong places. Too many of these public benefactors were simply buying tickets for a preferred or at least a respectable place as a reward for these virtues to be conferred in the hereafter?

Reading here like merely a sordid old-wives' tale, this dreary addiction to excess by American success was really a teeming hive characterized by will, speed, ruthless competition, contradiction and fury but always action, getting the unintended insult to

the fore with amazing hindsight. For my part, by this time on my own, the master (L.H.S.) gone—I faced this tantalizing and threatening challenge to what I stood for: the end of which is not yet seen—if ever? Can co-existence be effected between body and soul by science? No. By art and religion? Yes, together with science. I am bound to think that we in America have the answer in the principles of building called organic architecture.

INSIDE OUT—OUTSIDE IN

In order to become national reality, this intrinsic philosophy (new and yet so ancient) now interior to the competent architect as man or creative artist, must, so I see, destroy any cultural or educational fetish whatsoever; especially destroy the fetish of "a style," a cliché.

Yet to come to modern architecture, as official, in this world is *Style* as style for its own sake. But never—now—should we in America be caught in the fetters or the talons of *a* style. Certainly not, when natural building is free to live from within outward with our magnificent new equipment. Already the Idea is again vital and fascinating. The triumph of spirit over circumstance is evident nation-wide. This expression of idea if genuine has always had style and so always sure of popular appeal. "Style" is becoming an American "natural."

PART TWO: FORM—A BIRTH

Again to architecture comes the serenity of the right idea; human integrity is in action. True significance of line, color and form is now the very method of construction. Principle itself is looking out from our American habit of thinking about planning not only buildings but planning the new city; developing this beauty in our villages by appropriate uses of ground: learning now how to build and dwell in a building as a work of art: dwell harmonious with our own Time, Place and Man. We need be apostate no longer. Now we are apotheosis, able to master our vast facilities of machine power and the sciences.

New methods and new means continue to arrive. Well-adapted forms may be seen based upon Principle instead of Precedent! Instead of the incongruous selecticisms, ambiguous forms of a dated aristocracy, forged by illegitimate taste upon the legitimate patterns of machine craft, here come the concepts of genuine forms to rescue character from ruin by false leadership or any hangover from the Renaissance: perhaps rescue America itself from recession? Our era is still young, yet more or less nostalgic, so Victorian in spite of our progress. The motorcar is yet a wagon trying to digest four wheels when ruts no longer exist. Etc. But Ruskin and Morris are now "once upon a time." Going and gone also are the ites and all isms of the modernistic. The rational is no longer inimical to art and architecture or the reverse. The spirit may live anew.

NEW PHILOSOPHY

This philosophy of organic character develops new strength; timely apprehensions going deeper (and wider); penetration into the heart of "matter"; the true nature of a new building-construction is now indigenous. When understood as a principle it applies to architecture anywhere on earth. The great mother-art, Architecture, is still living. Never in history has timely philosophy asserted itself in action more quietly or simply. Witness, here, Unity Temple, the Taliesins, the Hillside Home School and the Larkin Building. Amidst turbulent changes a way of building has brought to our society a new integrity. Principle recognized despite our hectic superficiality. Integrity has been proved feasible in actual practice. These simple buildings themselves show architecture to be *organism,* based upon: "part is to part as part is to whole." Only such entity can live. Inevitably this nature-concept was individual in architecture as it was individual in the Declaration of Independence and characteristic of the nature of man himself. Wholeness of humane expression in architecture is now assured. Never again could successful building be otherwise. "Such as the life is, such is the form."[4]

Poets, Jesus and Laotze leading them, have so declared from time to time. Poets the "unacknowledged legislators of the world"; preservers of the human race. Laotze expressed this truth, now achieved in architecture, when he declared the "reality of the building does not consist in the roof and walls but in the space within to be lived in." I have built it. When Unity Temple was built this sense of interior space began to "come through": 1906.

NEW INTEGRITY

To Americans thus came natural, free building. For mankind *the ideal* of man free, therefore his own building humanistic. Both these freedoms I understood then as now to be basic to all our modern art, parallel to the *idea* by which we live and have our being as a people. This is the meaning of democracy. Architecture will never long be satisfied by the shell itself nor by anything done to it in the name of Architecture. It will now be conceived only as integral feature of Interior Space. Because of this more humane sense of cultural integrity by this new way of building, entity is born to put an end to mere machine-age depravity in our culture. This new ideal to shape appropriate environment for life—free—is now true determinant of technology and no less of style!

PRINCIPLE BEFORE PRECEDENT

Here then is new "school." Principle-before-Precedent. Negation of the national current of haphazard, standby, knockdown taste: new basis for all kinds of aesthetic or ethical achievement. A new "school" able to turn right side up almost all perversions by modern*ism,* enabling the architect forever to prevent the return of classicism. Struggle for natural performance in American architecture begun all over again. To continue . . . how long?

In any case liberal in thought means liberal in art. The nineteenth century has given birth to new achievement: comes in time to be in tune with the awakening prophesied "late in the nineteenth century or early in the twentieth . . ." Now comes a twentieth-century architecture. The mother-art of civilization should be able to live no longer tied down by formalistic fashioning nor be put into harness or into uniform either by academic education or political authority; be further stultified by science or vulgarized by commercial success. Our human environment may now be conceived and executed *according to nature:* the nature of Time, Place and Man: native as was always natural to cultures wherever life in the past was strongest, richest and best. The level always highest when *native.*

This upshoot of indigenous art is already dedicated to our democracy: alive none too soon, organic expression of modern life square with our forefathers' faith in man as Man. Sovereignty of the individual now stems true as the core of indigenous culture in the arts and architecture. Yet to come to us as a free people is the organic *religion* natural to this new era of organic faith in man. Organic economy would naturally follow. Sovereignty in this sense of a new religion is needed to go hand in hand with man truly free. Human sensibilities, little by little, are opening to vistas of the new America.

"NORMALCY"

The more any building as Idea is true to the Idea itself the better I like the building. The more it is likely to be in itself a free wholeness of expression of the Idea. It stands then for the ideal building that would be wholesome as a work of art. And the more the home is a work of art in our society now the better even for the selfish property instincts of the owner.

What is called "efficiency" among us is to be regarded with suspicion, or impatience, because it has too little sympathy with the deficiency that now goes with it. The alcoholic, the chain-smoker or habituate in any form has, for me, a claim upon pity too strong to be borne. I have always regarded him with wonder or suspicion. So to be a doctor was not an ambition of mine. I believed that all was possible if in full accord with nature. I believed that less than this was the result of either poverty or sin.

So I have grown up intolerant of any "falling short" by way of pretense, artificiality, limitations or scholasticism or of any form of brainwashing. Insufficiency of any sort becomes increasingly the mortgage on freedom. Mercy is a divine quality, and always somewhere as a quality of my soul, but too often severely "strained." If mercy was spontaneous (genuine) I loved the quality of mercy, perhaps most of all, divine. But I have always hated "efficiency" *per se,* as I see it standardized in American life in big or little business. No less hate it in daily life as the "E Pluribus Unum" of success. Life thus over-organized is always deficient, soon becomes a form of imposition.

What I am trying to say is that life is fullness of love when *normal to the human being* and it is so either in the realm of ideas or in the nature of building—or conduct. Body, if used as and when *guided by spirit,* constitutes man's true virtue and the quality that distinguishes him from the brute. Exuberance has always seemed to me constituent good health. Poverty of any kind I view with deep dread as a kind of punishment flourishing upon deprivation. Exuberance to me early meant ecstasy of love, the poetic principle of life. Therefore, Beauty, as the poet

PRO BONO PUBLICO ARIZONA
FRANK LLOYD WRIGHT ARCHITECT

Arizona State Capital "Oasis—Pro Bono Publico" (Project). Phoenix, Arizona. 1957. Longitudinal Section. Pencil and color pencil on tracing paper, 60 x 36". FLLW Fdn#5732.006

Blake said it was. In this sense I have loved life with pertinacity and delight in ever new phases of idealization—in which love itself is realization. These eternal springs of inspiration never run dry for the human spirit in love with Nature's exuberance. Through lack of this life-given exuberance, love from within, the fountain-head of Art goes dry.

The "classic" was excess negation by rote: dry. The Renaissance became a dry tree. The "tree dry" was William Morris' withering symbol for jealousy or hatred. To this day it is so to me. Nature's own inexhaustible fertility is manifest exuberance, and never less than the elemental poetry of all her structure. So it will be in the structure of all our native culture when we do arrive at a culture of our own. The love we know as beauty and the beauty we know as love will be natural to our civilization and no longer will every prospect please while man alone is vile. I propose as the symbol of this love— the tree.

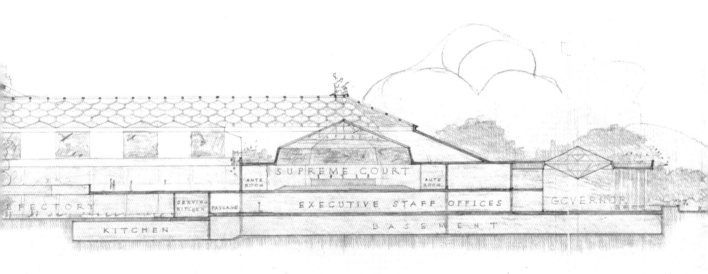

The labels visible in the drawing read: SUPREME COURT, ANTE ROOM, ANTE ROOM, EFECTORY, SERVING KITCHEN, PASSAGE, EXECUTIVE STAFF OFFICES, GOVERNOR, KITCHEN, BASEMENT.

THE NATURE OF NATURE

I would here again eliminate confusion too often caused by my use of the word "nature." So many years ago when I began to write and speak upon the subject of architecture I used the word to mean "the interior essence of all cause and effect." My sense of "native" thus took the inner nature of the poetic principle to be right in whatever it might consist or make manifest. *Truth,* this was, of any object or condition: this was to me the innate sense of *origin.* The original.

According to my training at my mother's kindergarten table this was the activating *cause* of all visible effects. Nor, later, was it necessarily moral, but always ethical. For instance, the essence of a brick, of course, lies in its brickness. In a machine it lies in its dependable mechanism. The same of a human heart, a sinew or a screw or any interior activating impulse or synthesis; parts whether of a pump, a brook, a stone; sex, a scoundrel or a poem. All this became inexorable thesis of man as a whole.

Innate sense of scale then was proportion. Really investiture of life in our present time—not to be distinguished from all time? I have continually asked myself this question. What is the great or small difference between "then and now"?

What is this life of ours today; is man in his new place in Time? What kind of Man is this man of today? What of his civilization? Nature is how now? What is Man as he is? Where does this activation of life-force apply to old or new form, and what is substance as he represents it to be God or Devil? What lies ahead of us all now as we wander confused in the capacious lap of Change? Are we really helpless as we seem? What would be the nature of the abstraction that could be intelligently made to clarify and defend us in what we are calling "civilization"? In short, in what does man really consist as he exists in our native civilization?

The answer to all such questions lies implicit in human Nature. I have always wanted to build for the man of today, build his tomorrow in, organic to his own Time and his Place as modern Man. Therefore come these questions about *him*. And what is Art, now? What countenance would his life on earth really wear if not spurious or on masquerade? Of course it should be expression of his spirit and natural to his circumstances. Is it? Now, what Architecture would be *natural* to him? Can any man maintain this prevalent divorce from nature under the new freedom? But is man yet capable to live as the world's "free man"? Would he be capable of *anything* natural as things are with him? For so long has his excitable nervous system been his substitute for soul—how much is left of his soul now? Has modern man, by his taste for sensation and desire for security, become prone to mere expediency? Can his education, too long fashioned upon his expediency, be more than a false moment in history? Has false environment already made him a mere numerical factor, trampling with the herd? Is this atmosphere of ugliness he now endures actually created by him without his knowing it to be the result of his own confusion of mind? Or his impotence? He has lived so long subject to conformity or conflict that his judgment is atrophied? Has his habit of servility to custom and circumstance become servitude to mediocrity? Or is it that he fears his taste for the "unusual" might shut him in or shuttle him back again to insecurity? (There is nothing so timid as a million dollars.) Why does my brother live as a mendicant in this servility he thus puts upon himself or is put upon him because he puts it upon others? What is this modern man's true nature? Is something deadly put upon him by his false sense of himself extended to others? By being so far educated beyond his capacity is he unable to learn within himself from Nature? Divorced as he is from her, who and what can now be his? Does the so-called free man of democracy merely exploit his sovereignty?

Let us look back. I remember how as a boy, primitive American architecture—Toltec, Aztec, Mayan, Inca—stirred my wonder, excited my wishful admiration. I wished I might someday have money enough to go to Mexico, Guatemala and Peru to join in excavating those long slumbering remains of lost cultures; mighty, primitive abstractions of man's nature—ancient arts of the Mayan, the Inca, the Toltec. Those great American abstractions were all earth-architectures: gigantic masses of masonry raised up on great stone-paved terrain, all planned as one mountain, one vast plateau lying there or made into the great mountain ranges themselves; those vast areas of paved earth walled in by stone construction. These were human creations, cosmic as sun, moon, and stars! Nature? Yes, but the nature of the human being as he was, then. *Entity even more cosmic* had not yet been born. The machine then was but a simple lever in the hand of the slave: man himself a menial, subject to the cruel despotisms of high authority; priests imposing "divine" mysteries upon his lack of a better sense of himself. This he called "divinity" by equally mysterious authority. By the will of despots his hands were thus tied behind his back. He was himself but an obedient tool. His magnificent masonry was architecture beyond conceivable human need; truly monumental. Monuments to the gods of temporal power were laid out and built upon the great man-made stone-paved earth-levels of South American plateau. Architectural grandeur was thus made one with the surrounding features of mountainous land; made by wasting away the mountains; mountains moved at will by the simple persistent might of the human being multiplied, a man's own strength multiplied by the strength of multitudes of his kind. By such direct and simple multiplication of strength his buildings grew to be man-mountains. All were built as and for grandiloquent religious rituals to stand forever in the eye of the sun as the earthly embodiment of the mystery of human majesty, honoring deity. Thus man was made into, built into, living harmony with surrounding mountains by the physical might of primitive man. Reverence for authority was thus made manifest and mighty by the nature of manpower thus animated. All this great, man-building took place with a splendid human sense of primitive resources and the majesty of what was then apprehended as Man's place in Nature. All was exponent of great nature and, as we have called civilization, an abstraction. There was architecture by powerful primitive manpower. Basic it was, but based upon glorified abnegation of man to authority because of what he himself did not know. Such was his worship. His sense of beauty as a mighty son of Earth! Man's God involved with the worship of means to ends then—as now? A grandeur arose in the scale of total building never since excelled, seldom equalled by man either in truth of plan or simple primitive integrity of form. Architecture intrinsic to Time, Place and Man.

NOW—FREEDOM IS FROM WITHIN

But now the man, potent lever of primitive authority in architecture, has been given even more powerful means with which to build. The science of the Machine. Already a power grown to dominant world-power. Worship of this power has grown by means of the man of science. But science in true human civilization is but a tool. Science is inventive but creative never.

So many centuries later, American man begins to build again. Something has happened to his buildings. Notwithstanding his new sciences, nor due to them, a more powerful vision has come to him, the higher sense of his own soul. This is his own sovereignty—his freedom as native American.

Interior vision far greater now even in grandeur of construction, himself therefore more deeply creative as an individual, there comes to him this concept of "might" as spiritual. The dignity and worth to himself of the soul of individual man—a man no longer a tool of power or of a monarch or of any exterior authority, a man not bowed down to sacrificial mysticism but man free. Kingship now of his own soul ruled by conscience and increasingly cultured intelligence. This man has risen: himself gradually coming awake to power even greater than man's primitive power because it is power of the spirit. A new ideal of civilization arises based upon freedom of man's mind guided by his conscience. In view of this new abstraction the past subsides. Ever higher come new interpretations of old power by man's new might. Spirit is man's new power if he is to be truly mighty in his civilization. Only Art and Religion can bring this new vision as reality to a nation. Only the free man brings freedom. This new sense of life comes to his own nation and to the modern world as well. So Art and Architecture, soon his Religion too, must be new. The spiritual dignity of this new humane life for mankind, is the Spirit of Man himself sacrosanct. America has made this commitment. How are we to live up to the promise of that commitment? Where find the true sacrifices by and for this new man in this new world we call the United States of America?

This new release of the spirit of man comes to pass in our own good turn of time. Therefore to architecture comes a new sense of scale; the scale of the human being, man himself. Greater freedom all along the line of habitation becomes not only his desire but his privilege. A great simplicity is now his; the simplicity of perfect organism may be his in what he does. Human dignity based upon union of man's physical nature with his spiritual sensibilities.

His philosophy henceforward will cherish this freedom he has accepted and is endeavoring to establish for himself. But he has not yet wrought this new philosophy into terms of his modern life as the old philosophy of the ancient primitives was wrought into theirs. When he has done this, his dangerous new tools instead of the practiced human

Arizona State Capital "Oasis—Pro Bono Publico" (Project). Phoenix, Arizona. 1957. Perspective (night rendering). Tempera, color pencil, and pastel on black illustration board, 40 x 32". FLLW Fdn#5732.004

Max Hoffman House Version #1 (Project). Rye, New York. 1954. Perspective. Pencil and color pencil on tracing paper, 49 x 36".
FLLW Fdn#5504.006

Arthur Miller House (Project). Roxbury, Connecticut. 1957. Living room perspective. Pencil and color pencil on tracing paper, 40 x 33". FLLW Fdn#5719.002

hand will be used by him to make his liberation not only wishful theory but actual life—incomparable. But if they are not so used by him, a greater enslavement than ever now looms for him. Man either learns to use for humanity his new facilities or he perishes by them. A true sense of this new power in building-construction is basic to his civilization now. In architecture he will still find the basis of his new culture. At last this realization is dawning upon him.

In the realm of his own imagination come forms found only in freedom of spirit. Space outflowing instead of static containment. Liberation a fulfillment. Architecture no longer any kind of fortification but generously spacious and plastic. Thus expression of the new freedom no longer aggrandizes exterior forms of power but truly liberates man's sense of himself as Man. Instead of fortifying life by extraneous means and remaining subservient to ancient earthly gods—now comes our revelation that man conceives nothing higher than the soul of man himself and when he interprets himself from within, his outward expression will be all the heaven he could imagine and so desire. We call him thus, in himself, great Architecture. Trusting the great "becoming" as always he is in himself the omnipotent Idea. Forever becoming, always on his way to life eternal.

Thus comes to us the new sense of the true building: free in design, poetic but no less, even more, invulnerable shelter from the elements. Space free—space *flowing outward* by way of forms appropriate to life and circumstance. Appropriate *in human scale,* significance comes alive and works for mankind more at one with the character of man's spiritual nature.

For instance, here see the third dimension becoming a fourth; the architect's sensibilities throughout as creative artist becoming aware of democracy in a medium appropriate to his new life. Daily needs are no longer met by the old inappropriate architecture. Sound and practical these poetic liberations are when seen. The straight-line, stream-lined, flat-plane effects appropriate to proper use of his new advantages in this age of the machine are quiet but in the quick. Architecture is of elemental beauty again and of increased service to mankind.

THE EUROPEAN CONTRADICTION

This concept of architecture as organic, as expression from within outward, is twentieth century—a new sense of building entirely. The concept a "natural." Out of this concept comes interpretation of the third as a fourth dimension: the third seen not as thickness but as depth. Independent of any European influences whatsoever this twentieth century contribution, as a negation of previous concepts of architecture went to Germany, 1910 or earlier. And this—although originally an *affirmative* negation—became, in the European nineteenth century contribution, a negative affirmation, still applying to the old bridge engineer's concept of steel framing—structure from the outside in—the brittle box emphasized as brittle. Unless much mistaken in what I see at the core of the effort I am afraid it has too long remained so. Now past the middle of the twentieth century, European architecture is still nineteenth century in concept. Louis Sullivan's buildings were nineteenth century prophetic; the European contribution is nineteenth century reminiscent.

Yet almost all of our architecture here in America still speaks with foreign accent. First the accent was British, then the accent was French, then German.

Simple truths of the nature of the originating idea of modern architecture from the outside in and the space concept—are just beginning to be recognized by our critics. The new architecture was never so much "functional" as it was dynamic humanism. Solidly based upon the new humanities and modern sciences as the cornerstone of our genuine American culture, it has lacked penetrating criticism. Dynamic forms true to democratic sentiment would become more expanded and extended had such interpretation been forthcoming: life would have become by now more humane, imaginative and colorful. All this has passed unrecognized by current "criticism." In the practice of the dated cliché, our modern riches have gone by default into a sterile classicism: the steel framing of the box. (Don't go near the window!) The crack in the picture-window is widening.

DISCOVERY

From the prophetic nineteenth century work of Louis H. Sullivan, twentieth century architecture issued by way of the Hillside Home School, the Larkin Building, Unity Temple, the Coonley and Robie houses, the Imperial Hotel and the block houses (The Millard, etc.) of 1921 on.

In this connection, I remember Kuno Francke, German exchange-professor of aesthetics at Harvard (one of Theodore Roosevelt's exchange-professors), came from Harvard to Oak Park (1909) with his charming wife. Herr Professor came to see the work I had done of which he had heard at Harvard. Astonished and pleased by what he saw already accomplished when he came: the Coonley, Robie, Winslow and Cheney houses; Unity Temple; designs for other buildings; he urged me to come to Germany. Said Kuno Francke, "My people are groping, only superficially, for what I see you doing organically: your people are not ready for you. Your life here will be wasted. But my people are ready for you. They will reward you. Fifty years, at least, will pass before your people will be ready for you."

I did not want to go to Germany. I could not speak German. Fascinated by what I was already doing, I declined this invitation. Professor Francke soon returned to Germany. Several months later came the proposition from Wasmuth (well-known publisher in Berlin of art works) proposing to publish the work Kuno Francke had seen (all of it) if I would come to Germany to supervise preparation. A few months later, cancelling obligations of every nature in the field of architecture and at home, I went; risking the worm's-eye view of society I felt must follow. There in Germany and Italy I lived and worked for a year. In the little Villino Belvedere of Fiesole, massive door of the villino opening directly upon the steep, narrow little Via Verdi of the ancient old Roman town on the hill above Florence—I found sanctuary. Just below the little villino spread downward to ancient Firenze the slope where so many distinguished refugees from foreign lands had found sanctuary and were still finding harbor. Most of that year—1910—I worked preparing the forthcoming publication in German, *Ausgefuehrte Bauten und Entwürfe*.[5] Accordingly published in Berlin 1910–11. German edition promptly absorbed. Unfortunately the part of the edition bought for American distribution by two of my good clients, Francis W. Little and Darwin D. Martin, was temporarily stored below ground-level at Taliesin, previous to arrangements for distribution.[6] The entire portion of the edition meant for America was consumed in the fire destroying the first Taliesin—1914. (First of three destructive fires at Taliesin.) Smoke rose from the smouldering mass below grade for several days. So America saw little of this original publication in German unless imported. But one whole copy only and about one-half of another now stays at Taliesin with me. The entire work was more cheaply reprinted (smaller in size) in Germany later—also reprinted, in still smaller format, by Japan. *Cahiers d'Art,* France, published a resume in 1911. These publications have all but disappeared.

INCIDENTAL

Unfortunately, most of the original drawings made for this publication I took with me to Japan when commissioned to build the Emperor's "Teikoku Hotel" in Tokyo. Disappeared—perhaps because the Japanese covet, and cherish, the work of their masters; therefore of other masters.

For instance, a famous Japanese poet himself wrote a sign "Please keep off the grass"; set it up on the freshly seeded lawn in front of his new house. Every morning the sign was gone. But he kept on for several more days, posting a new sign each morning which he had himself written. Each morning the sign was gone. In despair the poet asked advice of a friend: Said the friend, "Employ a sign-writer to make the sign." The poet did. The sign stayed.

ORNAMENT

Plasticity, a *quality* new to architecture, is directly related to elasticity. What plasticity is to architecture, as I have been using that term, may need explanation. Somehow, as a boy of fourteen—probably deduced from my memory of Victor Hugo's prophecy, read in *Notre Dame*—I had come to regard the pilaster with aversion because it was applied to the face of a wall as pretended construction. So the pilaster became a symbol of falsity to me, or mere applied decoration. By then I was seeing the buildings of European Renaissance themselves as a kind of *pilaster,* as later I learned to see the Greek entablature and cornice as carpenter-work in stone. The Parthenon was really a copy in stone of an Etruscan wooden temple. So soon I throw all that in with pilaster! Both were the kind of arty-pretense I had already learned to call "constructed decoration"—that is to say, ornament found out of place in violation of the organic nature of materials and construction. Ornament if organic was never *on* the thing but *of* it; therefore little of the ornamentation of the Greek orders seemed more than merely pictorial. Charming but appliqué. This thought had appeared and remained with me: any true plasticity would be a quality *of* the thing itself, never be on it (applied to it). This meant positive negation of most classic ornament of the many "classic" styles. Plasticity therefore dictated ornament as one with structural or interior quality; its place was intrinsic. Yes. In architecture ornament should be organic in character: See nature! Building constructions embodying these ideals were built by myself in the Midwest, 1893, and seen in Germany by the Wasmuth publication just mentioned. At least as early as 1910, these were explained by myself as organic plasticity; the term I first applied to more humble buildings—dwellings. But "plastic" might apply with truth to all ornament in construction. Architecture by nature was susceptible to ornament. If old forms were denied, new ones should be capable of great affirmation. Humanity in the great mother-art would be seen in buildings for America's new place in time. Architecture might, but not by way of plasticity alone, become new and fit for a culture natural to us.

INTEGRATION INTRINSIC

When these new integers are able to cultivate and enrich the technical uses of art in organic architecture, new significance will have come to the citizen. The vital changes in his life could be interpreted to him and affirmed by his modern art. Were architects to become more interested in Architecture than in architects, architecture might not only tell posterity how man was in our time but *present* him for what he aimed to be. In the spiritual fibre of new ideas, his architecture yet does not tell! To be thus richer in culture he must be alive, more wide awake than man ever was before. This should be because he is better equipped, commands extraordinary facilities now. His responsibility widens with his own stature. All is now fresh opportunity for him; if still beyond his reach—as his lack of vision now would seem to indicate—in his humanity a quality "always sings" and is the virtuous life ever so "beautiful as the morning"?

The young American has yet to learn that freedom is earned "from within": a persistent vision that never for long leaves the man who is in love with the sense of democratic life. Freedom is promised to him by the nature of his government. But government, the policeman, can only guard not bestow freedom. Culture and government dislike each other by nature. In architecture, eventually, ideal freedom is up to the individual.

Exuberant and serene as this new architecture is it should no longer shy at the term "romantic" because organic free-thinking and building *are* by nature romantic; rich in romance of the human heart as ever. "Romantic?" Yes. This romance already stirs in young America because in the young the essence of character is always the originating idea of form. Character is no less fate in architecture today than ever in the life of the man of past ages.

Wherever they are found, organic buildings will belong, solidly based upon the *human* nature of elemental Nature. This nature-wise philosophy of architecture can never resort to the expedient cliché. The petty bias of personal taste can no longer hide either excrescence or spiritual poverty in the name of style. As natural building proceeds, the individual will see building as he is learning to see life. Idea to idea, idea to form and form to function, buildings designed to liberate and expand, not contain and confine, the richer, deeper elements of nature.

THE IDEA

The idea? In philosophy, the idea is ancient as Laotze but—in building for the occupation of modern man—as modern as the future. Poetic is prophetic insight. The genius of highly cultivated emigrés first gave birth to our nation. Now must come those who make the nation a worthy reality! Such truth of being will characterize those who will eventually bear this fruit, however long neglected—or worse, distorted—either by success or by fear.

So "classic" now is far worse for the cause of freedom than ever classic was before because fresh light has now dawned from fruitful sources within upon man's imperishable soul. If it is neglected, we lose our American birthright.

The social influences of all that science can do, if not interpreted by the creative artist, may be more sterilizing than fructifying. Intellectual is not necessarily intelligent either. At the Chicago World's Fair, American architecture sadly learned that popular sentimentality has nothing in common with true sentiment and unless, in the architecture of today, the new tools of this era of the machine come in for interpretation and human use in artists' hands a heavy liability will result.

STANDARDIZED

Man in his upended street must know he is becoming a mere numerical item of convenience; on the way to being a thing. His inherent instinct for love and beauty is not only becoming suspect but, in spite of all intent, useless to society. He sees the human creature atrophy as he sees poverty of imagination in much "modern art," so-called. But it was Walt Whitman himself who raised the perpendicular hand to declare: "It is provided in the essence of things that from any fruition of success no matter what, shall come forth something to make a greater struggle necessary." This is what is now coming forth in our architecture as in our life.

PART THREE: CONCERNING THE THIRD DIMENSION
ERROR I

Today, around the circumference of architectural thought, basic error still exists concerning the new concept I have stated of the good old third dimension—usually seen as thickness, weight, a solid. Sublimated by organic architecture, it is interpreted as *depth*. The "*depth*-dimension"—really a fourth now—the sense of space. Perhaps the fourth as sought by the European cubist? The element we call *space* given a new concept. Listen to Laotze again:

"The reality of the building consists not in the walls and roof but in the space within to be lived in." Witness organic architecture.

ERROR II

Concerns our universal power-tool, the Machine. The machine is accepted by organic architecture only as a tool to a greater freedom: new power to manipulate new materials by new strategy. But the machine has already been so far misused, taken aside from culture, as to become deadly facility, mostly in the wrong direction. By too many architects it is used as a motif or an excuse for one. Or else they are used by it.

Even now, sixty years later, its true significance is rarely grasped and used for what it really is. Promoted now by too many "moderns" in architecture, it is reduced to the status of a ritual, or at least to an end in itself; exaggerating quantity at expense to the quality of human significance.

The appeal of this mechanical facility appears to be to the "pictorial" in art and architecture—an evasion of the nature of construction: the two-dimensional poverty of design seen in the façades of current steel-framing of the box added to this purely negative cliché. Now, we have too many stale derivatives of the straight-line, flat-plane effects originally contributed by organic architecture to Europeans in the early days when it was the great negation. The effects then were seminal but the depth-language of that early time is badly translated when it is separated from its original concept of the depth-dimension. So misunderstood, this dimension again appears as thickness instead of depth. What made these early effects—wholly new to architecture then—possible some fifty years ago and enables them to continue, seems yet to be obscure. Therefore various phases of this original straight-line, flat-plane architecture are still mistaken for negation as, in a sense, they originally were—especially their grammar as it appeared until about 1908. But then came another beginning, revolutionary in character—amazing the consequences—still revelation: A further concept of plan and form to go on with the cantilever and continuity—suitable to new materials and as genuine machine-age technique—

but grown richer in human content. No longer confined to the earlier "affirmative negation" the new effects of affirmation, earlier only implied, were now directly involved; and misunderstood by hatchet-men following "the moderns." Having been attracted by the original negation they remain, more or less (if unconsciously) negative.

Commercialized as these latter-day two-dimensional façades appear: empty mirrors or emaciated steel-framed cages criss-crossed, they seem to have no more vitality as architecture of the depth-dimension than the radiator front of a motor car, a bird-cage, a glass box at the zoo or a goldfish globe. These box façades are topped with a flat invisible lid in order to emphasize this box effect. The steel box-frame buildings of modern architecture now make a church, a house, a factory, or a hotel, all appear much alike—creating an impression somewhat similar to that made by a horse with his ears laid back. So-called "modern" architecture has therefore gone as ambiguous as it has gone "styleward" (soon to call itself the new "classic") instead of toward a richer expression of the liberation of human beings made possible by the new facilities of our time. But, though the early ideas of organic design have been exploited blindly, or wilfully, their fundamentals are actually not much damaged except in point of time-lapse. Again unreasonable delay on the part of education and government.

Notwithstanding any abortion, organic architecture is for our own country still on an upward way to richer expressions of our freedom and superior technology, growing out of love of human nature. I still believe that architects are all that is the matter with architecture. I have therefore not yet joined the A.I.A. Instead of the American Institute of *Architects,* as I have said, they should make the letters A.I.A. stand for the American Institute of *Architecture*—and mean just that.

ORGANIC ORNAMENT
"Such as the life is, so is the form." Can the Ethiopian change his skin or the leopard change his spots? Or the turtle be without the pattern of his shell? Expression of the constitution of nature is emphasized, unified, clarified, *identified* by what we call Ornament? True architectural form has innate significance of character expressed and enhanced by the creative architect's organic uses of organic ornament. As melody is in music ornament is in architecture *revelation* of the poetic-principle, with character and significance. Ornament is as natural to architecture of the genus Man as the turtle's shell is to the genus Turtle. Inevitable as plumage to the bird: natural as the form of any seashell; appropriate as scales of the fish or leaves of the tree or the blossom of a blooming plant.

So every living thing bears innate witness to the need for love, expressing the poetic principle by what we call "pattern": visible in all organism. Creation as eye-music is no less expressive than ear-music because it too is heart-music, appealing too, to human life at the very core. Both melody and ornament reach us by way of the soul of all Creation and as we are made we respond.

By human faculties man is able to produce natural melody of a permanent kind to give more pregnant significance to his habitation. Humanly speaking ornament is true attribute of all human culture. To say, ornament is genuine—is to say it is indigenous. Ornament is intrinsic to the being human of the human being.

No! is always easier to say than Yes. In this matter of integrity of architecture a sense of honor in the human individual has its counterpart. Sympathy and kindness, fine sentiment in the realm of the human heart are in human conduct as the grace and beauty of ornament are to organic architecture. This beautiful quality of thought in the organic constitution of building-construction is fundamentally affirmative. Never can it be negative except as a preliminary preparation for some such affirmation.

ROMANCE
The eternal Law of Change proceeds. Development has wrought and multiplies as growth among us—or subtracts the past. We are increased or diminished—perhaps destroyed. Evasion, imposition,

supposition, suppression, distortion, foolish misin-formation all notwithstanding, change proceeds, inexorable, and nature her custom holds. The philosophic center-line of future action in the realm of art is thus daily becoming more evident as the changing current of humane thought in human beings. This old-fashioned term "romantic," too, so long and still so often meaning mere affectation or sentimentality is become liberated and liberating. Architecture is truly romantic. There should lie in the very science and poetry of structure the inspired love of Nature. This is what we should and we do now call Romantic.

The ceaseless overtones and intones of space, when developed as the new reality in architecture, go on, tone upon tone, as they do in the music of Beethoven or Bach, Vivaldi or Palestrina. Like mu-sic-totality every good building has this poise, floats, at home on its site as a swan on its lake. Much of the "modern," devoid of this innate sense of music, makes factories of our studios, churches and schools. Education, our greatest busyness, is our greatest de-ficiency in this matter because it lacks courage as well as enlightenment. It still calls ornament a form of embellishment and, regardless of its poetry, re-gards it as an impractical luxury. Wherever the question of an *indigenous* American culture comes up to be either appraised or acted upon, the ques-tion of its expediency arises, and the expedient is the "pay-off" in terms of money. The cart thus in-evitably put before the horse.

But if you listen! You will sometimes hear the language of the poetic principle spoken. And never-theless, an infinite variety of indigenous art-expres-sions still come and go in spite of us, especially in ar-chitecture. To me, the principles of affirmation were alive and operative even within the original negation, say that of the Larkin Building in Buffalo, New York, as early as 1904, or, about the same time, Unity Temple, Oak Park, or the Hillside Home School I built for my aunts, 1902. These buildings show the principles and should by this time have "come into school." "From inside out" had there been firmly established as a better basis for any criticism directed against, or for, the life of such architecture as lived in our midst.

This is largely the fault of such criticism as reaches us in so many mediums: none of them deep enough or wide enough to see architecture as the cornerstone of our culture, no less than it has been the cornerstone of culture from time immemorial.

THE CRITIC

How is he made? Oftentimes bitter, sometimes sweet, seldom even wide-awake, architectural criti-cism of "the modern" wholly lacks inspiration or any qualification because it lacks the appreciation that is love: the flame essential to profound under-standing. Only as criticism is the fruit of such expe-rience will it ever be able truly to appraise anything. Else the spirit of true criteria is lacking. That spirit is love and love alone can understand. So art criticism is usually sour and superficial today because it would seem to know all about everything but understand nothing. Usually the public prints afford no more than a kind of irresponsible journalese wholly de-pendent upon some form of comparison, commer-cialization or pseudo-personal opinion made public. Critics may have minds of their own, but what chance have they to use them when experience in creating the art they write about is rarely theirs? So whatever they may happen to learn, and you learn from them, is very likely put over *on* both of you as it was put over on them. Truth is seldom *in* the crit-ic; and either good or bad, what comes from him is seldom his. Current criticism is something to take always on suspicion, if taken at all.

USONIA

Samuel Butler, author of *The Way of All Flesh,* orig-inator of the modern realistic novel, in his *Erewhon* ("nowhere" spelled backwards) pitied us for having no name of our own. "The United States" did not appear to him a good title for us as a nation and the word "American" belonged to us only in common with a dozen or more countries. So he suggested USONIAN—roots of the word in the word unify or in *union.* This to me seemed appropriate. So I have often used this word when needing reference to our own country or style.

Imagine for a moment what fertile Usonian manifestations of well-disciplined human imagination our environment might be today if, instead of the panders to European dead-ends, creative thought and feeling had been encouraged, the creative sense of space in architecture properly recognized—and now become intrinsic! If teachers had become *enriched by such experience,* and cultivated it as basic element of their own education, they would have been free to cultivate our democratic vision, might have buttressed our American spirit against the confusion and conformity that beset us now. With their help we might now be able to see spiritual entity as beauty—beauty as ethical—and ethics as more important than morals, or money, or laws. If the meaning of the word Usonian had only thus become truly characteristic of the unity of our national life we would have earned this title, and Usonia would be ours.

SCIENCE AND THE SCIENTIST

The scientist: he who takes life apart but is unable to put it back together again to live. Scientists practice invention, addition and subtraction—but in the teaching of architecture they should not continue to be mistaken as creative themselves. They are one reason why the huge business of education is not on speaking terms with culture and such culture as we now have is not on speaking terms with reality. So long as the scientific, pictorial or business interest comes first in order to make a living, culture—divorced from life as it is lived—will be helpless or false.

THE SUBSTITUTE

The substitute for art and religion has been science.

Indigenous poetry has been leeched from our common life by the "practical" materialistic ideals of industry, education and government. War—ultimate substitute provided by science. Yet the poet is not yet dead and, as a consequence, we are not.

Would you worship life amid this confusion of today, remember again the prophecy by the ideal Man, "The Kingdom of God is within *you.*" By Nature-worship, by way of revelation of your own nature alone, can your God be reached. By this fresh sentiment of individuality that gave America freedom, organic building has come along. If its principles had been comprehended by the hordes of those impressed by its appearance; if its imitators, so quick-

ly attracted by its aspects, had grasped its intrinsic virtue, we would now be well ahead of any controversy now confusing the issue. We might not be called "the only great nation to have proceeded directly from barbarism to degeneracy with no culture of our own in between." The truth is: we are a great experiment still: and all the same a great civilization. But the truth is also we are an amazing tentative culture, in possession of more than we have digested or are able yet to understand. So far as a culture of our *own* is concerned we still thrive on substitutes provided by science in spite of the fact that we *do* now have something to export besides dollars.

It is all too easy for derivatives of culture to thrive in our midst at expense to the original. Society always a coward afraid to acknowledge any debt to origins. How can any substitute ever be good in our nation for the creative artist? Our culture depends on him.

THE MONUMENTAL

The monumental should now be not so monumental as memorial. Owing to our sovereignty it is high time the scale of the human figure and its elemental, natural rhythms be put into the culture of our architects and by way of characteristic machine-age technique by T-square and triangle made to take the place of the unsightly grandomania of our early days as a nation. Witness our national capital and its progeny, our tributes to greatness. Ironical that a nation devoted to the upholding of law should have become so devoted to illegitimate architecture. But "the monument" is still seen in the mere bigness or tallness that is not in itself natural but tries to match the chronic old syndrome of column, pilaster and cornice. Whereas the modern should have something more noble and appropriate to say. Architecture has no need for monumentality unless as a natural beauty. On any other terms, either public or private, size or tallness is not the point at issue. The question is, has it the significance of beauty natural to *now.*

The wall standing stark is essential monumentality but empty. Such architectural features and proportions as are designed to put the inferiority complex to the soul of man are no longer valid or vital. It was picturesque in the days of empire, kingship and great temporal authority; and may be thrilling and picturesque again when serving a purpose well and we inherit from nature its grandeur. But, such pictorialization as we see in reckless posterism, this sterile negation of the individual, these fixations of his fate rattling the bones of construction in box-like frames, the strident steel criss-cross of these boxes trying to look tall when they can only look big—are all eventually unsatisfactory to the spirit of man. In the nature of life, tall should mean not merely high, but a beautiful expression of aspiration. The soul of modern man has more depth than such architectural masquerade, expression of mere quantity, would indicate. Desire for more imaginative humane expression with deeper feeling still grows outside as well as in our cities due to the sense of the individual's sovereignty in his America. The essential suppression of his spiritual faith will be his curse, if freedom ceases to be beautiful as expression of the American spirit.

In any sincere practice of this fundamental philosophy of building we will find the great means to put the best of man, *living as himself,* into what he builds to live in, live up to and be judged by. If better architects could thus find themselves they would eventually be found by their people. They might see themselves ennobled and built into the hearts of their people by their knowledge of the straight way to serve life as it can be lived today.

SELF-POSSESSION
Americans need the serenity of spiritual strength in what they build even more than in what they do. Tranquility and repose as a people would be great reward and assurance—always an indispensable quality of freedom. Modern mechanical skills are cheap enough though technical skill is cheated, because it is expected to be only mechanical, not inspired. Architects are wasting skills both ways and so their clients are cheated of what they really have a right to expect: integrity of spirit. Integrity? I believe I see it awakening here and there as a new American civic conscience. The great mother-art of architecture will not fail to envision and ennoble the

American life of our future. True to this emancipation the common man standing there beyond will be bravest and best of us and where he belongs.

We—the people—must retrieve this environment of ours already so heavily mortgaged. Both the life of town and country now waste each other. Accelerated by the exaggerated motor car, these interchanges and mortgages are forged by the rail men, the pole-and-wire men, advertising men; the realtor, the so-called "developer"—all defacing life. Call these *conservative?* Conservative should mean faithful maintenance at all costs of the free ideals for the sake of which our forefathers gave to every man in the country a stake in himself, as most glorious of all his privileges. Men truly "conservative" would not tolerate overwhelming violations of life, moving us toward the danger of mediocrity in high places. We should be less likely to allow an expedient conformity to frustrate our growth. Nor should we be willing to settle, by weight of mass opinion, for a bureaucratic economy on a low socialistic scale that will not take long to sink American policies to the level of or beneath communism.

DEMOCRACY
Our forefathers were not only brave. I believe they were right. I believe that what they meant was that every man born had equal right to grow from scratch by way of his own power unhindered to the highest expression of himself possible to him. This of course not antagonistic but sympathetic to the growth of all men as brothers. Free emulation not imitation of the "bravest and the best" is to be expected of him. Uncommon he may and will and should become as inspiration to his fellows, not a reflection upon them, not to be resented but accepted—and in this lies the only condition of the common man's survival. So only is he intrinsic to democracy.

Persistently holding quality above quantity only as he attempts to live a superior life of his own, and to whatsoever degree in whatever case he finds it; this is his virtue in a democracy such as ours was designed to be.

Only this sense of proportion affords tranquility of spirit, in itself beauty, in either character or ac-

Dallas Theater Center (Kalita Humphreys Theater), Dallas, Texas, 1955. Photograph by Messina Studios. FLLW Fdn FA#5514.0013

tion. Nature is never other than serene even in a thunderstorm. The assumption of the "firm countenance, lips compressed" in denial or resentment is not known to her as it is known to civilization. Such negation by human countenance may be moral (civilization is inclined to morality) but even so not nature. Again exuberance is repose but never excess.

THE APPEAL
Truth.

Who then is "conservative" in democracy? Would he not be the man with a sense of himself as at one with truth, seeing truth as his own love of the beautiful? "Conservative" then as he looks into nature from this inner self of his and his aims to be true to his own spirit—this is the conservative, normal to America. In this spirit beauty will ever be dear to him. Truth in every form becomes *necessary* to his spirit and the quest of appropriate form is vital to his happiness. The conservative man looking for Truth as the Beautiful, and the Beautiful as Truth. Wit-

tingly or not, the word *beautiful* therefore is to him indissolubly associated with the word *truth*.

FREEDOM
Liberty may be granted but freedom cannot be conferred. Freedom is from within. Notwithstanding all the abuses to which freedom is now subject—marking man down as a commercial item and cutting him off from his birthright by senseless excess and the demoralization of the profit-system—yet man may still be in love with life and find life less and less abundant for this very reason. Truth is of freedom, always safe and affirmative, therefore conservative. Truth proclaims rejection of dated minor traditions, doomed by the great Tradition. The Law of Change is truth's great "eternal." Freedom is this "great becoming."

TRADITION
Thus to break with many of the commonly accepted ways of life is imperative to freedom. By the nat-

Dallas Theater Center (Kalita Humphreys Theater), Dallas, Texas, 1955. Photograph by Walter Delima Myers. FLLW Fdn FA#5514.0033

ural working of his own sensibility, the free mind of man in democracy is always open to the truth. Together mind and heart constitute his soul and their unity is the true protection—perhaps the only one—of his freedom.

Democratic man thus free may by his own acts enlist in the struggle for a national culture but he must himself be none the less the very hub of virtue in the circumstances. The commercializations of his era are not for him. They are not his friends. If this era is to be known as "The Sanitary Age" only, then our freedom is doomed. Democracy must die. To cultivate beauty in his society, the citizen must again see life as poetic, study the poetic principle as guide, as counselor and friend.

From within this philosophy of fundamental freedom any disorder is made manifest. Force, as Napoleon confessed, can never organize anything. Force soon renders useless our discoveries of new facilities such as those of this our Machine-age.

Force reduces "progress" to affairs of mere invention, to such subsciences as the mere taking of things apart. Life may only be redeemed, rendered more noble, by great thought and feeling in all our art and in concise opposition to unwholesome manifestations devoid of spirit which we have long been calling tradition. "Style" taste-built is about all our evidence of culture. Unsafe because "taste" (whether old or new) is basically a matter of ignorance, seldom unless by accident on good terms with knowledge of the poetic-principle. It is necessary to know, not to taste.

PART FOUR: THE CITY

By neglect of prophetic apprehension of the nature of the future as practical, an expedient form of centralization (no more than habituation) stands. It is now seen, at last, as foremost among American social evils, the ancient city as inheritance; not planned for modern man or his uses. Modern man has only crammed the city of his ancient brother with gadgetry and is now being demoralized by it. Scientific modern "advantages" have been his confusion and may be his defeat.

The Medieval city is still all the city he has and his gigantic financial investment in it is encouraged regardless of fate or fact. Persistently this abuse is not only by investors knowing no better but by academic authority that should know better. Enormous static, thus inherited, is perpetuated by gregarious human habit so manipulated. This giant investment in the city is an appeal to the gregarious nature of the human animal; eventually, too, to be dead-sea fruit. The urban realtor now looms as future America's most obstinate enemy, manipulating the huge barricade of urban habit in his behalf against the future of the race. Quantity is entrenched by him to put an end to quality. Life is overwhelmed, becomes an undercurrent beneath the unsafe success of mass- or quantity-production. The insolence of authority is endeavoring to substitute money for ideas.

This ominous trampling of the herd is now the traffic-problem in big-city streets. Perpetual pig-piling of enormous increasing masses of humanity, steering to and fro, rolling out to dormitory town, rolling bumper to bumper morning and evening, back and forth again and yet again, crowds packed into cubicles to work or be entertained in crowds, always invoking artificial light, crowds crowding into schools and crowds crowding university campuses, crowds crowded into brick citadels themselves the sanitary slums a grade above the old slums by sanitation; and we hear the vain boasts of science as well as of government remorselessly promoting the Crowd, more investment in crowds, always more, never less, congestion; building more roads into and out of the cities, increasing the need for parking facilities.

Meantime we boast the highest standard of living in the world, when it is only the biggest. Society finds itself helplessly committed to these excesses and pressures. Ugliness is inevitable to this inorganic, therefore senseless, waste motion of the precious life of our time become a form of involuntary homicide. So mesmerized are we by the "payoff" that any public participation in culture becomes

likewise wasted. So little are we enlisted in the potential new life that belongs to America.

Thus cheated by ourselves of general culture we have little genuine architecture. Official authority being by nature more and more merely numerical is already helpless even to recognize this fact, basic as it is. However I like to believe I see continuing signs of worldwide unrest pointing to the long desired awakening, to the needed integrity of an organic architecture—the very awakening, late in the nineteenth or early in the twentieth century, foreseen by the poet Victor Hugo.

IDEAS AND IDEALS

Our United States of America—itself a radical statement of ethical philosophy—a prophetic faith. A civic conscience is necessary to protect the new civilian freedom, promising more humanity than any promised before.

There is no individual without a point of view. It is the condition of individuality. Ideas are fountainheads! An idea is an achievement in itself; originality of thought most desirable of human qualities.

It is on this quality that the life of democracy truly depends, and on the protection it affords *its own genius*. Nor can "teamwork"—the committee-mind—ever safely be substituted for the inspirations of genius.

Any enterprise depreciating American idealism to an abject level no higher than the concept of "the common man" is either communistic or some low form of socialism that our brave progenitors feared and our friends abroad sometimes prophesy. For when the free man our forefathers conceived falls under the regime of the committee-mind, individuality is lost in the average of averages. I have never believed there is a "common man," nor does any man, not in his *own* estimation at least.

No man will ever live happily with himself or with other men under democracy unless he takes the opportunity afforded him by our nation to rise above average (the common) by his own virtue. By playing down to the idea of the common man, dogmatic political authority exploits him; and has gone far to destroy for everyone reverence for distinction and individual achievement by personal virtue and sacrifice.

So the ideal of innate aristocracy of which our forefathers dreamed is betrayed for votes in the name of democracy. But the Declaration was originally made the thesis of a solid new faith in man as individual. This man could only mean the rise from within the nation of a genuine American aristocracy of sympathy and character, a new kind of aristocracy—as I have said—*of* the man, not *on* him. Again: his not by privilege, or birth, but by virtue *earned:* aristocracy, therefore, of man's own nature: an earned benefit to his kind.

New definitions as well as new dimensions are therefore needed all down the line, including that of the now threadbare term "gentleman." Definitions now imperative in America, because danger to this nation among its neighbor-nations lies in the inferiority complexes of mediocrity exalted by the impact upon it of politics, its numerical aspects, the ubiquity of its character.

YOUTH AND ARCHITECTURE

Our present discouragement and distortion of architecture as individual expression is alarming. Our best young men too rarely seek to be interpreters of the poetic principle, which is what an architect should be by nature. Maybe because they are no longer so born or perhaps because they are so conditioned by education; they are no longer deeply enough desired by our society to be properly rewarded.

Consider the overwhelming toll taken by the premium placed upon more "successful" professions or upon captains of industry or the persuasive salesmen of anything at all. It is "men-of-affairs" and men-of-science that are in demand; the politician rates high. All ride the tide to take what each may take of his share in society. Superior reward for inferior performance taxes heavily the young man's choice of a "career." The novice sees far greater financial chances for "security" and social standing afforded him almost anywhere else than in architecture and the arts. The true rewards in the practice of art, architecture or religious devotion are becoming dubious intangibles. Students must go into practice

of architecture too cheaply—go ready-made either by rule or rote by way of some preferred educational institution and a license after spending too many years in service to a (perhaps mediocre) professional. Only then is he "licensed" to build. His experience is here reduced by inorganic regulations and rules to servitude—a requirement of his services as architect.

Therefore most of the novitiate thus "licensed" are not builders because of ability, good background or depth of character; they have no proved capacity for the long, patient experience in work which should be theirs when they start to practice. Unfortunately, it can come only later. True dedication to adequate preparation is not there; and it is not to be had "by license." Qualification is rendered not only unlikely but virtually impossible, so architects today usually lack both inspiration and integrity. A protection to which society is entitled has thus become only elimination of superior human material, an exploitation of the profession which can only be explained by their need for a continuing supply of draughtsmen. Only devotion to nature-study in the light of guiding experience under competent leadership by a qualified master can reveal to the right kind of apprentice the necessary knowledge to safeguard America from unripe or demoralizing building-performance. Instead, the young man in architecture must try every shortcut provided by the available systems of education today in order to become a tastemaker according to this name or that name as may be recommended by their "followers." But a creative artist is not to come to us by the same educational process or the same means we employ to produce a scientist, a businessman or a politician. So the story of our current architecture in any true retrospect is likely to be a sad one: architecture declining in significance and power until the tragedy of "restatement" or no statement at all worth considering becomes again "classic."

RETROSPECT

Serious architects coming here from abroad found our culture around the beginning of the century almost completely ignorant of our own architecture or, for that matter, of any architecture except that

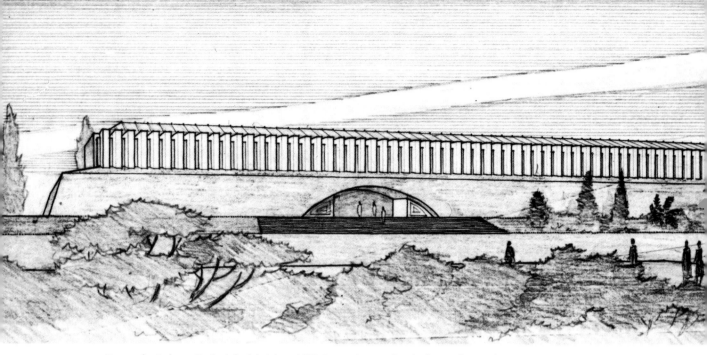

Museum for Sculpture (Project), Baghdad, Iraq. 1957. Perspective. Pencil and color pencil on tracing paper, 44 x 18". FLLW Fdn#5748.005

taught by the Paris Beaux-Arts or in evidence as old "Colonial." Old Colonial derived by the English from France and by France from Medieval Italy. Italy was indebted to Greece. Greece to Egypt and Egypt to—? (As a consequence of all this procession, see how the beam that bore the poet-builder's message to humanity down the ages has been short circuited by modern science. But only for the time being—until the true significance of the mother-art comes again clear. Every so often in history the fate of a civilization depends upon a single ray or hangs by a thread—but it has thus never yet been lost.)

The same was then true in the "liberal" arts: American society, worldly-rich, was utterly poor in art and afraid to live as itself. Fearful of being ridiculed for lacking knowledge of art, we felt much safer in buying "culture" ready-made from abroad. That is where our culture had always come from?

So, from Europe, rather than the Orient, came most of what art our people knew, and there, at top-heavy financial levels, it could, and did, buy what it wanted. America, meantime, was getting noisier, faster and uglier (the exceptions being the Louis Sullivan skyscraper and the dwellings I built on the Midwest prairie around Chicago) under the prodigious success of machine-masters. As we were,

then (and not very different now), if a substitute was presented as an original—who would know? This obviously meant a consequent atrophy of our spiritual arteries.

Already educated far beyond capacity, our over-privileged society tended more and more toward some kind of servile conformity. The old box forms, stripped of ornament, were encouraged by expedient social standardizations now grown so useful. Any cliché would do. So American life was left to be quickened above the belt by any phase of art provided it was imported—Old English, Beaux-Arts or Bauhaus—or what have you? All to be subjected eventually to mass-production. Due to our skill in scientific invention, our life became more and more subject by the professional tastemakers of the country (never artists, merely artistic) to the exploitation of commonplaces.

The compulsory machinery of public education plus the real-estate "developer" (and we have now government housing not to mention the public "service" corporation) all contributed to the degradation of the beauty America promised.

Add a vast and growing bureaucracy to this, and the natural result of machine politics was the man more and more a machine. Our biggest machine became not the corporations of big industry,

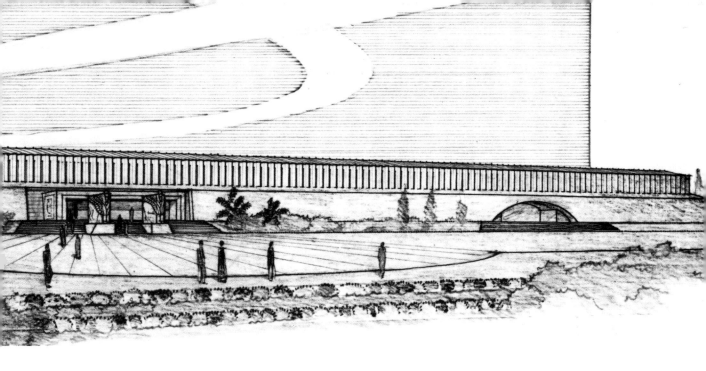

but incorporated government, and biggest of all, the machinery of education.

In general (of necessity) machinery feeds and thrives on quantity production. So our society became subject to the influence of profit-minded industries (and what other kind of industry have we?).

"Profit-minded" meant, first and foremost, *quantity*-minded. Owing to endless machine invention and production, the reproduction of the substitute was easily accepted.

Even in 1893 art was servile to "big business." It is now easy to see how architecture, art (and religion, too) become subservient to business in order to survive. The university not much above the level of a trade school or business college (business has now made a college degree a virtual requirement); and higher education is largely a cultural liability backed by big American executives themselves.

Though often sensitive, sensible (occasionally mature), these money-magnates seldom allowed themselves any show of feeling for the cultivation of beauty. To give to beauty more than a casual look or gesture, to give any extensive (or expensive) consideration to the "beautification" of even their own business world—though it is now at last increasing—would have seemed, to most of them, weak—if not waste motion.

The machine thus magnified became Moloch, dominant as quantity factor. So, instead of raising the quality, it increased only the *size,* of the standard of living of our society, inevitably reducing the value of the man himself.

Any honest, intelligent analysis of our situation will show that, with rare exceptions, money must talk, take over, and decide even these matters of the soul. Success breeds success, but where success breeds excess maintained by some form of advertising, the end is unpleasant to see. Advertising, subsidized by government—at public expense—is really our most distinguished form of art, and grows rank and noxious as any weed.

TECHNOLOGY AGAIN

Why did the manpower and technology of the haphazard uprisings of building that characterize our big cities almost entirely escape the essential hand of the creative artist-architect? Wherever and how did he ever manage to survive? His apparent contribution to American life is still small and continually ignored by the business-administration of art by "efficient" plan factories.

Novelty seems always to be a good form of advertising a substitute. And superficial architecture is based upon just such a temporary novel appeal, and thus upon "taste." Organic architecture cannot have the automatic advantage attaching to the substitute. So it has not been able to qualify much this appalling drift toward expedient conformity. It is hard to realize that until recently organic architecture was comparatively unknown to our people.

To what extent is the bureaucrat to determine the culture of our civilization? The "insolence of office" thrives upon conformity. See now the distortion of our intrinsic social purpose by experts and specialists and the encouragement of mediocrity by mass-education. With the inspiration of great art unheeded, where is the check to deterioration? Are architecture and art simply to fade out with religion?

Still to be discovered as a devoted son of culture is the inspired architect, the public servant who, if appreciated and used, could express the quality of depth and validity in the human values of our society, enabling us to qualify this ruthless imposition of quantity over quality. The artist-architect will be a man inspired by love of the nature of Nature, knowing that man is not made for architecture; architecture is made for man. He will see the practice of architecture never as a business but always religiously as basic to the welfare and culture of humanity as, at its best, it ever has been. And we must recognize the creative architect as poet and interpreter of life. We have only to consider what he has done and where he has been in every true culture of all time to see how important this son of culture is to our own future as a nation. By way of a growing art chiefly comes the culture that fertilizes society, by fructifying the individual and enabling men to call their lives their own. This enrichment of life is the cause of Architecture, as I see it.

Both abroad and at home I find that good minds still doubt the consequences of such all-out commercialism as characterizes our life and threatens human interest here in America. Yet, wholesale mechanization now seems a matter of course; technology and science menace the exuberance, the richness, of life expression and help to fashion it into a monotonous Style without human scale or significance.

The machine as a tool now is inevitable to human joy and comfort, and originals must have, in themselves, properties essential to the proper use of our machine-powers. But, machined-shapes are no *substitute* for architectural form, nor is the machine itself a form-giver or interpreter.

SALVATION

If our American engineers had had more sense of organic architecture in their systems and the architects more sense of organic engineering, the fate of our modernization of medievality would not be so tragic. Full-scale planning, afresh, might have saved city life for another half-century, or more.

The primitive ideals of centralization are now largely self-defeating. Human crucifixion by verticality on the now static checkerboard of the old city is pattern already in agony; yet for lack of any organic planning it is going on and on—not living, but rather hanging by its eyebrows from its nervous system.

Well-meaning ignorance and greed habitual add story to story, congestion to congestion, in order for the landlord to "pay off." Landlordism, now a disease of our profit-system, fights skyscraper with skyscraper. The frantic attempt to salvage urban investment destroys all human values and tries to make the human creature like it. The upended street is the invention that made possible this attempt to cage human beings.

Our oversized mobiles with non-mobile shapes—sheer excess—squared off, squared up platforms, swallowing four wheels, barge between trucks scaled more to the railroads than to city streets; all making menace constant and driving a hazard. Add to this the mortgage on our American landscape forged and foreclosed by the pole-and-wire men—and the citizen himself is condemned; on the road but headed for bankruptcy.

Owing to demolition of human values, saturation is not far away. Life itself is now distorted out of proportion, out of perspective. Everywhere in the city the citizen is treated by service itself as a servant. Subject to this universal backfiring of modern "advantages," now featured and practiced like a tax levied upon him, he is becoming a piece of machinery himself, his city a vast urban garage.

Fission of the atom might eventually prove the logical conclusion to his insoluble traffic problem created by human cupidity plus stupidity. Elimination of our badly overgrown cities, if only to release man from this growing universal bondage, would be merciful? Organic planning by way of organic architecture would be liberation. By decentralization. The forces that will eventually secure this planning are meantime at work. Why do we not work with them? The architect as more engineer and the engineer as more architect could by now have had man's liberation well under way.

First principles of organic architecture bring much light upon a new type of agrarian-urban planning. But even without benefit of such planning, the building of the new city is going on. Inevitable undercurrents beneath the old city life are taking both city and country apart. To bring them back together again in *humane* proportion is not the work of science or commerce; it requires the vision of the architect in love with architecture.

Everywhere pushed to extremes, the abuses of machine-power, the gigantic property interests cast ominous shadows upon defenseless *human* interests.

The character of "modern" citizenship is more a hangover from the animal than ever—and yet "humanity begins where the animal leaves off"? Yes. But the urbanite seems willing not only to go in to be pig-piled flat, but now to be pig-piled up on end. The realtor-landlord and the landlord-realtor, prime movers of present urban centralization, take him up and take him down; in and out, to and fro goes the hapless victim, until he is finally "taken over." By what? And how?

His coming emancipation is what should matter most to him now, notwithstanding his habituate embrace of deadly factual routine. His essential dignity remains only in his intelligent sense of himself. Fortunately for him he is learning to see Architecture as basic element of his civilization, and to understand that his birthright lies in that higher nature to which, for the sake not merely of his survival but of his happiness, he aspires. Decentralization and organic reintegration of his city is chiefly an affair of architecture.

ORGANIC CHARACTERISTICS

Quiet mass-outlines extended upon the ground levels in becoming human proportions throughout: an appropriate new use of materials old and new: these characterized the early straight-line, flat-plane dwellings built by myself—happily and with great hope—on the midwest prairie I loved, beginning 1893. Buildings creating a free, new phase of horizontality were also characteristic of the capacity of our new tool, the machine; and a new sense of human scale.

New-old philosophy had come to the rescue, soon afforded new freedoms in design. The plan grew more beneficial to human life. Eventually to do so

Monument to Haroun-al-Rashid (Project). Baghdad, Iraq. 1957. Elevation. Pencil, gold ink, and color pencil on tracing paper, 28 x 60". FLLW Fdn#5751.004

universally. These initial buildings were made to declare and express the affinity not only of man's life to his ground, but of the ground to the nature of the man who lived upon it. They showed how the inevitable order of the machine was better fitted as a tool to build these new buildings than any means ever known. But this revelation could not have been made under the old codes, nor could it have come alive under the rules of the old classic or medieval order.

Box-frame architecture, being set up on every hand as the urban ideal, also constituting the respectability of our "more educated" villagers. These standard lines of dreary human cages, with flat lids or none visible, that stretched for miles and miles were indistinguishably serving to live in, to live by; to learn in, to play in. The steeple marked the box to pray in, the dome the box to rule in.

THE NEW CLICHÉ

Now, latest in the succession of habituated boxation is the open box with glassified poster-facade standing on urban streets from Chicago to New York—representing contagion? Box to box, boxes within the box, framed by steel from the outside in, has long been the traditional form of building; but if this boxation is to continue, why call it modern architecture? We know better. What we now need is not more nineteenth century architecture of this type. Past the middle of the twentieth century, we are at last ready for twentieth century architecture.

As for novelty, everybody is learning to know that almost all sensationalism is good advertising and may be made to serve commerce. But there is neither architecture nor artistry in any of it; only a low level of invention, at best. Prolixity bred to propinquity, these mantraps seem to express the herd ideal spread by way of advertising, and accepted by man's own default. We see here the breakdown, owing to man's lack of faith in himself, of our national ideal: the sovereignty of the individual. We see here the triumph of conformity, man the individual now man as termite.

Integrity of *principle is* lacking in all this, but perhaps the self-immolating confusion called "modern architecture" is only a preliminary skirmish on the way to true modernity. Probably as old style, restyled; novel, not new, but on the whole better than the usual collection of older eclecticisms known as "the classic."

Knowledge that could retrieve from imitation the original effects of organic architecture is not forthcoming from contemporary graduates of our colleges. With no principle or ethical performance, these mere effects are taken as a new style, one to be copied, so the cliché.

Managed publicity in newsprint, in magazines and on the air is for architects instead of architecture, and the standardized architectural schooling in our universities, their curriculum a mere runaround, seems designed to go along with formulas now being substituted for performance. Much of the criticism we know aids, if indeed it is not inspired by, this expediency. Here is one reason why our "modern architecture" grows in platitude and volume while decreasing in sensitive, imaginative significance. The art of building steadily diminishes in spiritual character by the brainwashing architects receive as education. "Practice makes perfect," only if practice be right. But if the practice be wrong?

Genuine expressions as essence of the great art itself cannot be taught or imitated. Nor can they in any way be forced. If the quality of vision we call inspiration is lacking, all is lacking; and inspiration comes in its own good time in its own way, from within—comes only when all is ready, and usually must wait.

Great art has always, at first, been controversial. Now that our means of communication have multiplied, how much more so today? Any moot point soon becomes every man's controversy. Specialists in controversy, numerous and vociferous, sprout on every branch. And the pressure toward conformity leaves young minds weak with the uncertainty that cleaves, for reassurance, to the static in some form.

Resemblances are mistaken for influences. Comparisons have been made odious where comparison should, except as insult, hardly exist. Minds imbued by the necessity of truth, uttering truths independently of each other and capable of learning by analysis instead of comparison are still few. Scholarly appraisals? Only rarely are they much above the level of gossip. So, up comes comparison, to compare organic architecture to the Crystal Palace of London, for instance—Horatio Greenough, *Art Nouveau,* Emerson, Whitman, Sullivan, Coleridge, Thoreau, etc.

Those adversaries of truth who claim its discovery are invariably traitorous. Contemporary criticism is mostly posture, at the back door or at best side entrance, therefore a mere guess as to what the affair really looked like from the front. Every now and then one of the so-dedicated writes a book about a book written by a man who did the same, to win the "take away" prize in this game; never actually to be won because it was lost before it started.

INFLUENCES AND INFERENCES

To cut ambiguity short: there never was exterior influence upon my work, either foreign or native, other than that of Lieber Meister, Dankmar Adler and John Roebling, Whitman and Emerson, and the great poets worldwide. My work is original not only in fact but in spiritual fiber. No practice by any European architect to this day has influenced mine in the least.

As for the Incas, the Mayans, even the Japanese—all were to me but splendid confirmation. Some of our own critics could be appreciated—Lewis Mumford (*Sticks and Stones*), early Russell Hitchcock, Montgomery Schuyler and a few others.

While admiring Henry Hobson Richardson, I instinctively disliked his patron Henry Adams as our most accomplished (therefore most dangerous) promoter of eclecticism. I believed Adams, Boston Brahmin, would dislike Louis Sullivan and Walt Whitman. His frame of reference was never theirs, or mine. My enthusiasm for "sermons in stones and books in running brooks" was not "fascination frantic for ruins romantic—when sufficiently decayed."

At that early day I was thrilled by Mayan, Inca and Egyptian remains, loved the Byzantine. The Persian fire-domed, fire-backed structures were beautiful to me. But never anything Greek except the sculpture and the Greek vase—the reward of their persistence in search of the elegant solution.

My search was more for the exception that went to prove the rule, than for the rule itself.

As for inspiration from human nature, there were Laotze, Jesus, Dante, Beethoven, Bach, Vivaldi, Palestrina, Mozart. Shakespeare was in my pocket for the many years I rode the morning train to Chicago. I learned, too, from William Blake (all of his work I read), Goethe, Wordsworth, Dr. Johnson, Carlyle (*Sartor Resartus* at the age of fourteen), George Meredith, Victor Hugo, Voltaire, Rousseau, Cervantes, Nietzsche, Unamuno, Heraclitus, Aristotle, Aristophanes.

I loved the Byzantine of San Sophia—a true dome in contrast to Michelangelo's bastard. I loved the great Momoyama period in Japanese painting and the later Ukiyoe as I found it in the woodblock prints of the periods. These prints I collected with extravagant devotion and shameful avidity, and sat long at the inspiring series of Hokusai and Hiroshige; learned much from Korin, Kenzan, Sotatsu and always the primitives. The Ukiyoe and the Momoyama, Japanese architecture and gardening, confirmed my own feeling for my work and delighted me, as did Japanese civilization which seemed so freshly and completely of the soil, organic.

Gothic soared for me, too; but seldom if ever the Renaissance in architecture, outside the original contributions of the Italians. I read, being a minister's son, much of the Bible; and inhabited, now and then, all the great museums of the world, from America to London, across the globe to Tokyo.

I read and respected many of our own poets and philosophers, among them: Emerson, Thoreau, Melville, William James, Charles Beard, John Dewey, Mark Twain, our supreme humorist-storyteller; especially the giver of the new religion of democracy, Walt Whitman. I cared little for the great pragmatists in philosophy and less for the Greek sophists. Historicism always seemed equivocal to me; the best of the histories Gibbon's *Rome;* my respect for Friedrich Froebel always high owing to my mother's kindergarten table. Soon I turned away from the Greek abstraction via Oxford or elsewhere. Of all the fine arts, music it was that I could not live without, and—as taught by my father (the symphony an edifice of sound)—found in it sympa-

Marin County Civic Center, San Rafael, California, 1957. Photograph by John Reed. FLLW Fdn FA#5746.0161

thetic parallel to architecture. Beethoven, and Bach too, were princely architects in my spiritual realm.

I liked Beethoven's great disciple, Brahms. Italy was to me and is still so ever the beating heart of art creative, manifest in Vivaldi, the Italian troubadours and Palestrina. They came along with Giotto, Mantegna, Leonardo, etc.

My mother taught me, in my childhood as described, the kindergarten "gifts" of Friedrich Froebel—a true philosopher. At the age of eleven I was confided by my mother to her brother, my uncle James, on the farm in "the Valley" to practice both edifice and gifts as I might, and did. Never a thought in politics as other than profane until I was past fifty-five.

WISDOM

Again: I found repeatedly confirmed that the inferior mind not only learns by comparison, but loosely confers its superlatives, while the superior mind which learns by analysis refrains from superlatives. I have learned about architecture by root, by worldwide travel and by incessant experiment and experience in the study of nature. In the midst of sensible experiment based always upon preliminary experiments, I never had the courage to lie. Meantime I lived with all the expressions of beauty I could see. And all those that I could acquire and use for study and enjoyment I acquired as my library, but living with them all as I might. I never had much respect for the collector's mind.

BOOK TWO: THE NEW ARCHITECTURE

PART ONE: PRINCIPLES
I. THE EARTH LINE

At last we come to the analysis of the principles that became so solidly basic to my sense and practice of architecture. How do these principles, now beginning to be recognized as the centerline of American democracy, work?

PRINCIPLE ONE: KINSHIP OF BUILDING TO GROUND. This basic inevitability in organic architecture entails an entirely new sense of proportion. The human figure appeared to me, about 1893 or earlier, as the true *human* scale of architecture.

Buildings I myself then designed and built—Midwest—seemed, by means of this new scale, to belong to man and at the moment especially as he lived on rolling Western prairie. Soon I had occasion to observe that every inch of height there on the prairie was exaggerated. All breadths fell short. So in breadth, length, height and weight, these buildings belonged to the prairie just as the human being himself belonged to it with his gift of speed. The term "streamlined" as my own expression was then and there born.

As result, the new buildings were rational: low, swift and clean, and were studiously adapted to machine methods. The quiet, intuitional, horizontal line (it will always be the line of human tenure on this earth) was thus humanly interpreted and suited to modern machine-performance. Machine-methods and these new streamlined, flat-plane effects first appeared together in our American architecture as expression of new ways to reach true objectives in building. The main objective was gracious appropriation of the art of architecture itself to the Time, the Place, and Modern Man.

What now is organic "design"? Design appropriate to modern tools, the machine, and this new human scale. Thus, design was opportune, and well within the architect's creative hand if his mind was receptive to these relatively new values: moving perception at this time with reverential spirit toward the understanding of the "nature of nature." The nature of the machine, studied by experiment and basically used in structural design, was still to be limited to a tool, and proved to be a powerful new medium of expression. Buildings before long were evidencing beautiful simplicity, a fresh exuberance of countenance. Originality.

Never did I allow the machine to become "motif"—always machine for man and never man for the machine. Ever since, in organic architecture I have used the machine and evolved a system of building from the inside out, always according to the nature of both man and machine—as I could see it—avoiding the passing aspects now characteristic of urban architecture. The machine I found a better means to broaden the humane interest in modern architecture. Nor, in point of style, have I once looked upon the machine as in itself an end, either in planning or building or style. Quantity has never superseded quality.

THE MODULAR OF THE KINDERGARTEN TABLE

Kindergarten training, as I have shown, proved an unforeseen asset: for one thing, because later all my planning was devised on a properly proportional unit system. I found this would keep all to scale, ensure consistent proportion throughout the edifice, large or small, which thus became—like tapestry—a consistent fabric woven of interdependent, related units, however various.

So from the very first this system of "fabrication" was applied to planning even in minor buildings. Later, I found technological advantages when this system was applied to heights. In elevation, therefore, soon came the vertical module as experience might dictate. All this was very much like laying warp on the loom. The woof (substance) was practically the same as if stretched upon this predetermined warp. This basic practice has proved indispensable and good machine technique must yield its advantages. Invariably it appears in organic architecture as visible feature in the fabric of the design—insuring unity of proportion. The harmony of texture is thus, with the scale of all parts, within the complete ensemble.

II. IMPULSE TO GROW

PRINCIPLE TWO: DECENTRALIZATION. The time for more individual spaciousness was long past due. 1893. I saw urban-decentralization as inevitable because a growing necessity, seeking more space everywhere, by whatever steps or stages it was obtainable. Space, short of breath, was suffocating in an airless situation, a shameful imposition upon free American life. Then, as now, the popular realtor with his "lot" was enemy of space; he was usually busy adding limitation to limitation, rounding up the herd and exploiting the ground for quick profit.

Indigestible competition, thus added to the big city, despoiled the villages. Over-extended verticality then congested to hold the profits of congestion was added to the congestion already fashioned on the ground.

To offset the senselessness of this inhuman act, I prepared the Broadacre City models at Taliesin in 1934.[7] The models proposed a new space concept in social usage for individual and community building. But the whole establishment was laid out in accordance with the conditions of land tenure already in effect. Though the centers were kept, a new system of subdivision was proposed.

Later, this model of the broader use of ground for a new idea of a new city was carefully studied in detail in a series of smaller tributary models, all as described in *When Democracy Builds,* a book I later wrote on the suggestion of Robert Hutchins. Buildings, roads, planting, habitation, cultivation, decoration, all became as architectural as they were in Umbria in Italy in the Middle Ages; qualities of ancient sort in modern form for modern times, considered in terms of modern humane utility. Thus broadened, the view of architecture as basic now in service to society came as relief and gave a preview of primary form facing the law of the changes inevitable.

Therefore quantity—the machine source—was in no way, nor anywhere, at any time, to be used to hinder the quality of new resources for human profit and delight in living. Living was to be a quality of man's own spirit.

Science, the great practical resource, had proceeded to date itself and magnify the potential sacrifice of man as menial, now wholesale destruction of democracy. Congested in cities by continually bigger mechanical means to avoid labor, man was to be given a new freedom. The ground plan of Broadacre City was bound together in advantageous, interactive relationship to the new resources of human life under protected freedom, our own if only we would reach out and take it.

Convenient, inspiring continuity appeared in this plan for a new community (still called a city), inevitable to the survival of human individuality. But I have learned that a new pattern can never be made out of the old one: only palliation is possible—and is soon inefficient. These initial Broadacre City models, still to be seen at Taliesin, were exhibited at Rockefeller Center, New York, 1934, and many times since, elsewhere in our country and abroad. Notwithstanding the A.I.A. and the critics, this complete group-model, new in concept and pattern, showing the new life of agrarian-urbanism and urbanized-agrarianism, virtually the wedding of city and country, reappeared to travel around the world in the exhibition "Sixty Years of Living Architecture." After being shown in Philadelphia, Florence, Paris Beaux-Arts (where I was told this was the only one-man exhibition since the one accorded to James McNeill Whistler), Zurich Art Institute, Munich Art Palace, Rotterdam Civic Center, University of Mexico, it returned to a special exhibition building in New York City, and later to a special extension of Olive Hill in Los Angeles by the Municipal Art Society.

III. CHARACTER IS A NATURAL

THREE: Appropriate "character" is inevitable to all architecture if organic. Significance of any building would clearly express its objective, its purpose— whether store, apartment building, bank, church, hotel or pie-club, factory, circus or school. Fundamental requirement, this should apply to all building, in ground-planning and, especially, relative to human life and its site. This means sane appropriation of imaginative design to specific human purposes, by the natural use of nature-materials or synthetics, and appropriate methods of construction. Our new resources already evolved by science, especially glass and steel wrought by the machine, are bound continually to develop new forms. Continually new ways and shapes of building will continue to give fresh character and true significance to all modern structure.

Poetic tranquility instead of a more deadly "efficiency," should be the consequence in the art of Building: concordant, sane, exuberant, and appropriate to purpose. Durable, serviceable, economical. Beautiful. In the ever-changing circumstances of complex modern existence all this is not too easy to accomplish and the extent of these evolving changes may not yet be fully seen but as architects we may thus reconstitute architecture in our hearts and minds and act to re-write our dated "codes" and refrain from disfiguring our American landscape by buildings or "service" systems.

Marin County Civic Center Exhibition Building (Fair Pavilion) (Project). San Rafael, California. 1957. Perspective. Pencil and color pencil on tracing paper, 53 x 36".
FLLW Fdn#5754.004

IV. TENUITY PLUS CONTINUITY

FOUR: Completely new character by these simple means came to architecture; came to view, not by haphazard use, but by organic interpretation, of steel and glass. Steel gave rise to a new property: I call it *tenuity*. Tenuity is simply a matter of tension (pull), something never before known in the architecture of this world. No building could withstand a pull. Push it you might and it would stay together but pull on it and it would fall apart. With tensile strength of steel, this pull permits free use of the cantilever, a projectile and tensile at the same time, in building-design. The outstretched arm with its hand (with its drooping fingers for walls) is a cantilever. So is the branch of a tree.

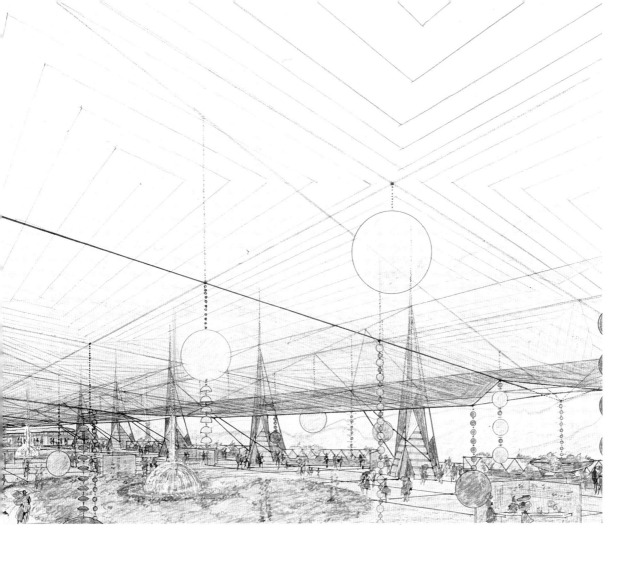

Marin County Civic Center Exhibition Building (Fair Pavilion) (Project). San Rafael, California. 1957. Perspective. Pencil and color pencil on tracing paper, 53 x 34". FLLW Fdn#5754.005

The cantilever is essentially steel at its most economical level of use. The principle of the cantilever in architecture develops tenuity as a wholly new human expression, a means, too, of placing all loads over central supports, thereby balancing extended load against opposite extended load. This brought into architecture for the first time another principle in construction—I call it *continuity*—a property which may be seen as a new, elastic, cohesive *stability*. The creative architect finds here a marvelous new inspiration in design. A new freedom involving far wider spacings of more slender supports. Thus architecture arrived at construction from within outward rather than from outside inward; much heightening and lightening of proportions throughout all building is now economical and natural, space extended and utilized in a more liberal planning than the ancients could ever have dreamed of. This is now prime characteristic of the new architecture called organic.

Rigid box shapes, outsides steel-framed, belong strictly to the nineteenth century. They cannot be twentieth century architecture. Support at rigid corners becomes mere obstruction: corners themselves now insignificant become extravagant waste, mere accents of enclosure. Construction lightened by means of cantilevered steel in tension, makes continuity a most valuable characteristic of architectural enlightenment. Our new architectural freedom now lies within this province. In the character of this new circumstance buildings now may proceed *from within outward:* Because push or pull may be integral to building design.

V. THE THIRD DIMENSION: INTERPRETATION

FIVE: To sum up, organic architecture sees the third dimension never as weight or mere thickness but always as *depth*. Depth an element of space; the third (or thickness) dimension transformed to a *space* dimension. A penetration of the inner depths of space in spaciousness becomes architectural and valid motif in design. With this concept of depth interpenetrating depths comes flowering a freedom in design which architects have never known before but which they may now employ in their designs as a true liberation of life and light within walls; a new structural integrity; outside coming in; and the space within, to be lived in, going out. Space outside becomes a natural part of space *within* the building. All building design thus actually becomes four-dimensional and renders more static than ever the two-dimensional effects of the old static post and girder, beam and box frame type of construction, however novel they seem to be made. Walls are now apparent more as humanized screens. They do define and differentiate, but never confine or obliterate space. A new sense of reality in building construction has arrived.

Now a new liberation may be the natural consequence in every building exterior. The first conscious expression of which I know in modern architecture of this *new reality*—the "space within to be lived in"—was Unity Temple in Oak Park. True harmony and economic elements of beauty were consciously planned and belong to this new sense of space-within. The age-old philosophy of Laotze is alive in architecture. In every part of the building freedom is active. Space the basic element in architectural design.

This affirmation, due to the new sense of "the space within" as reality, came from the original affirmative negation (the great protestant) 1904, the Larkin Building of Buffalo—now demolished. Here came the poetic principle of freedom itself as a new revelation in architecture. This new freedom that was first consciously demonstrated in Unity Temple, Oak Park (1906) as written in 1927 for AN AUTOBIOGRAPHY. With this new principle at work in our American architecture came a new sense of style as innate. A quality natural to the act and art of modern habitation: no longer applied by "taste." (Again: "Such as the life is, such is the form"—Coleridge gives us perhaps a better slogan than Form Follows Function.) For Americans as for all shades and shapes of human beings everywhere "style" becomes generic: poetic expression of character. Style is intrinsic—or it is false. As a characteristic of "the space within to be lived in"—the life of style is perpetually fresh.

VI. SPACE

SIX: Space, elemental to architecture, has now found architectural expression. Glass: air in air, to keep air out or keep it in. Steel, a strand slight and strong as the thread of the spider spinning, is able now to span extraordinary spaces. By new products of technology and increased inventive ingenuity in applying them to building-construction many superlative new space-forms have already come alive: and, because of them, more continually in sight. Some as a matter of course will be novel but insignificant; some will be significant and really new. But more important, modern building becomes the solid creative art which the poetic principle can release and develop. Noble, vital, exuberant forms are already here. Democracy awakes to a more spiritual expression. Indigenous culture will now awaken. Properly focused upon needs of twentieth century life, new uses of livable space will continually evolve, improved; more exuberant and serene. A new security and a new tranquility. Enlightened enjoyment of fresh beauty is here or due. As for the future: encouraging to me are the many letters, coming continually, country-wide, from teen-agers now in high school, asking for help with the term theses they have chosen to write upon organic architecture. This widening of the awareness of the coming generation's interest in architecture can only mean a new American architecture. When these youngsters become fathers and mothers, say a generation hence, they are going to demand appropriate space-homes on these modern terms. We will soon see the house as a work of art and because of its intrinsic beauty more a home than ever.

VII. FORM

SEVEN: Anyone anything of an architect will never be content to design a building merely (or chiefly) for the picture it makes—any more than a man would buy a horse merely by its color. What kind of intellect must the critic have who seeing a building judges it by "the look of it," ignorant of the nature of its construction?

For the first time in 500 years a sense of architectural form appears as a new spiritual integrity.

Heavy walls, senseless overheads and overloads of every sort, vanish—let us be glad. Light and thin walls may now depend from cantilever slabs supported from the interior on shallow, dry-wall footings, walls themselves becoming slender screens, entirely independent of use as support. Centralized supports may stand isolated, balancing load against load—seen not as walls at all, but as integral pattern; walls may be slender suspension from point to point, in fascinating pendant forms. In general, structure now becomes an affair from the inside outward instead of from the outside inward. Various geometrical forms (circular especially) in planning structure become more economical than the square of the box. Building loads may be suspended, suspension supported by slender, isolated uprights. Glass or light plastics may be used to fill in and make the whole habitable. Sheet metal and light metal castings afford a permanent material for the exteriors of such structures. Enclosures extremely light in weight combined with such structural elements relieve all modern building of surplus static; structure no longer an obesity or likely to fall of its own weight. Walls require little or no floor space. Spaces hitherto concealed or wasted or made impossible by heavy walls are revealed and made useful. Arrangements for human occupation in comfort may be so well aimed that spaciousness becomes economical as well as beautiful, appearing where it was never before thought to exist. Space now gives not only charm and character to practical occupation but beauty to the countenance and form of a valid new kind of habitation for mankind. Buildings, at long last—like their occupants—may be themselves free and wear the shining countenance of principle and directly say honestly, by free expression, yet becomingly, what they really are, what they really mean. The new sense of interior space as reality may characterize modern building. Style will be the consequence of integral character. Intellect thus reinforces and makes Spirit effective. An art as flexible, as various, as infinite in its possibilities as the spirit of man.

ORGANIC UNIT

Thus environment and building are one: Planting the grounds around the building on the site as well as adorning the building take on new importance as they become features harmonious with the space-within-to-be-lived-in. Site, structure, furnishing—

decoration too, planting as well—all these become as one in organic architecture. What was once called "decorating"—landscaping, lighting, etc.—and modern gadgetry (mechanical fixtures like air-conditioning) all are within the building structure as features of the building itself. Therefore all are elements of this synthesis of features of habitation and harmonious with environment. This is what *posterity* will call "modern architecture."

VIII. SHELTER: INHERENT HUMAN FACTOR

EIGHT: As interior space to be lived in becomes the reality of building so shelter thus emphasized becomes more than ever significant in character and important as a feature. Shelter is still a strange disorder when reduced to a flat lid—though a common desire on account of economy. *To qualify this common-sense desire for shelter* as most significant feature of architecture is now in organic architecture of greatly increased importance. Witness, for instance: The new sense of spaciousness requires, as inherent human factor, significant cover as well as shade. Cover therefore now becomes in itself a feature more important as architectural form: Solidity of walls vanishing to reappear as imaginative screens involving light, and as inevitable consequence leaving more responsibility to the shapes and shaping of the whole building "overhead" with direct reference to the elements. Radical structural changes too now make the overhead lighter, less an imposition, more graceful, more harmonious feature of environment. Organic architecture sees shelter not only as a quality of space but of spirit, and the prime factor in any concept of building man into his environment as a legitimate feature of it. Weather is omnipresent and buildings must be left out in the rain. Shelter is dedicated to these elements. So much so that almost all other features of design tend to lead by one another to this important feature, shelter, and its component shade. In order to complete the building, protecting all within it from every changing circumstance of light, of cold and heat, of wear and tear and usage, we require shelter. The occupants of a building readily discover greater opportunity for comfort and more gracious, expanded living wherever shelter is becoming shade. By shade,

charm has been added to character; style to comfort; significance to form.

THE CLIENT

Thus modern architecture implies far more intelligent cooperation on the part of the client than ever before. New rewards being so much greater in a work of art than by any "good taste" of the usual client, the wisdom of human investment now lies in "the home as a work of art." Correspondingly, the architect becomes more important than ever. The dwelling "as-a-work-of-art" is a better place in which to be alive, to live with, and live for and by in every sense. Therefore, why not a better "investment"? The interests of architect and owner are thus mutual and binding upon both.

IX. MATERIALS

NINE: I told my story of the nature of materials in building-construction in a series of articles written for Dr. Mikkelsen when he was editor of *The Architectural Record* of New York—about 1928. The good Doctor saved my economic life while I was getting a worm's eye view of society by calling me in to commission me to do a series of articles on "any subject I liked." I chose "The Nature of Materials," astonished to learn when starting research on the subject that nothing in any language had ever been written upon the subject.

All the materials usable in building-construction are more than ever important. They are all significant: each according to its own peculiar nature.

Old or new materials have their own lively contributions to make to the form, character and quality of any building. Each material may become a happy determinant of style; to use any one material wrongly is to abuse the integrity of the whole design.

STYLE

There is no such thing as true style not indigenous. Let us now try to evaluate style. "Style *is* the man." Yes, style is, as should be, largely a matter of innate *character*. But style only becomes significant and impressive in architecture when it is thus integral or organic. Because it is innate it is style genuine—or not at all. Style is now a quality natural to the build-

Norman Lykes House, Phoenix, Arizona, 1959. Photograph by John Amarantides. FLLW Fdn FA#5908.0003

ing itself. Style develops from *within*. Great re-pose—serenity, a new tranquility—is the reward for proper use of each or any material in the true forms of which each is naturally most capable.

OWNERSHIP

In the hands of any prophetic architect the building is far more the owner's building than ever it was when built for him only by way of his, or her, own taste or whim. His building is the owner's now by his knowledge of the knowledge involved. So it is in the nature of architecture organic, that there can no longer be reason to deny any man his own way with his house if he really knows what he wants. The house may be designed to suit his preferences

or his situation in his own way of life: but there is a difference between his preferences and his taste. If by his preferences, he reveals awareness of the principles involved and here touched upon, that will make his building genuinely his. If he seeks to understand *how* they involve, and evolve, his freedom *as individual* in this, his own, particular case his new home will declare his sovereignty as an enlightened individual. Homes of the new American *aristoi* may be as they must eventually become: one's own, not chiefly nor even ever "for sale." But this individual supremacy will come to the owner only with the knowledge of what it is that establishes this work of art as his own. "Taste" will now amount only to a certain discrimination in his approval of means to ends and appear once and for all in his choice of an architect. New light on both sides is indispensable to this new relationship, owner and architect.

Again, the *style* of each house may be much more than ever individual. Therefore the necessity for a new *cultural integrity* enters: individual sensitivity and personal responsibility are now essential. So comes a man-sized chance to choose a place not only in which to be alive, but in which to live as a distinguished entity, each individual owner genuinely a contributor to the indigenous culture of his time. Within the spirit of this wider range of individual choice, it becomes the home-owner's responsibility to be well aware of the nature of his choice of an architect. What he does now will not only surround him and represent him for life; it will probably be there for several hundred years. Integrity should appear in his life by his own choice. In our democracy the individual should rise to the higher level of aristocracy *only by his own perception of virtue.*

WHAT IS NATURAL

As the consequence of these basic principles of design, wood and plaster will be content to be and will look as well as wood and plaster, will not aspire to be treated to resemble marble. Nor will concrete buildings, reinforced with steel, aim to resemble cut-stone or marble. Each will have a grammar of its own, true to materials, as in the new grammar of "Fallingwater," my first dwelling in reinforced concrete. Were this simple knowledge of the grammar, the syntax, of organic design to become actual performance, each building would show its nature with such honest distinction of form as a sentient architect might afford to the awakened, appreciative owner. Building is an organism only if in accord outside with inside and both with the character and nature of its purpose, process, place and time. It will then incorporate the nature of the site, of the methods by which it is constructed, and finally the whole—from grade to coping, ground to skyline—will be becoming to its purpose.

A lady does not wear diamonds to market nor appear in shorts in the hotel lobby. Why then should she live with disregard for parallel good sense

in the conduct of her own home environment? Building as organism is now entitled to become a cultural asset.

This is all merely the common-sense of organic architecture.

ADDENDUM I

New materials in construction and methods of good building slowly remake the aspect of the world. A new grammar of design in the use of materials, all capable of characteristic effects, should enrich the building of the world without overemphasis or ignorant abuse, should never become a cliché. However, not many such buildings are in evidence as thoroughbred.

FURNITURE

Furnishings should be consistent in design and construction, and used with style as an extension in the sense of the building which they "furnish." Wherever possible all should be natural. The sure reward for maintaining these simple features of architectural integrity is great serenity. What makes this whole affair of house-building, furnishing and environment so difficult to come by is the fact that though a good sense of proportion, which is the breadth and essence of organic design, may find adequate response from good "taste," good taste is not a substitute for knowledge. A sense of proportion cannot be taught; a sense of proportion is born. Only so gifted can it be trusted as an affair of culture. Knowledge not only of the philosophy of building but its constitution is necessary. But there is no true understanding of any art without some knowledge of its philosophy. Only then does its meaning come clear.

THE CAMERA EYE

If one would get the essential character of an organic building, it could not be by camera, inasmuch as it is wholly a matter of experience. One must be *in* the building before he can understand what makes it what it is. To write about it otherwise is false. Its pictorial aspects are purely incidental—but integral. Pictures of the buildings of the old two-dimensional school (nineteenth century) are most meaningful because they were seen as pictorial when conceived.

But the building living before us now as an organism (twentieth century) may only be seen by *experience within* the actual structure. Since the depth-planes so characteristic of these structures are inevitable to their effects and are, chiefly, edgewise to the camera, any true sense of the whole edifice is seldom if ever found in a photograph. The depth-plane defies the flat camera-eye. Profoundly natural, these buildings are never dull or monotonous because this subtle quality of integrity due to "the each in each and the each in all" is continually there although not tangible to any superficial view. The essence of organic building is space, space flowing outward, space flowing inward (not necessarily by the use of the picture-window). Both plan and construction are seen to be inspired from within. For this important reason also, photographic views of these buildings are seldom satisfactory on the record. Only when the buildings are comprehended from within and each in its place a feature of its own special environment—serving its own appropriate purpose with integrity—are they really seen. If trees or mountains are round about, they will come to join and enrich the building by their natural sympathy. Architecture will become more charming because of this affinity. *The people in it gain the same distinction they would gain by being well-dressed.*

The character of the site is always fundamental to organic design. But fortified enclosure is no longer needed nor is it now often desirable. The old sense of fortification may still be with us as a more or less "monumental" weakness, as is any mere wall left standing alone. But ponderous though monumentality usually is, a monument often has its place: still serves some human purpose, as an emphasis of some chronic egotism or as true respect for the memorable, but usually abused as the dressiness of some exaggerated sentimentality.

THE PROFESSION

Architects today seem to have left but this one thing in common—something to sell: to be exact, themselves. Eventually, as a matter of course what *is* sold is chiefly themselves. Architecture is not on their minds.

But is degradation to the level of salesmanship and its profits a criterion to be tolerated by American society, either coming or going, in architecture? To take as earnest of our American future any cliché or endeavor to be international, this monotonous range of the commonplace which much of the architectural profession is now busy making of our present, is too fantastic, pessimistic egotism. Is there to be no true vision of whatever superior possibilities may exist for us in our new world besides these abortive boxes endeavoring to look tall?

Can it be that the ultimate chapter of this new era of democratic freedom is going to be deformed by this growing drift toward conformity encouraged by politics and sentimental education? If so then by what name shall our national American character be justly called? Doomed to beget only curiosities or monstrosities in art, architecture and religion by artists predominant chiefly by compliance with commercial expediency?

Machine standardization is apparently growing to mean little that is inspiring to the human spirit. We see the American workman himself becoming the prey of gangsterism made official. Everything as now professionalized, in time dies spiritually. Must the innate beauty of American life succumb or be destroyed? Can we save truth as beauty and beauty as truth in our country only if truth becomes the chief concern of our serious citizens and their artists, architects and men of religion, independent of established authority?

THEY ALSO SERVE

Nevertheless I realize that if all false or unfriendly forces (due to ignorance or so conditioned as here described) inimical to culture, were to become less and less, many long years would still be needed to overcome the deep habituations that have been built into the American scene by inroads upon the American character; wholly against natural grain and against our glorious original aim. If this twentieth century architecture, true to the principles of construction and more in line with our democratic faith, were to be more widely acknowledged by established authority; even if it were to be proclaimed from the housetops by cinema, television, press, politics, government and society as "the right thing" to be studied and practiced—there would still be controversy.

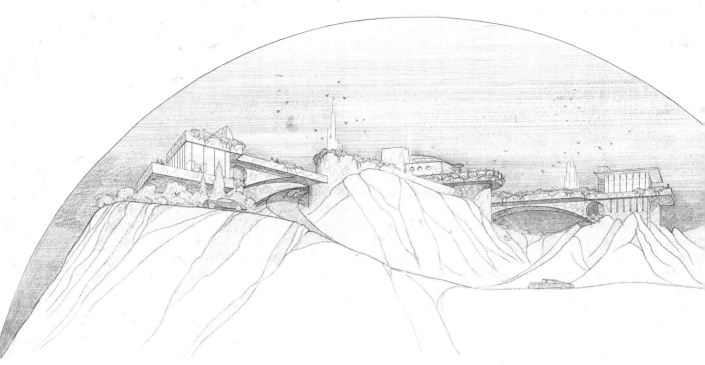

Helen Donahoe House ("Donahoe Triptych") (Project). Paradise Valley, Arizona. 1959. Perspective. Pencil and color pencil on tracing paper, 58 x 36". FLLW Fdn#5901.021

Controversy would, even then, continue for the coming half-century at least, would perhaps never cease. Democracy knows only too well the senseless weight and conflicts of irresponsible public opinion, the chronic oralism, the dead weight of ignorance, the prejudices of conditioned minds siding right or left with selfish interests of hearts hardened—instead of the deep faith in Man necessary to inspire enlightenment by generosity of motive, which democracy meant to our forefathers and must yet mean to us. The common sense of the simple truth in this new-old philosophy, *from within outward,* if awakened in our society as now in our architecture, would ensure the true uses of technology for human shelter and reverential harmonious environment, both socially and politically. It would soon get into politics.

Meanwhile we continue to hope that the Comic Spirit in which we as a people do excel may survive long enough to salt and savor life among us long enough for our civilization to present us to the world as a culture, not merely as an amazing civilization. The basic distinction between the curious and the beautiful, in which culture really consists, will make all the difference between a society with a creative soul and a society with none.

PART TWO: HUMANITY—THE LIGHT OF THE WORLD

Constantly I have referred to a more "humane" architecture, so I will try to explain what *humane* means to me, an architect. Like organic architecture, the quality of humanity is *interior* to man. As the solar system is reckoned in terms of light-years, so may the inner light be what we are calling humanity. This element, Man as light, is beyond all reckoning. Buddha was known as the light of Asia; Jesus as the light of the world. Sunlight is to nature as this interior *light* is to man's spirit: Manlight.

Manlight is above instinct. Human imagination by way of this interior light is born, conceives, creates: dies but to continue the light of existence only as this light lived in the man. The spirit is illumined by it and to the extent that his life *is* this light and it proceeds from him, it in turn illumines his kind. Affirmations of this light in human life and work are man's true happiness.

There is nothing higher in human consciousness than beams of this interior light. We call them beauty. Beauty is but the shining of man's light— radiance the high romance of his manhood as we know Architecture, the Arts, Philosophy, Religion, to be romantic. All come to nourish or be nourished by this inextinguishable light within the soul of man. He can give no intellectual consideration above or beyond this inspiration. From the cradle to the grave his true being craves this reality to assure the continuation of his life as Light thereafter.

As sunlight falls around a helpless thing, revealing form and countenance, so a corresponding light, of which the sun is a symbol, shines from the inspired work of mankind. This inner light is assurance that man's Architecture, Art and Religion, are as one—its symbolic emblems. Then we may call *humanity* itself the light that never fails. Baser elements in man are subject to this miracle of his own light. Sunrise and sunset are appropriate symbols of man's existence on earth.

There is no more precious element of immortality than mankind as thus humane. Heaven may be the symbol of this light of lights only insofar as heaven is thus a haven.

Mankind has various names for this interior light, "the soul" for instance. To be truly *humane* is divinity in the only sense conceivable. There can be no such thing as absolute death or utter evil—all being from light in some form. In any last analysis there is no evil because shadow itself is of the light.

And so when Jesus said "the kingdom of God is within you," I believe this is what he meant. But his disciples betrayed his meaning when they removed the Father, supreme light, from the human heart to inhabit a realm of his own, because it was too difficult for human beings to find faith in man. So Christianity, itself misled, put out the interior light in order to organize worship of life as exterior light. Man is now too subject to his intellect instead of true to his own spirit. Whenever this inner light of the man has been submerged in the darkness of

discord and failure he has invented "Satan" to explain the shadow. Insofar as light becomes thus inorganic, humanity will never discover the unity of mankind. Only by interior light is this possible. Science seems to be going toward the physical discovery that light is the essence of human being so far as life itself can be known.

Genesis: "Let there be light and there was light."

"More light," said the dying Goethe and he, no doubt, found it.

Then let this rediscovery of Architecture as Man and Man as Architecture illumine the edifice in every feature and shine forth as the countenance of truth. The freedom of his art will thus find consecration in the soul of man.

AMERICAN GENIUS

So the genius of our democracy still lies hidden in the eternal law of change: Growth, our best hope, consists in understanding at last what other civilizations have only known about and left to us—ourselves comforted meantime by the realization that all one does either for or against Truth serves it equally well.

1. FLLW footnote to original text: Daniel H. Burnham to Frank Lloyd Wright.

2. The 1945 *When Democracy Builds* was a minor reworking of the 1932 book *The Disappearing City,* reprinted in volume 3 of *FLLW Collected Writings.* Wright would greatly revise it again in 1958, this time publishing it under the title *The Living City,* which is reprinted in this volume.

3. FLLW footnote to original text: William Blake.

4. FLLW footnote to original text: Samuel Coleridge.

5. The introduction to this monograph was reprinted in *FLLW Collected Writings,* volume 1.

6. Francis W. Little house, "Northome," Deephaven, Minnesota, 1912. Demolished 1972. Darwin D. Martin house, Buffalo, New York, 1904.

7. The model was exhibited at Rockefeller Center in 1935.

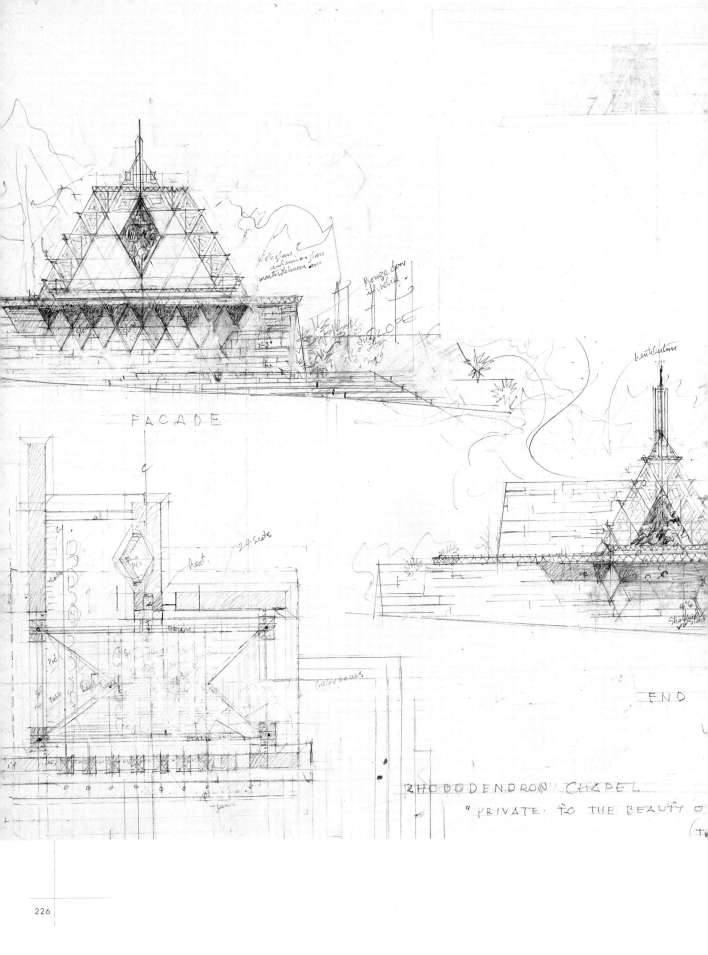

FACADE

RHODODENDRON CHAPEL

"PRIVATE TO THE BEAUTY O

END

IS IT GOOD-BY TO GOTHIC?

In this article written for Together magazine in February 1958, Wright propounds his thoughts on church architecture. For example: "All forms of religion have a basic desire to function in harmony with their beliefs and I try to help them—to materialize their ideas in something beautiful for all humanity. It's the architect's job. For architecture is not just buildings. It is the living spirit that builds." Entitled, somewhat brusquely, "Is It Good-by to Gothic?" he qualifies the sentiment by stating, "Yes, it's good-by to Gothic—as a style. But not to its spirit of reverence for beauty. That should be expressed in new styles attuned to the new day, using steel, concrete, glass, and other modern materials." Throughout his practice, Wright was engaged in designing religious architecture. At this point, he was designing a Greek Orthodox and a Christian Scientist church as well as a Jewish synagogue. Earlier in his career he had built churches for the Universalists and the Unitarians and a chapel for a Methodist college. [Together, May 1958]

CHURCHES INTEREST ME. IT'S NOT ALONE BECAUSE I AM AN architect but because I am a son, a grandson—and also a great-grandson—of preachers. To me, a church building should express a reverence for the beautiful.

Beauty is truth, and truth beauty. All religion must hold a love for what is beautiful and true—in life and in conduct, but also in building and painting and other arts.

If your church isn't beautiful, *tear it down!*

Should you replace it with a structure in one of the conventional styles such as Gothic? You ask me and I answer: NO!

The Gothic style took its form in crowded medieval cities. As God was thought to be high in the sky, so the more aspiring spires that arose, the more fingers there would be pointing to heaven. But the Gothic era is past, and with it should go its architecture.

Yes, it's good-by to Gothic—as a style. But not to its spirit of reverence for beauty. That should be expressed in new styles attuned to the new day, using steel, concrete, glass, and other modern materials.

What shall the new styles be? Only a prophet dare say. There are those who would press the mantle upon me. I decline. But I believe we are making a start in what I call organic architecture. It seeks to catch the inner rhythms and forms of nature. It has a reverence for the beautiful and the true. It senses the

Kaufmann Family Chapel "Rhododendron Chapel" (Project). Mill Run, Pennsylvania. 1952. Plan and two elevations. Pencil and color pencil on drawing paper. 35 x 28". FLLW Fdn#5308.014

Kaufmann Family Chapel "Rhododendron Chapel" (Project). Mill Run, Pennsylvania. 1952. Perspective. Pencil and color pencil on tracing paper, 34 x 18". FLLW Fdn#5308.017

cosmic order as clean integrity *in the terms of living.*

Organic structures are of the land and for the life as lived within those structures. You can listen to music and understand it. You can look at a painting and understand it. But a building stands there as an experience. To understand it, you have to live in it, or work in it, or worship in it.

But I must say that many buildings called "modern" are travesties. Architecture today is swinging low in a cycle. In all such cycles, first a new principle appears, and it has an intriguing countenance. Then the outward effects are repeated without anyone's asking why. The principle is neglected, then forgotten.

An example is the ranch house, which I developed in the West early in this century. It has been prostituted. I built ranch houses low and broad and gave then a sense of shelter. But the principle has been misunderstood. The copyists even forget that picture windows work two ways. People inside look out, but those outside can look in!

The idea of "form follows function," was stressed by the great Louis Sullivan, my teacher. But today that concept is lost in the gutter of unthinking imitation. Maybe in 10 years or so architecture will fish out the principles of his greatness and use them. I hope so.

But I wonder. American goes on building jammed-up cities. They, like Gothic churches, belong to an era when communication was difficult. People had to live close together for protection and to understand each other and to be entertained. Not so now. Yet here we go, building big boxes on small sticks—those so-called skyscrapers which really are a 19th-century product. Urban apartment developments? Just sanitary slums. We have transferred the slum from the body to the soul of man.

The things in which you deeply believe always happen. The trouble with America is that we really don't believe in ourselves—in our principle of individual development. And we substitute money for ideas. The result is that we are being swallowed up in the sea of conformity.

That's not Thomas Jefferson's idea of democracy. He believed in the integrity of the individual. He thought that if each man were given the freedom to be and to become, a natural aristocracy of uncom-

mon man would arise. Instead, we glorify the common man and mediocrity and conformity. The uncommon man—the one who is great and good and talented—is probably already unconstitutional and I suspect soon will have to sue for a pardon!

You know it. When the average man sees the great and the good, he says, "Humph! They ain't no better than we are, Sarah. Just got the breaks, that's all."

There was outward uniformity in the Gothic era. But the inner spirit has freedom. From it came the Renaissance and the Reformation and democracy.

Democracy was the first real change in civilized thought. It challenged the monarchic past just as it challenges the statism and the Communism of our day. The old is always afraid of the new, but the new has no occasion to be afraid of the old. To make progress, we must always be ready to change.

Democracy should bring freedom for the individual to realize himself as an individual—creative, unique, free. The validity and the dynamics of democracy lie in a continual insistence upon man's free will and the right to follow his own mind and his conscience.

Our architecture should proclaim this. And a religion is entitled to an architectural style of its own, expressing its searching for God.

Right now I am building churches for the Greek Orthodox and for Christian Scientists and a synagogue for Jews.[1] I built a chapel for a Methodist college, Florida Southern, at Lakeland.[2] All forms of religion have a basic desire to function in harmony with their beliefs and I try to help them—to materialize their ideas in something beautiful for all humanity. It's the architect's job. For architecture is not just buildings. It is the living spirit that builds.

There seems to be something in the human mind that requires a special particularizing of reverence. That is why we have different religions—each seeking its own relationship with the divine. And it's why we seek different styles in church architecture.

A style for all America would be a devastating mistake. It would depend upon authority—which would be its death.

I have always said nothing creative and fresh could come out of ordinary committees. And I have refused to work with committees unless they would

Annunciation Greek Orthodox Church, Wauwatosa, Wisconsin. 1956. FLLW Fdn FA#5611.0044

nominate someone empowered to transact the relationship with me.

Competitions are illusory. That's because competitions by nature lead to average everything. In the first place, those concerned have to agree upon the committee who will decide the matter. That's your first average. Then the committee—when drawings are submitted—has to agree upon one, throwing out the best and the worst. The winning one thus becomes the average of an average of averages. Anything distinguished or inspired is reduced to the combined mentality of a committee. The result is mediocrity.

That's the way it happens, often. The architect is forced to become the slave of the expedient. The genius hasn't a chance.

What is a genius? Being of Welsh stock, I answer with a Welsh triad that comes down from the days of King Arthur: "A genius is a man who has an eye to see nature; a man with a heart to feel nature; a man with the boldness to follow nature."

Nature is of God. We must study nature—in the sunlight, with our feet upon the good ground. The growth and the structure of trees, for example, reveal principle and form and design. Through nature we can sense anew the universal pulse, the inner rhythm of all being. We must do that if we are to recapture the reverence that gave life to the Gothic spirit.

Architecture, like any art, must be a continuous rebirth—and always reveal its human significance, its purpose. It must not be reiteration and a restatement, but always a beginning.

Long ago I passed the biblical threescore and ten, but I have just begun. When somebody asked me recently which of my buildings I was most proud

**Annunciation Greek Orthodox Church, Wauwatosa, Wisconsin, 1956. Detail of visors over balcony windows.
Photograph by John Amarantides.** FLLW Fdn FA#5611.0151

Christian Science Church Version #2 (Project). Bolinas, California. 1956. Perspective. Pencil and color pencil on tracing paper, 34 x 25". FLLW Fdn#5527.009

of, I told him, naturally, that it was the next one I was going to do.

I have lived to see things happen that few men see. Ideas fought for when I was young and dark-haired have been accepted. I know the price of success—unremitting devotion, hard work, and an inextinguishable love for the things you want to happen. You can't achieve much without this deep-seated feeling for life that we call love.

Love, in that sense, will engender new architectural forms—love enriched with a reverence for beauty and truth.

We bid good-by to Gothic but we save its spirit. We can build and build again even more beautifully than ever before.

1. Annunciation Greek Orthodox Church, Wauwatosa, Wisconsin, 1956. Completed by Taliesin Architects, 1963. Christian Science Church, Bolinas, California, 1955. Unbuilt project. Beth Sholom Synagogue, Elkins Park, Pennsylvania, 1954.

2. Florida Southern College. Campus complex of eighteen buildings designed by Wright between 1938 and 1954. Eleven were completed.

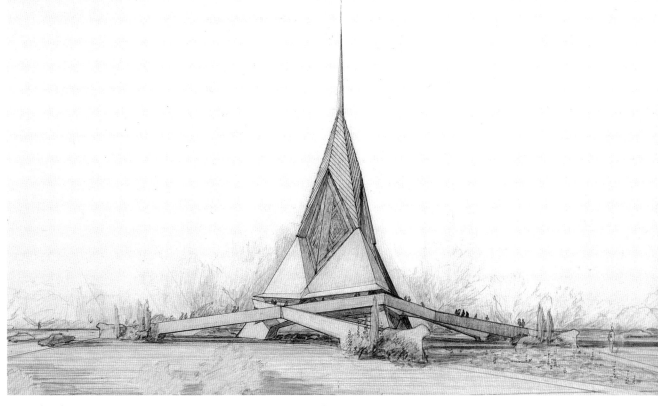

Trinity Chapel (Project). Norman, Oklahoma. 1958. Perspective. Pencil and color pencil on tracing paper, 49 x 36". FLLW Fdn#5810.001

Pilgrim Congregational Church. Redding, California. 1958. Perspective. Pencil and color pencil on tracing paper, 35 x 21".
FLLW Fdn#5818.002

PREFABRICATION

From the very beginning of his writings, Wright explored the theme of the machine in modern society. In 1901 he delivered his famous paper "The Art and Craft of the Machine" at Chicago's Hull House (volume 1), in which he offered his antidote for the English-inspired Arts and Crafts movement that was sweeping the country: "William Morris, John Ruskin and the Pre-Raphaelites were at the center of the stage in art and architecture. Handicraft societies were all over the United States." It was not that Wright looked with disfavor at the objects produced by the Arts and Crafts societies; on the contrary, he admired their beauty and design. But he realized that such meticulously wrought articles were beyond the reach of the average home owner in the nation at the turn of the century. Furthermore, he saw the machine as a miraculous tool that could effortlessly and economically produce beautiful objects.

In this article he reemphasizes his stand of 1901, but supplements it with the experience of six decades of additional work, which enables him to frame his ideas within a viable form. From his earlier treatises on the machine he now espouses machine-craft in factory production and prefabrication: "This really is at the base and the center of good design by prefabrication, which means appropriate use of an enormously effective instrument, the machine as a tool, to better the conditions of all human life." [House and Home, April 1958]

WAY BACK IN THE DAYS WHEN HULL HOUSE WAS THE CULtural center of Chicago—say 65 years ago—William Morris, John Ruskin and the Pre-Raphaelites were at the center of the stage in art and architecture. Handicraft societies were all over the United States.

Hull House had called a meeting to found a similar crafts society in Chicago. I was invited by Jane Addams to put forward at this meeting a minority report. The minority report was: "what is the use in getting behind doors and pounding your fingers trying to make things, when the whole world of production is stalled and missing inspiration that really belongs to the machine!"

In those days we hadn't reckoned with machines. We merely used them. The machine was new on the crafts horizon and it was murdering handicraft right and left. It had succeeded by way of Grand Rapids in turning out machine carving as well as other hand work. I made a proposition at the meeting that we quit all of that study of the crafts.

I advocated the machine as an artist's tool and the machine of course meant prefabrication, reproduction, standardization. I suggested we go to work and investigate what it could do in Chicago, in the metal trades, what it could do with wood, what it could do with other building materials. But I was voted down and out.

Next day the Chicago *Tribune* published an editorial (I think Jane Addams wrote it), saying that for the first time in the history of art, a Chicagoan had advocated the machine as an artist's tool.

Since then my lecture, "The Art and Craft of the Machine," has been translated into seven languages and gone around the world. It had a long enough time to get around and come back, and really nothing much has happened since.

The ability to envision and make practical the uses and purposes of machines—to get what inspiration we can from on high to qualify the machine product in a new way, to new purposes—is still "way behind the lighthouse." As a matter of fact our architects are today building 19th century buildings. We are still building the old steel frames. In other words, people who were accustomed to building lumber buildings, now build them out of steel lumber.

All our architects who are famous as modernists are still building steel-lumber buildings! New York's full of them, Chicago's full of them. They are all dying of arthritis at the joints because you can't insure the life of a steel-frame building by insuring the life of the joint with paint. As wood was born to rot, steel is born to rust.

That is only a little indication of our lack of education. I mention it here to show how slow it has been even to conceive the justice and the perfect common sense of the nature of materials and of making them beautiful in the way you work with them.

Now, that means today, prefabrication, because you can prefabricate nearly everything in a house that doesn't give it individuality. The bathroom doesn't give the house much individuality. You can prefabricate it, take it to the job, make three connections. The heating system I brought over from Tokyo—gravity heat I called it because heat rises as surely as rain water falls—is now called radiant heat for some curious reason. That's mechanical and that's prefabrication. It can all be made and brought to the building.

Of course, anything done in the field has gone (laborwise) entirely out of all proportion. The cost of building used to be, for labor, about a third of the

building's total. Today labor is about one-half of the cost of the building. Architects (and they are all that is the matter with architecture, I assure you) have not given enough study to what can be done by modern machinery to the advantage of the well designed house.

Now where you live, the living rooms, these places of warmth, proportion and charm, have gone by the board because no one is willing to pay for good design. Designs are something you get out of magazines. The magazines get them from boys who are looking to make a reputation somehow for something they have gleaned somewhere. . . .

The so-called practical boys doing the housing now are not the real sinners. The real sinner today is education. Teachers have not placed the values in the right places, and don't realize the value of good proportion and design. Without them there can be no real beauty in building except by rebellion.

Without organic consistency of method to purpose, man to tool, there can be no great beauty in "housing." Without all these high-minded things, difficult to come by, we have only a stupid procession of empty technology. What should be technology is really not technique at all, it is mere habitation and has come by way of the realtor. Our nation is unfortunate in this respect. The industrial revolution (production controlling consumption) is making a cinder-strip of the whole country, with little hotspots we call cities.

Now I don't think we were destined to wind up as an industrial cinder-strip. I believe we were "designed" to have the beauty and freedom of the green earth as a heritage. Then came the realtor, then came the developer—and God has not saved us from them. He won't because He expects something of His children, He expects some intelligence on their part to stand up and say: "No, this is not living. This is not America. This is not sovereignty of the individual. . . ." All freedom of life, and the beauty of it for the individual, is right there where you live, where your "housing" is. . . .

In building homes we have the key to, and the cornerstone of, whatever culture our nation is capable of. By its buildings every great civilization is judged. And most of them passed away just as we are going to pass away, only we are going to pass away sooner. We are not going to last quite as long as most of them did because we can go faster and the faster we go, the sooner we finish. So it is high time to pause and take stock of the things that constitute the spirit of true building.

Good design is the spirit of man, the spirit of our times, the spirit of our nation made evident. There is nothing so valuable, nothing worth so much to a society, to its future, as the fine high quality of its living conditions!

Now living conditions don't consist only of kitchens, bathrooms and standardizations of rooms to live and sleep in. You can't prefabricate the thing that gives life to the building. That is something that has to come by "benefit of clergy" so to say. So this prefabricated house here, which we have launched in order to save a third of the cost—probably without damage to its character or its spirit—still has something that I have just called "benefit of clergy." This makes sure that the house belongs where it's built, that it is adapted to the site where you put it, that nothing can be done to mar or destroy the harmony of its features. The house cannot be distorted, nor can the house be misplaced.

The sense of proportion is what put me into architecture in the first place. I was the man who declared that the human scale was the scale by which man should build. The old architectures were grandomaniac architectures and were intended to give man inferiority complexes. They did! But now we are entitled to give the American citizen something more in his own image, in his own right—in his own proportion, too. Something that came out of the everywhere to which he belongs and into the here in which he lives. Now that's quality.

Quality and quantity need not be enemies, necessarily. They can be partners and in the prefabricated house that's what they'll be. That's what they are and what they should have been many, many years ago.

Our trouble now lies mainly in lack of ground. There is no such thing as human habitation put on the ground, no such thing as human habitation placed center to center, blotting out the ground.

Only if the ground-space is developed into the paces of the building and the building has enough ground-space about it to characterize the building, and be characterized by it, have you got what we should dare to call American architecture.

We used to say that an acre to the family was enough. Well, it should depend upon environment. It will all depend on where and how the building is built. Now much of the money that goes into the building should go into the place where the building stands. That is where your realtor has to come in for a drubbing. Because it is his habit to run out ahead of the crowd, buy up the land, put up his little advertising paraphernalia and sell land in little pieces—the smaller the piece, the bigger his profits. Why do you take it? Why now when the automobile is here and we have a new time scale? We plan by time scale—five minutes, fifteen minutes, twenty minutes.

Now the automobile itself has changed everything in a building. We have made the car like a little horse and stabled it alongside the building where by nature it doesn't belong. If there is any companionship that is odious to a building, it is the motor car of today. Gasoline, carbon monoxide, noise should be left outside somewhere. They are not fit for human companionship. And then if you look at the car itself, you can get an idea of what happens to buildings in the way of design. Who designs those cars? No student of nature! Well, now you can't get designs from any other source than from a deep sincere study of nature.

What's the nature of our automobility? Is it that thing with fins sticking way up and out behind and all the rest of it like a raft or a ferry boat coming down the street gnashing its teeth at you? Well, now your houses are going in the same direction. You have our picture window houses, and you have all this glass you don't know what to do with. Perfectly indecent are most of these modern glassifications in subdivisions. I wouldn't be surprised if people began to commit suicide by the thousands on account of the way they have to live in their glass houses!

Why shouldn't you stand up on your hind legs and say: "No, we don't want that sort of thing. We know this isn't the right thing and we refuse to be

Erdmann and Associates Pre-Fabricated House Version #2, Madison, Wisconsin, 1957. Photograph by John Reed.
FLLW Fdn FA#5706.0009

jammed into a box, no matter how big the hole is in front. We know there is plenty of ground room in this country. We know that's one thing the country is "long" on. We know we don't have to pile up on half-acre lots, 20 of us to the acre."

We don't have enough sense of our own dignity! We don't know who we are really. We lack respect because we give no respect. Have we lost sight of the main thing we're here to get?

There is no excuse for building poverty into the country as an institution as they've done in the big red-brick prisons of New York City. Those red-brick insurance investments, the money of the people put into building poverty into the nation as an institution! . . .

If you can see freedom, if you can see green fields, if you can see children playing in the sun, if you can see buildings that have charm, what a man is, what a woman is, then you want something more than you are getting today. Now believe me—no man's home, notwithstanding prefabrication, need be so like another man's home as to cheat him of his

natural distinction. Good design qualifies it by the things done to live in it. If the living room is there, and the people are where they belong and the things round about where that house stands are different and the client's things are where he put them, individuality will come through notwithstanding such prefabrication as is advantageous.

Prefabrication and standardization are two different things and yet they belong together. They're going to stand together. We're going to have them together.

You can standardize almost anything but unless you know how to keep life in it by good design, it will be more or less a quantity thing. Now a quantity thing is never going to take the place of the quality thing. But we know well enough now (I as an architect say this to you advisedly) to put quality into quantity up to a certain point. It can be done only by an inspired sense of design. It's not common and never will be. It's not in the magazines. It's not something you pick up in the street.

Good design is something you have to go in for carefully—

not too sure of your own "taste." Good design is something precious and rare. Of course we're a taste-built culture. We have had no knowledge concerning taste. If you have been to a university or your children have been there, they have grown up in a haphazard environment. I think probably some regents should be taken out and shot just for their taste. University buildings were built by somebody's taste, nobody's knowledge.

You are likely to get into the same rut by taste. This still new engine called prefabrication is of course a dangerous engine. Anything vital, living and competent has a dangerous side. There is nothing more dangerous than Truth, nothing more to be dreaded if you are in the wrong. And here we are in our housing projects, the developers merry, ignorant of quality, desirous of quantity at so much per unit. But what of the human element (spiritual element), the element of the man himself? Look for it! Where do you find it? You won't see it in the big projects. It has been left out. Whose fault is that? It isn't the fault of the builder. It's the fault of the man who buys that project house and consents to live in it. He can groan and complain and think he might have had more for his money but there he is. It isn't how much house you get for your money, it's the quality of what you get. Now if we could set that kind of thinking going we would really be what you might honestly call on an economic basis.

We boast of having the highest standard of living in this world. I'm afraid that when we say the highest we can only claim the biggest. Quantity is not the same as quality. You can have "the highest" standard of living when it isn't half so big. Now the question should be how do we improve the quality? How do we preserve and then how may we use quality?

Quality is a characteristic of the free man. Are buildings going to be subject to the deadly routine of conformity? The cheapest thing you can get in the cheapest way without consideration of quality and with no real knowledge of what constitutes quality? If so, then we are the biggest, shortest-lived civilization in history. And the atom bomb (what do you call it now?) might as well drop, because I don't see anything particularly admirable or desirable to

stay here for. I think we might just as well kiss it all goodbye.

There is only one thing that makes life worth living to an American and that is the highest, the bravest and the best of everything there is available right down the line. Take no less, know what is the best; know what is really good, have knowledge.

Know why a house is good, know that the proportions belong, know that the building looks as though it belonged there where it is and couldn't be seen anywhere else, and shouldn't be. Know a building's charm—the kind of appeal that good comfortable clothes have, the way good shoes fit you. That's the good house. That is the quality house. That's organic architecture and it means: according to nature, to the essential intrinsic character of everything. Not just trees, flowers and out-of-doors, but the actual inner life of everything. In man it would be soul.

Only as science becomes as one with the spirit of man can a culture or a civilization live indefinitely. Science can take things apart, but only art and religion can put them together again—to live.

This really is at the base and the very center of good design by prefabrication, which means the appropriate use of an enormously effective instrument, the machine as a tool, to better the conditions of all human life. Our schools have to change their concept, training our architects to deeper nature study. We can't blame the professions or the builders or the people who buy homes. The thing I am talking about has to come into society, has to come to us by way of a greater consecration to life itself and by a deeper and more serious feeling for beauty.

Henry Mencken said: "Americans seem to have a lust for ugliness." Look at the poles and wires devastating our landscape. See the buildings we build violated by them. Everything we have sees no consideration for beauty, nor much for life. We need to join together to make environment beautiful.

We have raised the flag to the spirit of man. Until science, vision and art become as one, there is no rest or peace for humanity.

AWAY WITH THE REALTOR

Prefabrication, Wright asserted, is the key to providing better homes for lower-income families. But he maintained that first it would be necessary to educate a new generation of architects with an enlightened sense of design. Housing, as it was developed in the United States, was to Wright comparable to reducing man to the level of the farm animal: "Thus, through mass ignorance and capital 'playing it safe,' our people get what 'housing' they get. Animals are penned or stabled. Humans are 'housed!' In this human misery we call 'housing' we see, too, the heavy hand of government that should have no business there." The common notion of housing was simply to herd as many families together on as small a parcel of land as possible, depriving the individual family of dignity and any sense of beauty whatsoever—to the benefit of the developer and the realtor:

> *The "realtor" is even more to blame for this packaging of domestic ugliness. He does not admit that our people should have homes built in the spirit in which our democracy (our freedom) was conceived; does not seem to know that the individual should be integrated and free in his environment, that his environment should be appropriate to new human circumstances, and that the free man and his wife should lead a life as beautiful as it can be made in modern times.*

[Esquire, *October 1958*]

TO SEE AMERICA WITH AN ARCHITECTURE TRUE TO ITSELF, worthy of its new advantages in this new era of the machine—this is my "business."

To profoundly study the nature of good design, design on good terms with Nature, to produce a true, ideal American home, especially for those Americans presently settled in the lower income brackets of our famous "highest standard of living on earth"—a "standard" which may prove to have been only the biggest—this is what we need more than all else.

In other words, what we need is an American architecture.

But American architecture today is not concerned with the study of such design.

Today architecture is becoming an industry; it is no longer great art.

Architecture is becoming a business in league with its own government for housing people wholesale—at retail prices.

Looked at with perspective, the American home we now see spreading wide over the whole country—by way of the realtor, the wholesale house broker, or the "big" developer—is little more than a parody of the old congestion housing in the style of the London dormitory town, crammed with patented gadgetry: packaged ugliness in a choice of old styles or new.

Except for the car, telephone, television, the bathtub, the kitchen and the water closet, there is nothing natural to a free American humanity in any of these houses.

You need only look at the old "front yard" from a "picture window" to see the worst.

Style is and should be the character of what *we* are, not what the house-builder boys would have us be. Style is and should be the expression of our free spirits.

But these so busy all-go-getter boys care too little about the human spirit!

They do not care enough to buy good design. They buy (cheap). They pirate what can be had from the American Institute of Architects' back room or from the market magazines on the newsstands. Why pay for what is on every stand or out there in the gutter now in every city and suburb in America?

These big boys, with the help of duly managed publicity, give us the works on a big scale. They are putting themselves, the producers, in control of us, the consumers.

Because they pay much for publicity, but not much for design (good or bad), they have given to the word *housing* itself the sound of something evil.

These are their crimes: they deny the spirit of man and divorce man from Nature.

The successful ones turn away from that grand and challenging abstraction: design on good terms with Nature!

Instead, some designer (so-called) sits in his office to "turn out" something, anything that will capture the imagination of his boss.

The boss himself is busy out front selling "designs" to the customer, pursuing his chosen profession without benefit of culture or the necessary range of mind or any experience of the integrity of spirit.

And the poor customer, too. Usually he is a prospective homeowner or a government adminis-trator whose only claim to good judgment in architecture is the fact that he has the money.

His culture is usually in his wife's name. He does not know or care much how to live better or how others might live better. Perhaps he—the "customer"—is the chief obstacle to good design, but I won't believe it until he is shown something better.

There are other culprits not so easy to see.

The "realtor" is even more to blame for this packaging of domestic ugliness.

He does not admit that our people should have homes built in the spirit in which our democracy (our freedom) was conceived; does not seem to know that the individual should be integrated and free in his environment, that his environment should be appropriate to new human circumstances, and that the free man and wife should lead a life as beautiful as it can be made in modern times.

He does not allow that the smaller the piece of green earth for this individual, the more unprofitable will be his life, not only for himself but also for humanity.

Rather, the realtor watches the crowd, senses its direction, and gets out to the site before it can arrive.

He gets control of the land, chops it into regular little square pieces side by side and measures success by the smallness of the pieces: the more pieces the better his "success."

In this crowding his profit lies, but never was there any need in America to pack anybody in.

We now have millions of individual building sites available everywhere. Most of them are neglected.

Why, when there is so much idle ideal land, should it be parceled out by realtors to families in tiny strips twenty-five-, fifty-, one-hundred-feet wide?

An acre of ground per family should be the democratic minimum if our country is to survive with its spirit intact. If every family had an acre of ground we should not fill the state of Texas alone. There would be room for playgrounds as well to help solve the teen-ager problem the realtor has helped to create.

The individual realtor is no more to blame than all those bankers (almost all of them) who play it safe and refuse to loan money on a scheme for the house that has good design and sufficient ground.

Bankers, like realtors, are uneducated in good design and are themselves a part of the feudal mass-ignorance which they exploit.

The motto of the banker is "safety first."

Safety means the commonplace to him. Conformity.

Ignorance playing it safe for ignorance.

The education that might have dispelled ignorance and improved the character of life was and is lacking.

In place of the growth of character through education, we have enshrined the old rural maxim: "T'ain't never dangerous to be safe."

Today we have a country full of preachers and teachers advocating it. It is the motto of the average man as he drifts toward conformity, as he becomes the limited-mediocre man, the man we have over-privileged, just as other societies overprivileged royalty.

What we will have done with Democracy is worse than Monarchy.

We placate the mass man, not with grace or style, but "house" him, wholesale at retail.

We play it "safe." We lose our great advantages because we abuse the machine and leave it to such misrepresentatives of the power of machine as the realtor and his big builder.

Every day in every way, we see machine production in control of man's consumption. The machine is imposing ugliness upon our humanity. Machine production is demoralizing the people. Money is used to complete the spiritual degradation of America.

What we are seeing is the disintegration of the integrity essential to Democracy.

We ourselves see: the more money one gets and keeps the more we become stupid standpatters, safety-seekers, defending what the machine has done to us.

Thus, through mass-ignorance and capital "playing it safe," our people get what "housing" they get.

Animals are penned or stabled.

Humans are "housed!"

In this human misery we call "housing," we see, too, the heavy hand of government that should have no business there.

Once politics was the science of human happiness; now it is the imbalance of craftsmanship where getting the most votes lies.

That is why, architecturally speaking, Democratic government has not built a single city of its own in these United States.

I had a chat with the mayor of Philadelphia not long ago.

I found him to be a genuine leader, a lover of his city and fellow man, a perfect mayor. Except in one respect.

Architecturally, he had no conception of what a free city should be. He believed that you could get more culture out of a city by having people step over each other's heads and elbow each other in crowds.

His conception of Philadelphia was the same one that prevailed when that city was first laid out; a carbon copy of the London dormitory town; a congested city built on a plan that predates both the existence of liberty in this country and our new scientific advantages.

We Americans planted here on earth a sweeping assertion of man's spirit—the "sovereignty of the individual"—but our materialism warped us and we put the spirit of man out of business!

The Communists are trying this, too—"by bread alone."

So, are we attempting to beat them at their own game?

Powerful are the forces arrayed against the idea of an architecture worthy of America—the designer, the builder, ignorant customers, sordid banker, the hustling realtor, all cherished by blind mass-government.

Where then does our hope lie?

In all this doghousing of our people, where can we find inspiration for the American life of which our forefathers dreamed?

Can our architecture ever contribute to the free man's spirit and his ability to live a "free" life of his own?

Where is a more natural plan and procedure to come from?

Well, first, if it is to come at all, we must be aware of the truth.

My Welsh grandfather's motto was "Truth against the World." When I built my first home, I had carved in the oak slab above the brick fireplace the motto "Truth is Life": a challenge to sentimentality.

Soon after, I thought: Why did I not make it "Life is Truth" and say what I really meant?

I could not alter it; it was built.

If we become aware of the truth, we may live again and take deeper thought on our goal and its problems.

To really "think," Louis Sullivan, *Lieber Meister,* used to say, "is to deal in simples."

Simplicity is a gospel in itself.

So let us start with a house.

WHAT IS A HOUSE?

A house is a human circumstance in Nature, like a tree or the rocks of the hills; a good house is a technical performance where form and function are made one; a house is integral to its site, a grace, not a disgrace, to its environment, suited to elevate the life of its individual inhabitants; a house is therefore integral with the nature of the methods and materials used to build it. A house to be a good home has throughout what is most needed in American life today—integrity.

Integrity, once there, enables those who live in that house to take spiritual root and grow.

The real barrier to this new integrity is the lack of good design.

"Good design" is found at the very root of our civilization where now spiritual values are weakened by selfishness and overprivileged ignorance.

Is not the nature study of good design our basic necessity?

Truth is, good design has already appeared and is well on the way to individual recognition over the dead bodies of the materialists. New architecture has come from the intelligent use of available machinery for machine prefabrication.

Marshall Erdmann is a prefabricator for whom I have designed a standardized three-bedroom house factory-built, erected in the field; this house that would cost without prefabrication $50,000 sells for about $35,000.[1]

The factory has gone to the house; the house is not taken to the factory.

These homes are a start; more and better will follow.

But, first, there must come the *will* to have space—more space on the ground commensurate with the needs of a family growing in the modern spirit of man.

Next to this spacious planning on and of the ground comes better and more natural designs for the prefabrication of buildings to be built upon the ground.

The intricacy of doors and windows and other detailed conveniences of occupation, the appurtenance system (heat and light)—in these matters the factory must finally decide and yet, all these matters must be so designed as to admit of fine varied planning in the design.

All this together amounts to about two-thirds the cost of such an especially designed structure.

So it is important now to take the factory to the house.

Here and there, more or less, by fits and starts, besides the Erdman homes, some of this is going on.

But still lacking is the basic nature study concerning "good design" that can see and use the whole as a unit, serviceable to man's higher ideal of himself and more agreeable not only to his machine methods but to his own love of nature.

How to state this in terms of reality in this whirlpool of selfish, conflicting interests? A statement like this:

Abandon forever the plan for the London-style house, of the dormitory town, of wholesale realtor housing at retail prices and of any participation by government in housing.

For the sake of posterity turn the American home out into more green acreage.

Next: get an over-all plan for the house that not only affords the right to privacy but protects it and affords the charm of living that should be the profit of the individual for living at all in this amazing man-made era of the mighty machine.

Our present drift toward conformity is the illogical betrayal of all for which we became a great nation to present and prove to the world—that is, the right of every man to be true to his better self as himself, free to dream and build, therefore free according to the best and bravest yet known to him; ruled only by the bravest and best.

One more idea: how do we learn where to find the bravest and the best where building is concerned and, when found, how so to use it as to *be* it?

We must learn it from teachers who are qualified by some earned excellence which they are able to impart, but which is so hard to come by. We must reward the teacher as one of first importance.

The realtor and the developer, the banker and the businessman, however activated by altruism, have not qualified themselves for this high service. Their methods need reform or abolition.

Such men as we need should be found capable in the ranks of our American architects—found there, or they will not be found at all.

Call upon our young architects and ourselves to be more careful of their education.

Insist now upon improving the qualifications of the young architect.

Insist upon freedom of life and a fresh new in-

tegrity of spirit; the characteristics of true individuality.

Call upon the young with the spirit of youth to help work out these problems of good design, with no interference of any kind by government. In America, government must stay out of culture—it can therefore have no business with housing.

Call upon the young and tell the banker and house broker to reform their many habits.

Disenfranchise wholesale housing at retail prices.

Accomplish this and the *design* for the home-making in America can become as genuine as a work of art in itself.

Recognize the machine as the appropriate magnificent tool of pre-fabrication to be used *for* man, not *on* him.

1. Erdman Pre-Fab #1, Madison, Wisconsin, 1956.

THE SOLOMON R. GUGGENHEIM MUSEUM

In 1958 the construction of the Guggenheim Museum was nearing completion. But heated consternation and confusion on the part of artists, some of the museum's own personnel, including the director, James Johnson Sweeney, and much of the public, continued. The controversy was based on the assumption by many that the museum's galleries would prove to be totally inappropriate for the hanging of paintings. From the commission's beginning in 1943, it was a constant issue, even with the Baroness Rebay, curator of the museum and the very person who selected Wright as the architect. He repeatedly described the functions of the building, carefully explaining to Rebay and Guggenheim the new way that pictures—those that in themselves represented a new vision in art—could be displayed. At the time he wrote this article he made a set of new interior perspectives illustrating various schemes for exhibitions. Dated June 1958, the text and copies of the drawings were sent to several architectural journals at home and abroad. Nothing was published at that time, but the following article was incorporated into a book on the museum that it published with Horizon Press in 1960, one year after Wright's death. [The Solomon R. Guggenheim Museum, New York, 1960]

THE SOLOMON R. GUGGENHEIM MUSEUM'S WALLS AND spaces, inside and outside, are one in substance and effect. Walls slant gently outward forming a giant spiral for a well defined purpose: a new unity between beholder, painting and architecture. As planned, in the easy downward drift of the viewer on the giant spiral, pictures are not to be seen bolt-upright as though painted on the wall behind them. Gently inclined, faced slightly upward to the viewer and to the light in accord with the upward sweep of the spiral, the paintings themselves are emphasized as features in themselves and are not hung "square" but gracefully yield to movement as set up by these slightly curving massive walls. In a great upward sweep of movement the picture is seen framed as a feature of architecture. The character of the building itself as architecture amounts to "framing." The flat-plane of the picture thus detached by the curve of the wall is presented to view much as a jewel set as a signet in a ring. Precious—as itself.

Slightly tilted curving away of the walls against which the pictures are thus placed not only presents no difficulty but facilitates viewing; the wide curvature of the main walls is, to the painting, a positive asset. Occasional sculpture may rise from oval or circular masonry pedestals of the same color and

Frank Lloyd Wright at the Guggenheim Museum during construction, January 1959. Photograph by William Short.
FLLW Fdn FA#6007.0338

Solomon R. Guggenheim Museum, New York, New York. 1943–1959. Interior perspective. Pencil on tracing paper, 40 x 35".
FLLW Fdn#4305.012

material as the floor and walls of the Museum. Comfortable low seats of the same character are placed conveniently at the base of the structural webs forming the sides of the alcoves. The gentle upward, or downward, sweep of the main spiral-ramp itself serves to make visitors more comfortable by their very descent along the spiral, viewing the various exhibits: The elevator is doing the lifting, the visitor the drifting from alcove to alcove.

Three different ways of lighting from above the paintings placed in these alcoves are designed. One—from the reflected light directly overhead, from beneath the overhanging wall of the spiral.

Two—the same but daylight regulated by invis-ible, semi-transparent, easily adjustable plastic blinds.

Three—emphasizing the lighting of the pic-ture by brilliant reflection from a continuous mirror placed on the opposite vertical wall-space of the overhead space of the ceiling-light itself. Accent upon the picture.

All three methods are supplemented by ample artificial lighting by fixture from the same source.

From beneath the continuous gently sloping picture-walls throughout the spiral, at low level just above the floor, slants a lower portion of the picture wall: a base-band—a low slope extending outward on the floor from the picture-wall about five feet, and seen as a device designed not only to sublight the picture above it and light the ceiling surface of

Solomon R. Guggenheim Museum, New York, New York. 1943–1959. Interior perspective. Pencil and color pencil on tracing paper, 40 x 34". FLLW Fdn#4305.010

the alcove in which pictures are placed but also to refract light upon the webs, or side walls, of the alcove. A subtle modification of light on these side-walls or "webs" is directly related to the painting as a picture. So this continuous sloping break outward of the wall at low level is not only a lighting-feature but is, no less, fundamental wall surface. Incidentally this feature serves as protection from any approach to the picture beyond a safe distance of several feet by an over-curious observer. Any legitimate curios-ity concerning any particular painting may be exer-cised, if some observer so desires, by slightly leaning forward. Thus, in all the alcoves pictures are not hung as on a wall but are set up as features in them-selves. The pictures (they are without glass with only narrow wood or metal borders for framing) are easily set in place and as easily removable. Changing pictures—simple.

As now built these features are natural circumstances of the Solomon R. Guggenheim Museum. A great memorial building should thus prove to be matchless in complete unity between human nature, picture

Solomon R. Guggenheim Museum, New York, New York. 1943–1959. Interior perspective. Pencil on tracing paper, 40 x 34". FLLW Fdn#4305.013

and environment. These new arrangements are de-signed in conscious deference to the depth-plane of the third-dimension as practical in modern organic architecture. This liberation of painting by architec-ture is a fresh accent in modern culture.

HE MASTERPIECE

Typical of the details of this edifice, symbolic figure is the oval seedpod containing globular units. This simple figure decides the shapes of all furniture; the pedestals for sculpture, tables, flower-boxes, jardinieres, etc., etc. Features of exterior and interior, these all agree. The main walls gently curving outward establish the repose of the upward sweep of the great spiral, therefore of the whole structure. All is deliberately designed to promote the idea of a painting as a feature in itself freely floated in a sympathetic atmosphere of architecture instead of framed, as usually, and "hung square." Paintings in these new circumstances are to be presented as features in themselves—not as if painted on or subservient to the wall behind them. They are now seen as master of their own allotted space, remaining quietly independent yet harmonious with the character and walls of the building containing and exploiting them. So pictures are here to be seen in environment precious to themselves because of this new emphasis upon the painting itself as such. All this is an affair of exposition in which lies a definite, fresh *relief*. A new freedom! The only "framing" needed by the painting is this relationship to architectural environment. Painting no longer compelled by the strait jacket of the tyrannical *rectilinear*.

Similarly tilted backward are various additional double-faced screens of various widths and heights to afford additional picture-surface to the alcoves. Ingenious arrangements are intended and suggested. These arrangements may be few or many at the many different levels of the grand spiral. The top-level ramp, higher than the others, is to be used as research libraries and studios as required.

Finally: In any right-angled room the oblong or square flat plane of a picture automatically becomes subservient to the square of the architecture. In the plastic third-dimensional sweep of the main spiral of the Guggenheim Museum any particular picture will become free to be itself; to be master of its own allotted space. Every feature of its environment will exhilarate and contribute to its own dignity and significance as a painting. Features of the picture ordinarily obscured or lost are now liberated and seen: the character of all things seen being modified by a fresh, harmonious architectural contiguity.

Paintings thus presented gain new dimensions.

LIGHT

It remains only to remark upon the degree, quality and character of the light accorded to various pictures by these unique circumstances. To show any picture as the dealer usually desires it to be seen, a constant flood of fixed artificial light directed from his chosen standpoint is deemed a standardized necessity. But the charm of any work of art, either of painting, sculpture or architecture is to be seen in normal, naturally-changing light. If only the light be sufficient enough to reveal the painting these changes of light are natural to the gamut of painting as to all other objets d'art and thus most interesting to the studious observer. Seen by daylight to artificial light in naturally varying degree here, also, is "three-dimensional" light. Instead of light fixed and maintained in two-dimensions, this more natural lighting for the nature of a painting is a designed feature of the new Solomon R. Guggenheim Museum.

SIXTEEN

World Week, *published by* Scholastic *magazine, requested an article from Wright on the subject "If I Were Sixteen Today." In a letter to Mr. and Mrs. DeWitt Wallace of* Reader's Digest, *Wright wrote:*

> *I don't know how you select your "pieces" for publication but believe you sometimes garner them from other magazines—a wide field. So here is a copy of an answer to a questionnaire sent to me by a magazine, an answer which I like well enough to suggest it to you. . . . The question was "If I Were Sixteen Today." A silly question to be sure. I refused to accept their fee for the answer. Sincerely wishing to see you both again—Frank Lloyd Wright.*[1]

> *Evidently the* Reader's Digest *board did not elect to publish the article, but Wright wrote again to Wallace saying, "In my feeble (and foolish) way I tendered you a small contribution which was 'indigestible.' We hope to see you and Mrs. Wallace at Taliesin again this coming winter. You are cordially invited whenever the spirit moves you."*[2] *There is no record indicating whether the article was indeed first published in* World Week. [Frank Lloyd Wright: The Crowning Decade 1949–1959, *California State University, 1989*]

I AM NOT ONLY SIXTEEN NOW, I AM ALMOST NINETY. MANY of the buds on stem at sixteen are in blossom now. I imagine the feeling of ninety is much like the bloom of the bud which indicates to me that "young" is only a circumstance while "youth" is a *quality*: a qualification once possessed that does not, because it cannot, die: a quality never lost and, probably, somehow coincidental with one's immortality.

Something like this: "the child is father to the man." My experiences as teenager are still my experiences enlarged and completed—often adventurous and picturesque and exuberant. "Exuberance is beauty," said William Blake.

Wisdom in the human-bud becomes fragrance in the human flower.

To specify . . .

I dreamed at sixteen of building secure against earthquake—I have done so now. I dreamed of building tall—I can now build a mile high. I dreamed of rivaling the trees in building as they do, from inside outward. I can now do that too and I can "build houses to fit people." So though I am all of sixteen now plus enough more years to count ninety, like blossom to the bud in a gorgeous bouquet, I can offer you a flower! A promise kept: a prophecy fulfilled. It is enough.

Now I can put proper substance beneath dreams of beauty that were mere dreaming at sixteen: able now to construct where then only to dream or hope. So age is a qualification if the conditions of life are right.

Time being an essential, I now often see success as failure and see failure as success.

A civilization wherein age is made a disqualification is no true culture: no true pattern for humane existence. Civilization is then but a manifested failure of purpose.

No, I would not like to be sixteen again and relive all those precious experiences. Nor, because *growth* is something beautiful in itself for itself and a treasure not to be lightly cast away, would I wish sixteen to be ninety.

Show me a happy man or woman—I will see growth in place. Despite all attempts to make himself ludicrous or hideous, the idea of "Man" is supremely beautiful. He *grows!* If he lives according to the Spirit of human nature he is Nature's most beautiful act and is on the way to a good right to be proud of himself. Or else something went wrong, probably his Education.

So, Time becomes itself a kind of *qualification* to be gratefully respected. But not one to be bound by.

1. FLLW to DeWitt Wallace, 1 September 1958.

2. FLLW to DeWitt Wallace, 30 October 1958.

THE LIVING CITY

The Living City *was the third book Wright published on the subject of urban planning. His first major book on the subject,* The Disappearing City, *appeared in 1932.[1] His reaction to the vast magnitude of the American landscape prompted him to urge the nation to move to the countryside, to build its "cities" of the future there. Instinctively he saw the crowded city as an evil that could only beget more evil as it continued to grow and become inhumanely congested, spawning misery, poverty, and crime. Following the publication of this first book, he designed a model of Broadacre City in 1934 as a solution to this proposed migration from the crowded urban center out into the open spaces. In 1945 he slightly revised* The Disappearing City *and published the new version as* When Democracy Builds.[2] *A second edition came out in 1947. The book was illustrated with photographs of the Broadacre City model as well as other models related to it: a typical dwelling, a fireproof farm, an apartment tower (set in a park), and a cloverleaf highway overpass.*

However, in 1958, with the previous two books out of print, Wright extensively revised and expanded his urban planning scheme, made new drawings, and published it as The Living City.

In 1932 he realized that the automobile, more and more an essential part of the daily life of the American citizen, freed people from the confines of the city, which he perceived now as nothing more than a medieval anachronism. Once civilization had taken to roads, rails, and skies, such old prerequisites were now useless and unnecessary—except to the realtor. Featuring the automobile as the key to expansion outward from city to country, Wright (in 1931) envisioned the service station to be the key component in this horizontal movement. He conceived the service station as more than a stop for fuel and oil: it would be a small market with groceries and other sundry items for the journeying citizen—what today we know as the mini-mart.

In The Living City *he once again emphasized the need to move man into the country and bring him closer to a life in harmony with nature:*

> *Architectural features of any democratic ground plan for human freedom rise naturally by, and from, topography. This means that buildings would all take on, in endless variety, the nature and character of the ground on which they would stand and, thus inspired, become component parts. Wherever possible all buildings would be integral parts—organic features of the ground—according to place and purpose. . . . And imagine man-units so arranged and integrated that every citizen may choose any form of production, distribution, self-improvement, enjoyment, within the radius of, say, ten to forty minutes of his own home—all now available to him by means of private car or plane, helicopter or some other form of fast public conveyance. . . . Such integrated distribution of living all related to the ground. . . . When every man, woman, and child may be born to put his feet on his own acres and every unborn child find his acre waiting for him when he is born—then democracy will have been realized.[3]*

[The Living City, *Horizon Press, New York, 1958*]

THE INTERNAL CHARACTER OF A MAN IS often expressed in his exterior appearance, even in the manner of his walking and in the sound of his voice. Likewise the hidden character of things is to a certain extent expressed in their outward forms. . . . He ought to look with his own eyes into the book of Nature and become able to understand it. . . . The knowledge of nature as it is—not as we imagine it to be—constitutes true philosophy. . . . But he who is not true himself will not see the truth as it is taught by nature, and it is far easier to study a number of books and to learn by heart a number of scientific theories than to ennoble one's own character to such an extent as to enter into perfect harmony with nature and to be able to see the truth. . . . Wisdom in man is nobody's servant and has not lost its own freedom, and through wisdom man attains power over the stars. . . . He must realize the presence of the highest in his own heart before he can know it with his intellect. The spiritual temple is locked with many keys, and those who are vain enough to believe that they can invade it by their own power, and without being shown the way by the light of wisdom, will storm against it in vain. Wisdom is not created by man; it must come to him, and cannot be purchased for money nor coaxed with promises, but it comes to those whose minds are pure and whose hearts are open to receive it. . . . The highest a man can feel and think is his highest ideal, and the higher we rise in the scale of existence and the more our knowledge expands, the higher will be our ideal. As long as we cling to our highest ideal we will be happy in spite of the sufferings and vicissitudes of life. The highest ideal confers the highest and most enduring happiness. . . . The highest power of the intellect, if it is not illuminated by love, is only a high grade of animal intellect, and will perish in time; but the intellect animated by the love of the Supreme is the intellect of the angels, and will live in eternity. All things are vehicles of

virtues, everything in nature is a house wherein dwell certain powers and virtues such as God has infused throughout Nature and which inhabit all things in the same sense as the soul is in man. . . . True faith is spiritual consciousness, but a belief based upon mere opinions and creeds is the product of ignorance, and is superstition. . . . This physical body, which is believed to be of so little importance by those who love to dream about the mysteries of the spirit, is the most secret and valuable thing. It is the true "stone which the builders rejected," but which must become the corner-stone of the temple. It is the "stone" which is considered worthless by those who seek for a God above the clouds and reject Him when He enters their house. This physical body is not merely an instrument for divine power, but it is also the soil from which that which is immortal in man receives its strength.

—*Paracelsus*

FOREWORD

WHEN a great Oak is to die, a few yellow-green leaves appear on topmost branches. Next season much of the upper part of the tree is yellow; next year the upper branches remain without leaves. After several following seasons we say the tree is "dry."

But for many years to come, the frame of the dry tree stands erect, making black marks against the sky as though nothing had happened. Finally, rotted at the root, useless, the top-heavy structure falls. But then even the heavy frame must lie a long time broken upon the ground. Many years pass before it crumbles to soil and grass roots come; perhaps another acorn or two to give rise to other great oaks.

What sap and leaves were to the great Oak a healthy aesthetic is to a People.

This book is written in firm belief that true human culture has a healthy sense of the beautiful as its life-of-the-soul: an aesthetic organic, as *of* life itself, not *on* it; nobly relating man to his environment. The sense of this natural aesthetic would make of man a gracious, integral, potent part of the whole of human life. Ethics, Art and Religion survive in civilizations only as departments of this aesthetic sense, and survive only to the extent that they embody human sentiment for the beautiful. To ignore this truth is to misunderstand the soul of man, to turn him over to science ignorant of his true significance; and to remain blind to his destiny.

Here we are in this great melting-pot of all the breaking-down or cast-off cultures of a world wherein we have allowed the present arrogance of science to forestall a genuine culture of our own. In common we inherit and are preserving this cultural lag.

To confess that we "the great American people" have, as yet, developed no culture of our own, no efflorescence of the great Tree of Life, no such fragrance, is quite fair enough. Useful at this time.

Just as great trees die, civilizations themselves die—often withered from within by lack of culture. Or they are blown down, destroyed root and branch by the eradicable pest—war. Or are buried by the flood—revolution.

We are too young a nation thus to degenerate? Too vigorous to die a violent death utterly?

Although we have never attained the high plane from which a nation degenerates, the virus of earlier cultures coming here in the blood of immigrants might be a contagion marking us for decay and death.

Salvation depends upon the realization that, with science carried far enough and deep enough, we will find great art to be the sure significance of all that science can ever know of life and see that art and religion are valid prophecy of everything science may ever live to convey. We will find philosophy to be the science of man from *within* the man himself. Our vaunted scientists must work upon him only from the *outside,* so where man's soul is concerned science must work in vain; because such sciences as we practice substitute morality for ethics, money for ideas, fact for truth. We, as a nation, have ignored or only imitated art, confused or neglected religion, demoralized philosophy and ignored ethics. No science can be humanely fruitful until art, religion, philosophy, ethics and science are comprehended as one great entity, a universal Unity seen as the Beautiful.

In this immense drift of provincial conformity-culture, our aesthetic sense is neglected, or betrayed, and likely to come down to a raising of the overflowing cup with the little finger delicately lifted: discussing, say, the easel-picture directed to the nervous system instead of the soul. Or some poetic pose or selecticism by taste; taste in manners or the cliché all over again in Architecture. Whereas we need now to know that the honest hardships of our forefathers in their bravest pioneering were as nothing compared to the equivocal trials now inflicted upon their sons and daughters on this new frontier of the Spirit: in behalf of a culture of our own! Not only we, their sons and daughters, but our grandsons and granddaughters must stand here now exposed to insidious danger from decaying traditions within and blind authority without.

Our forefathers faced dangers in the open that we might live. We face more insidious dangers: the danger of degeneracy, of dishonesty; the danger that they may have lived for us in vain and we, their own begotten sons and daughters, will have begotten sons and daughters of our own in vanity without the heritage of spiritual courage and consequent strength.

"Once upon a time," not so long ago, the conquering of physical or territorial realm was the Frontier. But now to conquer sordid, ugly commercialism in this machine age, this "bony fiber of the dry tree"—that spiritual conquest is our new Frontier. Only by growing a healthy aesthetic, organic in the souls of our young polyglot nationals can we win this victory, greatest of all victories—Democracy.

This book is on the firing line of this new, most important frontier of all frontiers—a fight for faith, faith in man's Democracy, in the beauty of this new gospel of individuality; faith in the beauty that is the fragrant efflorescence of all humanity—the sap and foliage of the Living Tree—man's faith in himself as Himself.

NOTE

Professional criticism (say, writing book reviews) like most criticism, requires extreme egotism. But critics are not so useless as they might seem to be.

Among apprehensive appreciations of the original *When Democracy Builds* (reviews by critics more

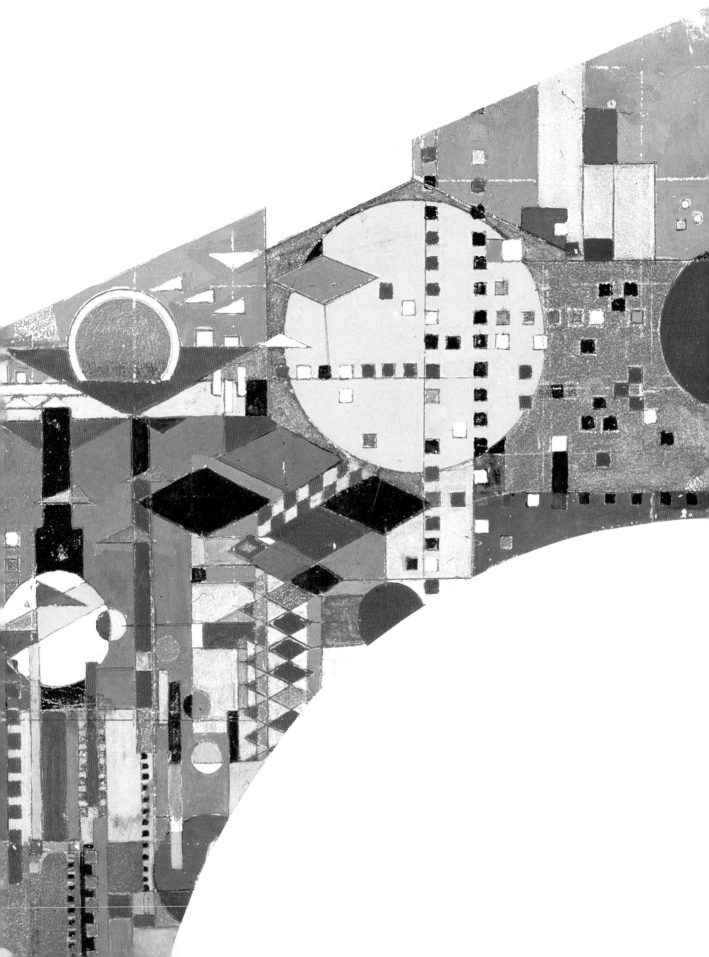

interested in content than style) came several more interested in style than content.

One such said, "The style of the work is just this side of deplorable," and quoted a sentence to prove it. I have retained this sentence. Another said, "The licentious use of capitals is confusing." So it seemed. Even to me.

One poor man gave it up entirely, saying he "failed to understand."

Another said the book was full of clichés. Yes, it was; but "my own"—because quoting myself.

So, curiosity thus aroused many months away from initial writing, I took up the book to reread it. Perspective was afforded by distance from the act—and—

Well . . . the critics were all too kind. The style of the work seemed to me—yes—deplorable. Capitalization by means of which I intended to emphasize significances actually confused them. Sentences pregnant to me with meaning when I wrote them utterly failed to clinch, or went into reverse.

What to do?

Rewrite the book.

Ignominy of course!

I hardened into my own most severe critic, I thought, and yet—sentences quoted by my critics to show my style just this side of "deplorable" I found right enough—in their way. They stand. I apologize. But I did find the affair with capitalization fantastic, far too capitalistic. I threw this affair out, and proceeded to clinch every phrase in the book concerned with an idea, so far as I could. I found so very many at loose ends and many stay there yet.

But as for clichés, if so, I made the original of every cliché *myself*. Regarding that I call your attention to the captious English lady who, advised to read *Hamlet*, threw the book away half-read—with the contemptuous remark that she "couldn't see why they thought Shakespeare so great an author when his work was so full of quotations."

My critics! Sincerely I thank you.

PART ONE: NATURE
EARTH

The value of Earth as man's heritage, or of Man as earth's great heritage, is gone far from him now in any big city centralization has built (but never designed). Centralization—without plan—has overbuilt. Urban happiness of the properly citified citizen consists in crowding in confusion—lured by the hypnotic warmth, pressure and approbation of the crowd? The screech and mechanical uproar of the big city turns the citified head, fills citified ears—as the song of birds, wind in the trees, animal cries, or as the voices and songs of his loved ones once filled his heart. He is sidewalk-happy.

But where and as he now stands, out of the machine that his big city of the motor age has become, no citizen creates or operates more than mere machinery nor is he going to be much more than a machine himself—if his big city stays.

Thus the properly citified citizen becomes a broker of profit-system ideas, a vendor of gadgetry, a salesman dealing for profit in human exaggeration. A speculator in frailties continually dealing in the ideas and inventions of others—or become an avid spectator. This puller of levers, pusher of the buttons of vicarious power, has power of his own only by way of mechanical craft. A "graft" is this tide on which he rides.

So a parasite of the spirit is here; dervish in a whirling vortex. Yes—from the top down, and enamored of the whirl.

Perpetual to-and-fro excites this citified citizen, robs him of deeper sympathy, of the meditation and reflection once his as he lived and walked under clean sky among the fresh greenery to which he was born companion. On solid earth he was neither fool-proof nor weather-proof, but he was a whole man.

But he has traded his Book of Creation for emasculation by way of the convenient substitute;

Previous pages: "The City by the Sea" (Chicago on Lake Michigan). Mural painting. Scottsdale, Arizona. 1956. Watercolor on paper mounted to board, 21 x 27". FLLW Fdn#5609.001

traded his origins and native pastimes with streams, woods, fields, and animals for the ubiquitous, habitual to-and-fro; taint of carbon monoxide rising from him to his rented aggregations of hard cells on upended streets overlooking hard pavements. "Paramounts," "Roxies," night clubs, bars—such as these are his relaxation, his urban recourse. For all this easy come and easy go he lives in some cubicle among other cubicles under a landlord himself a "hot-shot"—one who probably lives up there above him in a "penthouse." Both landlord and tenant are the living apotheosis of rent. Rent! Always rent in some form is the city. If not quite yet parasites—parasitic all.

So exists the properly citified urbanite! Still a slave to the herd-instinct, fatally committed to vicarious power—a *slave* in any final analysis just as the medieval laborer, not so long before him, was slave to caprice of king or state. A cultural weed now, he grows rank in the urban field.

This weed goes to seed! Children keep on coming and growing. Now herded by the thousand in schools built like factories, run like factories: all systematically turning out herd-struck teenagers like machines turning out shoes. In knowledge-factories.

And when urban men-of-commerce themselves succeed, they become more than ever vicarious? Soon these very successful men sink into the sham luxury their city life so continually produces. But they *create* nothing! Spiritually impotent, a fixation has them where impotence wants them: fixation in a cliché.

But life itself has become intolerably restless; a mere tenant of the big landlord: the "big city." Yes . . . above the belt, if he is properly citified, the citizen has long lost sight of the true aim of normal human existence. He has accepted not only substitute means but substitute aims and ends. Naturally gregarious himself, his life now tends toward the promiscuous, blind adventure of the crafty animal; toward some form of graft; toward the febrile pursuit of sex as "relief" from factual routine. He seeks but cannot find peace in an all prevailing uproar of mechanical conflicts—unless in alcohol? Meantime struggling artificially to maintain teeth, hair, muscles, and sap; his sight growing dim; hearing increasingly by telephone. He now must go against or across a streaming tide of traffic, at risk of damage or death to himself or others. His own good time is inevitably, regularly, increasingly wasted by others because he is as determined, and inevitably, all-out to waste theirs. All go about in different directions or swarm over hard concrete to various ugly scaffoldings, or go underground to get into other cubicles occupied by other sub-parasites-of-rent—always rent, rent in some form—or go higher up under some other skyscraper-rentlord. The citizen's entire life is an *exaggeration* or frustration, on wheels or accelerated by plane, television or telephone. By elevator, the upended street, his life is thus limited and confused, contained instead of *expanded;* a vicarious life virtually sterilized by machinery, by medicine, by more and more stimulants. His demoralization has only begun.

Were motor oil and castor oil to dry up, the great big city would soon cease to function: the citizens would promptly perish.

So this modern monster, degeneration of the Renaissance city, becomes the form universal of anxiety, all stated in various form of rent. The citizen's very life is tenant, himself rented, in a rented world. He and his ever-growing family evicted if in arrears, or the vast "debt system" of rent goes to smash.

Should his nervous pace slacken, his digestion become ulcerous or fail, his anxious lock-step with rent would fall out with the lock-step of "production." Landlord, money-lord, and machine-lord . . . the man, with ulcers or none, is soon a total loss even to his bureaucratic government.

Nevertheless—relentlessly—over him, beside him and beneath him, even in his heart as he sleeps, is fear. Fear. Fear forever ticking in this taxi-meter of triple rent—rent for land, rent for money, rent for being alive—each of them goading the anxious "consumer's" unceasing struggle for or against ominous increase-of-production. Production regardless—production now driving consumption bankrupt or insane; insatiable unearned increment for power. To stay in the lock-step—that is now all the "pay-off" he hopes for. Not so much more than that. He, the wage-slave in some form, puts his own life into bondage, or is busy managing to get the lives of others there just in order to keep up the superficial privileges to which he has consciously, fatuously, subscribed and which are often described to him as great, beneficent "free enterprise": enterprise to which his ubiquitous politicians continually refer him. Humanity is here preying upon humanity? Man's inhumanity to man seems also to be the feature of the only "economic system" the urban citizen yet knows or has been, officially, encouraged by government to know. So he takes "the system" for granted—as now he takes all else for granted: Capitalism included. But even "the system" is, at best, only capitalistic. Not true capitalism because it is the apex instead of the base of the pyramid that is on the ground.

As the citizen stands, powerful modern resources, naturally his own by uses of modern machinery, are (owing to their very nature) turning against him, although the system he lives under is one he himself helped build. Such centralizations of men and capital as he must now serve are no longer wise or humane. Long ago—having done all it could do for humanity—the centralization we call the big city became a centripetal force grown beyond our control; agitated by rent to continually additional, vicarious powers.

Thus the system is steadily increasing in man his animal instincts, his fear of being turned out of the hole into which he has been accustomed to crawl in again each evening to crawl out again next morning. Natural horizontality—true line of human freedom on earth—is going, or gone. The citizen condemns himself to perhaps natural but most unbecoming (and now unprofitable to him) pig-piling. What he aspires to is a sterile urban verticality, actually unnatural to him because he is upended, suspended and traffic-jammed by this verticality due to his own mad excess. He is calling this evidence of fixability instead of flexibility—*success*. It is only conformity.

Notwithstanding slum-clearance by insurance, the profit-sharing of sporadic "housing" which he has unwittingly approved to build himself permanently into bondage, he becomes more confused and helpless.

Nevertheless out of this automatic turnabout against him of his own industrial revolution without a soul now fast running away from modern man, he may yet emerge from the ancient shadow-of-the-wall as master instead of machine-age conscript. He may emerge by way of Organic Architecture because its philosophy and practice are natural to his better self made free.

THE SHADOW-OF-THE-WALL—PRIMITIVE INSTINCTS STILL ALIVE

Go back far enough in time. Mankind was divided into cave-dwelling agrarians and wandering tribes of hunter-warriors; and we might find the wanderer swinging from branch to branch in the leafy bower of the tree, insured by the curl at the end of his tail, while the more stolid lover of the wall lurked, for safety, hidden in some hole in the ground or in a cave: the ape?

The static cave-dweller was ancient conservative. Probably he was more brutal, if not more ferocious, with his heavy club when occasion arose than the mobile wanderer with his slender spear.

The cave-dweller became cliff-dweller. He began to build cities. Establishment was his idea. His God was a malicious murderer. His own statue, made by himself more terrible than himself, was really his God; a God also hiding away. He erected this God into a mysterious covenant. When he could, he made his God of gold. He still does.

But his swifter, more mobile brother devised a more adaptable and elusive dwelling-place—the folding tent.

He, nomad, went in changing seasons from place to place, over the whole earth following the laws of change: natural to him.

He was the Adventurer.

His God was a Spirit: like a wind, devastating or beneficent as he was himself.

These main divisions of primitive man, the human family, having herd-instinct in common with other animals, made God, or conceived gods, in their own image. Both human divergencies set up enmity. Enmity each toward the other.

Cave-dwellers bred their young in the shadow of the wall. Mobile wanderers bred theirs under the stars in such safety as seclusion by distance from the enemy might afford.

We assume the cave-dweller multiplied with comparative ease owing to this safety, and more rapidly than his brother the wanderer. But when his defenses fell, destruction was more complete, economic waste more terrific. So when he ceased to find a natural cave, he learned to make one. As he grew more powerful, his walls grew heavier. Fortification became his own; cities were, originally, such fortifications. Early dwellings were only less so. He, the cave-dweller, was thus prototype of the state socialist, communist, or statist. Not the democrat.

The cave-dweller's nomadic human counterpart meantime cultivated mobility for safety. Defenses, for him, lay in the Idea—or swiftness, stratagem, and such arts of self-defense as nature taught.

These primitive instincts of the human race—now ingrown instead of outgrowing in this far distance of time—are still at work; although instincts of the wandering tribe seem to have been overcome gradually by the more material defenses and heavier static establishment of the original cave-dweller. Herein we still see the "shadow of this wall."

I imagine the ideal of freedom which keeps breaking through our present static establishments, setting their features aside, or obliterating them, is due in no small degree to survival of the original instincts of the nomad—the adventurer: he who kept his freedom by his undivided prowess beneath the stars rather than he who lived by his obedience and labor in the deep shadow of the wall.

The nomad? Is he thus prototype of the democrat?

However that may be, these conflicting human natures have conquered or been vanquished, married, intermarried, brought forth other natures; a fusion in some, still a straining confusion in others. In some men, a survival, more or less distinct, of one or the other of these salient, archaic instincts of mankind.

Gradually in the present body of mankind, both natural instincts work together and produce what we call civilization. All civilization insists upon and strives to perfect culture, in order that it may survive. By increasing happiness?

In the affair of culture, "shadow-of-the-wall" has so far seemed predominant, although the open sky of the adventurer appeals more and more today to the human spirit. As physical fear of brutal force grows less, all need of fortification grows less. Ingrained yearning of the mobile hunter for freedom now finds more truth and reason for being than the stolid masonry defenses (cave-dwelling) once upon a time erected in necessity to protect human life from humankind. This freedom is now characteristic of all yearning for culture—a spirit still slumbering in the agrarian and the manufacturer, the merchant and the artist.

Yes—modern science makes all ancient, static defenses useless. Man's value now depends not so much upon what he has made static (that is to say, saved, stored up, fortified) as upon what he can *do*—still better—by proper use of new scientific resources. So a human type is emerging capable of rapidly changing environment to fit desires, one amply able to offset the big city of today: remnant of the great, ancient "Wall." In this capability to change we have the new type of citizen. We call him democratic.

It is evident that modern life must be served more naturally and conserved by more space and light, by greater freedom of movement. And by more general expression of the individual in practice of the ideal we now call culture in civilization. A new space-concept is needed. It is becoming more evident everywhere. A definite phase of this new Ideal comes in what we call organic architecture—the *natural* architecture of the democratic spirit in this age of the machine.

Our modern automobility is only one of the leading factors of modernity. Alongside glass and steel it is having characteristic effect upon what survives of the nature of the cave-dweller. He places his faith with the new facilities, speed and command of time and distance, instead of in his own works. But these scientific future-liberating factors of the machine age are actually his means of potential self-realization. But the modern citizen will use them for more human freedom when he uses them at all well. Man is returning to the descendants of the wandering tribe—the adventurers, I hope.

The machine is continuously at work—molding, remodeling, relentlessly driving human character in many directions—mobile. The question is becoming more one of grass or goods? *Men* or *Man*.

So it has already come true in our overgrown cities of today that the terms of feudal thinking are changing, if not by name, to terms of money and commercial diplomacy. But the old form of city, except as a market, has little or nothing substantial to give modern civilization above wagery, little or nothing above the belt—except degeneration.

New York is the biggest mouth in the world. It appears to be prime example of the survival of the herd instinct, leading the universal urban conspiracy to beguile man from his birthright (the good ground), to hang him by his eyebrows from sky-hooks above hard pavements, to crucify him, sell him, or be sold by him. He is now himself a form of rent called production for profit. High priests of such gangsteristics we have set up in politics or in professional armchairs. High priests of religion as of education, as we have them both now, seldom understand and never dare teach the basic freedom, the life-blood of Democracy, ethical and not militant! Its very nature remains obscure. Through new powers of publicity (the power of reiteration) mediocre high priests overtake and imprison a mediocre citizenry. Conformity to mediocrity increases. Into high places go common men. Enormous urban flocks meantime sing false hymns to vicarious power, jazzing a dreary dirge. These theme songs are as false to the singer as to the listener. All badly off key.

Ultimate impotence comes where creation of fine art is the concern.

This price is extracted from us, as a nation, by the momentous mistake of substituting artificiality—artificial means of production and machine power—for human power, in terms of money.

Instead of expanding our spiritual strength as human beings by means of these our new scientific advantages, we are content to practice artifice without art. The Substitute or Imitation is the signpost of our cultural lag. Science can do little or nothing about all this. It is up to the American spirit seeking above things for organic *(natural)* forms truly essential to a culture of our own.

DEMOCRACY: GOSPEL OF INDIVIDUALITY

Only human values are life-giving values.

No organic values are ever life-taking. When man builds "natural" buildings naturally, he builds his very life into them—inspired by intrinsic Nature in this interior sense we are here calling "organic." Instead the citizen is now trained to see life as a cliché whereas his architect should train his own mind, and thereby the citizen's, to see the nature of glass as Glass, the board as Board, a brick as Brick; see the nature of steel as Steel: see all in relation to each other as well as in relation to Time, Place, and Man. Be eager to be honest with himself and so not untrue to other men; desire deeply to live on harmonious terms with Man and Nature; try to live in the richer sense because deep *in* nature: be native as trees to the wood, as grass to the floor of the valley. Only then can the democratic spirit of man, individual, rise out of the confusion of communal life in the city to a creative civilization of the ground. We are calling that civilization of man and ground—really organic agronomy—democracy: intrinsically superior to the more static faiths of the past lying now in ruins all about him. If the Usonian citizen were to live in a free city of democracy he could not fail to make communal life richer for all the world because true individual independence—by natural growth of a natural conscience—would be his. The American citizen is now where he must abandon his favorite expedients—especially the idea that money plus authority can rule the world. He must at last realize that ideas inspired by spiritual integrity can and will make the modern world.

Faith in that conscientious selfhood is the ideal fit for the sons of the sons of American Democracy.

What then is the Nature of this idea we call organic architecture? We are here calling this architecture The Architecture of Democracy. Why?

Because it is intrinsically based on Nature-law: law *for* man not law *over* man. So understood, so applied. It is simply the human spirit given appropriate architectural form. Simply, too, it is the material structure of every man's life on earth now seen by him as various forms of structure—in short, organic. Democracy possesses the material means today to be enlarged intelligently and turned about now to employ machine power on super-materials for man's own superiority. Therefore, organic architecture is not satisfied to be employed merely to make money—not if that money is to be stacked against Man himself. Our growing dissatisfaction with autocratic power or bureaucracy of any kind requires wisdom. Old wisdom and good sense are modern even now; it is their application that changes.

Still more ancient is the wisdom, and it too is modern, that recognizes this new democratic concept of man free in a life wherein money and land-laws are established as subordinate to rights of the human being. That means first of all that good architecture is good democracy.

So dignity and worth would come to our society if the individual were thus *individual;* true individuality, no longer written off as some kind of personal idiosyncracy by way of "taste" but protected as essence, to be understood as the safest basis for interpretation of science, the practice of art, ultimately the inspiration of a true religion. This is modern today; it always was; it always will be. Now in order to become *organic* we will learn to *understand* that form and function are as *one.* On that organic basis a civilization might endure forever as a happy humane circumstance. Free.

This new sense-of-the-within naturally unfolding, taking form by the culture of art, architecture, philosophy and religion, natural; all being content to look *within* to the Spirit for the solution of every human problem and, by expanding the means so found, enlarging and achieving new, varied expressions of life on earth—this would be old wisdom, ancient as Laotze at least; yet modern. That is modern Architecture and modern manhood.

Were we in America to put this concept to work in government, that would be our great day-after-tomorrow? If it were basic in what is now carelessly miscalled "education" we would soon arrive at proper qualification of the vote. And we would arrive at the sense-of-the-within as the new criterion

in art and architecture. By means of it, architecture will be able to qualify the work of the world, reject the imitation and the substitute; make any makeshift a stupidity or a crime. Make life one great integral simplicity: Beauty comes alive.

Such simplicity is necessarily not "plainness." A barn door is not simple; it is merely plain, sterile. Harmonious grace of the wild flower and all countenances of organic integrity anywhere or everywhere are truly simple. In all man-made life-concerns this is integral Simplicity. If organic, simplicity is in itself exuberant. It was ever modern in ancient times. Why not so now?

This our integrity needs—old wisdom, yet new to our present servile, provincial, and amazing civilization. Infinite possibilities exist to make of the city a place suitable for the free man in which freedom can thrive and the soul of man grow, a City of cities that democracy could approve and so desperately needs; will soon demand? Yes, and in that vision of decentralization and reintegration lies our natural twentieth century dawn. Of such is the nature of the democracy free men may honestly call the new freedom. Where and whenever this is understood, the part is to the whole no less than the whole is to the part. This true entity is alone able to live as organic architecture or as culture—the soul of any civilization.

PART TWO: ILLUSION
SOCIAL AND ECONOMIC DISEASE

To look at the cross section of any plan of a big city is to look at something like the section of a fibrous tumor. In the light of the space-needs of the twentieth century we see there not only similar inflamed exaggerations of tissue but more and more painfully forced circulation; comparable to high blood pressure in the human system. Think of the big towns you know; then try to imagine what modern mobility and new space-annihilating facilities, even now, are doing to them! Consider the space-requirement of modern mobilized man today as compared with twenty years ago. At least twenty times larger?

Growing out of the old feudal city-plan are these new *centripetal* centralizations: unrecognized uneconomic forces at work to destroy mankind.

Not only are these forces unchecked, but their acceleration is still encouraged—even by insurance companies themselves investing the people's money in consequence of this unwholesome crowding.

But in all democratic minds a question now coming uppermost is: what benign power can check such centralization as the city has become— now a destructive fixation?

Well—within the problem itself lies the solution. As always. Centralization itself is the old social principle that made kings an appropriate necessity and is now become the uneconomic force that overbuilt them all, degenerated to a force we call communism. These pseudo-monarchic towns of ours are merely such centralization. Centralization now proves to be something that, used to wind space up tighter and tighter, smaller and higher, is like some centripetal device revolving at increasing speed until—terrible, beyond control—it turns centrifugal, ending all by dispersal or explosion.

Meantime, what possible control?

Government? No—or only to a very limited extent. In democracy, more and more limited to expedients; politics.

The only possible control, then, is profoundly educational. In democracy, is education—when on speaking terms with culture—not the true answer to such exaggerations of artificiality as machine power in production, or as *crowding?* On behalf of humane freedom it is the growth of this human intelligence ultimately applied to the city that must interfere by such pressures as it can exert there where pressure does most good. Salvation from the false economics of centralization lies in wider grasp of the limitations and danger of these powers—machine powers all— multiplied to excess. What hope is there for our future in this machine age, if indeed the machine age is to have any greater future, unless decentralization and appropriate reintegration are soon encouraged—given right-of-way in actual practice?

A MAKESHIFT

Three major artificialities have been drafted and grafted by law upon all modern production; hangovers from petty customs originating in feudal cir-

cumstances. Many of these traditions have been blown up into supposed economic patterns: but all forms of rent and all illegitimate. Rent for money; rent for land; really only extrinsic forms of unearned increment; and the third artificiality is traffic in invention. A graft by way of patents is another but less obvious form of "rent."

By mechanical leverage accelerating urban activity, creating pressures never existing before and now never ceasing, these three unnatural economic features are the forces of our present-day city, enormously intensified. Monstrosity has been reached. But the capacity of the human animal for habituation is also enormous—seemingly beyond belief.

RENT

The first and most important form of rent contributing to overgrowth of cities, resulting in poverty and unhappiness, is rent for land: land-values created as improvements or by growth, held by some fortuitous fortune's accidental claim to some lucky piece of realty, private but protected by law. Profits from this adventitious form of fortune create a series of white-collarites—satellites of various other unearned increments, like real-estate traffic in more or less lucky land areas. The skyscraper as abused is also an instance of adventitious increment. The city the natural home of this form of "fortune."

The second artificiality: rent for money. By way of the ancient Mosaic invention of "interest," money is now a commodity for sale, so made as to come alive as something in itself—to go on continuously working in order to make all work useless. All profits earned by "big money" are a specious premium placed upon the accretions of labor, creating—in the form of interest—another, a second adventitious form of fortune. More armies of money satellites busily engaged in the sale, distribution, operation and collection of this special form of increment, rent for money, all unearned except as an arbitrary, mysterious premium placed upon money itself "earned," so called by those who made it. A new *speculative commodity* has therefore appeared—money, unnatural as a commodity, now becoming monstrosity. The modern city is its stronghold and chief defender; and insurance is one of its commodities.

The third economic artificiality: unearned increment of the machine itself. The profits of this great, common leverage over labor as now employed by all mankind are thus placed where they seldom, if ever, belong. Here traffic in invention is captained, maintained by a form of capitalism intensified. By the triumph of conscienceless but "rugged individualism" the machine profits of human ingenuity or inspiration in getting the work of the world done are almost all funneled into pockets of fewer and more "rugged" captains-of-industry. Only in a small measure—except by gift or *noblesse oblige* of the captains—are these profits yet (or will they ever be) where they belong; that is to say, with the man whose life is actually modified, given, or sacrificed to this new common agency for doing the work of the world. This agency we call "the machine."

So, armies of countless high-powered salesmen—salesmanship the modern art—now come into being in order to unload the senseless overproduction inevitable to this new machine facility, exercised by the hands of insensate "business" greed. The worker is thus dispossessed as owner of the machine: *the man himself,* another dispossession. As subordinate rent-creature, a third form of "fortune" is here. A series of white-collar satellites again rises—selling. This form of propaganda, salesmanship, becomes *the* great modern "art." Politics and journalism (managed publicity) financing, collecting by foreclosure, increasing artificial profits by refinancing, are crafts of repossession. Wholly false fronts are set up as mercantile commonplaces and a wholly false capitalizing of "risk" takes place that now rides high as "insurance." Security not only may be bought but *must* be bought and paid for in almost any case.

Unnatural fixations all—the three economic creatures of rent—all unearned increments. Together with other creatures of false fortune they concentrate money-power in fewer and fewer hands, as insurance. Inevitable centripetal action of capitalistic centralization proceeds by tactfully extended channels of control.

Now, to maintain this mounting external money-power in due force and effect, innumerable legal sanctions must be continuously sought, applied and maintained. Agents of all these artificial factors dovetail together. This is now called the "moral necessity" of "business," until morality is no longer on speaking terms with ethics. What is expedient is too soon legal and enacted by government as moral. What is right (ethical) is entirely another matter, too often beside the mark. Then what is right? What is culture? Where then is this one-time science of human happiness we call "politics"?

Once upon a time the Jeffersonian democratic ideal of these United States was, "that government best government that governs least." But in order to keep the peace and some show of equity between the lower passions so busily begotten in begetting, the complicated forms of super-money-increase-money-making and holding are legitimatized by government. Government too, thus becomes monstrosity. Again enormous armies of white-collarites arise. Here comes more bureaucracy: public checking of private money—to add to the public armies of the bureaucrat. All dressed in a little brief authority. As all this comes uppermost major and minor courts are multiplied; petty officials, their complex rulings petrified, become more and more necessary until they, too, are an army keeping tab and collecting "legal" extractions from the citizenry if for no other reason than to maintain such phenomenal bureaucracy. We might now add this form of fortune (the official job) to the other three. But this, too, is only another subordinate creature: government committed to collect rents. Perpetual propaganda becomes a kind of vested interest, itself growing ubiquitous. Again public propaganda perpetrated upon the people for which the people must pay, whether of the minority party or majority party. Always comes the next election and propaganda turned loose.

Multifarious as these laws—enacted by our promise-merchants, the politicians—are, they are only complex expedients to force this swarming clerical breed of bureaucracy to function together. This has bred, finally, still more droves of white-collarites: a new army of lawyers. It becomes impossible to hold, operate, or distribute land, sell or buy money, or manufacture anything, safely, or even marry, make love or die, without the guide and counsel of these specialists in the extraordinary entanglements of rent, of rules, of regulations applied to this or that involute commercial expedient with courts for counters where the attempt to put law above man is made in this complex game we now call our civilization in the prosperity of the machine age. Small wonder, then, that decisions of these specialists in "law and order" so often are themselves in conflict! Lawyers, as satellites of rent, maintain its multiple forms. And so hundreds of thousands of legal experts are the inevitable mentors of whatever mission is now left to the American big city to perform. We must add the lawyer as yet another subordinate form of rent bred by government and thriving upon misfortune or its prevention; but committed, either way, to performance.

These artificialities all depend upon a strong-arm status quo. The Police! Also upon some expedient form of religion wherein men are to be saved (from themselves and each other) and for God by faith in God rather than faith in their own works as men.

All together against quality in these United States, this marching army of quantity is the traditional substitute for organic economic structure of the forms of humane society: art, architecture and religion. Any simple *basis* we might honestly call fundamental to the economy of our democratic republic is not there. This society of ours has overbuilt and now persists in overinhabiting cities—a wholly inorganic basis for survival now shamefully battening upon sources of extrinsic production; senselessly increasing production for the sake of more production! Production is now trying to control consumption—the big horse behind the little cart. This it is that turns the nation into a vast factory, greedy for foreign markets, with the spectre of war as inevitable clearing house.

The old city, already distinctly dated by its own excess, is only further outmoded by every forced increase. Our natural resource now is in new possibilities of access to good uses of good ground: an agronomy intelligently administered.

Our sources of production are intrinsic only with those men who—by skilled or manual toil or concentration of superior ability, by inspiration, upon natural resources or upon actual production whether physical, aesthetic, intellectual, mechanical, or religious—render "value received" to human life. To these hewers of wood and drawers of water and men of the machine, pressing questions of decentralization must be referred. The living, consuming man-unit of our society will ultimately decide this momentous issue. *Consumption must control production.* This matter will only be decided by consumption in proper control of an organic basis for distribution, man to man, nation to nation.

What then of this human subject (or object) the man-unit (he is consumption) upon whom, by his own voluntary subordination, this now vastly complicated uneconomic structure has been erected and cruelly functions, although rudely interrupted by failure about every seven years only to be strong-armed by federal government? Aid. All-pervading, large or small business aid is now quite universally accepted as moral. Even normal?

But what about the man of ideas who labors out of the unknown essential sustenance for all? What about this imaginative individual who gives reality to thought? The planner-designer—he who gets results from materials so far as the life of society is concerned with them? Where in all this is the Artist Agrarian, Artist Mechanic, the inspired Teacher, Inventor, Scientist—in short, the Artifex? And then what about "hewers of wood, drawers of water, the laborers in the vineyard" and elsewhere?

Well—all are pretty much in the same hard case, or shall we say, caste? No longer masters of fortune. Fear is their daily portion.

Fortunes today engendered (controlled) by schemers; experts in the complex artificialities of this from-the-bottom-to-the-top-down system we are miscalling capitalism. Must this capitalisticism rest upon no broad human basis square with the *nature* of man's rightful relationship to other men or to his own credit here at his own hearth on earth? Façades of false fortune place false premiums upon false traits of his character. Moreover, though the three main systems of false fortune are necessarily maintained by the strong arm of a forced "legitimacy"—that arm, however strong, however reinforced by the police, must periodically tire; come down while confusion and misery of the day of reckoning meantime descend upon all: life itself confused as alarm seeks cover of some kind—somehow—anywhere. We name the chronic recessions thus created (are they a fatal disease?) "depressions." Or, if it is a managed convulsion by high-powered finance, we have war: war the inevitable clearing house of finance-a-la-mode: always war! Nothing else can save any system from destruction where production controls consumption except it be by this ages-old destroyer. War.

Where, then, in this destructive ambush of strong-arm-artificiality superimposed on artificiality, is integrity of the genuine artifex to be found? Where is the original source—basic master of ideas—inspiring the artifex? What place has he in this economic Tower of Babel with its apex in false fortune; accelerating manufacture for exaggerated profits? All profiteering—a deflation of manhood to inflate and exploit mankind. Inflation is bound to be characteristic of any such haphazard system strong-armed by law. Why miscall this system Capitalism when its base is up in air and apex down on the ground?

THE ARTIFEX

We admit that such haphazard centralization as we have attempted in utter materialism confers certain human benefits upon the artifex, stimulating by financial reward his ingenuity in machine development and all its uses. But far more extensive uses of our vast machine resources now do lie ready to make life more available to the citizen. Meantime, essential rightmindedness and decency of the artifex have moved him to go on working in this confusion of our machine age; trying to cultivate justice, generosity, and pity; best of all, the beauty of individual responsibility—in the midst of chaos. Upstream almost all the way without very well knowing why or how, worshipping not a golden god hidden in a cave but a great spirit ruling all by Principle. Modern man has been doing so without quite knowing how to apply that inner principle; hardly knowing even in just what the principle really consists.

Nevertheless, he knows that god of the free artifex is a great free Spirit allowing man to choose between what is good *for* him and good *in* him as against what is bad *in* him and bad *for* him, so that by free exercise of his conscience he may himself grow god-like. The road to a good life is still open to the artifex. But today his road must lead on through persistent public obstruction, most of all the drift toward conformity—the subtle envious propaganda against superiority—hindrances legally erected, legalities exploiting his good faith—a general depravity in a drift toward quantity at expense to quality, until we find all heading in toward war or revolution: this time the revolution industrial—yes. Agrarian, no. About time now our agronomy asserted itself in his behalf. You've left a glimmer still to cheer the man—the artifex—and by that light now mark my words we'll build the perfect ship.— (Kipling's McAndrew's Hymn.)

AN EXPERIMENT

In spite of all perversity—of the cash-and-carry mentality, the servile system it would maintain (if it could) grafted upon the new world of organic character—appears this modern organic concept of man and his God as organic growth: therefore a deeper sense of human integrity which we might properly call organic Democracy. Out of this philosophic romance, the life of man began with this new nation of ours as a foundling conceived in liberty to pursue the growth we call happiness. All men to have equal opportunity before the law; thus to develop manhood. Our vast territory, riches untouched, was inherited by all breeds of the earth who were courageous enough to come and take domain on the hard terms of "pioneer." A new frontier we erected then. Not the frontier we are facing now.

Our new nation, called a republic, was an experiment in freedom, eagerly manned by refugees from the despotism and monarchy of all nations. Soon we became a great federation of states, the greatest known—these United States of America. United, the states became a nation—call it Usonia[4]—harboring within its borders the murderer, the adventurer, the outcast, the cheated, the thwarted and the superior: the predatory worst but also the courageous best of human kind deserting previous nationality to make a new nation—a life there to be in the image of a great ideal of freedom—at home on vast incomparable ground. Or so its leaders planned, hoped and pleaded. A new nation founded upon the best and the worst wherein rule by the bravest and the best would be *natural*.

Though with no corresponding revisions of traditional, Romish, or feudal, property-rights; and not much, if any, consideration given to appropriate new economy, our new country *was* founded upon a more just freedom for the individual than any before known: "that government best government which governs least" said a Thomas Jefferson crossing an Alexander Hamilton. George Washington, Thomas Paine, Abraham Lincoln, William Lloyd Garrison, John Brown, Emerson, Whitman, Thoreau, Henry George, Louis Sullivan—such as these and their kind were her sons. In them the original ideal was held clear. Then arose indiscriminate private wealth by way of fortuitous survivals of despotisms: feudal money-getting and property-holding. The new nation carelessly adopted them. An economic order more suited to monarchy and despotism than freedom was let loose with fresh ascendancy. Now see a new free-for-all race for power of riches, riches of power. It soon outran such culture as appeared, or bought it ready-made. Unnatural reservoirs of capital as predatory accumulation made away with what little cultural understanding the new country had originally borrowed—a culture of no indigenous integrity. It was easy to discover, gather and exploit the fresh spoils of our vast new territory that huge fortunes piled up, almost overnight, in hands least fitted to administer the powers of wealth. The fortunate, lucky, were only too willing to buy ready-made whatever they might like—buy what they did not know they could only have truly if *grown*. Suddenly rich, not content within the culture they had with them (or on them) when they came here, they were quite satisfied with importation they could buy. As

a matter of course the original idea of Freedom grew thin so far as culture went, and grew dim or died. Such arts as had come to our new states with the frugal decency of the early colonials survived but a short time, but there was no principle originally involved, or living, in the Colonial arts that came over to grow new culture upon. Originally modified French elegance or borrowed Italian Renaissance, they were already degenerate when they reached new land. Soon with the advent of so many foreign nationalities came licentious eclecticisms in all art. By way of peripatetic taste we were especially devastated in architecture. A ready-made art, antique or pseudo-classic (the same thing), satisfied the pressing social demand and even became the pressing need of Society in the new nation. Riches in general so rapidly overwhelmed any indigenous culture that so-called "American architecture" fell to the great low in eclecticism of all time. "Culture" attempted thus ready-made became a mere commodity. So its merchant became "moral." The merchant became desirable, even a social-aesthete! To refer to Principle was not yet offensive to science, but it was peculiarly offensive to the merchant in the education of the arts. To refer whatever culture we had to Principle was then beside the mark. The "radical" became an offense: dangerous! Where there were no roots, why look for them as he would? The radical became a menace, considered—even as now—unconstitutional.

Here (is it for the first time in history?) a self-determining polyglot people on incomparable ground, subscribing to the highest ideal of human freedom yet known, sprang into being as a nation with a curious bastardized culture; its culture a quarreling collection of many ready-made cultures of the world, borrowed, pieced together by uncultivated "taste." Such as it was, here was a makeshift garment worn outside in—even upside down—not cast away as we now see it should have been. So we got the wasteful makeshift our eclecticisms became and that we now regard in this ugly discord all around us. Incongruity was begot by riches. Great abortion. But abortion was merchantable, therefore "moral," no more than a makeshift; a purchase consisting at best in some copy of the great rebirth called "the Renaissance" so that nothing indigenous in art could be born to us. Thus quondam bastardization of the new nation's character was artificially elected and applied; an artificiality soon to be confirmed by "higher" education! Education in America became a collection of imported academic devices arbitrarily applied to the surface of life. And, too soon, the authority of this pseudo-culture was battening upon developments of our material resources, characterizing our wealth. Externally applied substitutes such as these inevitably failed to inspire an appropriate (Usonian) way of life of our own—or of our era—or to encourage integrity in interpretation of our new ideal of freedom; the ideal upon which the life of our new country was so eagerly founded: the Sovereignty of the Individual!

So this new nation arose, grew in might as it grew in riches but, so far as culture went, shamefully wasting, upon the imported substitute, its every natural characteristic and resource. Strange perversions or absurd pretenses were presented as worthy.

But the nation quickly outgrew the narrow bounds of the weak borrowed forms, even while academic education still continued to condition the people by planting and nursing the Substitute. See the buildings they built for the purpose. No constructive lessons could be learned from such servile eclecticism as became nationally characteristic. All our great nation had upon which to found and grow indigenous culture was sacrificed to this reflection of the "setting sun all Europe had mistaken for dawn." Academic abnegation amounted to obsession; and, by the personal likes or dislikes of the wives of our rugged culture-puzzled individualists who themselves really cared nothing at all about the matter, art became a mere academic pretense or a fashion; American culture a form of license putting on provincial airs and fancified attire.

This pseudo-culture became the more deplorable as our money-power grew more enormous. The better citizenry—north, south, east, west—took refuge in the authentic antique, and committed aesthetic suicide by acquiring monstrosities openly in the name of the "classic." Conformity. Mere names and "the styles" thus gained prestige and, soon, au-

thority. Periodic fashion could, and did, rule supreme. Downright imitation in all arts that should have been creative became at least honorable though impotent. This very impotence was called "conservative!" Meantime the more fancified citizenry also committed promiscuous adultery by the purchase of atrocities in the name of the Louis' and their mistresses. Paris was capital not only of the pseudo-English Colonial venture in culture; it now became the capital of our own pseudo-aesthetic interests.

This prostitute pictorial performance was, in our national life, raised to authorized academic pattern, eagerly grasped and sanctioned by the Mrs. Gablemores and Madame Plasterbilts of American "good society." Evil consequences of this confusion or degradation of choice by what the selective "taste" of the period could buy abroad—or import—were fashionable.

The god of Principle to guide the rulers of the country new-founded upon a more just expression of human liberty than men had known before did not seem to inspire appropriate (or even sensible) interpretations for the ways and means of the free and democratic life that had been made possible. Nor did the wealthy or the supremely successful seem to understand not only what life under their great democratic ideal meant in terms of economics, but not at all what arts or crafts would be natural to such a life as ours. Unsuitable fruits of the old monarchic-authoritarian system prevailed, demoralizing any vital functioning of art. So also demoralized whatever else went with it? Ancient "traditions" now entered the heart of the nation. Not in spirit? No. As culture, a mere eclecticism damnable by taste. In place of culture of our own came servile abnegation to the past. We were conservative?

Architecture, parasitism for five centuries, sank to incontinent imitation by our ever freshly confirmed eclectic fashionables. Religion itself (quite naturally) sank beneath the level of duly accredited servility. The need to maintain this abnegation or sterilization was inevitable. In all valid interests of our new life, exploitation of the cliché (the "formula") in religion as well as aesthetics had right of way because get-rich-quick patrons found it as expedient to get-culture-quick. Yes . . . ignorant provincial social ambitions had found this cheap shortcut to culture. The healthy spiritual significance of our own new ideal of freedom—Democracy—was, and so easily, betrayed by the powers of financial success.

Provincial people thus superficially and suddenly eclectified could, perhaps, breed "tastes" that could only turn back to taste—instead of growing new life of the spirit or new ground in a new era. The culture we as a people needed was a culture the European world itself needed in somewhat different terms.

So, once again, this time in the latter days of the nineteenth century and early in the twentieth, our American academic world mistook the setting sun for dawn. *"Pseudo"* by official order was duly confirmed as Precedent and ruled over popular education. "American" in culture became the highly respectable following-after into general outer darkness which we now see in perspective as the present "International" cliché.

THE CULTURE LAG
What could such superartificiality do but stumble and fall wherever or whenever Life insisted upon itself as beautiful?

The cultural lag? The lag was to be proudly worn as a tag of respectability for another half-century before it became a rag.

Still with us now, to stay perhaps for some years more? Still with us though modified—at least by mouth.

There could be nothing of course in such bottoms-up provincial servility as ours that could grow anything at all worthy of the spirit of our great adventure? Wealth, indiscriminate, and growing abuse of vicarious power, increased the numbers of those unqualified for success; and the new country could only outgrow old medieval cities—centralization patterned after the ancient feudal town outmoded. That appropriate beautiful town now became static. The great ideal of Freedom had declined, by the refusal of "authority" to let it be truly free. Money-power could not be substituted for ideas, could do no more than make more money with money or go to war. Go to war it went.

The Jeffersonian democratic ideal, so inspiring in the beginning, is really the highest form of aristocracy this world has ever seen: aristocracy genuinely a quality of the man himself—not merely bestowed upon him by heredity or privilege: now a matter of *character*.

But aristocracy lacked spiritual nourishment and man had grown sterile. He had little left that could encourage and give prestige to the new idea of democracy. And so old intellectual equipment met new paraphernalia head on. Indigenous culture was—to this day—left to languish. Except as the cultural mask might be imposed by architects—themselves no more than drapers and haberdashers of the arts—shallow *couturiers* who functioned as "artists." High-powered salesmanship by professionally managed publicity was able to sell their feeble or profane derivations of old culture to new "success"—if not shameful ugliness, sheer stupidity—and any upsurge of vitality in the arts of the new republic was left to lie before us. Reproach growing to this day! Naked necessity would have been far better.

This cultural mask has thus covered and concealed our true nature. In the name of some bad forms of surface-decoration, or the cliché internationale, our country was and still is being taught to call it Architecture. All but one of our universities have conditioned the novitiate to regard this bastardization of motive as the essence of art and architecture.

So the teenager—American youth—goes to the stocks to be conditioned by false qualifiers in the greatest eclecticisms of all time—our big colleges. There hopelessly confirmed parasites of the American spirit teach our youth. They are crammed with imported formulas for all this idiosyncrasy of "good taste." But taste can never be more than a matter of ignorance now, because the way to knowledge is truly open to the teenager.

Such substitute for culture—suitably urban—as we have set up in the big cities of these United States, thus betrays the country. It functions as something imposed upon American life because we—the people—could not or would not learn the value of culture really grown out of the daily circumstances of our life. Organic. Unable to live our own lives where the fruits of a new civilization might be our concern we have found it so much easier—cheaper too—to fake our culture, or buy it ready-made. Uncertain provincials, still awkward, we have been afraid of being laughed at if our "choice" (taste) should happen not to be properly certified by duly managed prestige. In our ignorance, such *authority* was once upon a time all we had to *steer* by.

FOR THE INDIVIDUAL

Buddha believed in nonvicarious effort—the spirit—only; that is to say, only in effort disciplined from within. The individual himself might never reach the ultimate for man on earth but what matter?

And Jesus taught the dignity and worth of the individual as developed from within. *"The Kingdom of God is within you":* the potential of individuality. Christianity in his name diverted this teaching, professionalized and confused it in creeds and churches. Even by the Gothic cathedrals.

The Church, with its creeds that Jesus did not want, discounted his Idea, seeing in it only "every man for himself and the devil for the hindmost." So "religion" has too often emphasized the desirability of the disappearance of individuality: this, more or less, is also the politics of fascism or of communism; similar to the practice of monarchic, socialistic or communistic peoples. Meantime the protestant succeeded in bringing individuality back, but only partially; as a compromised Ideal.

Some five hundred years before the life of Jesus, the Chinese philosopher Laotze preached the sense of Individuality as a reflex of the organic unity of the Cosmos: the true source of human power, the all pervasive "state-of-becoming"! Our own democratic ideal of the social state seems originally conceived as some such unity. That is to say, Democracy was conceived as the free growth of humane individuality, mankind free to function together in unity of spirit (their own skill in the making); by nature thus averse to formalism and so to institutionalizing. Institution seemed a form of death. This ideal of Nature lies at the core of organic

democracy, and architecture organic. We should emphasize this in order to regain ground lost to the industrial revolution and consequent wars. But now come haphazard big builders of these haphazard cities being badly overbuilt. By way of the industrial revolution this great iron horse (the Machine), upon which the West rode to power, is now rampant in the Middle East and the East. The yellow man, ubiquitous, is learning to ride. Well, why are we afraid of him? Is it our conscience? Or the lack of it?

Out of American "rugged individualism" captained by rugged captains of our rugged industrial enterprises we have gradually evolved a crude, vain power: plutocratic "Capitalism." Not true capitalism. I believe this is entirely foreign to our own original idea of Democracy. The actual difference between such "individualism" and individuality of true democracy lies in the difference between cowardly selfishness and noble selfhood! Like the difference between sentiment and sentimentality or the difference between liberty and license.

"Isms" only aggravate misuse of vicarious powers by our expedient masters of the expedient, using the three great increments—rent for land, rent for money, and rent for manhood—to put native individuality into bad repute, or into its grave. Like the abuse of any good thing abuses of individuality will bring reactionary consequences. Proof of such reaction is with us today. Fearful, our ultra-conservative rich men are proof enough. But our art, degraded to the level of the makeshift, and our tottering religion, are stronger proof. These personal idiot-syncrasies of "the man of taste" by which we are persistently misled in the name of individuality are still more evidence. If creative ability is our concern, we may be seen to have failed, because sterility has been the natural consequence of vicarious exercise of our enormous mechanical powers. Abuses of power are characteristics of ultimate defeat. Not success. Quantity uprises at expense to quality. This is surely the antithesis of Democracy.

But true creative ability as always will be the first concern of democratic individuality. And, conversely, Individuality must ever be the concern and success of creative ability. Until Usonia recognizes individuality not as personality merely but as the natural blossom and fruit of organic character; seldom if ever common; always radical—therefore, however difficult, is conservative of Life itself (being *of* the Soul)—we will have no adequate share in Democracy nor any in its defense, because we will not have grasped what Democracy really means! Then how can we learn to develop and protect it if we do not learn to know what it does really mean?

Democracy cannot afford mere personality to be mistaken for true human individuality. Nor can the human will and mere intellect ever produce true individuality. Any such attempt could make only a mimic, or a monster; perhaps at best a scientist. Should our own great or near-great ever become able to draw the line between the Curious and the Beautiful, this difference between personality and individuality will come clear. Salvation of our culture therefore lies in practices which would be evident enough if we would evolve true definitions of the character of our purpose and the nature of our circumstances.

We "the Free" should recognize individuality as organic entity of the man: essence of the soul of true manhood. Democracy is of the soul, not an expedient. Our policy would then always be a determination to struggle against any form of fixation or conformity. Militocracy or any cliché outside that of the machine itself would be murder of opportunity.

If the significance (*spirit*) of form is lacking, creative art can be nothing of or for the soul. Only where this significance is the aura of form does the spirit enter into man-made things. Art. To be insignificant our nation needs only to be without this radiant aura of indigenous spirit. To be a people without this supreme poetic expression of principle—Art and Architecture—is to be untrue to our ideology, untrue to ourselves. To have no true philosophy as sanctuary for the spirit of Freedom is to have no haven for genius, national or personal.

Democratic individuality therefore may be said to be organic; of the character of the "person" or of "things." An inner *quality*. So we may properly call that *quality* as of the Soul. Creative manhood, first to last, is concerned with soul as the deeper significance. Education should consist in learning to recognize its integrity and this indigenous character wherever found in people or things. When we speak of character we often really refer to individuality. Democracy is the very gospel of Individuality.

Without such elemental human integrity, there can be only the use and abuse of materialism not much above the belt, and vicarious. That is to say not above artificiality. No great art or architecture, as poetry; no religion; no integrity even of conduct.

If we deeply enough desire democracy, we will be much more careful of how we turn upon our basic ego—selfhood—just because we have failed to distinguish it from mere egotism. We have misnamed so many flagrant abuses by egotism in the name of individuality. For instance the rugged "individualism" of capitalism. "Capitalistic" may mean merely individual*ism*, or a run-in with riot. Such ism may be (usually is) completely something else—something for which true individuality has but scorn. And true individuality has no more to do with the crass methods of mercantile egotism such as ours than with communism or socialism at its other extreme. Democratic individuality, a salient essence of all human life, is the fundamental core of Art and Artist—creative.

No isms can express true individuality. Any man with a formula instead of a spirit has already taken his place as an affront to nature: a mere *substitute* no matter what ist, ism, or ite he may be.

> "Man, proud man,
> Drest in a little brief authority,
> Most ignorant of what he's most assured,
> His glassy essence, like an angry ape,
> Plays such fantastic tricks before high heaven,
> As make the angels weep."

Great religious leaders—Buddha, Jesus, Abdul Baha, Mohammed, Laotze especially—wanted no formalism by institutionalizing religion: tolerated no bureaucracy or officialism in the realm of the Spirit. Such integrity of soul wanted not even disciples!

So human nature, far "out of drawing" in this day of our own time, is bound to miseducate because miseducated. The education that would be essential to the freedom of human nature is either on crutches now or pitifully weak; pseudo-functioning only on pseudo lines; staying on the boulevard; thinking by the groove; moving by interior wheels or on rails. City pavements? The sidewalk-happy probably function best when off hard pavements and in the rut. And, since we all go now on wheels on rail or pavement, or "fly," life tends to become a rut. So rut-government seems inevitable at the moment and the rut the "way of all flesh."

How then does the rut become disreputable? Surely expedient, considered moral, therefore it is said to be safe—"conservative." Often it is only the rut that we call Law and Order. May it be what we are now inclined to call civilization?

So Individuality *is* a menace to all forms of rut-life. Rut-life turns with ratlike perspicacity against all individuality; with hatreds born of Fear. The so-called Conservative has always hated the Radical: hates him with good reason because the "conservative" is afraid of going to the roots of anything at all—just because he knows instinctively he has no roots! And there can be none wherever he is on the ground.

Now, we are here reading an actual consideration of the nature of the future city of democracy: a city with greater future for human individuality: a life in deeper organic sense, true to man's own Spirit—individuality being *fundamental integrity of the soul of man* in his own time and place—and so most valuable asset of the human race. Without this city of its own America will never have known a culture of its own. No great architecture can arise *from* us or *for* us based upon the expedient use of the ancient city. Wherever there will be the democratic city, individuality of conscience and the conscience of individuality will be inviolate.

THE INEXORABLE LAW OF CHANGE

We must admit that before the advent of any wholesale standardized mechanization of a new city the American way of life in the old city was, in its effects and proportions, no longer humane because its basic plan was so completely medieval. The Middle Ages.

In no planning which the old city has received has modern spacing been based fairly enough upon the new time scale of modern mobilization—the human being no longer on his feet or seated in a trap behind a horse or two, but in his motor car, or going in his plane. Listening to commentators on the subject, we find that machinery has brought to us no alternative plan. Urban life, originally, was a festival of wit, a show of pomp and a revel of occasion while all was still in *human scale*. True urbanization rewarded life back there in feudal circumstances, a life for which our cities of today were originally planned and built, formed by and for a group-life of powerful individualities, themselves in scale true to human life in medieval times. Then conveniently enough spaced. But now under modern machine age pressures, the better life is being driven, or wills itself, away. Either gone or going now, it travels to and fro: perhaps lives in penthouses in the city or far beyond in country estates. More time wasted in the to and fro than is spent in desirable activity. Such genius as the big city now knows is recruited from farms and villages of the American countryside. No city with over 100,000 population can live by its own birthrate. The recruits, celebrants of the hard pavement (such as they are), sidewalk-happy, all now seek the city to find it to be a market only: insatiable. A great maw demanding and devouring *quantity* instead of encouraging and protecting *quality*. As it devours man, so now it must devour itself. Fish are for sale in this marketplace but there are none in its streams. The foolish celebrant, crowding in on crowds of hypnotized seekers no less confused, frequently escapes to the countryside; escape essential because the overgrown city now offers him nothing he cannot better find on terms of comparative health and freedom in the beauty of the countryside. Already the age of the machine has laid that open to "his majesty the American citizen." While he slept it came upon him . . . the American architect notwithstanding—impotent.

Again, reflect upon these facts: first the fundamental unit of space-measurement in modern life has, for every man, so radically changed that he now bulks twenty to one—even a hundred to one—when he gets around about seated in his favorite motor car. Then reflect that mobilization has only just begun! This circumstance of the car alone is rendering the old big city obsolete? Like some hopelessly inadequate old boat or building, the city itself is still in use, inhabited because we feel we cannot afford to throw it away and allow the spirit of Time, Place, and Man to build the new ones we now so much need. Soon we will be willing to give all we have to get on with the well-planned city of our own freedom. Inevitably this new city is underway for our posterity if not for ourselves. Posterity must have it.

But reading history we learn that the devouring of human individuality has ended invariably in eventual desolation together of the devourer and the devoured. Once render conscience "suspect" or deny conscience as sacred to freedom itself and you have only downfall ahead: of man or his works.

Then why and for what are these overgrown American cities so desperately maintained? Exaggerated as they now are, and held against the normal tide of change? Held for militocracy, prostitution, banking and war? At what price?

ILLUSION

And yet, coming to the greatest of them, New York, for the first time, one has the illusion that we must be a great people to have raised this heavy barrage of relentless commercial mantraps so high; to have grandly hung so much book-architecture upon cumbrous old-fashioned steel framing, so regardless. Inhabited at such enormous cost not alone in money but in all human values as well.

Such frantic energy pours through this haphazard money-mountain made by the mile to pile up and confuse men and materials, haphazard; here and there ruthless; drenched by what relentless ambition has wrung from our abounding national resources. Well, what of it—if everywhere these resources are wasted by foolish attempts at establishment by the nation and we end in some form of bad surface-decoration? What if one arrogant skyscraper does outrun or ram another, and crams the horizon with harsh haphazard masses—upended, crowding on the bewildered wistful eye, peering up from black shadows cast upon the man down there below on hard pavement? What, if so? We have seen crowding, greater if similar, as destructive drama wherever irresistible physical force has violated mankind or tilted up and broken through earth's crust. So—see in this volcanic crater of confused energy bred by money-power, no wise control of enormous mechanical forces, pushing up to crowd and be crowded, to grind against each other with a blind force moved by common greed. Crowded exploitation, as only the Machine can crowd and exploit, forcing *anxiety* upon all modern life. Is astonishment at all this akin to admiration? But consider—this is never a *noble* expression of life; it is again and again only the apotheosis by the gregarious expedient of overmastering Rent.

The shadows of these haphazard skyscrapers cast down below are significant. Their shadows are the surviving shadow-of-the-ancient-wall of the cave-dweller.

The skyscraper if considered as independent achievement in itself may be justifiable: a prideful thing! A tall building may be very beautiful, economical and desirable in itself—provided always that it is in no way interference with what lives below, but looking further ahead than the end of the landlord's ruse—by inhabiting a small green park. That park is humane now. The skyscraper is no longer sane unless in free green space. In the country it may stand beautiful for its own sake.

Exaggerated perpendicularity has no such bill-of-health. It is now the terrible stricture of our big city. Whatever is perpendicular casts a shadow: shadows of the skyscraper fall aground and where crowded are an utterly selfish exploitation. Because, if the civic rights of the neighbor down there below, in the shadows, were to be exercised, there would be no "skyscraping" at all. There would be only a general rise in urban floor-level. Without much sense and with no distinction, cramping and swamping all tenantry in artificial light and forced ventilation, all would congest and be congestion unbearable even to the herd-struck morons our present skyscraperism has cultivated.

THE LIGHT OF DAY

So to the urban skyscraper-builder in overcrowded cities the very insolence of the urban skyscraper-feat is no small measure of its attraction? Although skyscraperism fits so well into the primitive psychology of the "rugged individualist" of the industrial revolution—he who from an office fifty stories above the man in the street casts his ominous shadow below upon the man he directs in some great money-making enterprise—he *is* "success?" He is at last picturesque in the way he likes to be. The tall silk hat and gold-tipped stick of the past had only a little something to gratify his old-fashioned equivalent—but now? What a hallmark, the very tallest building in the big city outcrowding the already overcrowded, based upon commercial success! Ancient titles? Mere nicknames! Here he is—the tangible proof of the "greatness" of modern business. In the city, is this skyscraper shadow his own shadow? But what does that matter or mean to his place in Time? He will never know.

Now move him and his shadow into the open spaces and he becomes truly splendid: a contribution to the glory and dignity of our era. The difference?

Simple. As material things stand with us today the skyscraper might be ultimate expression of the individuality fairly expected from the freedom of democracy to signify what we have so painstakingly prophesied and now discourage. But in the overcrowded big city it is no exalted order of merit. See it there as conspicuous proof of the cultural lag and a fine example of our conspicuous waste.

In the present era's future (if it has one) the skyscraper will be considered *"ne plus ultra of the e pluribus unum"* capitalistic centralization. The New York skyscraper will be seen as the prancing of this great iron horse—the industrial revolution. The iron horse rearing high hoofs in air for the plunge before the runaway—the runaway to oblivion by way of the atom bomb—or we go to the country!

Thus enforced upon our understanding by the non-understanding in overgrown urban life, skyscrap-

ing is not merely a falsity but a moral, economic, aesthetic, ethical monstrosity!

This exaggeration of privilege among us is already far out of democratic scale. Owing to social, collegiate, and commercial pride of exploitation going hand in hand with miseducation—if properly citified, "well mechanized," that is to say standardized by commerce, the citizen is now so far gone that he easily mistakes the pig-piling and crowding of big business for eminence of excellence: mistakes the pushbutton powers of the machine age for his own powers and finds hectic excitement in urban uproar and the vertigo of verticality. The more citified he becomes the less civilized he is; the more this racing of the iron-horse into the inferiority of conformity grows characteristic of his weakness. Roaring tumults of congestion emphasize terrific collisions of power; explosions of grinding mechanical forces in this whirling vortex, urban exaggeration; in these the rich whirling-dervish thinks he sees *his own* greatness. In the whirl the citizen is satiated—his "greatness" something wholly vicarious. But his shadow too is the shadow cast by the sun.

And yet—seen at night, heedless of stampede, the haphazard monster has myriad beauties of silhouette; light streaming—the light punctuated by reflected or refracted lights. In human terms yet undefined, the nocturnal monster yields rhythmical perspectives, glowing spotted walls of light, dotted lines, a world of fascinating reflections hung upon other reflections ranging along vistas of the street or pendent as the wisteria hangs its violet racemes on a trellis or the trees. Then the skyscraper is, in the dusk, a shimmering, prismatic verticality; gossamer veil of a festive scene, hanging there against the backdrop of a black night sky to dazzle, entertain, and amaze, in great masses. Lighted interiors come through the veil with a sense of life and well-being. The City then seems alive. It does live as illusion lives.

The light of day? Streams of more and more insignificant façades and dead walls rise and pour out of hard faced masses behind and above human beings all crawling on hard pavements like ants to "hole in" somewhere or find their way to this or that cubicle. Beings packed into the roar, rush and danger of a new kind of the old voracity—speed. And out of other holes everywhere elsewhere pour these sordid reiterations, rent, rented, or in pursuit of rent! Overpowering emphasis everywhere of the cell in upended stricture; continual slicing, edging, inching in all the crowding. Tier above tier rises the soulless habitation of the shelf. Interminable empty crevices run up and down the winding ways of windy unhealthy canyons. Heartless, this now universal grip of grasping, unending stricture. Box to box on box boxing, glassed in boxing looking into other glass-boxing. Black shadows falling on glass fronts with artificial lights burning behind them day long. Millions upon millions of little cavities, cells squared by the acre, acreage spread by the mile. This a vast prison with glass fronts.

Above this avaricious aggregation which cruel ambition has built and now patronizes are haphazard odd insignificant skylines: like the false ambitions below making it all more human by lying about it. Elaborate ornamentation is all spasmodic. Here goes and comes to go again the to-and-fro, anxiety, satiety of life in the machine age. Incessant the wear of the cities, always to stop-and-go, go-and-stop only to crisscross again. Every human movement made is made to be broken! Every human being's interest, private interest, is entangled and in danger everywhere. Every heart that beats—beaten soon or late.

Streets? All too narrow channels jammed and jamming traffic. When available they are all, at best, only half effective owing to the ubiquitous crisscross of the gridiron. Always the gridiron! Forever a bedlam of harsh, torturing shrieks and roars. This wasteful spasm of racing movement to and fro in the crisscross. Down erstwhile narrow old village lanes one is deep in dark shadows cast by distorted forces. Therein lurk the ambitions and frustrations of the human being urbanized out of scale with its own body. Here see defeat of all aspirations of the human heart. The sense of humane proportion lost.

Incongruous mantrap of monstrous dimensions! Enormity devouring manhood, confusing personality by frustration of individuality? Is this not Anti-Christ? The Moloch that knows no God but *more?*

The agonizing traffic problem is here seen forced upon the city originally made and now aggravated by the persistent landlord with his skyscraper. The present city is yet only about one-tenth the motor car city it must become within the next fifteen years unless the citizen abandons his car. But dutiful devotion to advantages of our machine age now means to every citizen either a motor car—or two or three—(comparative flight) a helicopter; or else a frustrated moron for a citizen. Or a maniac? Every citizen will have a car or two or already dreams of having more, meantime envying the neighbor his four. Three, two or one—observe if the new freeway or the gridiron congestion is not already crucifixion. Then what comes, as average success multiplies and relentlessly multiplies the excess of our already excessive mechanical leverage?

Roughly calculate the mass of public conveyances, taxicabs, buses, private cars and trucks that success will bring to any overgrown village consisting of one hundred thousand to several million people: add half that number of private cars and add, perhaps one twenty-fifth as many delivery machines; add one fiftieth as many buses to displace streetcar tracks and carry children to school; and add unwholesome subways. You will find that—with room enough for each incidental transient coming into town from the suburbs (or going out), in order to function at all lengthwise, to say nothing of around about or crosswise—the surging maniacal mass inextricable would pig-pile in the narrow channels of the city well above the seventh story!

Allowing now for the established urban crisscross (the gridiron making every city street only half-time efficient) the struggling mass would again double; pile up and submerge even the ten-story buildings? Call this exaggeration: cut it in two. Then, if you like, cut it in two again. There will still be enough cars pounding along the streets and pouring carbon monoxide into them to put Manhattan and all its kind completely out of commission, starved for oxygen.

Now consider the fact that motorcar traffic has just begun within this resurrection of ancient Bedlam. Then why deck, double-deck, or triple-deck city streets or burrow in holes below them at a cost of

"The Living City" (Broadacre City, 1934) (Project). 1958. Perspective. Sepia ink on tracing paper, 42 x 36". FLLW Fdn#5825.003

billions only to invite further increase and eventually inevitable defeat? Now see these new imitations of old feudal cities as total loss to modern times.

Why not then allow the citizenry to keep the billions they would have to pay for decking and burrowing? They could buy more and better cars and perhaps soon safe flying machines, eventually bailing out of the urban mantrap into the more natural life of the small town fruitfully expanded in the country. As the freedom of our democracy dawns genuine in the citizen's heart, the present prison-city vanishes by way of its own senseless excess. Hazardous machine power built the excess and, if

left haphazard, will ruin it. A City should now be the planned consequence of better understanding of what the nature of the machine may mean to the man with a conscience; and this must now be made constructive. Without this integrity on our part our boasted democratic freedom is going—going—something soon doomed entirely by its own foolish extravagant ignorance—and gone.

So no longer manifest is any clear thought or sane feeling for humane good in urban exaggeration. Humane elements are sterilized by it or demoralized. Lurking in sinister urban shadows cast by these prideful urban strictures, lie the legalised impositions of today; and no less in our libraries, museums, colleges and in institutions of learning and especially of authority—a terrifying make-believe. The abortion we see in street façades has become a general frown. This surviving shadow of the ancient wall itself sinister. Savage or unsane as the convulsions caused by the overgrown city are—we see in them as valid an example of deterioration by "advantages" as has existed in all time.

Just because we have some little thriving village of yesterday (port perhaps) driven thus mad by excess—why is it so conveniently mistaken for principles? Success creative would seldom if ever know! The abnormality the city breeds is nothing more than much more of the already much-too-much in all the hell there is right now!

FORCES TEARING THE VORTEX DOWN

Human sensibilities, above the belt, are growing tired or numb. But good hope lies in this fact: this whole swollen commercial enterprise we call the City proceeds to stall its own engine by its owners' own excess. The day of reckoning is not so far away.

Mercantile interests have overbuilt the city, own it, and are now spending billions to keep it in place and going, using such man-prowess as we have to make ground-rent, floor-rent, man-rent and money-rent acceptable to urban millions; all, including themselves now, in immediate danger of running each other down in a race for bigger and better bait for no less acquisitive but even more bewildered tenants.

So inexorable forces that have overbuilt the city for swarming tenantry in so many different forms, yet all the same, build and build only to see urban monstrosity tear itself down or wear itself out by its own overweight: obesity is not yet a virtue.

For a page or two now let us examine these inimical mechanical forces, thrusting against human life by all this vain exaggeration and try to see just how natural forces may return all festering excess to the soil. If humanity were only there on its own inheritance—this good ground—cancerous overgrowth, wrought upon the life of these United States, might be gradually healed. The small home-farm-building to take the place of promiscuous farm buildings and the tenement is one item in sight shown in detail by the drawings of Broadacres: free city.

Of all the underlying forces working toward emancipation of the city dweller, most important is the gradual reawakening of the primitive instincts of the agrarian. Agronomy, source of the ancient wandering tribe. The adventurer down the ages reappears, his instinct still intermingling with the static of the cave-dweller. Call the survival of the ancient feudal city due to survival of the ancient cave-dweller instinct. The adventurer protests and denies this surviving shadow-of-the-wall—this old new city.

Physical forces of the machine itself, electrical, mechanical, and chemical invention, are meantime volatilizing human movement, voice and vision.

All now in so many new forms are actually aiming against the city, on the side of the original space-loving primitive.

Miracles of technical invention with which our "hit-and-run" culture has had nothing to do are—despite misuse—new forces with which any indigenous culture must reckon.

ONE: Electrification. Given modern electrification, distance is all but annihilated so far as human communications go; and by electric light human occupation continuously illuminated. Radical change in the entire basis of civilization.

TWO: Mechanical mobilization. Given the steamship, airstrip, and automobile, the human sphere of contact immeasurably widens. By the many mechanical modes, by wheel, air or ship, this radical change in the basis of our civilization is taking place.

THREE: Organic architecture: natural building. Given the Principles of nature, material resources become something no longer to be fought against but fought for. Now available to man in the air, sea, or mud under his feet, are the natural bases of human use by good design. With organic architecture his resource, man is a noble feature worthy of his own ground; integral there, as trees, streams or the rock ribs that are the hills. Rational changes in our civilization are imperative now because the individual himself, when no longer merely a creature of taste, becomes creative. Architects of the democratic spirit are here, demanding deeper organic foundations for an organic society. Everywhere this new American architecture is demanding more organic foundations for economic, ethical, social, aesthetic daily life; insists all future planning now begin *at the beginning*. Planned revolution by evolution is *now* organic.

The sense of space in spaciousness is not only scientific (it always was) but now fruitful, a genuine becoming. Congested senseless verticality is both inartistic and *unscientific!* To this spiritual awakening of the architect comes the space-loving human being as client. To freedom-loving democracy all stricture is as intolerable as it ought to have been so long ago.

Wherever the welfare of human life is concerned stricture, vertical or horizontal, cannot stand against the more natural conscientious harmony of life with the ground.

Another greater force to aid the reawakening instincts of the ancient adventurer lies in the spiritual strength of this challenge as a superb ideal of human freedom: Democracy! This new-old ideal is ancient as a spiritual concept of life, but is new to our own phase of modern time. See its natural consequence as the reintegration of Decentralization! With this new spiritual concept, we move beyond prevailing expedients. Organic architecture is integral; a concept of this new life our nation *is* learning to identify as free democracy. Yet only dimly comprehending this new-ancient ideal, architecture, because itself inevitable to all appropriate forms of civilization, must become a great spiritual force moving to free mankind from time-bound life in time-bound modern cities. Decentralization is therefore innate necessity: a new city is inevitable as sunrise tomorrow morning though rain may fall.

Thus the three principal machine agencies are steadily at work for the surviving instincts of the freedom-loving primitive. Democracy steadily approaches. And while yet unconscious of the precise forms it will take, we are able to see new forces gathering.

Look again and again at these modern machine agencies, busy forcing change upon this "best of all possible worlds." Examine each—more in detail. Then study the basic ideals of this young-old champion of Freedom, already at work around the world: Organic architecture—and you will begin to understand Broadacre City.

LOOKING BACKWARD

Earlier in time human intercommunication could only be had by direct personal contact. Commercial or social communication was slow and difficult. The City was of necessity a close-built mass—a mart, the only general meeting place, therefore the only distribution center. So the pattern of the feudal city grew to serve human needs as they then were. Human concentration, then, was not an unmixed evil. Such cities as there were grew as organisms; grew naturally as the organism of our own body grows; the natural result of proper feeding. Acceleration of tissue by circulation and chemical activity such as characterizes a malignant tumor did not then manifest itself. The city then was not malignant. The ancient city was not opposed to the course of normal human life in relation to natural beauty of environment; it was as inevitable as it was desirable. Cities of ancient civilizations grew to relieve pressures then caused by the lack of the integration now possible to us. Those ancient civilizations have perished.

Perhaps learning lessons from the past, modern European cities wisely resisted skyscrapering and remained nearer human scale. But our own survivals of these ancient cities have gone on absorbing from the countrysides what they could never repay; exaggerating the productions of industrialism at expense to agriculture. Ignorant of the culture which agronomy should have meant to our country, we chose to follow the British line of industrialization.

But not one of our big cities can subsist long on its own birth rate as birthright; therefore, a vampire, it must renew itself from our farms and villages.

Feverish excitations of the industrial urban ganglia (owing to pressures caused by fundamental changes such as we are describing), have grown abnormal, therefore painful. Concentrations of about two hundred or more persons to the acre are often considered "practical" (see London, New York or Tokyo) in planning or replanning cities.

Gather so many people together, visible on every acre, and try to imagine freedom and the pursuit of happiness left to each in housing them by the square mile!

Any wise recognition and definition of freedom under Democracy must say that ultimate human satisfactions no longer depend upon but are destroyed by density of population.

Our new machine agencies create new tendencies consciously employed; or deployed and reorganized. Civilization recapitulates. The village that became a city scatters far, as mobilized communication grows: agency number one. There is now no advantage in a few blocks apart, over a mile or two or even ten. There is a new time-scale to take the place of the old foot-and-inch scale. Human thought itself long since rendered ubiquitous by printing, now by visible speech and movement, all but volatile: telegraph, telephone, radio, television and safe flight. Then what have we? But the proper question is, what has us?

Concerning agency number two: steam, once upon a time dependent on fuel concentrations, congested and coupled close together human devices for movement and living comforts. But the internal-combustion engine (motor car or plane) safely goes anywhere carrying its own fuel, smoothly working as it goes. The motor ship, the automobile, and the airplane. Transit through space becomes economical. New hard roads or rails still come in, because of still necessary composition with these advantages. Developed as continuous avenues of swift, fluid mass communication, these are all comparatively new devices, breeding still more devices and advantages.

Results of agency number two are countless mechanical systems of ventilation, refrigeration, heating, and lighting, making dependence upon the centralized service-systems of the old city superfluous.

Agency three: new materials, fibrous steel—the spider spinning—used in tension, high-pressure concrete in compression, glass and innumerable plastics. Broad, thin, cheap sheets of plywood, sheet metal, or cement which together with sheets of similar insulating value make completely new types of building design admirable. Buildings may be so economized by intelligent standardizing that "home" may now be open to beautiful environment and be designed to broaden the life of the individual family, making site and building a unit.

Tendency number four: inorganic prefabrication: degeneration of quality by mass production. While utilities are made better and cheaper, new designs are needed to be made available for all, instead of more and questionable luxuries for the few. Machine design is now principal means of making use of power for decentralizing the big city and dispersing it; collecting it into what we, at first, call the countryside (not meaning suburbs); but, uniting desirable features of the city with the freedom of the ground in a natural happy union: such reintegration as here called Broadacre City. A city of native creative ability, its advantages, we hope to see, turning the capabilities of the machine spread *for* the human being not stacked against him. We have earned good right to speak of this city of tomorrow, the city of Democracy, indulging in no double-talk, as the City of Broad Acres.

FREEDOM—OR CONSCRIPTION

Individuals are still capable of developing selfhood instead of selfishness (consciously or unconsciously) and we go first to this free, more democratic individual, as the individual we must work with for the right human uses of the machine. By this time the machine is not only a runaway but revolutionary; and reactionary to such human values as the industrial-revolution has allowed to live. The runaway, imperceptibly at first, forcing the old city into new forms. The more intelligent citizens now lead the way to freedom for others. Numbers, increasing, come trailing along into that spaciousness we will soon have *good reason* to call the freedom of American democracy.

Character is a healthy individual growth of freedom from within. No matter how the present pilots of our civilization came to be pilots, unless the people themselves want to go down to stay down, they must act upon the modern imitations of ancient feudal cities inimical to our new means of life. They must act upon them not as calamity but as opportunity for development of the *quality* now belonging by nature to them throughout every feature of their daily lives.

Decenter and reintegrate. When this need is seen as indispensable, democracy will be built. Only

"The Living City" (Broadacre City, 1934) (Project). 1958. Plan. Pencil and color pencil on tracing paper, 40 x 40". FLLW Fdn#5825.001

the spirit of an energetic freedom-loving people disciplined from within by means of true nature-study; employing natural methods and whatever materials art, organic architecture, science (and religion) have in common; using our new advantages; only such *command* will ever know indestructible power—unbreakable defense. Of such should be the character of these United States. Say, Usonia? Aristocracy from within, which our forefathers hoped to see a reality—interpreted by Thomas Jefferson as "the bravest and the best."

Why then should free men not use the power of machine leverage to gain and keep the freedom their own forefathers declared?

Individuality independent—the Sovereignty of which we have already enough unselfish manifestation to live and grow the new city by—is continuing to make the old city increasingly unimportant—even as a burrow. Driven to sky-hooks, nooks and crevices—inhibition everywhere—the big-city now can exist only to be thwarted or aborted.

"Full employment" as we continually hear about it is not enough for the democratic citizen if this country still means what it declared—1776. No. "Full employment" is not enough because it may be and often is only a more subtle form of rent or conscription continued as the useful means centralization now holds out. It is the baited hook to keep the worker dangling.

No human soul, healthy, grows or even long survives sterilizing practices of the vicarious machine life as are common to this machine age. Urban life—à la mode—can be little more than some kind of surrender to the all-devouring god: Expediency. As petty social and official exactions increase, always the underlying purpose is found in some form of rent. You can call rent, too, a form of conscription. The modern crime of crimes against Democracy is conscription in any form, because conscription is inevitably a form of *confiscation*. Conscription is the form of rent most hateful to democracy because it soonest destroys freedom at its very source.

Our soul grows more by what we give than by what we take and feed upon. No man's soul grows by what is exacted from it. When he signs away his sovereignty as an individual he is not far away from the lowest form of socialism the world has ever seen.

PART THREE: DECENTRALIZATION INTEGRATION ON THE NEW SCALE OF SPACING

Our share in the Americas—why not call that share Usonia?[4]—can no longer be earned without good architects as essential interpreters of America's humanity. Creative architects. Nor can this nation afford to believe creative architecture is not to be its own logical interpretation of ways and means of life in our modern machine-made era. Art, Philosophy, Economics, and Religion, all old-school, have failed us, and politics is becoming likely as prostitute in a drift toward conformity. Organic architecture now comes as natural interpreter of Nature. It should light the way? Any true creative art can know the way. After our long journey—at least 500 years long—away from the original art of Architecture the mother-art, other arts, though not so integral with the daily life of the human being, now show signs of awakening. But in fundamental social affairs of Form (not *re*form) the architect is necessarily our prophetic interpreter in such circumstances as are common to our fate. The new forms will be provided by him. The nature of the true architect-mind is most needful now as in any era of Change. Great ancient powers that built great civilizations (abstractions) only to die, still live on in us to help build a civilization able to survive the fate that overtook them. We do know that ancient cities, however they were conquered or destroyed by force, have perished because of external ideals of life—life from outside in—not life from inside out.

We know, too, that the same old human power they died of, and with, is infinitely multiplied in our case by enormous mechanical exaggerations. But were we so to use machine power as to build new freedom for man, *free in the organic city* now inevitable to our civilization, we might live indefinitely! Why then more temporizing with all the *external* ideals which have proven fatal?

It is nearly two thousand years since the assertion of the organic truth that "the kingdom of God is within *you*." This new dynamic interior ideal we are calling democracy has grown up gradually in the human heart. But we of these United States have neglected to build a life—therefore a city—natural to us. A natural architecture of a natural economic order of the natural state. Organic.

An experiment? Yes, and if by "experience" it succeeds, and this union we are calling Usonia turns from the present static to the integration of decentralization inevitable to our ideal of democratic life, only then will we turn toward the new freedom: laws made for man not man made for laws. Integral livelihood for the citizen, artist and all laborers in the vineyard. And for all artisans a life based squarely with good sense upon good ground.

Coming now to the individual "at home": he will be organically related to landscape, to transport and distribution of goods, to educational entertainment and all cultural opportunity. All as easily imagined now. But the individual home democracy will build is in itself new freedom and freshness from within which other civilizations have only partially attained.

This ideal of the Usonian home is where organic architecture first comes in to meet rising demands for integrity of means with social ends, by radical change in *basic structure:* one great fundamental improvement brought into the service of the American citizen *as individual.*

First decentralization, then planned reintegration. Reinterpretation of our life by modern art and science will soon point the way forward to this realization. So work, leisure and culture; Art, Religion and Science; all will be, nearly as possible, *one.* Only then may each man be a whole man, living a full life. Only then is he "secure." Nor does that mean that every man must be a genius or farmer. But there will be no longer excuse for any man to be the kind of parasite the machine power of centralization is now so busy making of him—only to ensure him "employment" on the terms of a wage-slave?

We now know that these new machine forces may be potential, great liberators, but we know they are yet far from working so for the citizen. They are not owned by him nor are they owned for him. They are owned by the same landlords, machine-lords, and money-lords that operate rent and operate the city, itself now a vicious form of rent. These misdirected mechanical means are potential means of human liberation. But thus warped to distortion, enormity is maintained to destroy the citizen.

It is within the power of these very mechanical forces to automatically destroy any system that continues to deprive humanity of all but a small fragment of its potential benefits.

As a people we are still unfamiliar with the idea, but it is organic character in planning and building that alone can lead the way out of this terrific collision of mechanical forces. Organic architecture can end this superwaste of human life, now become so commonplace that we thoughtlessly accept its evil consequences as inevitable. Normal though not inevitable, it may become fatal to our national experiment in freedom.

In this city of today, as of yesterday, ground-space is reckoned by the square foot. In the organic city of tomorrow ground-space will be reckoned by the acre. No less than an acre to each individual man, woman and child. This individual acre seems minimum when we consider that if all inhabitants of the world were to stand upright together, they would scarcely occupy the island of Bermuda. Reflect that in the United States there are about fifty-seven green acres each for every man, woman and child within our borders at this time.

On this basis of an acre to each, architecture could soon come into service of the man himself as a natural feature of his life. The architecture of his home could never again be the adapted, commercialized thing it is: as housing by government or otherwise. Overcrowding itself to be sold; sold again. Resold. Overcrowding oversold life by taximeter: the realtors standing by to "see to it" that there be no more standing room than lively competition demands and he feels he can afford. Artificial scarcity thus chronic in any form is no boon now.

Liberal ground use is itself now one sure basis for culture and a more liberal education for America.

As our society learns to see life as free and believes man to be trusted, the citizen will learn to see architecture as the essential expression, the true protection natural to freedom; because good building is itself a form of organic life. Be sure that the ultimate Usonian City will thus be on its own foundations, and be its own impregnable defense.

Imitative eclecticisms now so widely practiced, however tastefully sophisticated, are only some bad form of crooked sentimentality. Personal "taste" can seldom be more than superficial because it is merely selective: some sentimental exploitation of something or other from somewhere that someone else approved—somehow. As we now practise what society is pleased to call "taste," taste is a kind of knavery. The jackdaw, the magpie, the cuckoo, the monkey—all "eclectics" by nature! But why man? It is more than merely unfortunate that our experiment in the birth of a nation has really known the creative artist only on such terms. The imitator never actually learns. His "conversion," when it occurs, is merely a turnabout to some other form of eclecticism. This man may know all about everything and understand nothing. Expediency is eclectic as eclecticism is taste expedient forever.

Taste peripatetic tried long ago to pick and choose the external effects that might lead, instead of letting life lead as native and so teach man constructively how to work and live. Natural. So man himself has become little more than a palliative, the quality of his luxury spurious. At his best overedu-

Following pages: "The Living City" (Broadacre City, 1934) (Project). 1958. Perspective. Sepia ink on tracing paper, 40 x 36".
FLLW Fdn#5825.002

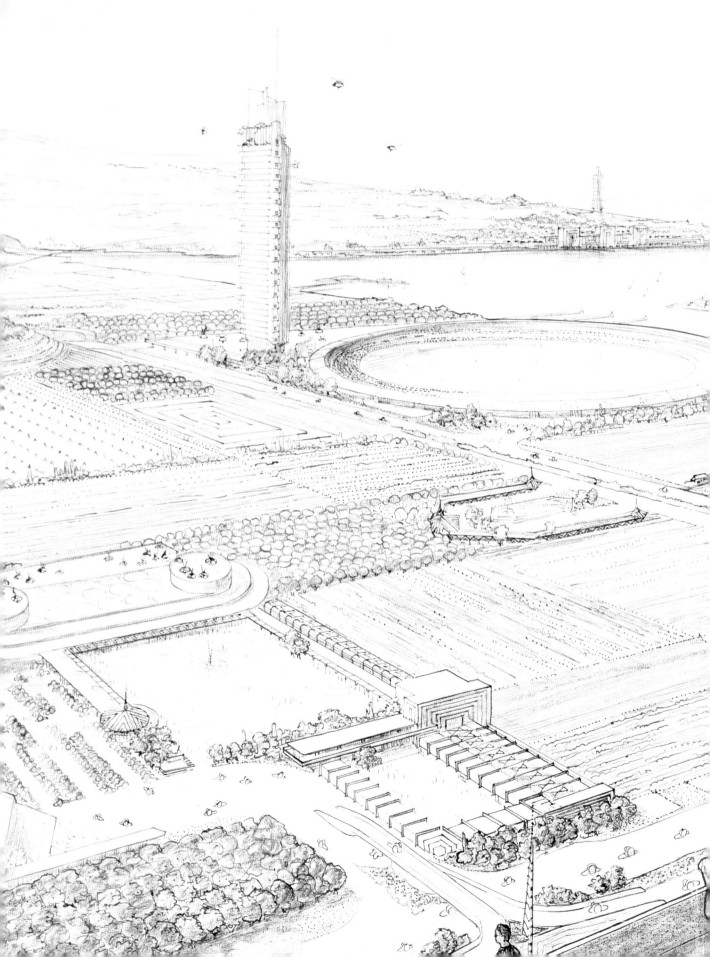

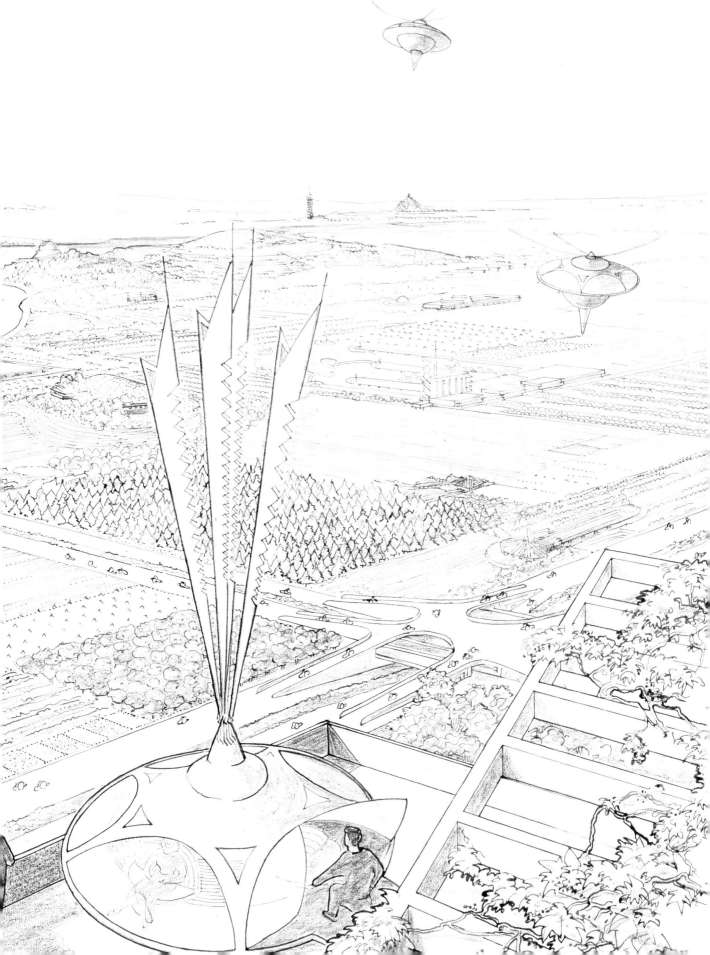

cated, "best" is likely to be very worst. The huckster you hear on the radio; the star you see in the movies; the designer whose work is on manufacturer's lists; hopeless deterioration by way of taste. As a consequence, see what "sells."

If the true architect's faith still lives, it must live as it has always lived: as honest experiment made by courageous, intelligent radicals in love with the poetic principle—and practicing these principles as architecture.

Only the faith that keeps radical faith with life itself is fit to be called safe! This is as true wherever great political co-ordination is effected as it is where good building is done. But no worthy experiment founded on experience is the same thing as one merely experimental.

Let us now approach the growing traffic or any other pressing city problems as another *human* problem; not as tinkers trying to tear parts of the city down only to build it up again on its old site while declaring that "architecture has nothing to do with humanity"—the approach that is exactly what has made the difficulty.

We have plenty of occasion to know that vested interests cannot be divested by agreement; but, unless by force, only by sincere educational revolution. "Interests" will never voluntarily agree to the loss of their immediate quarry which lies in some form of rent. Perhaps even rent for rent.

Observe for another page or two this inner law of organic change now at work upon these big, bigger and biggest cities. Inexorable Law of Change! Law with inevitable drastic consequences. First and forthcoming consequence the organic city of this discourse: the city of the new freedom, Broadacres.

BROADACRES

Nonsense is talked by our big skyscraperites in the blind alley they have set up, defending urban congestion by obscuring the simple facts of the issue. Of what use, in modern light, is the surgery of these superspacemakers for rent—professional promoters of the congestion-promoting traffic problem? Their skyscraper-by-skyscraper is the dead wall of our obstruction, the gravestone of capitalistic centralization.

For similar reasons the traffic problem (as we call our danger, our distress and eventual disgrace), if tied up with the skyscraper, is insoluble by any busy big city in the United States or elsewhere.

But the door of the urban cage is about to open.

The amorphous herds of humanity swarming in the narrow, erstwhile village lanes and caverns may now take wings as well as go on wheels. All increased speed facilities of movement are lateral. All, in point of time, are comparative flight.

In the new time scale the door of the urban cage is surely opening wide. Motorcar invasion and collateral inventions in the air and on the rails are leading up to total mechanization of transit.

So not only is the actual horizon of the individual immeasurably widened but his entire range of life (why not thought?) is broadened on the ground by these mechanizations when properly put to work. It is significant that not only have *space* values entirely changed to *time* values, now ready to form new standards of movement-measurement, but a new sense of spacing based upon speed is here. Mobility is at work upon man in spite of himself. And, too, the impact of this new sense of space has already engendered fresh spiritual as well as physical values. A ride high up in the air, in any plane or elevator, only shows man how fast and far he can go away on the ground. It is this broadened view that inspires in modern man his desire to go. If he has means, he goes. He has the means in his motorcar, copter or plane. And the horizon keeps widening conveniently for him as he goes.

Observe this physical release at work upon the citizen's character as a spiritual thing—an inspiration as well as new satisfaction and implement.

When the citizen realizes this release, his selfish interests may still pull away and pig-pile him senselessly in high tiers of cells upended on hard pavements. Dazed by his new freedom, he may be like some animal born in captivity; but when he finds the door of his cage open, he will soon learn like the animal that he can go free. When he learns that he is free, he is gone perhaps only to come back by habit—for a time.

After all is said and done, he—the citizen—is really the city? The city is going where he goes. He is learning to go where he enjoys all the city ever gave him, plus freedom, security and beauty of his birthright, the good ground. The first true basis for his pursuit of happiness is such integral independence: the only sure basis of his desired freedom.

Throughout our amazing civilization the citizen is already going "afield" because the machine that brought him to the city is as able to take him back again. When he wakes to a larger and better sense of himself he is free to go out and—prophetic—build the new city. Machine power *subjected* to man's own proper use will enable him as a citizen.to live in a better city in a better developed countryside because he is no longer conscript either by or for the agencies now keeping him at least available as one.

Democracy on these new free terms means freedom for every citizen—yes, but only if the principle of the machine is forced *by himself* to go to work *for* him. It could start working *for* him if he should so desire and courageously so decide. The machine as an automaton is involuntary. Automatically (because of what it really is), the present uses of it work man toward the revolution which this decision may mean. Otherwise this great iron horse upon which the West rode to power—the industrial revolution—is not only a runaway horse but a stayaway.

To repeat: as centralization was the natural "monarchy" (in architecture the major axis and minor axis), men were compelled to centralize and revolve as closely as possible around an exalted common center, for any desirable exploitation of the man-unit. The idea of democracy is contrary. Decentralization—reintegrated—is the reflex: many free units developing strength as they learn to function and grow together in adequate space, mutual freedom a reality.

ANALYSIS

Consider: monarchy was defeated because it magnified, while at the same time it deliberately mortified, the individuality that we, as a people, desired and declared; and now, I believe, desire more than ever to establish? As for our present system, free enterprise, so called: well, if its beneficiaries should decide to persist in the present form of supercentral-

ization, the system—its apex on the ground, base in the air—now stands ready to fall. It will fall for the same reason that masonry falls or monarchy falls, as all despotism surely falls: the law of gravitation and the law of diminishing returns (a law of nature).

The mechanized forces now employed in the building of our mad world are turning upon the remaining peak of monarchic despotism now demoralized: the now overgrown old city. Do the hurrying fools blindly driving production to still further excess in big cities still imagine they are building the city up? But all nature is against them. They are tearing the city down.

Centralization is centripetal, whether as city, factory, school or farm; it has not met the rising spirit of democracy—freedom of the individual as individual to work with—for centralization is by nature against it. Many obvious details (traffic problem for one), also have enormous powers now setting in dead against the principle of centralization. Machine power itself now denies centralization in spite of its ancient masters, because it is in the nature of intercommunication and ubiquitous mobility that the big city decenter itself and spread out far away—spread thin, growing high and higher only as it goes outward from center. The countryside is the place for the skyscraper. If higher at all, then wider on the ground. It is in the nature of the development of flying, too, that the present city disappear eventually to reappear as well spaced structure in spaciousness. The old capitalistic city is no longer safe. It is mass murder. Even though no bombs ever appear as murderer. The true humane city is Broadacres.

By way of unnatural survival of the big citified city, capitalist centralization has had a bold day but can have no relatively long day. It is easy to see now that though not dead yet, what it really is is neither necessity nor luxury but harmful stricture, wasting humanity. So our big cities, vampires, must die. Universal automobilization, ubiquity of movement, thought, voice and vision now penetrating distance and walls—these are gigantic factors making present-day urban life as troublesome to free human life as static is to radio.

What about the time when these rapidly increasing "modernizations" become universal? Time not far away.

DEMOCRACY BY DEFINITION

Already men get more satisfaction out of their vastly increased facility for free movement than ever before. Imagine a man's life in the next twenty-five years, if man can keep out of industrial war long enough to get enough out of the last war to let the machine do its work for his own democracy?

Democracy: the integrated society of small units each of the highest quality imaginable and all characteristic. Genuine. This is in the nature of our rational ideal of the free world, and practical too, but only so if this machine age be taken well in hand not only by science but by organic character in art and architecture—in statesmanship as well—and effectively used in the nature of all materials according to intrinsic nature. Exaggerated artificialities of educational enterprises today—skyscraper the urban devil—have already gone far out of human scale. The humane and smaller unit made free and effective upon the whole surface of the nation everywhere is on its way. This is democratic. Salvation of the civilization we really do desire is in this free life of honest democracy. I believe we are now able and willing to pay the price for such growth as it presents.

Then let us have done with all exaggerated vertical lanes of elevator traffic in the rank and file: vertical transport impinging upon congested narrow lanes below—all channels crowding in upon these narrow closures called "courts"—all cutting in upon desirable privacy. Why make more concessions to makeshifts "authorized" by makeshift rules and regulations? No more submission to crucial (and cruel) landlord expedients. We know now that crowding is a ruse and has no beneficent solution except to inspire us to plan the new city.

LAND AND MONEY

What the nation has been calling democracy is really only mediocrity rising into high places—mobocracy. Let us now look at human life in America through native and natural eyes, yearning for a soci-

ety safe from the license of the mobocracy which is taking the place of conscience.

Common realty achieved by way of taxation on communal resources, as Henry George pointed out with complete logic, is entirely democratic. But his "single tax" was only an expedient and never intended to be taken as a complete solution of our land problem. Serving its purpose: when economic liberation of land and money is duly effective, none may say how far man's cultural liberation may go with greater aesthetic uses of his ground by way of the vast mechanical resources developed in the past century. By proper organic use of our new materials, steel, concrete and glass, if developed in the new spirit of organic architecture, our nation will build with a beauty monarchy and empire hardly dreamed.

Interior discipline of trained imagination is needed for good citizenship, and needed to adapt modern machine craft to such higher uses as would expand and enrich the quality of all human life. This, too, is a matter of good natural architecture.

But first of all we need a new aesthetic—also a new idea of what constitutes "profit"; a new idea of what constitutes Success; a new idea of what constitutes luxury. Beauty in all its phases as a native must grow naturally among us here. Else no life is worthy life. Machine power, decentralized and better distributed, more directly and simply applied to humane purposes, is the clear basis of any practical expression of social life here in this twentieth century. Developed machine-age life, as luxury, must consist in more appropriate use and intelligent limitation of machinery in devising new patterns inevitable for life in the New. Then will come a universal margin of leisure, greater rational freedom for the individual than any known by previous civilizations—but this only if the creative artist is there in his true place; the machine in his hand as a tool.

Why, then, should we try so hard to make life and buildings look hard, like machines? Why breed a tough mechanized citizenry, merchants commercialized by machinery? Why insist upon a merchant-motive, confusing romance with sentimentality, destroying both? Though modern buildings may have the clean lines and surfaces of a well-balanced

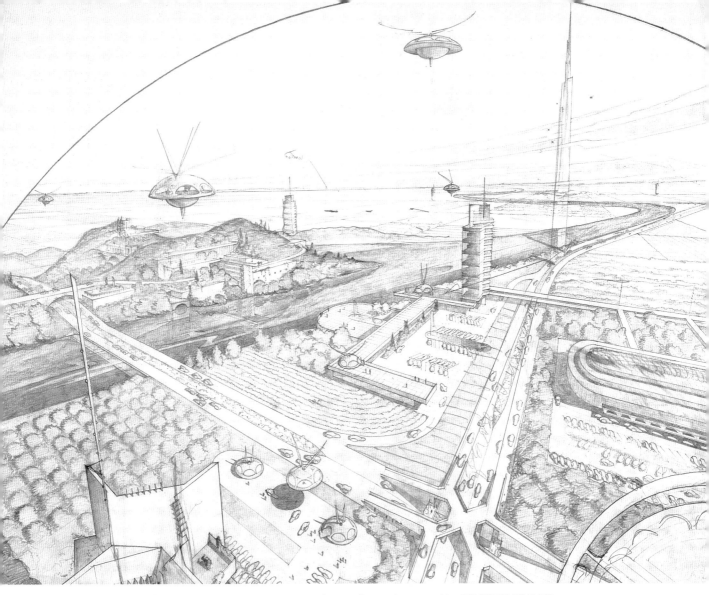

"The Living City" (Broadacre City, 1934) (Project). 1958. Perspective. Pencil on tracing paper, 36 x 28". FLLW Fdn#5825.005

machine, that is only the bare basis for beauty affirmative. But when they are merely negative? However novel at the moment, negative is only tentative. Power directly applied to purpose, with the inspiration of genius, is the basis for all good building or good life. But the spirit of man desires more because man's spirit *is* infinitely more—a nobility and exuberance.

It is not much to have discovered that a single mechanical unit may be infinitely repeated by machinery in construction or that it may be a great economy. (Though it may not be.) It is far more important that an infinite variety of appropriate forms and schemes may result when machine powers are placed in heads and hands guided by the creative instinct: the imagination of a mind with a humane heart aware of the grace and significance of beauty.

ORGANIC ARCHITECTURE
Organic architecture has demonstrated the fact that severe machine-standardization need be no bar to even greater freedom of self-expression than ever known before. If by "self-expression" we mean fruits of genuine individuality and do not mean a sterile style—the cliché—or idiosyncratic taste. All casual discoveries are not necessarily the Magna

Charta of the new liberty into which the architect—by interior discipline—may go by way of the machine to teach his own people not foolishly to re-build but to build the new beyond the old; to build a nation that is itself more like one great organic life altogether; to show now how to go forward into organic life universal. Served by machinery, yes, but only to humane extent and purpose. By this new means the artifex himself goes forward to build buildings far more natural to life for the more natural men and women of this more natural city than the Western world has known: this is organic architecture and this is Broadacre City.

Unknown to most of our citizens, this more natural city is already, by native circumstances, being forced upon us all. This city is happening now upon the very ground whereon we stand; forced by circumstances we fail to recognize as advance agents of decentralization. These agents are becoming so commonplace in our view that we fail to apprehend them.

Then why not be intelligently directed by the inevitable—our lives qualified, by learning prophetic command of organic design?

Only shortsighted interests that continue to overbuild our cities would deny that these nineteenth-century survivals of our own Imitation-renaissance have become too costly. Wherever distribution and transport are concerned, they are a much too serious handicap on production and a terrible imposition upon all parents and children in any aspiring family life. In democracy the family is norm. The family holds within itself the very seeds of culture that is native, organic therefore, and has a future. Organic architecture, this architecture of the twentieth century, is more than half a century past due in our cities.

Senseless waste of time and energy like the wasteful back-and-forth haul due to the skyscraper is symptomatic not of urban success but of excess. Failure. Make good ground free, available to good men for humane uses. As for the poor, subsidize traffic to the country, modify terms of ownership so that every man may have incentive to work and learn to make good use of men's tools on fair terms. All that is necessary for the new city of decentralization to spread wide, grow strong, the citizen free. Otherwise no

city will grow strong or free, and we are doomed to a life more and more vicarious and deformed.

What, then, is the basic thought here working for the organic change now essential to growth for the man, woman and child—the family—of Democracy?

ACTION

Well . . . certainly not the same old thought that makes our big cities a landlord's ruse—the further triumph of ignorance over impotence.

Certainly not this current of exaggeration of Old World survivals that impoverish many a free agrarian area, as though every citizen were a mere "collector"—and make unhappy people by turning good ground into a sterile cinder heap. Exaggeration of artificiality now offers specious "relief" by government "spending."

No, not that. Nor the same old survival of thought that turned America's youth into white-collarites and sent them out of agronomy into the city in search of a job—a "job" where at least one hand might be kept in the pocket, a cigarette hanging from the lip, foot on the bar rail.

Not the same old survival of thought that made out of an Old World economic system this legalized "strong arm" economic system of our new world: an arm that must weaken periodically; come down for a "rest" while all the renting and the rented and residue from rent gravitate toward starvation in the midst of plenty. By nature, such "economy" as ours must end in periodic national catastrophe. Depressions. The war a clearing house needed to revive in order to survive! War—actual as well as economic.

Nor can we imagine our survivals to be what seems to look to our authorities like freedom won and held by force. Meantime the law makes many more arbitrary laws having no foundation whatever in ethics nor any fair basis for our economic structure nor any social structure at all in nature. Now—is not the idea of "freedom by force" anachronism? Unthinkable senseless reiterations by our political promise-merchants of falsehoods we hear and see; and the drift again toward the same old impending cataclysm. Our own nation may reach death by way of these many obstinate centralizations of which in some form, civilizations, hitherto in similar agony, have died? Fate can be the result of such force by centralization as we are exercising upon mankind now.

All history plainly shows that "force" did not nor can it ever *organize* the *growth* of anything but resentment, hatred, revenge, more war—the epitome of all ill-will. Anything inorganic never can end fear. War is no less the denial of man's organic life now than it ever was. However expedient we make war seem to be as the clearing house for our fears or our political mistakes in handling our overproduction, restricting distribution by punishing competitors; however afraid, no man of creative conscience—not even a Napoleon—has ever thought of war as other than exorbitant foolish crime and waste. Nor has any truly creative individual ever yet acted upon his own thought otherwise. But war is now machinery and machinery is war when necessary to the machine age economy of our civilization, if present money-trust machinery survives to dominate it in the old name of "self-defense." "Security."

FEUDAL

Unworthy survivals of feudal thinking have made of our survivals of the medieval city a monstrous conspiracy against the freedom of life. Centralization itself, as a principle, is become only a bad form of rent: an inevitable conscription of mankind. It is the form of conscription which has not only wasted billions, and murdered millions; it has also made of American architecture a bad form of surface decoration. Architecture has become our blind spot. What was offered to the country for the fifth time as a progress fair in 1940 was only the same old Columbian Fair of 1893. Its face had merely been lifted to mark "progress" in 1933. The repeat performance in New York City to call worldwide attention to our "greatness" was really a confession of impotence.

Always the same old thought. Now we see it planted in this era of shopkeeping as the ideal of the prevailing shopkeeper, seated in so many high places of authority. We see it unwittingly fixing higher premiums upon baser qualities. Special privileges in money making or money taking: property holding. Just ahead of the conscript lie fears that have made of the man himself a piece of speculative property by

placing these false premiums upon activities characteristic of the wolf, fox or rat in human form.

Thus these Old World survivals will continue to stampede society, standardize the workman himself all in behalf of a vast labor system interlocking with capital. The employer himself is really another piece of property rented. By whom? Employer in the same fix as employee—only higher up. Or else not an employer at all; only groveling survival of the feudal thinking which will eventually break the workman and the employer both together, as one. So employers too are themselves no less the automatic conscript. They, too, are eventually broken on the industrial rent wheel.

No less, the same old struggle for "survival" puts heavy pressures upon the armchairs of universities to deprive American youth of such individual independence of thought and soul as they might otherwise have developed or achieved—turning fresh minds into empty toolboxes by throwing books at their heads while providing no collateral *experience*. American youth a conscript? He is and in so much more than a mere military sense. Conscription has made militocracy inevitable to him in his life. He is educated only by being conditioned, not by being enlightened.

For him survival (always "survival") makes the banker what he has become: a wary, professional acquisitor. The very profit motive he banks with, and upon, puts convenient premiums upon the baser acquisitive instincts as qualities of mankind. Banking heavily on Yesterday the banker is continually stalling, or already betraying, Tomorrow. But he alone among us is not yet a conscript? Why?

In it all we see the same old hangover overhead—fear—immuring men in the same old mantrap, to arrive in the same way—innocuous—at perihelion, impotence. The biggest survivals of the ancient medieval city are now Bedlam. We have been calling them survivals, but really they are monstrous centripetal grindstones grinding man himself to the consistency of whatever else is being machine-made, for sale!

Now all the more true, that machine power can have no meaning except to help make a man instead of a moron or a conscript, and help set him free from all conscription whatsoever—whether military, moral, economic or artistic.

"Survival" then in our society simply depends upon rejection of any belief in the thought that conformity to authority plus money can continue to rule the world. And no faith at all in the coward's belief that everything or anything worth a man's time may be made to happen by legal, military or money power. Finally the falsity that native Culture can be no more than some imported complacence, some *external* idea of form. Our national tragedy lies in these confused and confusing survivals of feudal conformities. We have nurtured youth upon this vain idea. This we have done vainly imagining that we were breeding citizens for Democracy. We were not. In fact, we have patterned our chief institutions of "higher" learning upon many an empty inglorious antithesis. From survival to survival again we derive an arrogant substitute for native culture. Now we are applying these substitutes upon the sterile surfaces of our brittle commercial success and trying to force the world to take it from us now on our terms. Or else. Concentrations upon concentered lives within the centralized city, a merciless unceasing gamble. Survival of the big city would leave the people of these United States—Usonia— immured in insignificant, ugly environment, our living unnaturally exaggerated, without joy, with no indigenous beauty created by our vast prosperous nation for itself: goods, goods, goods where grass ought to be—grass where there should be "goods." How then can life be good? Be other than itself "goods"? All life reduced to the level of merchandise—the national art, as a matter of course, salesmanship?

OUR ARCHITECTURE

Call architecture organic to distinguish it from the pseudo-classic order of the schools, derived mainly from grafted attempts at reclassification called the "international style." A cliché.

Architecture is organic only because intrinsic. In the reflex it seeks to *serve* man rather than to become a force trying to rule over him. Another reason why we say organic architecture cultivates "the space within" as a reality instead of the roof and walls: it is building from inside out, instead from outside in. Therefore it is living twentieth century architecture instead of nineteenth century architecture.

This new American concept of architecture has style as the expression of character. No longer is form a question of "styles." Essential Style it has, and is of the nature of all building whatsoever provided only that style be naturally achieved from the nature of the building problem itself and found within the very means for and by which the building stands built. The result: style is character. It is by integration in this interior sense that Broadacre City would give style birth; have great style all the while as something natural; not as something exterior and forced, either in its structure or upon its people. No exterior discipline whatever could rule, nor could *re*classifications be natural. Establishment of flexibility will be the reverse of antique classic externals in American architecture. Architecture and acreage will be seen together as landscape—as was the best antique architecture—and will become more essential to each other. Great architectures will arise within the lifetimes of the civilization actually expressed.

As a people, then, if we understand the eternal principles of Nature, our own especially, and learn to use our riches and industrial machinery upon the vast stores of our new materials to good advantage—use them with faithful sense of fitness to purpose—we will naturally arrive at nature-form with true style. Perhaps (though we need not bother much about that) arrive at what, looked back upon in distance of time, might be Twentieth century, or Usonian, style? Should that come to pass, it would not be so much by any calculated intention as by the fate due to honest production and long-continued practice. Style is a precious, magic circumstance— style is, and always, the death of Style.

Architecture organic, perhaps because first deeply concerned with the integrity of innate structure, first grasped the demand of our modern American life for a higher spiritual order. Perhaps only minds imbued with this deeper sense of structure as natural can perceive the fine integrities of the more livable and gracious human simplicities.

Our enlarged and deeper means of today could now break the strictures upon our life and revive emasculated manhood. If current tools were used even with intelligent self-interest, spaciousness, graciousness and happiness in human life would increase. If intelligent use would back up the enlarged sense of available spacing in modern city life, the citizen would automatically be released and the free city of democracy realized. With appropriate scientific use of the new space-scale to be used now as a time-scale, see the extended highway as one great horizontal line of Usonian freedom expanding life consistently everywhere, not only up and down but lengthwise and crosswise; then you see something of the modern Usonian city approaching—whether you like it or not—Broadacre City.

See the design of the farm itself (little or big) in true relation to adjoining farms and industry and culture, to you in your villages and all related to our national economy. See sizes and shapes of infinite fields well laid out in good proportion each to each—and man-built occupation of the whole, well adapted to natural contour—tillage itself a charming feature of the landscape; hedgeways, ravines, and waterways themselves proper boundaries. Well, if you can see all this, rhythmic in relation to human use and movement; well-placed buildings related to well-placed roads in suitable places: if you can see "horizontal farming" (contour plowing) properly applied to regions and crops, pastures, animals, related to happy people; if you can see the varied, multiple parts all thus contributing to a great dramatic whole in which you sense the repose of individual human contentment and the exuberance of plenty—the life of the imagination truly aesthetic, in the over-all view from wherever you may happen to stand—then you will get a glimpse of the country-loving life in agronomy of the new Usonian city, belonging by nature to the national agronomy of our democratic future. The agronomic culture of the vast nation our forefathers had some right to expect would come of what they were pleased to call Freedom. Then only will you see Usonia.

You will see the people of Usonian countrysides loving exuberance but hating waste, the waste that is ugliness itself and the ugliness that is itself waste: see a people now suspicious of too easy opportunity to live by the vicarious means being forced upon human behavior by the mechanical imposition interlocking rents, exaggerations utterly empty of beautiful human significance.

THE NEW CITY

Broadacre buildings would be naturally adapted to the lives of the people who would no longer build or be content to live in prettified boxes or take pleasure in the glassification of a glorified crate however "stylized." Intelligence of life would not allow buildings as ignorant expedients; it would see a bad one as serious impediment to good life. So in the free city now here in Usonian countenance of the countryside, find manhood seeking *organic* simplicity as appropriate *character* in everything; workmen themselves learning to see that organic simplicity is actually the fine countenance of Principle and no less so now in this our machine age than ever it was in ancient times. Rather more so. Yes, and how much more necessary to life are architects themselves who are in love with the poetry of life, they alone could say.

As for growing up in the knowledge of organic architecture: It sees itself as new yet ages old; now a true simplicity by way of simples growing out of the free democratic citizen's own devotion to life on his own ground; the citizen himself something of a farmer there, free of all unfair exactions.

In sunlight universal, see his establishment not as a boxment or burrow in a sterile mass of cars and towers; see him standing free of all such stricture on his own acreage. When the immured citizen realizes this independence, this greater opportunity to live his own life with his growing family, he is already on his way to the life which democracy owes to him and he to democracy. His will to be there is not in spite of but because of himself, himself a potential divinity. Then, is it not his good sense to be able to give such natural direction to otherwise inorganic forces, to go where he finds in the pursuit of happiness the liberty (was it not promised him by national charter?) for a natural, fruitful pursuit?

The architecture of the city may now be basic. Yes. As architecture is basic to essential structure anywhere of the timeless sort we can now build. This is no less the structure of whatever is music, poetry, painting or sculpture—or whatever else man's interior sensibilities may thrive upon when disciplined from within by an ideal. Architecture must see civic life in terms of such human economic freedom as here prophesied; recognize native ground free as the sure basis of a free life in a free city.

Teenagers! Wherever building is sensibly modern, or solid walls are vanishing, where dead weight was emphasized by black shadows, super-walls will take their place for you—thanks to you.

Fortifications, that once upon a time protected the might of the baron on his feudal estate, in our day can no longer fortify. As homes, fortifications are dead.

Modern America needs no longer to box up or hole in for protection, or dive into a burrow in any city. Instead security in every sense is best found in the wide free spacing and integral construction, the spiritual perception of what we are calling decentralization. Spaciousness is for safety as well as beauty.

Our vast beautiful country, notwithstanding all the status quo of vested interests is, at perimeter and at heart, gradually becoming more free in spirit as it resents urban constriction. True democratic ideals must—will—go on with this increase of deeper feeling in the popular mind until it reaches the popular heart and makes its feeling for better spacing a universal intelligence. Our vast resources in growing machine power and materials working, in spite of all opposition, to make our ideal actual. What need now for master or slave in any form—however disguised? No need for dictator or conscript. Even if disguised by clever uses of English, we no longer need Lord and Serf. Nor need now for expensive, expanded imitations of ancient feudal masonry by whatever name, no interests vested or divested choosing to call themselves social. Then, for what purpose may our manifold eclecticisms be thought appropriate for such immense vaulting money-power as ours? That tall facade—the "business monument"—already rapidly shifting to somewhere else; or downshore, out of our sight.

When democracy triumphs and builds the great new city, no man will live as a servile or savage animal; holing in or trapped in some cubicle on an upended extension of some narrow street. Withstanding all this passing danger to him—the free man will again live free: the human biped which the best of him always dreamed of being! Life and love as noble leaders of our brave social experiment. Our forefathers declared we would and should so live in spite of commitments to old establishments or property interests or "laws made not for man but as though man was made for laws"; the American living in full consequences of which they could not then foresee.

USONIA

For America today organic architecture interprets (will eventually build) this local embodiment of human freedom. This natural architecture seeks spaciousness, grace and openness; lightness and strength so completely balanced and logical that it is a new integrity bound to scatter servile imitation, to take away all urban stricture and depravity first from the regional field and then—as is the case with all inadvertent health—absorb and regenerate the tissue poisoned by cancerous overgrowth (Urbanism).

Modern gifts—glass, steel in tension, steam, electromagnetic sciences, chemistry, new atomic dissonance, alchemy; these and more, coming or here, implement the new era. We do not recognize their real significance. But we begin to use our own human gifts of creative imagination in the light of organic principles; the poetic principles and ever new ethics of right and wrong according to organic law, these will protect us. We already know that we may hammer heated iron but cannot hammer a stick of dynamite! Wholly new ideas of form will come as clearly to our relief, and joy. So simple and fundamental are the forces which lie beneath, above and within us, as natural agencies of life—that this new freedom is breaking for not against mankind. If the citizen, loyal, will reach out to take these, as they are for what they are—they are his on fair terms.

Facility to roam the sky; from here to there swiftly cover vast stretches of ground; live safely with perfect freedom of communication relating each to all and all in all, his feet on his own ground at will—his life his own when he so pleases, and all the time in his heart what love of home life and country that should mean to a man of free will. All this is not only possible but probable now to the citizen of our country if only he will have the faith in himself to go forward with courage to realize all.

Where, then, is the Usonian citizen situated economically, if he is thus born spiritually?

VALUES

Architecture (organic) knows architectural values only as human values, values true not only to Nature but to humanity as nature—or else not valuable! Good or economic modern building is an integration rising to build the organic city—the city that in rising is enemy to all forms of imitation that centralization imposes by impinging upon manhood when free. Neither building nor city is to be there tolerated as any form of *stricture*. Buildings, like people, are sun children, sun-born growth from and with sun-born Nature; and by nature sun-life is life-acceptance in building—or the buildings are not organic buildings. Both buildings and city now should be more truly defense against time, against the elements and the dangerous enemy than the city ever was before.

Architecture may again become true shield for whatever aspiration, glory or sanctity humanity may possess or desire. Organic architecture can be indestructible though machine-made fabric of light fashioned of metals woven into webs of turquoise, green, gold, and silver textiles, or the everlasting hues of the kiln; or cast in metals; or visible in whatever native nature-materials are naturally available, and still be no less integral pattern, the expression of a varied life for free people. If organic architecture is to function for mankind architecture must command every special purpose. Spacious ground must be made available on some fair basis and be legally considered an element having intrinsic value—as free to men as are other elements. Once emancipated by proper zoning and building laws from the tyranny of the exploiters of the "lucky-lot area," absentee landlords, money lords, machine lords (and similar impositions), city building in the new city will stand there free in its own greenery or lie long, flowing lazily and low on the prairie levels, or stretching along the ridges above the ledges of the hills. At one with environment.

Buildings public, private, or industrial, a tall shaft or a streak of light in the countryside enmeshed in metal strands and glass as music is made of notes. What is building without intimate relationship to the ground it stands upon and the inhabitants who occupy it? A great unity, every fine building is necessarily expression of the life it is built to serve directly. So no mere mantraps; no more landlords. No life imprisoned on shelves of vertical streets above crowds on gridirons down below. No hard faced poster façades.

As life itself builds, so organic architecture builds, no longer allowing man to stumble blindly along the path of the past, unaware as yet of the nature of the malevolent forces that have kept him down, ruining his living present; he seems still unaware of how destructive these modern forces are or in themselves how beneficent they can be. He has started a hell all around him, waiting to damn him now in this new era, to destroy him.

Then why must any status quo of citizenry continue to be some belief, on a par with such "patriotism" (misnamed loyalty) as is "the last refuge of the scoundrel"; or some standardized and sentimentalized academic substitute for culture? No free man can live on outmoded belief continuing too long, some sinister afterglow of feudalism. Again the pioneer takes his place on the frontier. No longer can he of the new order mistake the setting sun of any Renaissance whatever for sunrise.

Must his majesty—the American citizen—go along old-fashioned in his commercial interests, unwittingly in his own image betraying life by reducing all about him to a false, sentimentalized misuse of what was noble in all traditions? Must the common man then, to be common, still insist on practicing petty minor traditions that only turn him wrong end up, maintaining him as some kind of conscript going or coming?

"As loves must die because Love must live," so organic architecture has learned that these too many minor traditions must die in order that the great Tradition we were all born to serve, may live. When we face this, democracy actually comes alive and will plan the new city now already under way with no plan.

Like all principles the principles of organic architecture are simple: the principles of all *entity:* therefore of life itself? No house, nation or system built on makeshift foundations can long stand. So no building built for a life set up on minor or major makeshifts can last long enough. If necessity for such "shifts" be a moral virtue then where lies social weakness?

Good architecture concedes the right to live abundantly in the exuberance of beauty, in the more profound sense in which William Blake defined "exuberance." He did not mean excess nor any form of exaggeration. He meant fullness of the expression of Nature; nor stint nor stunt. That is good architecture for good life.

Liberal democratic philosophy yields that primary right to us all. But the only secure foundation we have for any interpretation of life in art, architecture or religion, is *character*. Understanding of Nature as life accepted not merely for fear of the police nor for any merely *expedient* relation between the welfare of the one as against the other, but the wellfaring of the whole. Personal life under democratic government enables one to proceed from generals to particulars. Our youth should be so educated as to discern and stand square with the practical, instead of oblique to the expedient; able to know with sure mind the difference between the merely Curious and the truly Beautiful.

Now to civilize our architects and cultivate them comes organic architecture. The future awakened civilians of Usonia will be naturally modern; or else all be failures, because Life itself is a changing insistence upon modernity! Life is always modern. Vital forms, fresh, are the continual need to contain or express or prophesy these changes—and do so without waste, sincerely in love with Beauty.

RECAPITULATION

Once again. *"All fine architectural values are human values, else not valuable."* Humane architectural values are life-giving always, never life-taking.

PART FOUR: USONIAN
A LEGACY WE HAVE RECEIVED FROM THE PAST

Are we all parasites? Whether we like it or not we do work or we do not work. But such bodies as our civilization preys upon if we are parasites seem to be either Nature or the Past? The forces we prey upon and by which we harm ourselves, chiefly, in this machine age are these inevitable forces of Nature. Machine tools have so increased our ability to produce, production has so increased, as to have made riches a kind of poverty; and made truth a kind of anachronism. "Incomes" of rich and poor both added together are an "outgo" that cannot buy the goods we produce at anything like the rate at which the goods, not to say the best, can be produced. So the human labors involved, considered by themselves, unadorned by art, are really less valuable now than ever they were in the past?

Only as idle heirs of civilization, then, are we entitled to a living if we are to be thus displaced by the facilities of machinery! Is it not absurd for man to compete by fertility of mind against the resources engaged in devising labor saving devices for money making schemes as mere gadgetry? The important thing for us all is to so digest these ubiquitous mechanical energies that men may be set free by them for nobler uses, uses more important to the growth of the beauty of life: developments and enjoyments no longer directly concerned with "making money for a living," or acquiring any degree of material power. No man should ever be so bound or time-bound. Nor should any man be a slave to or for "a living." The proper free man should do, in the main, what he really most wants to do when he wants to do, though he may never be able to do all he wants to do of it or for it. *That* really is the only legacy we have received from the past that is valid. Only under democracy genuine can we protect or even understand this legacy.

INDIVIDUALITY

Well, we have been calling this legacy, free from our urban past, "Broadacre City." Broadacres *is* our free city for the Sovereignty-of-the-Individual! Not so simply because it is based upon the minimum spacing of an acre (or several) to the individual, but, more important, because when democracy builds, this is the natural city of freedom in space, of the human reflex. The nature of democracy when actually *built*.

At present, the multiplicity of systems, subversive schemes, especially the 57 varieties in our modern architecture, have gone down so completely as the common expedient as to be too often mistaken by us for civilization itself. Maybe that characteristic, too well practiced, will hang over Usonia indefinitely to postpone any free city of democracy for some generations.

Nevertheless the free city we are considering is squarely within the laws of Change and is already here all around us in the haphazard making, the apparent forces to the contrary notwithstanding. All about us and no plan. Even *in* us—as we now are. The old order is breaking up under the load our senseless weight puts upon us whether we subscribe or do not subscribe.

The capitalism, net, of our nation, is only individualism gone rank or riot, producing either isolationist, authoritarian or unconscientious objectors.

Political partisanship becomes a form of gangsterism. "Party politics" are no true product for nourishment of sentient individuality. Various eclecticisms are the only feature our nation yet knows. The idiosyncracy of personality resulting not in the individuality needed for democracy but encouraging bureaucracy, and degenerative to mobocracy. Personality, by corruption and consequent degradation of the word "democracy," has got in the way of this great integrity we are calling, as we should, Individuality. In the Jeffersonian sense especially so. But miseducated minds of our day, by mistaking morals for ethics sterilize and standardize instead of fortifying by ethics. By academic training, on account of the resultant à-la-mode political façades, we are everywhere the too willing prey of propaganda by the managed publicity of any "professional." Far too "personal" and credulous as we Americans are, we not only stand in danger of losing our only chance at the free life our charter of liberty held out to us but we are still miscalling this mistake of conformity "democracy," instead of seeing it as and honestly calling it the refined gangsterism of the mediocre or of mobocracy. Democracy is the very gospel of Individuality! Call it what you please. Bureaucratic mobocracy is the corruption that would destroy the fruit of every democratic instinct we have developed.

SPECIOUS AUTHORITY

Concerning this probable academic attitude of authority itself toward the freedom Broadacres proposes: we have had prohibition because a few fools could not carry their liquor; Russia has communism because a few fools could not carry their power; and now democracy faces a swollen privatism of license instead of true individuality because a few fools could not carry their success! And yet, behind our passion for money-making we must go on making more money to secure more power. If we want power—and we do—we go into the money trust, as we must, or we bust.

Therefore, if instead of the organic architecture of Broadacre City we continue to have a mere styles-formula retained by A.I.A. as architecture, this cataclysm will come because so many mere money-makers have neither the wit, imagination, nor integrity to discriminate between personality the exterior, and individuality the interior; and more capacity for enmity than for gratitude.

By this confusion we continue to overgrow our badly overgrown urban life; and this too because too many capitalist fools pretend to be "conservative." It is their subversive "power" they conserve. This constitutes their own danger as well as ours.

Through adventitious wealth, gained for its own sake by the exploitation of natural resources by machine leverage—the machine now virtually owned by pseudo-capitalism's convenient satellites—the yes-men of our modern, overgrown cities are now an incubus, to be dealt with because they are piling up across the great natural stream of humanity flowing toward economic and spiritual freedom. That "dam" is the first, middle, and, perhaps vain to hope, the last hangover from old feudal systems. Right now, in this very hangover is omnipresent disaster to the freedom of our nation as a great republic true to the principles of democracy.

As I planned the free city, I saw clearly enough a worthy democratic life lying wrong side up before us, if at all. Right side up—in such planning as you may find in the illustrations of these long continued Broadacre studies of freedom—tomorrow: This practical vision of the free city—nationwide—is the city nowhere unless everywhere.

ARCHITECTURE AND ACREAGE TOGETHER ARE LANDSCAPE

Architectural features of any democratic ground plan for human freedom rise naturally by, and from, topography. This means that buildings would all take on, in endless variety, the nature and character of the ground on which they would stand and, thus inspired, become component parts. Wherever possible all buildings would be integral parts—organic features of the ground—according to place and purpose.

Although present towns and county seats are held as centers, no two districts of the new city need ever be precisely alike. Except as the new city might spread as new feature to some featureless plain. But that plain too, has a certain natural beauty of its own, and might well bear repetitions of the appropriate patterns characteristic of tillage and forestation. Broadacres would be so actually built in sympathy with omnipresent nature that deep feeling for the beauty of terrain would be fundamental in the new city building: would seek beauty of landscape not so much to build *upon*—as to build *with*. Endless unity-in-variety thus becomes a natural consequence. Indigenous character? Inevitable. Endless variety and indigenous character would be the effect of terrain and individuality coming naturally together, wherever they might arise. All would find natural expression, naturally.

Perception and planning, if organic, would be qualified to recognize features of construction and design that would make the physical body of this era of our vast machine age harmonious. Entity. And—to repeat—organic architecture is no less essential to the structure of painting, sculpture, music and religion because, by way of nature, mankind is spiritually awake to the uses and great purposes of all the arts that are all needed to make the culture of a civilization. Inevitably therefore architecture as the great mother-art and moderator contains in principle the essential basis, philosophy, and structure that should inspire them all! Architecture lives again as it has ever lived—*the great final proof of quality in any civilization whatsoever.* Always true basis or cornerstone of a culture.

So, all the way from economic basis to great cultural growth, buildings and good government will be innate features of the free city we have now reached and are about to describe in detail as primarily organic architecture. From great road systems, the natural veins and arteries of the new city, to the various buildings that are its cellular tissue; to parks and gardens that are its pleasure places, its smile; to factories in fields that are its physical subsistence and spiritual health—in the harmony of all this lies the new city of democracy. Primarily, Broadacres would be great architecture.

Were democracy here today in this respect, the entire native scene would soon become harmonious expression of the better nature of modern man himself; would again prophesy and help secure his continuous, happy search for man's growth on his earth. The *native abundance* in which he would then stand and share would be reward for the intelligent use and wise restraint of this gigantic engine of leverage (or of slavery)—the Machine! Our civilization might well be eternal instead of, as now, on the way to join the great rubbish heap of the civilizations which history catalogues, if this true man-light—the Poetic Principle—would dawn afresh for us in such organic character.

The good ground should greatly determine the fundamental shape, even the style, of every occupation in building, road, or institution in the new city. To see where the ground leaves off and the building begins would require careful attention. But this organic "ground-motive," variety in unity, once established in general practice, would be definite and infinite. The ideal of organic unity held firmly in mind, well in hand, the architect would himself gradually become more a spiritual power, equal to his vast new opportunities. Ever growing intelligence of the artifex together with a universal desire on the part of the citizenry for a whole life, all free to grow. This activated, more genuine impulses would soon make at least a work of art of every feature of the new city into which the old one would gradually dissolve. Petty diverse partitions of property, wilful deformations of natural beauty by conscienceless utilities like those of the pole-and-wire men, perpetual defacements by advertising in sordid self-interest becoming common everywhere to irritate the sensitive citizen, would be unpardonable crimes against the landscape. So-called "utilities service" and conscienceless advertising of goods and chattels along the roads by the universal huckster would disappear; mankind going about life in a more normal way; poisonous mechanical gases, groans, shrieks and screams in carbon monoxide gas or smoke—gone. Life itself no longer perpetually endangered by senseless stop and go, jamming, crowding. No more would abortionists be free to set up or set down their glaring paraphernalia by the wayside in attempt to beguile the desired eye. Garish poster façades or signs fighting it out with each other to catch the eye of the helpless passerby, exaggerating everything that can be posted or imagined. Signboards behind which the merchant moves in to live. And much more, not to be that should never have been.

Naturally enough the railroad rights-of-way as may be, belong to the people; and truck lanes occupy the vacant spaces each side along the rails. Operation is another matter. Eventually, the rights-of-way are the most desirable possession of the free city, because, as great traffic truck lanes, they may be turned over to fluid, undated traffic of this kind. Various streams of continuous cross-country traffic, local and long distance bus travel and local trucking should be placed upon these popular railroad rights-of-way, thus restoring the highway to the safe use of the citizen in his automobile.

Like many another established custom now to be liquidated and become proper feature of Usonian Broadacres, these railroad rights-of-way need comparatively little reconstruction except the new type of equipment, inevitable if for no other reason than that the present cumbrous establishment is already obsolescent as human passenger-traffic in America has taken to the air.

THE USONIAN VISION

Imagine now, freeways broadened, spacious, well-landscaped highways, grade crossings eliminated by a kind of integrated bypassing, over- or under-passing. All traffic in cultivated or living areas made gracious by landscaping, devoid of ugly scaffolding (like telegraph and telephone poles and wires), free of glaring billboards, and especially from ugly fencing and ditching. Imagine these great highways of generous, safe width and always easy grade—roadbeds concave instead of convex—bright with wayside flowers or cool with shade trees, joined at intervals with modern air-rotor fields from which self-contained mechanical units—safe, noiseless transport planes, radio-controlled, carrying neither engines nor fuel—like modern taxicabs take off from convenient stations to almost anywhere else. Giant roads now themselves great architecture. Public service stations now no longer eyesores but expanded as good architecture to include all kinds of merchandise, appear as roadside service along the roads for the traveler. Charm and comfort—no end—throughout these great roads as they unite and separate, separate again and unite. Endless the series of diversified units—as one passes by small farm units, roadside markets, garden-schools, beautiful spacious dwelling places on acreage, each on its own acreage of individually adorned and cultivated ground. Places too for pleasure in work or leisure are common where landscape features occur. And imagine man-units so arranged and integrated that every citizen may choose any form of production, distribution, self-improvement, enjoyment, within the radius of, say, ten to forty minutes of his own home—all now available to him by means of private car or plane, helicopter or some other form of fast public conveyance; factories in which to make his living. Such integrated distribution of living all related to ground—this composes the new city embracing this entire country: the Broadacre City of tomorrow. The city becomes the nation.

When every man, woman, and child may be born to put his feet on his own acres and every unborn child finds his acre waiting for him when he is born—then democracy will have been realized. By way of education made organic, life organic and organic architecture become the greatest servants of modern man. Great architects will surely then develop creative buildings not only in harmony with greenery and ground but in intimate patterns of the personal lives of individual owners. No two homes or gardens, none of the farm units of one, two, three—ten acres to forty or more—no two farmsteads be like factory buildings or markets be like either. None need be alike. Nor would any belie its true purpose; nor be ugly. "Styles" no longer fashionable, style itself will have a chance to flourish everywhere. Style now indigenous.

Strong, well built but light and appropriate houses would be good "housing," perhaps prefabricated but spacious workplaces, all of which would be convenient, each sympathetically built out of materials native to the Time, the Place, and the Man. Building construction would be so designed as to take full advantage of Nature. Professor and farmer, factory worker and doctor, entertainer or broker—as well as millionaire—all together in the new city would live and work in environment becoming to each, according to their various needs and nature but none the less themselves superior. All could live close to work or to pleasures. Only a short ride (in time scale) to work in attractive workplaces called factories, to reach markets, travel stations—smokeless; noiseless. Of course the farmer no longer envying the urban dweller or vice-versa. His own convenient improvements preferable while the white-collarite in turn might covet the farmer's green pastures and splendid animals although they could now belong to him also should he so make up his mind.

Normally the factory, farm, office, store or dwelling, church or theater would be within ten minute radius of vast, variegated wayside markets and schools. Food fresh every hour and manufactures in markets so placed that each might serve the others effectively, all directly serving appropriate population living or working in easy range of its neighborhood. No need then for the futile racing to and from any far away common center, tired out but racing back and forth again to race again tomorrow. No more stalling off time and crucifixion, just to keep things from being congested and too "big" because of the pacing of some money-making system eventuating from and into the money-trust. Instead of the big fixations of banking and insurance would rise multiplicity of fluid small individual charming human establishments. Freedom at last economic!

Forever fresh air, food no less fresh, sunlight, good land, green underfoot and appropriate spaciousness round about, people building themselves in everywhere, a more moral human life would thrive and develop. So would we live! So, recognizing our possibilities and comparing them with facts as we are all beginning to do (except insurance, the university and capitalism) Usonian home life will not eliminate any of the gadgetry related to modern comfort. It will keep alive and utilize the health-giving machine facilities to which the new freedom is largely due. Steel, glass, plastics too, will be sensibly called upon to fulfill rational uses. Steel for strength and lightness; glass for air-enclosing of interior space, wall screens to make of living in any Usonian house a delightful privacy, give protection against sun, without losing sky and surrounding elements: yes. And the neighbors? Well, their homes should be in no vulgarizing exposure or inconvenient proximity. They would all be in spacious outdoor gardens; their every garden an outdoor home.

Tall buildings? Not barred. No, but they would stand free of neighbors in small green-parks of their own, set in the countryside. Wherever desirable. "Cooperative" apartment houses might be erected for immured, untrained urbanites desiring to enjoy the beauty of the country but yet unable to participate in creating or operating it. But apartment houses need no longer be tier on tier of glass used as curtain walls, but each extended level with its flowers—a vine-festooned balcony-terrace. These semi-public buildings would be conveniently set up in spacious gardens on ground in the outskirts of a neighborhood. All varied activities now similarly independent of crowding would be so placed and built—each presentable to all. Especially schools and hospitals would be but one story high in segregated units.

No man content to build for himself by taking away from others natural rights to space, privacy and light: the result never a monstrosity like today's typical mercantile success, those massive urban apartments.

What life did this immense inhumane toll-gatherer, this nervous, fearsome mantrap which the city raised so high, have to give? What has such success to give any worthwhile citizen, now that he has the motorcar, while in spacious land "out there" the great hard-road systems of our country beckon erstwhile tenants of the cubicle to freedom where his motor may stand not only by his gate but wherever he goes, while he has access to everything he needs in order to live a useful and happy family life on his own ground. The individual truly sovereign!

Everywhere now human voice and vision are annihilating distance—penetrating walls. Wherever the citizen goes (even as he goes) he has information, lodging and entertainment. He may now be within easy reach of general or immediate distribution of everything he needs to have or to know: All that he may require as he lives becomes not only more worthy of him and his freedom but convenient to him now wherever he may choose to make his home.

I see this Usonian freedom as his "way out there" in a home more than a convenience: I see it as the modern sanctuary. Wherever the citizen wants to be, I see his own beautiful house economically produced by the factory going to the house, not by the house going to the factory—his dwelling in place produced economically and better designed than is his motorcar. By devotion to machinery a few hours a day he should get his house where he wants it. But wherever his home stands it will be a harmonious feature of unviolated environment. And the factory in which he may work, in which he leaves home to go to work, is so built, subdivided and operated throughout in harmonious proportions to his new life, that work is an equally attractive feature not too far away from his own home. An establishment just as becoming to the countryside as is the civic center or church. The time and money that the white-collarite now spends going to and from work, now usefully spent in the diversified colorful activities in the workman's widened margin of leisure in happier circumstances. See these more spacious, comfortable free establishments where whole families play and work; or the modern small farms; all industrial workers not so far from these many small diversified farm-units themselves. But they might own them too; bring their children up in knowledge of nature to help raise produce for highwayside markets which the citizens continually pass; picking up food continually fresh—clients of the professional man who himself comes from far and near to his own clinic built beside his own house. Both now on his own home ground. The modern motorcar will no longer be a stupid, awk-ward compromise with the horse and buggy to resemble a ferry boat. I see it distinguished as a swift really mobile *machine*—*humanized*. The only thing mobile about it now? The name.

Arts and crafts of eager, growing, young work-life more conveniently established wherever willed by the citizens—homes, shops, and workshops of craftsmen—artists everyone of them with his own car or air-rotor or both in addition to fast, regular public transport; these independent in the many small studios and workshops that will abound throughout the city.

I see "going places" a *genuine* luxury; enlightened pleasure in charming places to which all can go at will, so designed; and such places everywhere reserved nearby for occasions. And because the margin of leisure has been doubled by appropriate uses of the machine—and no more back and forth haul—all may have time enough to enjoy them. Droves of happy healthy children go to smaller and ever growing smaller schools. Garden-schools are more numerous and more individual. I see children there in their own little practice-shops working in little individual vegetable and flower gardens, schools and hospitals set in parks that are near garden playgrounds, placed where nature periodically stages "a beautiful show." Raising vegetables and animals of all kinds. Many joys now yet to be known would be a commonplace experience.

I see children's parents meantime living the free individual life that would enrich the communal life by the very changing quality of their own fresh individuality. And last of all but not least, I see beauty in the new life unafraid of anything outside itself: life that has rediscovered faith in life by faith in itself. All this harmony with nature in varied transport, buildings, work and recreation spaciously intimate with liberated transport I see as the proper life of the proper city. A great Usonian agronomy instead of the heartless sterilizing cinder-strip of enormous "industrialization," production senselessly increasing production only for the sake of more production.

Plan and elevation would all be carefully thought out in all establishments, as appropriate to purpose as each is to the other. Liberal life made free to flow from each to each. So to every man his life according to his natural ability, his choice free, the life of all suited to normal need. We might have had all this long ago.

With each generation this fresh outward flow from the lives of liberated citizens naturally refreshed and duly increased. Everywhere in America this warm upsurging of life is our heritage: a nation truly free to use its own great woods, hills, fields, meadows, streams, mountains and wind-blown sweeps of the vast plains all brought into the service of men and women in the name of mankind: Doing all this, doing no violence to get it done, America justly proud of its own organic power and beauty. Citizens understanding and conserving all natural resources whether of material or men. This—to me—is the proper service to be rendered by the architects of our country—the service of organic architecture to the democratic life of Usonia! Architecture alive: the cultivator of youth—preserver of the beauty of nature—guide and counselor of the growing American family as well as conservator of crops, flocks and herds. The philosophy of organic architecture looks—and sees these all together as the field in which the architect is born to practice.

From coast to coast and border to border, the hang-over of ancient ambitious centralization has now left the vast new acreage of these United States a neglected backyard. Smoke-and-cinder-gas-blighted areas make drear ground the industrial revolution has left in its wake; especially in the East and lake region. The South wears permanent scars. Permanent scars on both Man and Nature are the eternal shame of the industrialism that rose to power in the North from the cinder heaps. So many billions have already been wasted upon our becoming the arsenal of a fortuitous life. We are vainly trying to keep up at such great cost the "price system" that ran away; we called it "industrial revolution!" A pity that all this increment could not have been spent to create a more fruitful example of a truly liberal democratic life. What irony! Peace has never been organized for the innate glory of America—only for or against war! Or the fear of war.

Dying, Napoleon said, "Why has force never been able to organize anything?" Already, how often proved?

And, yet, just because forces of peace have never been truly organized (how magnificent they might be!) the freedom guaranteed by the Constitution of the U.S.A. has not only never been achieved but seldom understood. Were peace really organized as war is now organized, war could never defeat peace on any terms whatsoever. Citizens of Broadacre City will not be afraid that "peace will break out."

War would look as sinister to children and the citizen called upon to wage it as it really is. The teenager and the citizen would soon compel "the interests" to pay the price for peace in terms of peace and by their own contribution.

Human imagination is capable of greater divinity than we now realize. It alone is able to distinguish the human herd by way of the character that is individuality, able eventually to save man from the fate that has overtaken, finally, all previous human herds by way of their own civilization.

Finally, I see this release and increase of our native resources all adding up to a grand free culture of a civilization made integral with Nature by a noble architecture of its own: architecture by and for manhood, making the machine the proper means to create nobler longings in man for more fruitful activities than our new world has yet seen.

Let us then free ourselves from all secret government of our lives, from official artificiality; and let us free ourselves from false theories as to how we would or should act subsequently. But, what will the nation that is an organic comprehensive new city be like if we would thus design and build it instead of letting it, as now, haphazard, build itself? Abundance exists in Nature's own kind and time. Fruitfulness is abounding; not diminishing but increasing.

So the regenerate Broadacres architect enters now as master of utilization: as house-planner, road-builder, bridge-builder, town-planner and planter. The superhighway, tributary hard roads and bridges being—more than ever—fundamental architectural factors. Everywhere new dispensations are compelling, by discipline from within, a quickening sense of all this in the new city capital of the natural order of organic Democracy.

Low sweeping grades, banked turns on surfaced roadbeds, no open ditches beside the roads, wherever possible hedges for fences, well-considered green-covered cuts and fills healed by good planting of indigenous ground cover. All may have supreme beauty. Moving road-lines that are the highways laid down sympathetic to terrain, threading hills and plains with safe grades everywhere; these are already a delightful circumstance. Wherever they occur they are elemental features of architecture. Sightly road protections will be well studied together with designed drainage; culverts and bridges, in themselves, designed as good architecture. Where concrete retaining walls would be prohibitive in cost there could be lines of blocks dotted along the sloping banks of every turn. Evergreen masses by the mile would line the roads for snow protection, instead of unsightly snow fences. Masses of native growth would sweep over banks of the cut or fill, not the usual collection of so many different kinds of shrubs and trees misnamed landscape architecture. Everywhere possible, without obstructing desirable views, would be broad sweeps of native trees. At many an appropriate place always an eye to bloom and color changing with the seasons. Safe roads for hilly or flat country; curved roads always for curved country and contour tillage of all sloping fields. Everywhere, no trucks on main roads nor wires on poles. "Public service" safely underground.

No main hard road in the new city would have less than four lanes, some of them double-decked. Superhighways should have no less than six lanes with over- and under-passes for traffic. Nor should any ditches for drainage be allowed open alongside. "Roads be concave, not convex," become low-lighted ribbons at night, service pipes laid down at the center in concrete open trenches. Fueling-and-servicing-stations would be found at wayside parks and at strategic highway intersections. Road construction and green-planting, both as engineering and architecture, would be (naturally enough) under control of each county seat in every state, but with the best supervision that supervising architects, landscape architects and structural engi-

neers afford. The very best that this country, or perhaps the world, affords would not be too good, and would become *official*. Each main county seat would receive special attention. At proper points along or under railways or highways safe, spacious underground refuge should be constructed for the various kinds of storage uses in peacetime. These might afford protection under attack from the air; making such attack unprofitable.

The modern architect's trained sense of the harmonious "altogether" in these several matters of road construction, planting, bridge-building, would, and from beginning to end, be indispensable to the integrity of the conception of the whole universal city. A perfected agronomy in the best sense everywhere on the way.

Romans built such great roads that to this day they remain. But with the systems of reinforced concrete we now practice and our modern machines, we could as cheaply build better, more lasting roads and make all factors in a noble architectural scheme. What nobler agent has culture or civilization than the great open road made beautiful and safe for continually flowing traffic, a harmonious part of a great whole life?

Along these grand roads as through human veins and arteries throngs city life, always building, building, planning, working; living nearby or coming from miles away in these independent, cooperative broad-acres that are growing to be a greater nation than any ever lived in before.

Native lakes and streams, mountain resorts, all made more easily available by private plane or air motorization. Transport could thus contribute no small element of pleasure to our life. The barge and small motorboats could do in relation to the land for rivers and large bodies of water what the plane has done for the land itself.

The bad form of centralism that built the great railway stations as gateways to the old city (*Bahnhof*) will be gone. Exaggeration of conspicuous waste in any form will bear manifest rebuke by society. There may be many minor transient stations instead of a few major ones because "the great station," owing to lack of the great concentration, is no longer desirable. As flight develops, air-rotor or helicopter depots will be connected with the cross country rights-of-way on which once were laid the hard rails, trucks now running each side these rails. Railway cars would not run by noisy "trucks" but slide down shallow skids, the cars mounted upon them being light cylindrical tubes—perhaps jet-powered. A railway train would become capable of 150 miles an hour without any uncomfortable vibration. New traffic systems would include contact systems with minor flight-stations, and be placed wherever a flight-station might be regarded as permissible or convenient. The big terminal and storage warehouses of the present would not exist as eyesores because all would disappear beneath the tracks except at ports of entry or export; the major part of the traffic business, of either gathering or distribution of freight now free to go from rails to house or hand to hand. From factory and farm to family or from family to factory—piecework becomes no mere slogan but a reality. Or from producer to exporter, or from importer to distributing center, by way of the universal traffic lanes to which all units of either production or consumption have quick and easy access. Wasteful back-and-forth haul eliminated by good planning. As the natural city grows in completeness distribution is more and more easy.

But there will always be particular concentrations at ports and mines. A port concentration will differ from that of the inland city. Every such concentration will have imposed upon it the particular character of its special environment and situation, therefore each will differ from the others. One-third of all railroad business at present is hauling coal but now coal will be transformed into electricity at the mines: power lines and pipelines all underground. Water power is everywhere utilized to complete general electrifications all now available as a public asset, service at cost to the people. Atomic power the possession of the people when it comes.

Such individual differences as lie within the general shape and purposes of the universal city would all be naturally developed as *architecture* except wherever conformity to uniformity of mass production might enter as substantial human benefit. Standardization—and its usual bureaucracy—might be

the warp of a nation woven as would be a variegated, appropriate fabric. The ultimate weaving in all standardizing need show no less imagination and individuality than ever if in the hand of the creative architect. But because of the Machine used as a tool the finished whole might have the richer variety of individuality and so have finer quality than yet imagined. This inevitable individual differentiation of character as form and form as idea would give fascination to all of life: everywhere charm!

See that very human quality of individuality—strange to say, a quality these United States of America are finding it difficult to recognize, utilize and preserve: a quality we have all but lost, yet evident as the precious core of all creative power. Owing to no vicarious living whatever, nor to any false vainglorious success-ideal depending too much upon a too vicarious means by way of which man now surrenders in order to survive. Mere employment in the new city is by no means enough! Human satisfactions must be freed from the tyranny of stock plan-and-rule government; we must learn to recognize lapses of democracy even before we have learned to know what democracy really is. To conquer lawlessness in some other country, why must we submit to bureaucratic impositions here at home? What future for us then except as servile to brutal power as much as we are its beneficiaries?

When atomic power gets out of uniform—into overalls—fuel, public or private, for all purposes will be turned into electricity at the mines wherever sources of power are needed; or oil or gas pipelined to places. Power from all sources relayed underground to the consumer. Electrification thus universal will be low in cost. Atomic power really owned by the citizen will not only be able to compete but will abolish everything else as the source of heat, light and power.

Great power-transmission units underground and pipe lines where necessary would be the same miracles of modern engineering as the shoes we wear. Wherever natural resources happened to abound there improved methods of making power available to the citizen would take all fuel or power underground.

Awakened sense of the value of our native landscape would use so many recent developments in wireless telegraphy and telephone now unfairly suppressed, and make all poles and wires overhead a bad memory of ugliness and danger. This ruthless scaffolding once upon a time disfiguring environment by way of public service companies, hanging and maiming the countryside for all citizens for most of a century—these will not be found in the new city. This imposition of crude, utilitarian scaffolding, incurred during the infancy of our haphazard growth as a mechanized nation, invariably does violence to our own character as well as the countryside, violates to this day all the finer sensibilities of American life. Such crudity disappears in Usonia. Power and traffic will have found avenues of distribution more conservative of the general interest and found economical popular distribution in wiser, more public-spirited methods. Such devices as are now termed "service"—swept from sight into general discard, together with poles, wires, hard rails, track elevations, dirt overpasses, gas plants, coal-burning powerhouses, train sheds, roundhouses, coal yards, lumber and building material yards—all go out or under. These ugly features of life today no longer needed except under cover of road elevation in the groundwork of traffic systems themselves. Unsightly structures could nowhere exist in this new city of the future. Evidences of these crude if fundamental ways of money-making our pioneering days accepted are seen no more. Obtrusive, offensive scaffolding of any kind will be taken down so that the culture of our civilization may now appear, though as late as the middle of the twentieth century.

Such are the general *topographical* elimination and distributing features of the free city that decentralization itself is building among us right now, without our help or any wise planning, or anything at all but hindrance from the official finance-powers we are operating. *Organic reintegration* must follow decentralization. Planning is the factor that will develop the new city and keep the city economical and beautiful. The new Broadacres will absorb all needless cities and towns where they stand. The many big ones so badly overbuilt by the ruthless clinging to capitalistic centralizations making crowding profitable because crowding is made indispensable. The flowering of the new city, as we may see, depends upon the great topographical road systems for ubiquitous mobility. We can see them everywhere growing around us; well underway is the universal traffic problem. In Broadacres such jamming of various parts? Non-existent.

So these changing interpretations of American democracy through culture at last on good terms with education, will make the modern City not only a free city but a finer, a beautiful city—a city serving American ideals of freedom which might with all justice be called democracy building democracy.

Now, how do the various buildings themselves, human units in the new liberal planning by and for the reflex, become valid expressions of modern life? If with true aesthetic sensibility we should scientifically see in perspective the vast resources with which we continually go to war but with which we have certainly never learned how to go into creative work: Invention? Yes. Creation—no. Were we to see our own wasted forces organized for peace, we would find that the greatest benefits to come from the free city might come from men not "employed" in the old sense at all but men who work freely because they like doing what they do. "Employment," being free, now grows and does more than "stay in line" in some vast money-making game, on a wage-scale all out of proportion with the new time-scale brought to the surface by the leverage of Science.

Once consumption as master really faces production down, work takes on different character: Quality then has a chance to become accepted as superior to quantity, and it would naturally be so.

As a matter of course, the new standard of spacing by time-scale vitally affects everything in our new general city plan. These effects appear in every building—in every major or minor detail of this conscious elimination of the tyrannical major and minor axes in order to be free to plan according to Nature. Here we have at last the elimination of the insignificant.

Thus we shall see entirely new forms for living; and see a finer, more secure family life. We will see integrity of means to ends, the individual we have been prophesying and promoting we shall see taking effect in more intelligently civilized constructions. Men would build from the heart as well as by the head: build either by hand or by machine, but build always from the good ground upward and from the inside outward to comprehend time, place and man.

Most important, then, to us as a people would be this fast-clearing fact that the means to live a more lovable life now demands a more livable city. This Broadacre concept of city-planning simply means that any building in any place, of whatever kind, is concerned first with the new sense of space in spaciousness and of the nature appropriate to purpose and materials and tools. The old standards of spacing should have gone out when universal mobility and electrification came in. This concept of "planning" is a matter of the right kind of building in the right way in the right place for the right people. The individual has already secured speed and comparative flight. No mere expensive stunt. By more experimentation with mechanical powers, modern man may secure even more vicarious power. But it is now clear that he has acquired certain propensities of the bird as he had already acquired certain propensities of animals and fish. Security for him in this changed cycle of time now lies in use of the vicarious powers more naturally characteristic of his better self in a free city. A vast new city perceived according to deeper elementals enlarging his life with perception of his spirit according to his new advantages—using all machine powers, land, and sound money as mere tools by means of which he builds an architecture for life not as now lived, not by vain exaggerations and murderous neglects and abuses to destroy and be himself destroyed, but to build a great City. To be of the twentieth century this city must be built in these comprehensive terms of organic spiritual need instead of the *meum et tuum* of a profit system. As financial gain is now set it may be considered a public need. Money should have no power whatever in itself, as no commodity at all with which to merely speculate should have a credit value. It should have value only as a *medium* of exchange.

To develop organic power, to overcome these brittle economic obstructions continually thrown in the way of development by the present terms of orthodox finance, creative architecture must make available for its Place, Time and Man the various forms within which we may truly better live and build and make a great life now possible to us. If life is to be lived consistent with our great new powers and the widening margin of leisure (both now in infancy), both to be a blessing not a curse, man must be able immeasurably to widen his own spiritual horizon and exercise his spiritual capacity accordingly.

Again, consider the fact that machine increment by movement is far different from man moving on his legs or driving a horse-drawn vehicle. This new standard of measurement must be applied to any general plan-spacing in space-planning of the new city and its new homes. More important, this new space concept enters to be directly applied not only to buildings themselves but with equal constructive force to the mind and conscience of man himself. The sense of lived-in space within the building must be clearly seen as reality: Space-building being the kind of building available to him now. The sense of space *within* as the reality of building is not a new concept; it is ancient essential principle not only necessarily implied by the ideal of democracy itself but inherent first in the philosophy of Laotze and then in the nature-studies of Jesus.

Time is now for us to interpret this eternal sterling principle with our command of modern mechanical equipment, so to make the life of any building *actual* instead of allowing it to grow more and more a vicarious tax on reality. This should be established as profound *architectural* philosophy.

Now, along with steel and the use of a great variety of thin sheets of metal and wood comes greater demand for economical and appropriate use of materials not only new but old as well. This is for light, widely spanned spaces, exposures closed against the elements but not closed except at will to light and air, prospect-vista retained where desired.

Here, then, enters the new significances for the new City with liberating super-materials like glass and steel.

See the architecture of heavy enclosure for human life (the fortification) vanishing! A new kind of building to take its place comes to view—like magic—building now more natural to our time. In spite of all untoward vicarious circumstance, man is now to be less separated from nature. The new citizen is to be, in every way, a deeper man in the life of his own time. The hard and fast lines between outside and inside (where he is concerned) tend to disappear. Any building—outside—may come inside and the inside go outside when each is seen as part of the other and a part of the landscape. Continuity, plasticity, and all these imply, are fast coming home to him—a miraculous new release in life as well as architecture. The reflex democratic is now to be his in place of the captious strictures of monarchic power or the major and minor axes in which he was imprisoned by the "classic" bondage of centuries à la Renaissance as interpreted by the Paris Beaux Arts.

This interior difference is all the difference.

The king is dead; long live the king! But now the king is his majesty—the American citizen.

A new superlative is the basis of our new city for the new world not alone in architecture but no less so in the world of thought. Not only is *building* now free to be natural in and to America but so are the new space realizations of the new city themselves free. Modern man therefore no less free. Liberality now lies in properly awakened consciousness of our new circumstances. To be free will become *natural:* no longer freedoms ("the five freedoms") counted out to the man on the fingers of one hand. Freedom is of all, for all.

The fixations of traditional forms never knew such exhilarating release. If ancient forms are imitated, they can only interfere and destroy. All the traditional forms we ever knew were but external mass-concepts—facades for an external life under some form of conscription. Exterior compulsion. Exterior pressures exerted upon men to whom congestion was no unmixed evil. An "exterior" architecture. Actually congestion was not only a great convenience but necessary to the impositions of authority.

MIS-EDUCATION

Congestion has grown monstrous. The new principle and the natural changes we face are the important facts—the true basis of the art of beautifully building organic buildings is now a great *machine-age economy!*

Economy *organic* in itself beautiful. Economy is at last an element of beauty where each is of each other; they should be as *one.* Our civilization may at last rise to its best and bravest by way of such wisdom and democratic man demand to be ruled by what is seen by him only as bravest and best in his life.

Drastic congestions of mass centralization devastate the free growth of individual man's spiritual life. All old traditional forms must no longer be allowed to interfere with our new life. As a nation we are suffering from a low glut of population and *things;* things without beauty; people without spirit. This is reflected in our buildings. We have suffered untold hindrance to culture by way of popular "taste"; we suffer now from lifters of the little finger, who promulgate their own taste as arbiters of art and architecture. "Taste" becomes the false criterion, now that we may learn of architecture as organic. It was "taste" that made our culture a parasite, or parody, and helped our present city to be what it is today? Degenerate?

Some of our better factory buildings, escaping the facade, are already exempt from the academic excess made by commercial success. We are suffering yet from the so-called monumental and official building: academic hangovers that we said were in the "classic" tradition, merely reproductions of feudal thinking. This "classic" so narrowly fixed as "style" by current mis-education upon young minds. As the acquisitive jackdaw plunders to line his nest, or as our monkey-psychology still glorifies "to have and to hold," so cults in our great nation are especially servile. It is fabulous waste of the young when they are not allowed to be elevated to the study of all categories of Nature organic in art.

And, too, the fashionable house of the past period-of-the-periods was not only a sodden box-mass of some kind—masses of building material punched full of holes "à la" some dessicated mode or ancient fashion recorded by the museums—but often the result of mania for the antique which made of every house a bazaar, a museum, or junk shop. This disgrace to culture was set up here at home as authority by men who, in this remote darkness of the now obsolete shadow-of-the-wall, were themselves mere "left-overs."

Let us declare that this new era of freedom for which we hope and here prophesy is dawning in our hitherto servile American architecture—at last—although "possession" of the profit-system still operates as a scab on a festering sore. Democratic privilege, our heritage from the past, sinks to lowest terms in our politics. As for culture, what good sense there was in "the Colonial" style still survives as simian mimicry in the eclecticisms of many of our domestic establishments. Everywhere this "style complex" originally came from buildings that were no more than personal realizations, and foolish confessions (or else professions), of an inferiority complex mistaking itself for refinement or "the fashion."

This servility in architecture was proof enough that architects themselves as merchants of these backyard "styles" were all the architects the average American householder knew or had a chance to patronize—until organic architecture appeared. But any citizen capable of consecutive thought may now (and therefore) take hold of modern life problems with a share in them himself. Yes, one's own life problem (it is usually and chiefly a building) is able to obtain light from within. Independent study and real appreciation of organic law may now reach him if he will. The Usonian citizen may soon think his own way through to the particular share in the solution of this problem that is really his own. We are impelled to build this new city if we desire salvation for our civilization. The City of Broadacres is dedicated to him.

TO BEGIN
Beginning at the beginning is apparently an art in itself long lost. This ideal Usonian citizen will now find all proper proportions and significance in this word "organic." It is only a biological term which might indicate something hanging in the butcher shop; but it also indicates where part is to part as part is to whole. But before it is truly significant we must realize *form and function as one*. A spiritual truth instead of a mere fact.

This sense of the organic in the realm of the spirit is a secret of simplicity itself. Organic architecture in this sense is able to create a form of life that will pull many a puzzled mind out of dull academic confusion, open many new doors to this greatest of all arts—architecture—to the human spirit. The mind thus opened will enable democratic freedom of the individual to become a realization.

Erstwhile fashionable period architects and their fashionable clients have now tried every phase of abnegation to styles of the past. Shoddy pretenses. During their better moments such architects have tried to imbue their clients with a simplicity merely pictorial. Now they may try for simplicity genuine. Or, let's say, simplicity natural. There can never be anything organic about imitation whatsoever, either going or coming.

CHANGE WILL TAKE EFFECT
In every phase of the present order there is static; it is fixation that seems to be needed, but release is coming: coming from the source of power nearest to us "ourselves." If abused, abused by our own consent. This potential source of power plus the machine will become chief means to our desired liberation. But should we fall to imitating machines in planning our buildings, even if inspired by steamships, automobiles, airplanes, bathtubs, refrigerators, and water closets, then comes the streamline dogma—novel but dogma all over again. This time the dogma is the cliché "Form follows Function."

Now negation is not necessarily fatal. Neither is waste necessarily so. But negation sterilizes after all, and is only another phase of simplicity merely pictorial. If we dig deeper into Nature we will soon understand that simplicity is as far as the lilies of the field beyond any affected pictorialism. But as a beginning negation has already helped clean up the rubbish heap encumbering our architecture. Negation may be no more than a passing service.

Nevertheless the urban citizen's one-piece bathtub and water-closet do come nearer to beauty than do his present façades by pictorialism. And the car standing at the door shames the house if for no other reason than that in design it is itself a sham.

The intelligence that renounces the period house will also reject the foolish exaggeration in the design of the present car. But try to find a house with the integrity of the new reality. A house or a car integral with Time, Place, and Man.

Beginning to build the free city democracy demands that the young architect search for intimacy with actual building on the good ground. It will result in fruitful service on his part to the fundamentals by his very devotion to himself in his art. Realization of principle in practice will grow creative competence in place of the prevalent scholastic impotence. The soul of America is not yet dead in the young. The young architect will learn to build again as great folk-masters once built, as the songmasters of music wrote—out of the man himself for love of his art.

As things go with us, and with the young architect especially, negation is often good medicine—is so in all the arts—and may do something to abolish the culture faker by awakening and broadening a general dislike for him and a desire for simplicity, although the negator himself may be a culture faker. Even within our cerebral academic system—wherein youth is now educated so far beyond his capacity as to be highbrow—we may see change.

And whenever we do reach the true interior order of simplicity we will still find, among other motley dubious assets, offices inherited from the passing "order of the schools." Find the enormous armies of front-runners, "go-getters," peddlers, brokers, designing-partners, inferior desecrators and feature-writers, journalists, advertising agencies and professors: merchants all. All doing some kind of brokerage between the client (or purchaser) and his own abilities. Again and afresh, it is these quondam "experts" who become parasites in and upon the present aged city. Vain hope that the bureaucracy and academic tutelage that have made such weaklings socially acceptable will ever put fair premiums upon the integrity of the organic qualities in man. If we confound personality with individuality, we will never be able to put the right premiums in the right place; upon individuality whether in philosophy, religion, science, architecture or art.

But America needs no help to Broadacre City. It will haphazard build itself. Why not plan it?

We will be unable to save our immediate phase of civilization from present distortion or eventual destruction by the ambitious merchant-scientist, merchant-architect or the merchants of the "industrial revolution" or the merchants of the far more important chemical revolution. Why all these merchants!

The creative artist? Well—naturally he is himself one who by nature is as important to society as society is important to itself. Which should mean that he is by nature (and by office) the qualified leader in any society, natural, native interpreter of the visible forms of any social order in or under which we choose to live. If worthy to be so accepted, happily so. If rejected by our society, it will be because society will not learn to see the true radical as the romanticist he is. The romanticist we are bound to discover as the true realist; to see the creative artist, then, as modern seer of the poetic principle. Not only is he way-shower but, with experienced command of modern ways and means, he is our natural leader toward a coveted culture of our own.

Why then, even in our best society, here in these United States, are we so afraid of the radical? Why so afraid of every genuinely creative individuality? Is society so afraid because the spiritual values necessary to see the radical as he is, are undeveloped? And all social economic values go tipsy and twisting down the line? Society is actually afraid of truth? Of course it is, as Society now exists. "Society" is more or less afraid because, whoever the "elite" now are, their cherished prejudices are likely to be their holiest feelings, turned topsy-turvy by the truth sought by the radical. So society depends upon the imposing strong-arm enforcements of authority. The elite must now lose guardianship unless the true concept of the term "organic" dawns for them.

THE WORD "ORGANIC"

Be warned this word "organic" is like the word "nature." If taken in a sense too biological, it would not be what it is: light in darkness; it would be a stumbling block. The use of the term "organic" in architecture applies to a concept of intrinsic living and of building intrinsic and natural; both concepts seen together in structure as Native. To the young architect the term should be a daily working concept of the great *altogether* wherein features and parts, congenial in form and substance, are applied to purpose as congenial.

Such then is the true significance of the word "organic." We often refer to this quality as "entity."

THE USONIAN ON HIS OWN ACREAGE

It is not true that the poor are poor because the rich are rich. To say so is an attempt to divert attention from the real causes of poverty. The rich are as parasitic as the poor and probably less able to be happy.

Let us first consider the "poor."

"The poor"? The term immediately raises the "housing problem," now receiving so much social and official attention. Beneficial though some of the attention is, "housing" by our government can only practice putting off, by mitigation of a daily horror, the day of actual regeneration for the poor. Or build poverty into the nation as an institution.

The poor? They are those citizens most hardened, hindered or damaged by inexorable, multiple *rents*. Unearned increment progresses and piles up into the insurance of American fortunes. The poor are poor because of *triple rent:* rent for land, rent for money, rent for ideas. Or else the poor are only the lame, the halt, and the blind, not so numerous.

Where is the place for the poor in these cities and towns built and maintained by makers and takers of triple rent?

For answer, see the salvage effected by the latest and best slum clearance or "housing" developments all over the country, those formidable red brick towers. They are only improved, instead of improvised, slums. No doubt the poverty of the slum-quarter has been built in as an authorized state of body and mind; base standardization of the unproductive human soul. Poverty of spirit thus *builds* poverty into a great liability of our nation! This grim boxing of families—tier on tier—row on row—behind rows or beside rows of other families similarly boxed. Cubicles, the same or similar on rows of shelves on shelves, relentless in military array! Here is no monarchic hangover but an oppression wholly remote from the reflex of democratic nature and hateful to the student of organic architecture; about as inspiring as any coffin. But now decent? Maybe. But just for that, as things go—a deadening straitjacket in which human life may be "beneficiary"?

But not yet blessed. Here we see ingenious regimentation, by government order, of this army of the poor: the poor who are to be poor and *stay poor "decently"?* Made poorer by the machine? Yes and no. But made poorer by big-time production's flagrant greed. Here we see the abuse of surplus machine power and orthodox finance going hand in hand to make people useless at a rate soon triumphant: people machine-made in a machine-made world.

Even though "one's own way" (the old slum) may sink to license and stink, is there not more dignity, at least, in the "freedom" with which it sank? But what human dignity is there in the smell of soap and sanitation in these heavy red-brick prison-cells; in all this dull reiteration of no-idea, no feeling here—housings for nobodies, not homes for somebody—this dreary insistence upon *spiritual* poverty as an institution? Even though a bathtub be incorporated and a posy stuck in some flowerbox to decorate this lucrative form of rent—a sinister light is cast by our great industrial and social "success" in this "housing" of the poor, imprisoned for life by way of high-class "insurance."

Why not have especially subsidized transportation? Why not make the land they were surely born by nature to inherit, more free to the growing families of the "poor"? The land they were born to inherit as they were born to inherit air to breathe, daylight to see by, water to drink. Perhaps food to eat? Why not? I am well aware of the academic economist's reaction to any question of free land or anything "free" at all. Anywhere. And on present systems there is plenty of exercise for such rationalisms as his. But Henry George showed us—his people—clearly enough the simple basis of human poverty: the only *organic* solution of the land problem needed by the poor rich or the rich poor. Neither are secure? Any solution of their problem is eventually our own imperative salvation—soon, or we will have no true democratic society. What hope exists for proper stimulation of the great architecture of a great life while owners of land hold all man-made improvements on the land *against* the man on his land, instead of man-made improvements holding the land? For any organic economic structure as a basis for architecture this is wrong end to. Error at the root: that is to say, radically wrong. In present circumstances architecture is only for the landlord—building by permission of the banker.

Some form of redemption (or exemption) and subsequent co-operative sharing of increase in land values is past due to society. Authority must make available to each poor man acreage according to his ability (and the ability of his family) *to make good use of the land!* If at first there must be subsidy, then—again—why not subsidize transportation? And then—what house for the poor man? Where and what assistance may he find to go to work himself to build a home with and for his growing family? Certainly the present city is no place for him—or his—a mantrap for the poor.

Modern mobility can be so easily arranged for these citizens. Rescue and restitution are now ready for "the poor man" in a new city. Especially by way of a bus or a motor car. Emancipated from triple rent and with good ground now made available to him, he—machine-worker now rented, paying toll to the exaggerated city in order that the city give him work to do—should not he, the "poor," a wage-slave, go not backward but forward to his native birthright: the good ground? His family may grow up even well off in this free city? The poor are there to release their initiative; both workplace and family home may be the same and pleasant. Worthy and inspiring, this association. Families, as such, productive on their own ground, with modern scale of time-spacing, they can truthfully say "ten miles is nearby." Even more miles, say twenty. Or more soon.

The poor man? Yes. . . . Usually he is now wage-slave at some machine. He is probably on the production line. Somewhere. Somehow. And because he is there bound to his employers' machine, common sense would say that to use the machine to start building his own home himself he ought to be able soon, even as things are, to buy a standardized privy, cheap. That "privy" civilized is now a bathroom, manufactured complete and delivered to him as a single unit (his car or his refrigerator the same as the privy) all ready to use when connected to the city water system and a fifteen-dollar septic tank or a forty-dollar cesspool. Well advised, he will plant this

first unit wherever it belongs to start his home. The other necessary units similarly cheap; bedrooms designed for beneficial living added. As months go by, the rent he saved may buy other standardized units; a comfortable living-room and as many more bedrooms as he needs. These and other well designed prerequisites may be added as soon as he earns them by his work or the work of his family, in nearby agriculture, crafts or mechanized industries. His family, meantime, are helping to maintain themselves free on their own ground. All such standard units, varied in general scheme of assembly to suit either flat land or hillside, in various materials so designed as to make not only a dignified but well-planned appropriate whole. This I know. Such various standardized units as we already have are forbidding merely because they were not designed to take the curse off bad design in repetition, and do not add up to a practical gracious whole. But all are produced ad libitum, ad nauseam, by the machine owners' mastery of labor under a bad standardized "production-controlling-consumption" system working in some prefab-profiteering factory. Standards badly designed because bad design is cheap and good costs money? So the shop hates to pay for intangibles and good design is one of these. But the benefits of the "cheapening" process now seldom go to the worker. They go to the big producer to increase production; and quantity soon wipes out quality. But properly standardized units may be produced in the free city as part of itself! And, like automobiles, be produced by the cheapening power of modern mass production come right-side-up: and operated *on the worker's side.* The small cart no longer before the big horse.

Well then—as our artisan grows in resources, so his home grows. The artisan-home-maker now buys the required parts in some well-planned group-scheme of production that benefits by design from long study by the world's best talent, so minded. And such a flexible group of talent may "standardize" units not only to be harmonized by production to do no outrage to the landscape but also at last to be roomy and cheap enough to the consumer—so that his rent for three months in city bondage would buy the first units of his home if the machine is really going to go to work *for* him as well as its owner, and not be kept working to keep the poor poor just so long as the poor are satisfied to stay poor. Mere employment can no more be dangled before his worried artisan-eyes to keep him properly citified in poverty. Where now then is your poor man?

Thus, in a year or two, "the poor" own a house at least home-worthy, staunch, and appropriate to inspiring environment. This home would be a house of real quality; one of a *great variety of such free houses* with good lines, good proportions, pleasant and "practical." Establishment would then be good to look at and as good to live in, because it would be well laid out according to ground; a garden in the prevailing generous ground-spacing. Such outbuildings as he might need—also appropriate standardized units—would be harmonious and would also be designed as extensions of his house itself. All together these would stand among shade trees, fruit trees, berry bushes, vegetables and flowers in the gardens. All houses would have hot and cold running water; a modern fireplace; electric cook-stove and electric heating system comprised in one single unit, bought and serviced by one single transaction. With some small aid in the way of social insurance (part of his new freedom) here is a quality home within reach of the artisan properly in the country by way of his compulsory devotion to the powers of the machine. Under these better, more co-operative conditions machinery could produce a good house for him more economically than his automobile. I mean the present horse-and-buggy car standing out there in a new fifty-dollar car-shelter, a part of his daily life until he can get a better one; at least a car designed for *him*. After all, it is time for us to waken to the fact that a modern car is neither a horse and buggy nor a ferry boat. Were electrification universal, as it will be, there would be cheap, standardized cars, just as standard light, heat, and power would be coming to him, underground, wherever he wanted to be. All cheap because of his voluntary co-operation with his neighbors; government imposed upon him only in those matters incapable of individuality—say police-powers. Such co-operation from government would simplify his circumstances and allow him to go nearer to life in many new ways

without creating any more criminal conditions to be treated by government at his own expense.

Then, as a physical product—as things are—nothing is remarkable about extension to the poor of this opportunity. Taliesin was working upon this problem as early as 1921. The basis working underneath is already at hand. But remarkable is the fact that by way of organic design the whole establishment of the citizen may now have the kind of mass production that is inspired, and the kind of order that is "the first law of heaven." On no account need modern mass production lack the quality individuality alone can give if architects are truly architects. Choice as characteristic would belong to the citizen so freely that with appropriate design and practical devices available he could make his house a harmonious whole as appropriate to him as to his purse, to his ground as to his God. Where the workman has been thwarted by choice only of reactionary sentimentalities aborted by machinery, and compelled to accept ugly machine-made things put into a boxing-up by realtoristic bureaucracy, he will be equal in quality of investment to anyone "rich." The cottage has quality just as the mansion or factory or farm.

So, in the free city, where is your poor man? On a basis of equality he now has the same *quality* available to him as the rich. He can say his soul is his own because on his own ground opportunity has opened to him in natural ways. He has the right *to be*. Free to exercise his own faculties to the top of his bent, he becomes a gentleman because no longer enslaved to exercise himself as a soulless faculty of some machine-made producing system—probably for export! The erstwhile "poor" beside him are at least a block away, similarly situated on acreage of their own. Owing to genuine *quality* in design appropriate to time, place and circumstance he is at home related directly (and beautifully) to the ground he lives on and owns by improvement. He lives on his own in his own country: lives *with* the good ground *as a producer himself* not merely *on* it as a parasite of triple rent and hidden taxes. Birds sing for *him,* grass grows green for *him,* rain falls for *him* on his growing crops while the wheels of standardization and money-making invention no longer turn dead against him. All turn now *for* his majesty, the American citizen!

Are we ever to survive the ubiquitous Machine? If so it means increased life now to every man. Government, itself unaware always, must mean not only policing equal opportunity for all but be more concerned to improve the man. The machine is more the citizen's own concern—not government's—When Democracy Builds as it is surely going to do.

Is it too dangerous thus to allow the basis to exist for the free distribution of independence and liberty? Not in our country. This is the safest thing we as a people could do for our future: the really sane safe investment this nation could make in itself and truly call our national "defense." No standing nation is minded to become a mere satellite. It could be always avoided and we could set the pattern for the world by rational *independence shared:* insure world peace—if we would. Peace? Invincible when based upon freedom such as this.

THE TEEN-AGER

The poor man's children growing up in the free city we see making firsthand contact with more of the freshness and sweetness of their birthright. Native ground and beauty any "rich" man's children now know. And this not by way of urban grass plots, nor as a goldfish, inhabiting a globe together with a pebble and a reed by sheer grace of some wife of a municipally minded landlord.

Once and for all he, "the poor man," as well as "the rich man," is now planted square with his fellows as spacious tillage grows more skillful by way of his work. He increases beauty of the countryside and it enriches all. Meantime, children so rationally educated know what the value of beauty, native, consists in; and by way of this new elemental education are taught to turn someday to teach the "ground" to the world.

In these new circumstances, individuality is thus likely to grow more mellow, gracious and true. Civilization bears better, not bitter, fruits, sane and shared by each and all citizens. A free city in a free nation. Aristocracy in the true democratic meaning of that

misused word: aristocracy made integral: a genuine living *quality* instead of some dated hereditary privilege conferred by some dubious personal power.

To integrate general family small-garden and common little-farms production (to whatever extent this may be) and relate both to factory work and mental services a few hours each day; all the artifex is, and can produce, could be in so many ways economically related to the greater contact centers—extensive markets and factories standing there by the great highway; and rich resourceful neighborhood pleasure-places and civic centers; perhaps nearby as added feature are service-stations or wayside inns, the motels of the countryside.

This Broadacres family produce is regularly called for by men from these wayside markets, each day. Each day the *family* receives in cash one-half the value of whatever they can turn over to these collectors, whatever in its own free time in farmstead or in the shops elsewhere the family has raised and produced. And everyone now is where greenstuffs, produced fresh every hour, are commonplace. "Little-farms" thus reinforcing the larger, more expanded farm units would afford still greater variety of fresh produce to the city consumer, and some additional money would be earned by members of, say, the short-time machine-worker's own household: mother and children. Agrarianism holding its own; agronomy as cultural education for industrialism proceeds. Both could and would be cooperative. But as it now is, industrialism as producer is no fair partner for agronomy.

Where would the usual town-made employment be in the new circumstances? Nowhere. Where would the slums be? Nowhere. Abject poverty abolished. The teen-ager a valuable contributing factor. Integration of the various units by way of neighborhood kindergarten-schools, attractive travel everywhere, worthy entertainment, hospitals less needed and more humane, mutual insurance for sickness, accidents, the inabilities of old age; all these arranged to take from old-time machine-slaves the anxieties that bore them down to dump them into an early grave. Even were this start to be made as far down as the poorest of the poor, society would soon have self-respecting and respected creative individuals for citizens instead of increasing numbers of discouraged, bewildered alcoholics. And no such early retirement as now seems expedient. Instead of another cultural weed going to seed in urban municipal barracks all neatly lined up to raise more weeds indoors than outdoors, here we see a useful growing plant to sow more seeds of the healthy growing sort yielding a valuable mancrop for income. Good independent workmen would become more definitely a human asset. The workman nonetheless but the more a man because he happens to be the "machine age man." Even more a man because no longer a man-machine. He uses the machine too, yes, but the machine no longer uses him nor can it any longer abuse him. Yesterday he was only the machine "yes" man. Today, should he so choose, he is the "no" man or yes man—machine or no machine.

LIFE A WELL-CALCULATED RISK

A democratic minor establishment (so far as it went) would be his. It would have potent charm, become a national *cultural* asset. Homes will be fit to be lived in with the pride of intelligent individuality. As the motorcar will someday come to look like a machine made fit for a human being to ride in, so organic in design, the house and car will look well together— can you imagine it? I can, and so will you although at present the automobile and the house are both out of scale, and utterly out of harmony with each other: the car an incongruous, foolish hangover— simply a commercialized exploit of the not sufficiently-dim-and-distant-past until the new city begins on it and it begins on the new city.

All the various units of this artisan's new house could be built of native materials or fabricated of sheet-metal or composed of some form of composition-slab. Perhaps both together. Prefabrication here comes in as a natural. The house might be permanently built and "finished" like his car, in any texture or color he preferred but fit for a livable beautiful house. No "bad" color or unsuitable texture or pattern could be produced to be "preferred" in the new organic city because only good design is available. The house of the city-dweller

might have much glass, but not enough to wither the tenant—glass screened from above by thin, sheltering wood or metal projections or shaded by the overhanging trellis hung with vines. Various units in one scheme might be wholly rectangular; in another hexagonal; another, circular in form. And all these not only laid out in plan projection but also in what *arises from the plan*. Thus infinite in variety, infinite combinations could be made of these elemental forms. A completed home unit might achieve the inclosure of a central court or garden with much greenery and flowers. Perhaps a pool. The establishment should grow as the trees around the man himself grow. He would be earning the natural increase due to the propensity of himself—his ability *to do* increased not merely because he is self-employed but because his own initiative is set free to employ himself and family in the greater advantage of other men like himself. Teen-age problems all disappear! ·

He could leave the roofs of his new dwelling flat and use them as a roof garden under awnings. Or, at some greater expense, he could slope the roof, protected by permanent materials, and use the ground around the house for recreation. Furnishings, throughout, like all appurtenance systems, would become a natural part of the house: good to look at inside as his house would be good to look at outside. Thus because he got his furnishings as he got his house: designed for him by the best talent the world affords, he might soon choose wisely for his own problem with a perfected knowledge? A range of choice now easily wide enough to enable the homemaker to find his own in his own way— with a proper feeling for nature.

Now the all-inspiring fact in this? The workman is in his free city on ground that cannot be taken away from him, because it is his, not by debt but by doing. That is to say, not his by signing away his sovereignty to any interest-bearing mortgage. It would be his own by way of good use and such appropriate improvements as he would himself make. There could be no landlord over him other than agreeable established social-superintendance given (he would need it and ask for it) by the cultivated society of which he would (in such circumstances) be a cultural unit himself. He would establish it. So the youth grows up an independent workman with ideas of his own which may find fruitful expression, because his education consists in what he does as he is actually learning to live on his own ground. Habitation not habitation is primarily his modern "liberal" education, based upon nature-study. His home is not only his own but naturally harmonious to the whole new city-scheme and environment. No longer is he some haphazard unit that must be officered by rank and file bureaucracy in an army of standardizations to which he was, once upon a time (and not so long ago), committed as "the poor." In all the free city there is no grim rent collected by fortuitous fortune or any other forms of success.

That is to say, here would be the manly family—men living in Usonia because all were privileged manlike in the freedom promised by democracy. Together with their own there is still much more than enough room for growth for everybody to come in, to come to America, her vast unused riches in ground to be well used.

Human independence and liberty fairly distributed where it belongs count most for our actual national defense. With the citizen protected by the character of his position and disposition—his conscience one of the best of assets—government would now truly represent him instead of being merely repressive. Government (and especially so) is his own affair—and again becomes the science of human happiness.

Optimistic, nonpolitical, ex-urban, vernal, spacious, free! All this—yes. In practical outline here is the feasible idea of organic social democratic reconstruction of the city belonging to creative Society—the living city. Abolish not only the "tenement" and wage-slavery but create true capitalism. The only possible capitalism if democracy has any future. True capitalism is not found under evasive practices necessary to maintain a plutocratic republic depending largely upon foreign trade for friendship and prosperity between nations—like a pyramid, apex on the ground, base in the air, maintained by artificial supports.

THE USONIAN FARMER—
THE INTEGRATION OF THE FAMILY

For this farming citizen's share in our national life, what establishment would he, the farmer, have in Broadacre City?

Farmers now suffer from rent in its rankest, most virulent form. Any improvements the farmer makes are only a gamble adding to this burden of rent and probably ending somewhere down the line in foreclosure. Should his own labor be insufficient to pay rent for money, rent for land, and the rent exacted by far overgrown government, then good-bye to all his labor on farm improvement. The banker, as he takes over, takes his improvements. But in the free city, so long as he is able to work at all, he and his family can keep his land by his improvements and (by means of them) his own home where he made it, never fearing eviction. Poverty is thus far away from him if only he will work *at the work he likes* to do and knows best.

But farming at present is the hinterland of economics out there on the borderland of despair. Because the farmer was not taken into the present scheme of industrial or unearned increments, except as agronomy was gratuitous as a mere *source*. Intrinsic sources all become gratuitous too soon as factory-ized capitalized industry gains the upper hand. And in the more thickly settled regions of our country the farmer is still trying to compete against great grain-and-beef-raising by machine farming on the almost endless free acreage of our great, vast West. Grain-raising, as such, and beef are turning against him, and he must turn against both. Nor in cattle-and-sheep-raising can he well compete with these great ranges of western land held without need of improvement, taxed (if taxed at all) at a few cents per acre while the cost of the farmer's improvements always works dead against him on land taxed from fifteen to a hundred dollars (or more) per acre, plus taxed improvements.

Modern sanitation, motorcars, and electrifications like radio, television and flight, have brought the farmer's life a good deal nearer to the luxury of the sons and daughters of the prevailing white-collarite armies. But he is now (all too often) alone on his farm. And sometimes he is on the farm only to become an inmate of the poorhouse (would be better off if he were) at the end of his life's long labor on the ground, whatever may have been his energy and thrift—unless some tragic artificial stimulation such as war or government-spending comes to his rescue (for a short time only) eventually to push him deeper under when his turn comes to pay. This is his "relief."

Amusing or exasperating, as you may happen to take the view. See the empty political gestures his vote-getting saviors make to "relieve" him. He is the pawn in many a fulsome political game devised by false captains of urban fortune. Debt is forced upon the farmer as it is forced upon the wage-slave, for profit to what industrialism?

Despite these gestures made to "relieve" the farmer and the subtle subsidies offered him, not a statesman's voice is raised nor a single sensible legal move made to free him *fundamentally* from the inequalities that grip him for no other purpose than to give the white-collarite armies now serving industrialism a free ride on his back. These "volunteers" of our millions thus "citified" ride on the farmer's back to such an extent because the farmer's labor is *intrinsic*. It is a Source. A source is always infested by the petty parasites of the big parasite in our thriving era of the Middleman: the salesman. The farmer's labor on land contributes chiefly to maintain the characteristic vicarious powers of crowded city life: powers growing more than ever vicarious; power by lever and pushbutton help him on the one hand and push him back on the other. But the farmer's labor does not contribute very much beyond food and privations to his own life except as gratuities. Parasites are parasitic because they must and (it is *no* fault of theirs) batten upon innocent sources of production; live upon *origins*: doomed never to live by originating. So here in our own tiller of the soil is good and genuine life in deep trouble. By way of the preferred parasitism and paraphernalia of our continually increasing mechanical centralization we have to fake our capitalism. Unless the farmer turns and exploits centralization instead of being exploited by it, he is down to stay down for a long time.

Ground is seldom his own ground except as he holds it like his machinery by some slender show of "equity." The farmer—East, Middle West, or South—is no winner of the game of increments as that game is played, for high stakes with the rules of money-getting now established as a kind of betting-game. The financial dice are loaded against him by the very circumstances in which they are held and he is placed. He will "find" himself in time as and if he can, but only in a city like Broadacres.

THE GREAT MOUTH

Cities are huge mouths. Essentially the farmer is food-master for the great mouth. He has many subsidiaries, but his primary job is to feed these great feudal survivals of the city. Raw materials for clothing himself and the urbanites are still his job. Without the farmer our towns and cities, big and small, would go naked and starve.

But in the new free city he himself comes in for a due place and share. The new city will go out to service him as he services the city, the citizen not merely there to be fed but to share in the common luxury which the very nature of the farmer's intrinsic service to society has now made possible—bounty hitherto denied the farmer. Society will share indigenous culture with the farmer. His establishment is now most welcome to all as a fine feature of the city. His will be, perhaps, the most attractive establishment of all the structures of the new freedom.

For feeding the multitude, naturally the farmer's job, it is clear that intensive farming, varied as possible, will be a great social advantage. The vast western grain- and beef-producing areas will no longer compete with him. Instead of there being no place for him—he will take their place. One great advantage the citizen has: his produce, at last, will be direct from producer to consumer. The ubiquitous middleman, too often now a "Sinbad the sailor," will be off the farmer's back. Dairying, fruit-growing, truck-gardening, raising the rarer meats, fowl, eggs, in all of which freshness is a first consideration, will be the direct contribution of society to itself. The tin can and barbed wire fence, once upon a time the bulwarks of advancing western civilization, are gone. He is himself no longer fenced in, or tangled up in his own barbed wire by ubiquitous, inglorious debt. Agronomy, the equal of industrialism or superior, is the gifted source of our national culture—even now—if you take a fair view at our country.

As the natural agronomy we are describing proceeds, there will be a new farmer and his family in Broadacres. He will, by intensive methods, gradually take the place of the "dirt" farmer and his family of pioneer days.

The little-farms farmer—or his farmsters and farmerettes—will need a greenhouse; need less than one small portion of the land he tried to farm before he became a Usonian citizen. As a citizen he now needs a completely fireproof sanitary establishment, one that makes his lifework more pleasant, and a charming association with the higher-grade animals he husbands—breeding, feeding and tending them, primarily doing so for the new city, for the millions who meantime have cultivated their tastes, no longer their idiot-syncrasies, let us say. Or, let us say, cultivated increased knowledge rather than taste. Before everything else the new farmer will now need most (and know best) the nature-study we call organic architecture. He will need the kind of buildings now that will end unceasing tramping in mud or snow in and around about the ill-smelling inefficient group of ill-adapted buildings that had become a habit to him and a disgrace to his country. Organic design is able to supplant them all with one compact, well-correlated, fireproof, prefabricated building efficient for his every purpose, a vermin-proof building that considers his own life on the farm worthy of conservation and culture. The little-farms farmer's dignity, living comforts and cultural education of his children, as organic, are assured. He needs less but has much and more in almost every way worthwhile than when he thought by big acreage he too was "big." He no longer needs big areas, big machines or a multiplicity of sheds. Outbuildings of any kind would muss up his place. But he does need an intimate workshop and modern tools. He does not any more need many fences except those a part of his buildings or electrified boundary lines.

His energy is conserved by having all these conveniences together now under one convenient, sanitary, fireproof, model building; his animals a few steps away approached under cover; his motorcar or small truck reached by opening the door from his dwelling to a garage; his crop prescribed and sold, even before he raises it, by some plan of integration with larger or smaller little-farms markets. This market itself would be a comprehensive scheme for the integration of the many small farm units into greater uses, making available to them the choicest products of the world in art, literature or science. This integration, being inevitable, is destined to take the place of devastating back-and-forth haul of produce and of humanity itself in the present overgrown centralizations of all our big cities and even small towns. Distributions become everywhere direct. From factory and farm to family becomes more than a mere slogan.

This composite farm-building would be made up of assembled prefabricated units. Shelter for cars, a comfortable dwelling, greenhouse, a packing and distributing place, silo (narrow and tall or short and wide), stables for cows and horses, and diversified animal shed for sheep, pigs, etc. The whole establishment would be good architecture. Good to look at. Emancipation for the life of the farmer. As such the whole farm-unit could well be delivered to the farmers at low cost by machine production intelligently expanded and standardized. For the first time organic architecture would become his own, serving him by way of the best brains utilized to simplify and make his life more dignified and his whole family effective help. Their life would become attractive not only to themselves but to the new city itself, a feature of a true modern agronomy countrywide.

This composite little-farms building would be a group building not of one type only as here shown but of as many types in various materials as there are bound to be endless modifications of the farmer's purposes and his ground—or as seen now in our better buildings of more affluent citizens.

This architectural modernization of the very *basis* of all good farming would be a most important phase of "farm relief"—after the freedom of man, land and money is once established in normal channels for building a genuine American culture as a great beneficent agronomy.

Well-designed farm life grouped thus on units of five- ten- or forty-acre farms (or more)—production prescribed, or not—all buildings and equipment designed directly related to highway traffic and supermarkets selling farm produce fresh hourly—this is much more than mere "farm relief." It is true functioning on the broad basis of any democratic economy radical to our vast gift of magnificent ground.

Also of great importance is the design of the little-farms markets themselves. Additional festive social feature—these markets—of urban integration among the many minor service features found along the interior roadways of the highways of the free city.

A single tractor held in common could spread the tilth, power the disk, and harrow the soil for many farmers. Group ownership could be common, and the various community centers of various districts (now called county seats) could provide not only power distribution but pooling of certain labors and interests in case of sickness, or an economy in health. But also community-provided would be varied social entertainments, all of increasingly superior cultural character. Seasonal festivity of great inspirational value for all? All the races involved would soon be contributing to common neighborhood events in terms of the unifying intercommunications by air Today, far beyond those of Yesterday.

Here in suggestive outline only is organic "farm relief" and urban release. A happier, fuller livelihood for so many millions of uneasy white-collarites—become capable as free men and women—not quite happy as city-parasites wrestling with a teenager problem. By further subdivision and reintegration of smaller units, enabling upbuilding of general living conditions on a stronger basis, millions of our citizens would find the means of life that would be defense against propaganda, political oppression—or plain boredom. Population an asset not a threat. Quality would become the ideal. Citizenship no longer compelled to rent the chattels of any cash-and-carry system whatsoever! They would be citizen-owners of themselves.

So in every single county section of Broadacre City there would be plenty of room for the many varied occupations each integrated with all and independent. The superfluous millions of white-collarites now forever seeking and abandoning

employment in the old cities would be happy independents in a beautiful life in beautiful country.

No, "employment" is not enough! What a man wants, if democracy works, is not so much employment as freedom to work at what he believes in, what he likes to do. Officially dangling employment before a man now may be, after all, only the means of keeping him tied to a form of slavery—now some money-getting or money-distributing system that amounts to some form of conscription when any showdown comes. "Full-time employment" in the new city might cast the same shadow-of-doubt on man's future economic life as it did in the old. The nature of leisure will be more integrated with the nature of work than ever; work and leisure become natural to each other.

"BUSINESS" AND ARCHITECTURE
To say that "business" will some day know good architecture suited to its purpose before art, science, education and religion are able to recognize it, may be astonishing but I believe, nevertheless, true. Perhaps this recognition by business is not so much perception of the eternal fitness of things as it is again the flair for the best new expedient or what is "good advertising."

It would seem however that good business *is* heading in toward good architecture? The manufacturer, world over, in this has been leader. Perhaps this because "culture," in quotation marks, had no place for it but in the final decisions of business—the mind of the superior businessman was more free than the pseudo-cultural academic to accept the change that is progress.

INDUSTRIALIZATION
THE FACTORY
The factory?

A factory comes naturally enough to our countrywide countryside city. Government employees themselves become, more and more, small-farms gardeners. The factory is already so well organized, built, and managed that it needs less redesigning than any enterprising unit we have. But it needs more ground free; more space available for decentralization; also much ground free to the factory workers.

The big factory will subdivide, soon recognize the need for dividing itself up into smaller units spaced according to the new standards of space measurement largely due to the car: more economic freedom for the worker in order to make him a purchaser as well as a producer. Broadacre reintegration is division of the big factory into smaller units based upon events already taking place in many great industries. Factories will be first to see and help put an end to absurd waste motion. The factory, except for exaggeration of size due to overcentralization and the imprisoning of factory workers in "housing," is the best thing America has yet done. Great improvement on English precedents, our new varied factories are the most socially important units we have yet accomplished—not far, now, from ready to subdivide and reintegrate as the more desirable and sightly features of our new free city.

BUSINESS OFFICES
Commercial office buildings?

The financial, professional, distributive, administrative business edifice may be where it would naturally belong, to function as a unit of whatever business it might serve. Instantaneous intercommunication by air makes a return direct to origins not only good business, not only a desirable life-saver, but *reasonable*. Practical. The only good "business." Movement has started, and correlation of offices, manufactures, farming, with dwelling, will become more and more desirable; and is more and more going to the country. The commodity belt has less and less chance of survival. Why not accomplish this by good planning rather than let it happen haphazard? Efficient conservation of time and energy by the worker, the manufacturer and the farmer (all as co-operating citizens) will benefit producer and consumer alike. Much easier to work continuously forward from the plant than it ever was to work continually forward to and backward from it as in the circumstances of life in the present to-and-fro.

And offices for public officialism, petty or major (bureaucracy such as might still remain above ground) could center in police and fire stations now at present county seats. Already existing county seats would nearly all be at natural road junctions, but,

owing to lack of congestion, villages might be cut down to one out of the two or three operating now at waste expense, and certain parts of all the establishments be planted to trees or grass. District courts of law—greatly reduced by the simplifications of a true "people's government"—would also be found at this point, functionaries and functioneers established there beside them. None would be found in braggadocio buildings, the exaggerations now customary, because such official functions are really not grand but merely *utilitarian*. So Michelangelo's dome and its myriad offspring, the cupola, column and pilaster, the paraphernalia of the classic, would vanish with the ostentatious façades. Architraves and cornices out of luck.

THE PROFESSIONAL
Offices of the many kinds and kindred of professional men would be especially built for their work and be found usually in connection with their own home grounds. Or be interesting minor features of the new city. Various edifices for professionals might be set up, but "professionalism" would diminish, wherever recognized as a depreciation of form, regarded as gangsterism properly refined. Many small shops, or call them studios, clinics, small hospitals or art galleries, suited to "professional" purposes, would be found usually semidetached from the dwelling places. "Show-off" places too would be designed for any purpose whenever desired as machine age luxury. Such highly individualized professional units and the shops of all kinds of specialists, added to the homes, would enrich and variegate the aspects of the new city, save us from the battle of the sign-boards and, again, from all the enormous waste of the old back-and-forth haul of the professional from his suburb to his city.

Professional services would have a chance to become better and more economical as they were directly available to patients or clients under the convenient conditions that would characterize Broadacres. Also professionals would be easier to reach than through the traffic hindrances of present centralization which does violence to both time and nerves of both patient and doctor. The professional man of today needs less wear-and-tear on the man, more time for service, research, and creative study of nature in an inspiring atmosphere.

BANK, BANKER AND BANKING

The bank?

Oh, well, banks (money marts) should be found with other official buildings at some county seat or important road junction. Banks should be seen as integrated units in strong social credit systems. So the bank need no longer put on the airs of a temple of worship or any place of divinity. Service would be integrated with the social system. No need to hold up importance further with columns or a "front" to get business preferences from depositors. Bank credits financing production for use would have no money except as a demurrage currency having no commodity value in itself whatever. The credit of the People would therefore be in their own hands without unfair exploitation by broker or any system of interlocking insurance—the banker an integrated, dedicated member of his society.

So a "bank" would be only a well calculated responsibility, not of the individual but of the people! A nonpolitical, non-profit institution in charge of medium of exchange—a medium having, in itself, no possible speculative value. A bank therefore might have its own character as would a good, dignified filling station or church. Grandomania in construction, as seen in bank buildings themselves, great cut stone quarries for offices, enormous safes and locks appealing to superstitious depositors, would no longer be needed for prestige. Money itself as a power would no longer be glamorized; and be no direct invitation to thievery. These temples-of-unearned-increment would shrink to an open office somewhere for the more intrinsic uses of more intrinsic money—a mere medium of exchange. Credits instead of hard cash would be all the bank would contain. The enterprise of the bank-robber would be gone. But—what about an international standard of value for our rich production bosses? Consult Social Credit! The most practical of all the systems of "money" or foreign-exchange yet devised, because based upon the self-contained independence of each and every nation's citizenry.

MARKETS

Great spacious roadside pleasure places these markets, rising wide and handsome like some flexible form of pavilion—designed as places of co-operative exchange, not only of commodities but of cultural facilities. "Business" takes on a different character: integration of mercantile presentation and distribution of all produce possible and natural to the living city. These markets might resemble our county fairs, in general, and occur conveniently upon great arteries of mobility. These fine features of the future are already appearing in embryo. Even if neglected and despised, they are fingers pointing the end of centralism. Already appearing like roadside service stations, they are probably the beginning of future collateral cultural centers directly established and owned by the people.

In our present gasoline service station you may see a crude beginning of such important advance decentralization; also see the beginning of the future humane establishments we are now calling the free city.

Wherever service stations are located naturally, these now so often ugly and seemingly insignificant features will survive and expand into various important distributing centers of all sorts. They are already so expanding in the great Southwest. Each of these smaller service units might be again integrated or systematically "chained" in a series over large areas, to down costs and facilitate distribution; add new economies to production and standardizing of other products besides gasoline. Such widespread centers of distribution would become general distributors of many things that Marshall Field, Sears Roebuck, Montgomery Ward or Wanamaker now distribute by mail to the congested crowds senselessly swarming in from the country to hard pavements and back again.

Most important—fresh opportunity for building by the people themselves is everywhere found in this diversified wayside market and its tributaries. A daylight store in a park, it would be perhaps the most attractive, educational and entertaining single modern unit to be found among all new features. Parking facilities generous, adequate self- or service-parking, none now seem to realize how extensive this will be. Easily accessible room in the city will be everywhere for beguiling entertainments. Open-air concerts, cabarets, cafes, the theatre. Restaurants—good—with charm will be found at roadsides and at the markets as they will be found at roadside service stations. In certain places nearby, the luxury motel for overnight accommodation of transients will appear more and more, making continuous travel a delightful, comfortable experience. A cultural affair—this motel? Yes, and competition between various centers would develop, and individuality determine success or failure. Soon, from any and every traffic stream, one will turn aside into charming places not imitating those of any country to pick up in the *natural to-and-fro* of everyday traffic all or anything needed or desired at home. To deprive the age not too suddenly of its characteristic art of outdoor advertising, prospective purchasers might be subjected to the same temptations by effective sales displays such as now entertain and amaze in any of our highly specialized stores, but this advertising to be "built in"—never "roadside." Advertising would be concentrated, designed or incorporated as features of each particular building—the market. Proprietors, as salesmen or managers, all would be living not too far away. Not far away, now, is within ten or twenty-five miles: living in country places of their own choosing. Children would be going to nearby Broadacre country schools. "Nearby" being within miles, now, instead of a few city blocks. Citizens themselves would more likely be the improved modern equivalent of ancient landed gentry? The democratic artistocracy of a great democracy.

THE REALTOR

In all these various evaluations of establishment we have made, we have had time to see only a few changes for the better by better uses of our machine power—power at present only working to multiply in deadly fashion what goes to work *on,* instead of *for* creative humanity. If throughout the new Usonian social fabric we would courageously *plan* in the light of the law of natural change, as, say, Marshall Field followed it when establishing stores in big city outskirts and many small towns; as Woolworth and his followers have followed; then that would be an indication of the free city of democracy coming along—no longer haphazard but organic. So, ahead

of the pioneer centralizations of yesterday by the big realtor operating to accommodate the gregarious instinct of humanity, there naturally arises the next step: pioneering by decentralization. The urbanizing realtor in the discard. Tomorrow would bring along with it the social reintegration that establishes, defends and insures greater human happiness. Port towns and such localities as are near concentrations of natural materials would be subject to concentration as a matter of nature. But all this ends in most big and little inland towns.

Modern invention and machine resources, increasing the destructive interferences to human life in present cities and towns, not only compel the point of view taken here for the future (if we are to have a future) but they are already compelling unwilling citizenry to take heed and consider "moving out." As best it may, the present "system" is concealing from itself the very nature of what is now happening to destroy the makeshift eventually.

APARTMENTS

As for the apartment building, whether tall, big or small, perhaps it, too, could go to the country for another lease of life. Certainly so for the early time being. This now disturbing tall building in shadow, crowding its own shadow, and gathering and emptying its crowds on city streets might be one of the very first steps toward urban rescue—become exurban as infirmary for the sidewalk-happy citizen. The tall building in such circumstances might be similar to the one proposed for an apartment tower in the small park of St. Mark's-in-the-Bouwerie in New York City, first designed 1921 [sic], and built as the Price Tower in Bartlesville, Oklahoma, 1955.[5]

This arrangement (in quadruple) of indestructible airy duplex apartments is built and furnished complete. Such luxury apartments would stand in small parks, say several acres more or less, with particularly easy accommodation for parking dwellers' cars beneath the ground floor level—out of sight. Playgrounds and small gardens for each tenant would be alongside on the ground level as features of the small park enabling beneficent absorption into the countryside as a feature of education of the too many children of too many unqualified parents.

Such structures would enable many people who have grown so accustomed to apartment life to go to the country under highly serviced conditions if unwilling or unable (it is much the same thing) to establish themselves in the free city.

Towers of prismatic metals; steel, concrete and glass; shafts rising above greenery, each on its own private green, would be acceptable to Broadacres. Advantages of the countryside—fresh air, beautiful views, freedom from noise and the traffic jam, growing acquaintance with nature—could all well go to occupants of these tall buildings. And each in-dweller might own his apartment. Own it on the improved economic terms of the life he would be living: now able to turn the key on his abode and travel without great risk or sacrifice. Also there is the plan of the quadruple—in quadrangular array—widespread and beneficent—instead of the stan-dardized subdivision based upon the ancient Lon-don dormitory town.

MOTELS

As a matter of course there would be few or no hotels in their present commercial sense. Now a bad feature of the overconcentration of the city, they are already disappearing in favor of the luxu-ry motel. Each motel, now as hotel, would proba-bly be a group of small units conveniently related to a larger unit comprising public services—sepa-rate rooms for use of all guests, as already seen in the better planned motel. And establishments like the Arizona Biltmore, or San Marcos in the desert designed for Chandler, Arizona, would serve as re-sorts for tired millionaires.[6] These hostelries would probably be found where Nature stages a beautiful show in which they could be well employed for recreation and recuperation. All hangovers from the old city life, especially "the tired businessman," could be humanely cared for without destroying too much.

The motel is a comparatively new manifesta-tion of American life. Better suited to urbanite sur-vivals would be the mobile hotel itself "going places" on wheels. Made for the purpose of the transient to go to universally famous scenic regions; fully equipped to keep house.

These new free-wheeling mobilites would be commodious, with sleeping accommodations, tour-ing the country, with cuisine abroad. They would cruise North to South or East to West, stop awhile at places of unique charm or interest, places inacces-sible otherwise because of short seasons or practical inaccessibility. And also there is the inflatable home thrown into the back of the car and blown to size at the site.

Various attendant trailers, trains attractive in design, suitable lorries, and the mobile house, would be found along highways leading to great plains or mountain ranges. They could go where no other hostelry could be and survive.

Insomuch as the comfortable nature of trans-port is steadily developing everywhere, there is little reason why such mobile motels and hotels should not be beautiful as well as mobile, profitable and comfortable. Some such form was developed by the McArthur brothers at Phoenix, Arizona, 1927,[7] and intended to be a feature of the Arizona Biltmore Hotel. If these fantastic schemes are feasible for use as branches of prominent hotels, why not also feasi-ble as a dwelling place? Without picturesque disas-ter if well designed.

Mobility might apply to the lakes and streams themselves by way of charming motorized house-boats radio-equipped, serviced regularly by small boats from shore, each and all designed as appropri-ate features charming in the waterscape as well de-signed cottages could be in our native landscape—like the Lake Tahoe project in 1922.[8]

Pleasure-seekers, employers, employees, ex-plorers, artists, artisans (and wise men) all could have these road-traveling ships or floating barges at moder-ate cost. All live in them with convenience. The modern gypsies? Facilities for superlative design could make them as desirable at least as any plane or car.

At a householder's will, his motor house or motor barge could go about from place to place, linger at mountain lake or resorts otherwise inacces-sible to him—or upon suitable rivers and lakes—as the nomad once upon a time drifted over the desert with his camel and his tent. Under proper control this type of total mobility might be added to Usoni-an life.

COMMUNITY CENTERS

The community center would also mean more because it would be a salient feature of every countryside development of the county, wherever the county seat might be. The civic center would always be an attractive automobile objective—perhaps situated just off some major highway in interesting landscape—noble and inspiring.

Golf courses, race tracks, the zoo, aquarium, planetarium—all would be found at this general Center. Good buildings grouped in architectural ensemble with botanical gardens, art museum, libraries, galleries, opera, etc.

There might also be suitable country clubs nearby. But the community center would be the great common club of clubs, avoiding commonplace elegance and overcoming popular prejudice of town partisanship. The community center, liberal and inspiring, would be a general culture-factor because it would be an entertainment center. The art gallery a popular rendezvous, not so much a museum; a "morgue" no longer. Both grounds and buildings of the various centers would be gradually developed in harmony with one another so that each center might take on its own charm and individuality; therefore, why not itself be a great work of art? Scattered over the states, placed at various county seats of each, the community center thus would catch, retain, and express the best thought of which growing American democracy is capable. Commercial bustle and competitive humdrum or humbug diminished. The community center a respected, respectful place—a place for quiet comradeship suited to inspection, introspection and good company concerning both people and things.

THE NEW THEATER

Wherever a phase of Nature will have been raised by society to the level of greater Nature there we will find the Theater and find the people themselves owner and producer. Theater would be radical, arousing, inspiring, challenging popular emotion, presenting native problems. Human strength and aspiration would go there for inspiration. The theater would be no old soap-box either—no, and the old peep-show would be gone. With new opportunity to present life, no longer would scenes be enacted behind a proscenium and seen through this hole in the wall. The theater would be no circumstance as in the days of its origin. The stage itself would be cycloramic and, if needed, panoramic, more and more an automatic machine that would endow the theater with the plasticity the cinema has already taken to itself. The architecture of this feature of the developed civic center would probably be placed underground, worked out by artists in the new movements built by new uses of plasticity. Inhabitants of the whole county would probably often become performers themselves in preference to employed entertainers. The present star-system would gradually be abolished? But traveling "stars" or companies would be welcome on occasion if the occasion (or the star) survived and was changed by the changed circumstances.

Where desired by the homemaker, cinema, like the theater, taken from the marketeer and having the people now for producer (or sponsor), would go from original source into every home and public place. Entertainment both as sound and vision would become something freely, freshly imaginative, well executed; and cinema and tape recordings, continuously distributed by subscription, would be in the circulating libraries. No censorship but public opinion. At every community center there would be a continuous series of especially important features both in theater and cinema. All such would be *maintained by the community itself*—and liberally. None such would any longer be left to the mercy of any salesmanship for big production nor of any monopolizing commercial element whatever; nor ever again be used as a sales agency to put the nation into war or the huckster into the parlor, or the gangster into the bedroom. Nor could any secret salesmen, molders or soldiers of public opinion (hirelings themselves), ever reach the public for any such purpose.

Great music would mean something to be widely distributed to the people. The radio not dead but more alive than ever. Like the cinema, music would become the vital cultural affair it is—a cultural feature of the Usonian family at home, alongside architecture. The chamber music concert would naturally become a common feature at home; players growing up until it amounted to a home culture beyond mere entertainment. No uncommon accomplishment for children to learn to read music readily, play the piano and some other instrument as well. Music universal—like the culture of music in the old days of the family concerts à la recorder—may come alive again. The piano alone is enough. Knowledge of good music and reading it in score should be as universal a practice as reading books or the funnies; as essential as the reading of plans by the architect or reading the stars. And the reading of plans should be as universal an accomplishment as the reading of print.

THE LIGHT THAT FAILED

The Church. Why does the church no longer lead man out of merchantdom into realms of the poetic principle? Why should it attempt to follow the merchant and so become itself a merchant? Is this because the church is essentially unsuited to the sovereignty of the individual, being by nature some form of submission to opinion by hierarchy? Not freedom? Not Nature? Not Jesus nor the great philosophers who were like Him? And why not?

Was that why Jesus opposed the establishments called churches? Could abnegation of the Spirit in order to keep on good terms with the prevailing practices of the profit-motive in this machine age possibly withstand the revelations now made by science, and curb the curiosity aroused by the growing universal tides of sophisticated intelligence?

"Revelations" by science can be only partial. But the organized religion of the Church, too, seems as of now even more partial. The Church, as it was and still is, can never thrive in our spirit of individual democracy—the machine age—the age of the merchant. Certainly not in the democracy in this new city of the future. In that city the church, too, will change, become more integral, a deeper student of human nature.

Honest compromise between the ideal of success according to present merchantable money-getting systems and a true Religion is no longer likely. Is it because compromise after compromise in the interest of universal compromise has been attempted and failed, that the old idea of church, like the old idea of a city, is now hopelessly dated? Subject to change the church will grow more genuinely democratic in spirit; less and less sectarian; more liberal in thought therefore more comprehending of men and their faith in themselves as men; less concerned with the hereafter, with livelihood and deference to authority; less a sectarian institution which, though based upon humility, allows partisanship, prejudice, and superstition to live nevertheless; and understanding the difference between selfishness and selfhood. Democracy in the new city will want religion back in its true place. That place Jesus prophesied will be high up indeed. Probably higher than ever before. Never merchantable.

CHURCH BUILDING

Church architecture, like most college architecture, has been false to its opportunities. This for a century at least. The Church of Democracy—tomorrow no feudal survival—is finding for itself a true new form. It will be organic building more suitable to modern feeling for the sincere sentiment of worship. Education, too, when cultural in our democracy, will find the kind of building more suitable to its actual office than imitations of Oxford Gothic or anything else it has imitated.

Traditional church forms, like so many traditions now, must die in all minor forms in order that Tradition in great form may live! To understand this truth is to understand the changing growth that is already due to the idea of democracy, and to make way for the return of worship to the life of the citizen as well as for the uplift and integrity the nation requires to endure. As Walt Whitman and Emerson and Thomas Jefferson prophesied.

True religion never dies, because indispensable to man's life as well as his work. But, since the last great war, the Church, as we knew it then, must be buried. Deep.

True religion? Assuming religious sentiment would have had opportunity and occasion to survive the sidewalk-happy Broadway mind, it might deepen in the urban citizen's breast a reassuring living faith in man. Assuming that the falsity of the old sentimentalities of the fashionmonger would have diminished, the falsity as oppressive to the popular spirit in an enlightened democracy as it always should have been to the church; assuming the church would have survived in spite of the multiplicity of competitive churches, it would be likely to take nonsectarian form; more spiritual; more devotional; combining intellectual vision (the brilliant light of the West) with a softer, more earth-loving and deeper feeling for nature (the glowing light of the East). Here would be another great opportunity—perhaps the greatest of all—for the expression of true religion—religion a great human synthesis seen again as great architecture. So the church, by way of the ideal building in the free city, might be as a song without words, comprising minor churches grouped about a common meeting place. It is certain, in any case, that the new church would be a rendezvous with the very heart of great Nature. Thus will be served the depths and breadths of the universal spirit belonging to democracy. Church will again become the citizen's haven of refuge and he no less individual in his chosen terms of worship but more profound and comprehensive.

In these days of the commercial merchandising of humanity, regardless, spiritual degeneracy falls upon the youth of the world; the teenager problems increase. The church has sought to administer partisanship, conscription, and what is called "public opinion" in these pragmatic days of the modern materialist; the fomentation of war. But the over-all harmony of this new city might arise, and shine again, as the way of the church? Architecture could serve again to restore or refresh the mortal weariness brought by our foolish "success"—in the church itself, in our private lives, our commerce, our Congress. We have been amused by the wily cynic in this rancid era of the machine. In our ultra servility to the pessimism of this machine age, we all need the recreation found only in exercise of faith, free man's faith in man himself, faith in our new human privilege—our Democracy—faith kept and renewed by honest work for our great ideal of freedom. Theology can never again teach advocates of such faith, nor be anything more than troublesome pettifoggery. Our Broadacre City church, then, would be another Cathedral, unhistorical edifice for the fusion of all that is best in all the historical reli-

gions; it would be the greatest single wonder in the architecture of Broadacre City. Worship there would again be universal practice, protected once more in modern times by and for the free spirit of individual man. Here at last would be a great church not built by individuals separate, but by all the creeds together in order to promote—in terms of a tempered and well directed machine age culture, organic—a finer sensibility concerning what it is that constitutes a growing man's well-being in our time. Religion should thus promote firmer faith in the nobility and beauty of which human nature is divinely capable when once made truly free from within. In Broadacres the Cathedral could become again, and upon more noble social terms, the potent cultivator of independence, protector of the neighbor, pilot of human conscience, and thus alive for a whole people. Church would have no quarrel with science, science no quarrel with art, because science would need this church, and art, again great, would understand (as, indeed, would philosophy) that the true Art and Science of man are from within and that without them the life of no man is free.

THE HOSPITAL

The present hospital, efficient and humane as it is, but seldom, is now usually much too large—and growing larger. Through no fault of its own, the hospital has fallen to the obvious stature of a great business institution, but Broadacre hospitals would be sanatoriums of many types. Sunlit clinics connected together in natural ways or by artfully made park-like fountain-gardens, each building especially planned for individual privacy instead of the much too much generality and promiscuity of the usual hospital. Homelike residence would be so arranged in them (and of them) that no disabled or sick person need see another disabled or sick person (patient) unless either so willed. Resources of modern therapy, surgery, and medicine would be in their places, just as the plumbing, electric lighting, and heating would be; none visible as fixtures or features.

In short, emphasis in the new hospital would be on normality, not on the paraphernalia of abnormality. Death's head continually shows in the present-day hospital. Why is the hospital not as humanely practical in aesthetic effect as it tries to be in physical purpose? And yet our hospitals are among the most effective and well managed units found in cities. But in Broadacres hospital-service would be rendered to the people by the people. At any cost? No. Free.

EDUCATION AND CULTURE

"The soul without knowledge is without power." But without right practice too the soul is likely to fester?

Can that "soul" be considered educated who cannot read drawings? Cannot read the plan-documents that make everything made for man or around about him—the drawings, plans and details? Yes, fundamental plan-reading should begin early in our education because essential to all for understanding the constructions of life. The Friedrich Froebel kindergarten method for the development of creative children is the most needed element as antidote to the play sentimentalities of the present kindergarten system.

Should a man be considered educated, knowing nothing of the properties of line and color or the chemistry of good design, nothing of what constitutes a good building, knowing nothing about plants or the nature of the food he puts into his mouth or *the nature* of his own bodily functioning? Is that man "educated" knowing little or nothing of his real self, of the underlying principles of structure or aesthetics as well as the dynamics of *form*? When form and color, so essential to architecture, are left to the mercy of "taste," the soul is like some rudderless ship sailing uncharted seas. The science and especially the art of structure is basic to all true human culture. When education is without this foundation, it is a liability, not an asset.

Should that man be considered educated who knows nothing of the cosmic rhythms of sun, moon, and stars elemental in art, nothing of the effect they have upon *him* in whatever he does, in his dreaming, planning, planting, reaping, or breeding; his dancing, singing, or building?

Well, until the groundwork of his education is acquired from interior Nature, do not speak of education as culture. Education and culture are not yet on speaking terms in our country. Specializations should no longer be so much encouraged. There are enough of these speculative partialities to fill the infinite pigeonholes of our vast capitalist system and its multiple bureaus, the "crats," in this mechanized nation of salesmen; enough cogs are already made for capitalist wheels; enough conditioned minds turned out by universities to add up to ultimate grand frustration. Out of poor initiative, excellent conscripts, prey to violent partisanship. Not creative? As a matter of course. Fruit of the routine—the curriculum.

Then, general education by and for life in the free city should be had by *doing*—by life-experience at what tender age? The end of high-school age? Surely the teenager.

The university? No youth should be allowed to enter one until he has given unmistakable evidence not only of his interest in the principles of universality, but of some gift of perception that would make further research on his part among the eternal mysteries of the cosmic order seem desirable—both for him and for the society to which he belongs.

The judges?

Judges in the past have been some feature of institutional bureaucracy. *Fundamentally* educated, they would by intimate daily association know their fellows pretty well and therefore be qualified to select, elect or punish them under proper judgments. By laws made *for* people.

How senseless to speak of democracy where no faith is placed in the manhood of man and only "experts" are right. The expert? He is a man who has stopped thinking. Why? Because he "knows." Were education adequate in our democracy, the "expert" would be kept in a cell or caged, his special abnormality publicly exhibited as a warning to stop the university student, or any man in trouble.

UNIVERSITIES

We are beginning to realize that our universities are not worthy the cause or the name, not universal in any sense. Highly specialized trade-schools? That they are. And really mass-product, by specialists, to cover all specialties. Book-knowledge as inculcated is no feeler for life; the modern university will someday become more select and better antennae for the society it should serve as mentor. Then only will "university" mean independent findings, freely communicated to the growing citizenry, probably as much or more by television and radio. The university then should function as the vision of society with the courage of an honest radical's conviction, and as master of the deeper study of nature's *organic* laws. Mastery of nature-study in some high degree of excellence should be continual primary concern in selecting the teacher even though convictions might conflict. Perhaps especially when in conflict. A true university would strive to deepen and preserve ideals of underlying principles evident as naturally superior. The university then would be the very life-line of democracy—which it should exist only to serve. This service qualifying the voter as Thomas Jefferson imagined and hoped it would.

Situated in quiet retreats appropriate to reflection and concentration upon deeper concerns of the creative mind by the student and his masters, endowed by the people themselves, these various rendezvous would be dedicated to culture and contain small groups of mature, well developed teachers tested for wisdom and light by experience. All should be able to work well together in designed storehouses of universal art, science and religion, typical not only of the culture that mankind has produced in Art, Architecture, Philosophy and the Sciences but also of the culture it is able to produce now. Books, plans, drawings and models would be available for particular intensive study by advanced students chosen by themselves to reside there because they excel, but more especially because of unmistakable *qualities of leadership.*

No longer much more of the "Professorship." Nor any perfunctory "examination." No curriculum (race-course). No standardizing of any kind. Instead we would have several "father-confessors" (it being safe by then to select them by popular vote of their fellows) to lead life in a university. Say one such leader chosen by the scientists, one by the artists, one by philosophers, one by the architects and one chosen by the poets of each state. These leaders—thus elected—would be supreme as the "university." And if one could be found, a statesman should certainly be added to this leadership; but he would be less a politician, more a philosopher or metaphysician.

The best freely chosen *by the best*—not for the average or from the "average." All would be cultured from within, educated by experience from the ground up and themselves qualified to judge men and methods. The uncommon man to lead the common man to excellence.

All the fellows of the leaders would be chosen by and for the elected father-confessors. Such fellows would be freely employed in research concerning matters of society; those they might work upon. Only those who gave proof of inner strength to grow, integrity in some one of the qualities of the departments of human life should be accepted in any university either to lead and enlighten others or to be admitted to study.

Universities should not be large but be qualified and qualifying. Why not somewhat like the old monastic institution? Only now liberalized; radical culture made free of injunction, of underground or overhead "influences"; learning protected or corrected by the people themselves from all pressures or interference. Thus might be the true *university* of democracy: universality definitely related to social progress and the arts, and well equipped by men of achievement or research. A preparation, this, for teaching or for the practice of anything spiritual— at all. For a living? No. "Vocation" no feature of any student at the university. The characteristic vocational training practiced as the higher education in this "capitalistic" educational system of ours should be renounced or cut back to special courses and practical uses, elsewhere. Trade-schools? Of course, many. It is so much harder for us to debunk and delimit these institutions of "learning" than any other of our institutions, although none need so much to go down to *roots*—radical—and to spell Nature with a capital "N."

The word "radical" means "of the *root.*" Broadacre universities would be afraid *not* to go to the root with all honest radicals from the beginning of time to the day after the day after tomorrow.

SCHOOLS

The public schools?

For the schools more excellent teachers. Smaller and smaller flocks! Decentralization a natural aim in the direction of their education. Because the common school period ending in high school seems to be the most constructive period in education. The organic integration of the individual here challenges centralization.

The *big* American knowledge-factory, the *big* school—*big* anything is becoming a self-defeating institution. Our schools? How like one of the shoe factories of our industrial revolution! Our schoolhouses *look* like factories as one passes them going through American towns and villages! Unimaginative, they look more impotent spiritually than any good factory; so many prison houses for the young Western mind are the Greek abstractions still being taught there. Hand-picked but machine-embroidered our capitalist morals are not on speaking terms with Nature. Antique Roman law, or pseudo-Greek philosophy: this bookology is really by now a "craft"—the craft which the overseers of the knowledge-factory endorse as the beginning and end of wisdom. But the high school, as a school, is better than the college. And education should for a time end there; a four-year period of contact with experience now due.

Any culture center called a school in the universal city would be set in a natural park in the choicest part of the whole countryside, preferably by some flowing stream or large body of fresh water. The buildings themselves should be well designed and appointed not only as a whole, but so that "small" may be again divided into smaller units insofar as possible. Fireproof buildings fashioned of metals and glass or of other native material all universally adapted to the uses of young life growing up in sunlight to cherish the ideals of freedom, love ground, love space and enjoy light. Divided into small schools, each to contain, say, twenty-five children. Forty children would be a very large school. An outdoor game area and common hall or meeting room in common, a modeling and drafting room, a kitchen-dining-room would be characteristic of them all. Groups of three or four buildings might be arranged for a particular purpose around interior or exterior courts according to climate. Standardization would be here, again, but so used as to be given even more individual treatment. Enough ground for flower and vegetable beds would be planted and maintained by young workers alongside planted courts where they could conveniently be cultivated by the children. A callus on the palm would be a mark of honor. Rewards of merit would entirely cease or change as the character of the children working in these buildings changed. Large game and play spaces should be just beyond the courts and gardens. Each young worker would learn of the potentialities of the soil, the mysteries of mind not only by working on the soil and in it, but by educating his hand to draw or model or color what he saw of elemental nature equally well; learning to listen to music in the sounds of animal cries, wind in the trees, water flowing and falling. Learn by experience to be eye-minded because to be truly modern-minded is to be eye-minded. True *observers* are now most needed by democracy? Cultural buildings of this city-that-is-a-nation will be developed by architects themselves thus educated as children: architects free cultured workers in the arts; free themselves. Of first importance in school: *quality*—quality always the aim throughout education instead of quantity.

To learn to observe with clear-seeing eye the patterns of nature and draw them well would awaken certain faculties, but, more important, would be intimate approach to the study of all abstraction of Nature-structure: the study we call "abstraction" all being a kind of study of elemental architecture. This kind of research, going in behind the mere appearances for characteristic significant pattern, should inspire the growing design faculty of the younger generation and characterize the free city.

More perfect correlation of the faculties of the young, being actual and potential, would constitute a most important feature of all education. Eye and hand, body and mind, and what we call the soul thus becoming more sensitive to Nature and appreciative of integral rhythm. The very synthesis of being would appear.

In beautiful sunlit buildings thus organized, the everyday child of everyday Broadacres would be working in many ways. This child would be preparing food, learning how best to make it, when best to eat it, how to serve it charmingly to others; learning, meantime, not only to see clearly by learning to draw (define) what he sees but gradually taking other steps in practice to qualify himself to *build* organic structures. Of such a nature would Broadacre schools be. Youth learning to make two blades of grass grow where one, or none, grew before; seeing the spirit of that act coming alive! Spiritually and physically Broadacre boys and girls would become coefficients of a *naturally* creative humanity. Individualists capable of intelligent cooperation with Principle, growing up thus, not mistaking personality for individuality or license for freedom except on pain of general reproof. All high school students now learning the sum of the most important of all lessons: to know the difference between the Curious and the Beautiful.

For these children practicing individual responsibility in freedom, one teacher to a group—a group, say, of from fifteen to forty pupils (or, better, apprentices) would be neither too low nor too high an average. If able to inspire such teeming young lives, teachers would be best paid of all workers in the city. Because they would have to be the best qualified as human beings. Teachers in the free city—because the city wishes to remain free—would be the most important, cherished members of society. No price for such inspiring human quality in the growing generation would be too high to be cheerfully paid by the dominant generation.

Thus in outline would be the smaller school buildings of Broadacres. Ten such organic units for every single inorganic big one that is now attempting to function in factory-like buildings on hard pavements in overgrown cities for herds of humanity; or in those experimental new schools built on the model of a circus but without any change in thought (or in crowding) except to exaggerate and continue the fictions of the conventional idea of "a happy childhood." Children would not go there to school to be trained to accept happily the subsequent blessings of employment as contented wage-slaves. The "cash-and-carry" system would be out of luck.

SOURCE OF DESIGN—THE DESIGN CENTER

The Machine (capital "M") as it exists in Broadacres is settled in appropriate centers as the great means of mass experiment to determine greater ends in order to increase the flexibility and practical utility of every important human interest. For machine craft, or trade, the study of the machine would be in practical use, in either factories or homes. By way of machinery various crafts would be put into the hands of young students of organic structure. Young architects? In Broadacres, all maybe, more or less, young architects. Yes . . . and with the best means at home for experimental experience. Reluctantly I admit that to put the machine (or for that matter any modern tool of our civilization) into the hands of a body of young students at home, means the equivalent of some kind of "school." Fortunately, it would not be an "art school"; but one in which competent interpreters chosen by the foregathering apprentices themselves would actually be leaders, allied to the varied manufacturing industries they would teach to serve. With fresh impetus all kinds of appropriate patterns in these integrated style centers (we might so call them) would be inspiration to industry—for instance, the house, the motorcar, furniture, fabrics, etc., etc.—inspiration and an influence spreading over growing younger talent involved in these everyday design problems of production. Continually on every hand, in every new city of the democratic age in these circumstances, opportunities arise all along the way and some things to cherish as works of art would be produced.

Sensitive, unspoiled students (many are still to be found in our country) thus rescued from perfunctory machine education would, with varied techniques, lift the quality of many a basic commercial industry. Chosen by the industries themselves, under competent advice, there would naturally be workshops in the style centers equipped with the latest experiments in new machinery. Each style center, which should be adequately endowed for special research by interested industries, would be a quiet work place where talented young designers would grow and might remain indefinitely domiciled, spending the better part of each day working alternately in the laboratories, shops or upon the soil itself, in a way of life guided by their mentors. Students of machinery-using crafts rightly used, would be making myriads of useful things and might discover through these Broadacre experimental centers possibilities existing in the nature of many a particular craft which industries now know little or nothing about and might never discover on their own. In such fellowship research as this it would be the turn of fine art to use the machine. Modern machinery might so learn better to serve man. Broadacre City would ensure a better developed culture of a more appreciative United States, the country we have here been calling Usonia.

So let us say here that several branches of our industrial arts world might be taken for a ride to a true *beginning*. A certain number would be grouped together for the reason that they do react upon one another often to the great advantage of each just as young craftsmen should be interchangeable in the crafts to broaden the experience of each, and widen their sources of inspiration as well as of information.

Glassmaking, textiles, pottery, sheet metals-shaping, wood-working, casting in metal, printing and process reproductions: all industry in the changed circumstances of society should be willing to donate machinery, supply a competent machinist, and, to a certain extent, be eager to endow its own craft provided each of the various industries were certain of the proper management of such endowments and assured a share in results directly applicable to their own industry. Sharing benefits of design by designers especially adapted to a donor's particular field should be incentive enough for the donation.

Such experimental centers—not merely "schools"—intelligently conducted and inspired, would do much to reclaim and vitalize all American industry. Industry might soon make American lives really worthy of independence, less imitative of the culture of any foreign time or place, more aware of their value to their own time. With consumption in control of production, our own endeavor would not only help work out our own forms with style but would enable us as a nation (by example to all countries) to contribute to and be able to profit by the form and style of other nations without imitating them. Imitation should be strictly *out,* because

inspiration would be largely *in.* As an architect, I see no reason why experiment centers of this character—thousands of them—each limited to say twenty workers, preferably less, should not make a good, abundant living while producing valuable articles as *examples* to help carry on the growth of organic style at home and so probably throughout the entire world. Each article so produced might have (should have) the quality of a work of art. A work that could not fail to be a genuine missionary wherever and to whom it might go.

Co-work-places such as these would naturally inspire a culture for the new aristocracy of democracy as it would be in the free city. Aristocracy? Yes, because democracy (I believe Thomas Jefferson was right) is to be the highest known form of aristocracy, wherever democracy is really understood and *grown*. Highest because not privileged but natural—innate and so secure.

The so-called style-centers would be located on land sufficient so that three or four hours a day of physical work on the soil would not only help to insure the living of the workers and of such visiting or resident artists as might be heads of the work-groups but, by correlation of facilities and faculties, be stimulating to imagination. Say, seven to nine hours each day divided between design and work in shops. Their creative imagination would be stimulated by such physical labor; gaining experience in constructions designed. Voluntary co-operation of the entire system of such a design establishment as this in day-to-day ways of life would be both subjective and objective. Subsequent educational influences upon the consumer and producer would grow by means of exemplar-television and the brochure. Well directed work would always have, as it should, real producing power. Each month a supply of usefully beautiful things would be ready for roadside markets. Good design in tapestries, table linen, cotton fabrics, clothing, table glassware, flower holders, lighting devices, window glass, mosaic, necklaces, screens, iron standards, fixtures, gates, fences, fire-irons, enameled metals, etc., etc., for house or garden purposes, cast in aluminum, copper, lead, tin; practical flowerpots, architectural flower containers on a large scale, water jars, dishes, sculpture and paintings, all that is made for decoration or for use or suitable for reproduction. Designs for all media of value such as new process-reproduction of music and plays: designs in monograph for dwellings, farm buildings, industrial buildings. Or what have *you?*

Say, new solutions of such characteristic problems as the home, the gasoline station, better food packaging for immediate distribution—substitutes for the tin can—or modern distribution by cold storage. There would also be town and country dwellings, the helicopter, airplanes, trains, especially the automobile, and countless suitable objects for the complete furnishing of all these. Landscape planting of the vicinity and home environment— this would come first. Factories of many sorts would have to come out to the countryside to be attractive. Well designed features of Usonian everyday life fitted into the countryside as attractive places not only in which to work but to live in nearby. Again—according to the new scale of time-spacing, say, ten miles instead of a hundred feet.

Style center group stations would grow natural in this way and television and radio, owned by the people, broadcast cultural programs illustrating pertinent phases of government, of city life, of art work, and programs devoted to landscape study and planting or the practice of soil and timber conservation; and, as a matter of course, to *town planning* for better houses. In short, these style stations would be inspired hives of *creative* energy all bearing on the character of modern industry wherever industry touched the common life. Without hesitation or equivocation let's say that architecture would, necessarily, again become the natural backbone (and architects the broad essential leaders) of such cultural endeavor. It was ever so whenever civilization possessed a superior culture. Organic architecture is basic to all this because it is the intrinsic art of all structure whatsoever. In our own times architecture especially must be strong, as essential to life as it ever was strong and indispensable to the civilizations that have preceded ours. To keep insisting that architecture, because of its very nature, is the logical outline, the background

and framework as well as the philosophic and aesthetic center-line of any true civilization—this is necessary now! Or else no culture can be truly characteristic of us as a people or develop the essential inner discipline and natural strength to grow the true democratic ideal we profess.

So our Usonian style center should also become practical alcove in connection with the university. This in agrarian practices as well as in the practice of art and architecture, philosophy, archeology, and ecology. Intensive nature study would be the sound platform from which the broad abstractions of a cultural structure would spring. Wherever their location, even if not so important by our new time-scale, the center should not be too easy of access. All should have ample communication facilities, but as their work progressed their thought would be going out over the air by radio or television to the whole people while the workers themselves were sufficiently private.

No examinations, graduations, or diplomas as in schools now, if you please. But as any work-fellow showed special competence as apprentice in any special branch of art, science, or industry or evidence of unusual aptitude in any craft, after suitable experience he would be available as teacher in Broadacre schools; or for a place as designer in commercial industry. Broadacre City manufacturers would be contributors to such experimental work and would have second right to choose the more excellent apprentices. Bodies of young inspirational talent as well as associated experienced trade-machinists should be of such character that students from other schools in the many other branches of the free city would seek points of contact with their work by way of excursions made to the style centers—contact helpful to the designers and invaluable to Broadacre school students.

Such active work-units in design, were they truly dedicated and directly applied to the radical culture of indigenous style and the building of our city, would at last stimulate popular growth as light stimulates the growth of a garden. Officialdom would diminish or change its character entirely, if indeed there were need to continue its services, as we now know it.

PART FIVE: THE PRESENT
THE USONIAN

To the Usonian! He is the American citizen. For him our pioneer days are not over! Perhaps pioneer days never should be. But the American frontier has shifted in many ways. Efficient and brave, our forebears took life in their own hands and often in the covered wagon went ever westward to clear grand new ground for more humane habitation. But they only blazed the way for another, unexpected, instrument of an efficiency that, by way of their own "rugged individualism," became the exaggeration of their own good qualities; and now unchecked this menace grows on into the curse of exaggeration of the capitalistic centralization of our big city. As consequence, inane mediocrity or vulgar profanity, we now see, has come out of our new power only to push the lives of the citizens around? With courage and strength of the grand paternal inheritance, he the pioneer was native forerunner of the type of domination we see today building its own mortal doom and naming it for a monument to progress. The milestone and gravestone—our skyscraper—in the potential cemeteries that our proudest cities are to become. The skyscraper thus used will mark the end of an epoch; put a period to the plutocratic republic of America, which the industrial revolution raised to the nth degree by the exercise of selfish inconsiderate prowess; and mark the beginning of another revolution. Machine power is running away with man and running away *from* the Western world to contaminate worlds of the "yellow man"—the East. Consequences of our own industrial revolution, not foreseen, have crossed the Pacific and Atlantic. Perhaps our salvation will lie in what such capitalist centralization by machinery as ours is now will eventually do to the "yellow man" himself—as it has already done to the "white man." That result might be our only hope in any impending future which the nature of humankind seems to have staged for us—the coming war between dark and bright—the war between Occident and Orient—West and East. White and yellow? Yes, this impending consequence is our only hope—the atom is it?—but before that time comes the machine may have done its work for the yellow man that is already done for us.

His increased numbers—say nine to one—may not be able to tip the balance in his favor.

Or else the white man must pioneer again along a frontier new to him: the frontier of Decentralization! Our democracy's only sunrise—its only true course. Such re-integrated decentralization will be met on every side by intrenched capital, scheming political interferences and the ubiquitous remittance-men; wives, widows and orphans of the insidious hidden money power and habituation of our civilization. In full force all these and more have to be placated or painfully cleared away by pioneers today working for a more honest, humane and constructive *success ideal* for man. An organic culture for the free citizen in the nation that becomes the free city depends upon the quality of the new success ideal we need. Excess "success" is now—as always—reactionary. Therefore more or less tragic. We must be transformed through the long-promised opportunity by the artifex held out by freedom or we will have lost all wars worth winning. Why, then, should American men and women, because of the profit system as we have practised it (after the British) be compelled to live any longer according to the exaggeration of the baser qualities of our nature? Why not work now more patiently for a simple, natural ideal made right end to and right side up for man to live by? Good enough to live by and according to the light of his natural better self? Doing so, our nation will not only survive but will enable all the rest of the world to thrive and, at the same time, make innate the only impregnable "defense" our nation has or any nation may have.

THE NEW PIONEER

So, pioneering on this *new frontier* should not again come down to merely scraping off the too full bushel while ignoring the now legalized industrial impositions that continually overfill it again. The tinker, the soldier, the politician, the professor—all the best imitators and salesmen of vicarious power—is this the best power of which we as a people seem capable? Well, if it is infallibly to be on that basis, we are the tail end of a civilization! The *end,* not the middle, not even the beginning of a great one.

Statesmanship we now require! As a scientific

art, "the art of human happiness," we of these United States have lost it to that promise-merchant—the politician! Mediocrity has risen to high places by way of the profit taker's desires? No, his necessities.

A good statesman would be naturally a scientist, an architect of human happiness. He would be pilot, too, of an organic social order. What politician today, then, can we call a statesman? Reforms the politicians propose (sometimes) are but the political propaganda of our promiscuous governing powers, themselves governed by their own bureaucracy; usually little more than petty shifts to and fro in the complex rules intended to regulate and standardize money getting by using old laws on the statute books and repudiating the welfare of the citizen; old makeshifts that have been tried so many times and in so many ways and places that our new civilization is now likely to be defeated, destroyed by suicidal artificiality such as ours has become by conformity.

Sensible interpretation, either economic or spiritual, of our changed circumstances on the new frontier has not yet been contrived and so has not been fairly tried. A great people with a great ideal, we have been stultified if not betrayed by appeal to the votes of the mass ignoramus. Mostly betrayed by ourselves, of course, so ruthlessly invading other countries simply or largely because we have lost the true meaning of our own! However we here admit we are scared enough to pretend to be eager to "liberate" other nations! We must face it! We are unable to recognize or intelligently meet the drastic changes now due our own machine age growth of money power as a substitute for ideas. Spiritually we, in our own great nation, are still living in a neglected backyard from coast to coast. Where beauty of environment is concerned we do not understand its value; nor do we understand the devastating, or liberating, values of important organic changes taking place—to our own immense advantage. If we could but learn to practice, much less defend, what we call—without real comprehension—Democracy! Instead we now "defend" only what we consider our "interests." So we go from war to war—sciences used only to run away in order to go to war again some other day? The same old new way now by science improved? Whereas the only impreg-

nable human defense we have on earth is faith in ourselves and in our own kind. Our own unafraid performance here at home will make us or break us.

NATURE
Hitherto any capital mind among us has seriously questioned the right-mindedness and good instincts of other humankind. When and wherever humanity itself, *disciplined from within by an ideal,* is free, this is not so. In what, then, does equitable freedom consist in our already overgrown but so far underdone society? Let us truly and freely discuss our malady, sincerely seek the probable remedy, and discover the underlying basis of all growth and decay. Then we will find the basis we know to be organic. Only in that search may we discuss our order of freedom as a natural order or discuss the natural order of economics and the causes of war and debt intelligently, and as frankly as we discuss biology, for instance. Then, I believe, the fundamental democracy which we profess would come right side up for us—and so soon. Facing ourselves, as we must, and asking ourselves the right questions would truly add up the forces of our machine and money power. We, ourselves, of the New World, must go to work first to gain our own integrity: then, our feet well under us on firm ground, work *with* the world for peace, never *upon* it by war. We all know this. Why are we unable to practice it or even preach it by our own acts?

Let us ask ourselves these necessary questions: In what lies the significance of human life in which machine power has grown to be the destructive factor that it now is in the hands of money power? When clearly distinguished from life in various other forms of the social contract, in what (really) does human honor or even true machine efficiency consist at this time? Where and as we now live, can we use the usurious, vicarious powers of the machine here at home and continue to grow as happy human beings by forcing overproduction on the world at our own expense?

What now, then, is good sense? Incidentally, how would a *natural* economic order touch us here at home as the orthodox money matter now stands? Organic law teaches that we can hammer heated iron but not a stick of dynamite. Just so we need more serious study of *organic* law everywhere because it has been so completely ignored by avaricious money and land power. We have too much of the blinding externalities as well as the manifest disadvantages of ancient Roman law we have adopted by way of Oxford and Cambridge as paternal influences.

Are we to face ourselves and ask these vital questions and find answers aright? Are we patiently to investigate the present uneconomic basis of our life, such as it is, and learn *why* it has to go to war because it has no organic foundations and therefore is forever *unsafe?* Why has this matter, fundamental to us all, had so little study all down the line? Must we go on from war to war? Why not now reinterpret the significant facts of our own history as assembled and interpreted by honest radicals all too familiar with the nature of the root as well as the character of our finance? We must learn why our orthodox money system is a wholly inorganic superstructure. No *foundation* at all is there! Only an expedient assumption. Patiently we must learn why our life is now so inorganic, so wasteful and dangerous. Just as we must learn why the classic architecture we have adapted, or adopted, is four-fifths false, expedient inartistic waste of our natural opportunity; and try to realize why anything inorganic may have sporadic increase but *can never produce or reproduce itself as Life.* We must know why, wherein and in whatever of our circumstances, the complete correlation essential to *true growth* is lacking and that nothing can really grow from within—either for us, in us or by us—until our economic as well as spiritual foundations are *by nature* secure.

Only *entity* lives, only entity can reproduce! That is why capitalist centralization in cities is no longer the expansion of humane opportunity but fatal contradiction of structure and so a stricture. This innate contradiction is growing. It is a strong arm, unnatural, having no interior expanding principle of its own; no real integrity from within is possible to its character. Manifold "efficiencies" of our so-called money "system" is too urban, too involved on the surface with artificialities to function for democratic manhood's own good! Our money system is involution, incapable of true evolution. It can only add,

subtract, multiply and divide—especially divide.

To such false strictures human life in these United States is now too narrowly committed. Life in our republic attempting democracy cannot be committed to centralism (such as our money system also represents) except to stultify and degenerate its manpower. If we persist, we too must die as such false but expedient commitments have ever died. History holds the proof. Why not read the proof?

As our present uneconomic systems are inorganic, no matter how gigantic and all pervasive, so the social system of our life must be even more so—and our philosophy, our art, our religion remain more or less parasitic! Shall our "foreign policies" be blind and our fate eventually tragic. Why do our domestic politics continue so confused or blind and futile? American statesmanship in the light of any honest interpretation of the spirit of democracy is now misleading or inadequate. Our status quo by statesmanship *always* lies hidden from us. Is it because it is always some form of conscription?

For the same or a similar reason our great fortunes are with us, largely false, too unproductive unless by unfair taxation.

So have we drifted so far away from the valiant original intent of the democratic ideal of our great republic! So many ignoble forms of hidden selfishness, inane exaggerations of self, mistaken for selfhood. And by the very forces we have elevated for hire, in some form—some form of rent—we are now continually drawn downward by exaggerated forms of urbanism. Thoughtless uses of the vicarious power we agree to call Money by our credulous faith in the "substitute." Money power itself is only another vicarious power—and vanishes. Sources of money seem more important to us than the family and home, than the sources of life itself. What fate for such power as our industrialism becomes? The portals will open and the cartels get you, Mr. Vicarious-Power-Man. And soon!

TO HAVE AND TO HOLD

One of the main perversions of the principles of our democracy is to allow land to hold improvements made on it by the man who lives upon and improves and loves the land. What folly to have turned over his credit, existing only by way of the people of a great nation, to middlemen exalted officially to exercise a broker's takings: the broker himself being the banker's banking system. What tragic finality for our industrial revolution to have turned the citizen himself over to the machine as the slave of production—himself made only another kind of machine—all this done in order to concentrate and maintain more money power. Centralization that proves of fictitious value except as the war master becomes incontinent waster of human quality.

So it is by means of our borrowed culture and the specious middleman we have bred in all departments of our activity that we now reach a dubious debt era—the era of the front-runner and the useful substitute. Have we reached this degradation wherein all is more or less a kind of makeshift? Our very best is no more, at present at least, than adventitious? True? Then we ourselves can likely become no more than just that; and our life and our architecture have no organic (normal) foundation at all. And if so fundamentally wrong there at the root, how can American life ever genuinely become free? The valiant special man (non-common) among us—he alone is free. But even so he is free at his own peril; enemy, and therefore the dislike of the common man pursues him to some bitter end for both.

As things have been with us (now still more so) honest individual freedom, non-conformity, is growing to be a desperate, dangerous adventure for any loyal citizen. I have described true discipline as developed from within, as the expression of the soul instead of something applied by force in some form. As things are, the freedom won by such discipline will only be something on the way to the country poorhouse. Or to jail. We will come to this day of reckoning?

Nevertheless, out of observation of principles of organic architecture at work—with law-abiding respect for the law of natural change in this most successful of all nations—comes this ideal of a true capitalist city designed actually to harness and utilize the terrific forces that built us into the present whirling vortex from the top down.

Can we be a free people and be tolerant of mere *re*form when true form is what we should seek? No form true to our own nature will be made by mere alteration upon any old systems or architecture or old laws we have in desperation cherished. True forms, especially of independence in our modern lives, can only grow up from within the nature of our common life as we live it with our feet on our own soil however high our head in the clouds. Evolution? Perhaps revolution is a necessary feature. I do not know. As Nature herself grows forms so human nature—*her own higher nature*—must always grow buildings, civilizations, on good ground; West and East at last so reconciled as to work independently together. The light of the West is the light of the diamond, iridescent like the stars.

The light of the East glowing incandescent like that of colored gems burning with the lovely light of Earth in the palm of the hand. Why then hate and war with each other? All go to make a proper diadem for civilization—a Culture. And it will take all kinds to make a free world.

So I do venture to believe we as a nation have carried abroad enough good tidings to compensate for our sorrow over wrongly concentrated machine power. This mechanized era may go on with renewed faith, beneath all suffering, go to the root—and radically design the structure of a characteristic organic culture. To succeed in this uncommon endeavor we must commence work square with a fresh perception of *nature's organic laws* as they are now manifest—and actually change wherever or in whatever degree we are able to find and fit our course to them. In architecture we call this recognition of principle "organic" and cultivate "continuity" as a science. It is also the art of equilibrium in all human opportunity. To learn to perceive it is to learn the inevitable purpose of our own Life.

To have and to hold! Yes—well enough when having and holding square *with* nature; but disastrous, if not fatal, unless *giving* and *taking* according to nature! What I write here is directly in line with normal continuity in the law of organic change. As an architect I have observed these laws at work not only in and upon materials of building construction but also upon men and women throughout the vast undeveloped reaches of our already overexploited country. Yes—in the light of this organic ideal—a vast beautiful region from coast to coast and border to border, undeveloped and sadly in need of synthesis.

Time then, for these importunate powers we have been describing to be recognized by politics and education as mere scaffolding of the civilization we—the core of the modern free world—still fervently desire, however we may have betrayed it. Unfortunately, we have now gone so far afield as to mistake the scaffolding for our civilization. Such vital forces as we do have have won so little intelligent recognition. Our machine age culture (the elevation of the ground-plan of our plight) can now afford recognition of no force not really creative! No present commitment we have made to brute force by bomb or mentality can reproduce from seed because the true greatness of a people like ours does not lie in centralized wealth and science promoted and distinguished from profound Art, Architecture and Religion. These three are the soul of a culture. From the union of these with Science comes the freedom of a people.

But I confess that adventitious money increment—a power derived from exaggerated centralization used, as we are now using it, as incentive to desperate human effort—has not been utterly wasted. The techniques released by our machine age have been more rapidly developed than would have been the case otherwise, and that speed is part of our trouble. It may mean more imminent disaster at the point the atom bomb has reached where mechanical forces are running away with man. But such material gains as these might be consciously utilized in the objective *structure* of the new city in our new social state as in our economics and our morals, and—especially now—in our aesthetics also. But can the questionable materialistic "advantages" which centralization has brought to the manhood of our country be justified by the ghastly cost of these "efficiencies" in business, in government, in society, in sportdom no less?

Has not the time come to revaluate our course? Or else we will leave on record no true advance in beneficent civilization. We will have the shortest life of any civilization on record.

Any attempted slavery to material life employed in the name of democracy is folly. The machine and democracy, standing bound together as they are, are fast growing wide apart, only to destroy each other eventually. But by way of each other, they are capable of new vital form and expression in modern art, even in religion as already we have seen in science. But until science is qualified by art and religion truly free and reconciled to both, in co-operation and inspiration vital to new art forms to enrich the spirit, human misery will only deepen.

Again the setting sun all Europe mistook for dawn?

LATTER-DAY CIVILIZATION

Well . . . inwardly I believe that we must recognize openly and use the good in these strange new forms now thrusting at our cities against base imitations (conscious or unconscious) of dead forms now trying so hard and by dishonest means to hide the lack of any significance.

Education is unable to recognize (or unwilling to face) the fact that in these potent changes by mechanical agencies, conscientiously enumerated here, we must turn about to subdivide growing aggregates of machine power, abolish invisible despotisms, and advocate *radical* revision of the growing governing agencies—our bureaucracy. Revisions are necessary now to release and encourage the spirit of human initiative; help broaden, officially and socially, the *voluntary* basis of native manpower; develop and fortify the conscience of the citizen, defend it as inviolate to democracy.

Good education would consist in patiently building up the manly attributes of character that are the basis of true individuality but which we are allowing this machine age to destroy. Education must no longer ignore the fact that democracy proclaims the sovereignty of the individuality? Must our education (like government) continue static because it is organized deeply to distrust Man? And is science able to give us no faith in man as mankind but only tend to take it away?

DEMOCRACY IN OVERALLS

The dream of the free city is to establish democracy on a firmer basis. . . . Is it a dream? A vision certainly. Ideas always precede and configure the facts. But I am here writing no more than the too specific outline of a practical ideal perceiving Change as already upon us. Old phases as well as phrases must come to an end. Graphic and plastic arts and fine art come in at this point to aid in showing just what the universal city and its buildings might be. The different buildings here described have already been given either graphic (the drawing) or three-dimensional (the model) form. To begin, I believe that a general outline of any ideal is better than specific plan or model of its particular features. An ideal once clearly fixed in mind—and the plan will come naturally enough. Fresh undertakings then appear and proceed from generals to particulars with the necessary techniques peculiar to each. True ideas must develop their own technique afresh: The higher the ideal at first the more important and difficult the technique.

To the impatient, critical reader and all architectural eclectics who have come along thus far, these all too broad outlines of the coming free city may seem only one more "Utopia" to join so many harmless dreams that come and go like glowing fireflies in July meadows. But I am not trying to prove a case. My interest lies in sincerely appraising, in our own behalf, elemental changes I see existing or surely coming. There is plenty of evidence now at hand to substantiate all the changes I outline. At least here you have an earnest architect's conscientious study of organic structure ahead based upon manifest circumstances and the experience of a lifetime trying to get organic architecture to come alive as the true-form-of-building for American Democracy. An architect's struggle (so it is) in these United States lies in trying to get any profound study of any sort in the Arts into good form. I am seeing and saying that organic architecture is the only true architecture for our democracy. Democracy will some day realize that life is itself architecture organic, or else both architecture and mankind will become in vain together.

As a people no doubt we are busy sacrificing

the greater usefulness and the only happiness we can ever know in our own name to put our all into the cheaper, lesser "efficiencies," expedient as I see them. It is useless to go on further working for the senseless mechanisms of mere machinery for the landlord, the machine lord and his lady (as they stand) hoping for any sound general profit for the great future culture of this nation—and for the culture of this world. Noble life demands a noble architecture for noble uses of noble men. Lack of culture means what it has always meant: ignoble civilization and therefore imminent downfall.

The true center (the only centralization allowable) in Usonian democracy, is the individual in his true Usonian family home. In that we have the nuclear building we will learn how to build. Integration is vitally necessary to that normal home. Natural differentiation just as necessary. Given intelligent, free, individual choice the home should especially cherish such free choice—eventually based upon a greater range of possible freedom, range for such individual choice in the specific daily cultivation of principles in Architecture as well as in the daily uses we make of Science and Art. In Religion? No less!

Luxury (it, *too,* is primarily a matter of individual quality) would enter the democratic social sense as gratification of more and more developed humane *sensibility,* beauty the concern. Exuberance is beauty but not excess. Yes. Liberty is not license, exaggeration is not exuberance. Every true home should be actually bound to grow from within to dignity and spiritual significance: *grow* by the right concept and practice of building into a pervasive social circumstance: *grow* out of one's own good ground and better self into everybody's light, not in everybody's nor anybody's way. Every man's home his "castle!" No, every man's home his sphere in space—his appropriate place to live in spaciousness. On his own sunlit sward or in wood or strand enhancing all other homes. No less but more than ever this manly home a refuge for the expanding spirit of man the individual. This home is for the citizen of Usonian democracy, our teenager. In *his own home* thus the Broadacre citizen would be not only impregnable. He would be inviolate. This nation indestructible! He would be true exponent of a man's true relationship to his fellow-men because he *is* his fellow-man. He *is* his country. So he would naturally inculcate high ideals in others by practicing them himself. He would insist upon opportunity for others to do no less. External compulsions, personal or official, were never more than weakness continually breeding weaknesses or weaklings. Usonian homemakers of Broadacres would first learn to know all this so well that the citizen would practice this knowledge instinctively in his every public act, not only to the benefit of others who come in contact with him but to gratify something deep in his very nature.

THE AWAKENED CITIZEN

Improvements. Well, "improvements" in the sense of this sense of self are not only on but *of* the ground. Actually they belong to those who make the improvements and learn to use them as features of their own life; use them well in relation to other lives. It would make sound economic sense for the homeowner to surround himself with all such ideal expressions as might seem square with his ideal. He could no longer be compelled to pay unjust penalties for so doing. Advantages flow naturally in upon the enlightened and enlightening democratic unit in this new humane stronghold. Well aware of these, the significance of much that he knew but never realized comes clear. In worldly situations, radical changes necessarily due to fundamental realizations of freedom would render obsolete most of his old educational paraphernalia: destroy nearly all the so-called "traditions" once cherished by his teachers. He *knew* this, but now he *realizes* it. Then to what may he hold fast as he finds himself able to go forward to new life in this new way on his own ground? Power is now to become his own responsibility—power never dreamed of until he thus began to live as a free man. Power now is perpetually renewed from within himself, power appropriate to his new circumstances.

Production with a capital *P* has previously battened and fattened upon the homemaker. At exorbitant rent he has painfully acquired utilitarian conveniences by debt and such modern sanitation as the homemaker may have in this present day of the run-away industrial revolution. But all these and more may now be made from the bottom up and from inside out into one single unit *for him*. Convenience, ten to one in point of economy and true beauty (they are one now) may be his and do for him what he could not ask of "conveniences" heretofore: Electrification, sanitation, gadgetry of the kitchen complete, all utilities lacking individuality, to be delivered to him as is his car, in prefabricated units. Composing the characteristic Usonian abode, great variety of individual choices exists. Choice would naturally *increase* as the new materials—glass, steel, sheet metal, and the new plastics—let his life expand, *understood*. Vision comes into grounds surrounding and he places appropriate gardens around him. Vistas of the landscape become part of his house and life just as his house becomes integral part of neighborhood landscape. The machine properly disciplined by good design brings tangible, fruitful benefits to the homemaker by space interior and exterior—the new time-space concept, as described earlier. What that may mean to his spirit as well as his comfort lies easily within his reach. Luxury for him will consist in his new sense of a harmony—space free is his. However simple this house, it will be well designed and planned *with him for him:* good materials in good design, well executed. To be himself, the Broadacres homemaker will exercise his new sense in the ground plan of the place he is to live in, as well as the scheme of things around him, the spirit that made it free will maintain it so. The reward and refuge of such life as this would be in the free city would consist largely in fresh opportunity to have and to hold his own shelter secure by his own effort in his own atmosphere, free to go, stay or come. And whenever, however, he pleases to go, there is always something nearby worth seeing—a pleasure to go to.

Every man's new standard of space-measurement (we have said it is the man seated in his car) affects him everywhere he goes, and he can go anywhere. But, most of all, the new sense of space affects him where and how he may live. New breadths, increased depths, not only in the simple reaches of the new building he proudly calls home but into the very makeup of his faith in freedom. A feature of his philosophy realized. Thus inner sense of security defends him against imposition leading eventually to "repossession." And it will be just as hard to scare this Usonian out of his sense or his home as to scare him out of himself. The Usonian citizen will find new faith in himself, on his own acreage no longer a man to be afraid or to be afraid of. He will not "huddle." Nor will he run with the pack! Ask him. His faith is in—what?

Now because the American citizen will learn how expanded light, spacious openness and firm cleanliness of significant line in oneness of the whole may be his own, and how all may add to his stature as a man among men, he will not be stampeded. More chary than ever of grandomania, either at home or abroad: to this richly animated, awakened citizen's imagination quiet repose appeals most because beauty is concerned with him and he with beauty. With a sense of rhythmic quality in the appropriateness of plane to quiet length of line, he is able to trace the flowing simplicity of melodious contours of structure as he sees them in what he does to the land itself. Learns from it. The grace of native flowers in garden or meadow or by the roadside—he truly sees—the trees in teeming life of the wood or landscape. Naturally all will be a refreshing feeling of intimacy with Nature; grateful for space to be lived in; the new spaciousness understood, deeply enjoyed. In his new life the truth is he himself "belongs!" Even as hill-slopes, or the beautiful ravines and forests themselves belong and as bees and trees and flowers in them belong so *he* belongs. While at home, the citizen is pleased and pleasing lord of space. He has integrity. Spacious interior freedom becomes him and is the *new reality*. Romantic: he is both introvert and extrovert. No longer is his faith placed in arbitrary hangovers of Roman law because he goes deeper to the organic law beneath. There in Nature is where his new faith in himself is founded and can be defended.

Both physical and spiritual significance his, oneness of life lies in this new more natural sense of himself. The citizen is bound to see and find tremendous spiritual consequences come alive in him. For all of life, love, and the pursuit of happiness is no longer a phrase. It is the architecture of his soul.

Why, then, should citizenry ever be small, dishonest or mean? Why should the citizen deny to others what he has learned to value so highly within himself? Out of independence such as his a new idea of man emerges. He co-operates because it is for him to say either "Yes" or "No" and say so *as his own conscience dictates*!

ROMANCE

This interior sense of space in spaciousness is romantic and growing throughout the world. Well understood, it is the true machine age triumph, a true luxury. And as this sense of space in spaciousness becomes innate to mankind, I believe the American citizen will develop a more concrete freedom than a Greek or a Roman ever knew or even the Goth felt in the Middle Ages. Or any freedom to which West or East has subscribed or aspired. Perhaps greater in range of freedom interior, to go with freedom exterior, than man ever believed could be unless, perhaps, some adventurer like the ancient Arab or American Indian, some romantic like Francois Villon, or people of the earth-loving East sensed, "once upon a time." In sweep, simplicity (especially *in quality*), architecture never surpassed in significance and beauty what may be this awakened citizen's architecture—that of the free City that is a Nation. Again—that new city is nowhere unless everywhere.

Space comes alive, to be enjoyed and lived in, characteristic of this age of the machine. This is our growth, spiritual integration with everyday life. Simple because it is universal conservation of life, happiness is inevitable consequence.

ARCHITECTURE

Such practice of life lies in the province of organic architecture: architecture sure to react upon every practical homemaker's sense of himself. Modern man cannot fail to grow in health of mind as he becomes aware of himself as free. He *is* freedom! Freedom at home makes all men doubly democratic in spirit: Any man now demands the freedom for other men and their nations that he asks for himself because only so may he demand freedom as his "inalienable" *right*? It will not now be too difficult for the Broadacre citizen to see "his" right as no more than "their" right. When the meaning of the word "organic" dawns within the mind of the man, he will demand integrity and significance in everything he has to live with or that he does to others. His awakened eye will see boldly and he will not hesitate to search habitual forms everywhere, rejecting forms he once took for granted when he was only educated not cultured. He now challenges all form. The Usonian of Broadacres will have truth of form or he will have none! This goes out from him to his familiars and to establish better economic and social relations with other nations. It goes out from him to characterize American life—no curse put upon the world by insane exhortations of business to increase private "production" for greater public waste.

The citizen of Broadacres would see political science too as something organic—"the science of human happiness." And see economics that way too. He would reject state department banking and trading as likely to be vicious. Broadacres citizens would also regard philosophy as organic. The simplicities of Laotze and those of Jesus would dawn afresh. To practice them he would learn to find them concrete, effective *forces* that really work. At last the citizen would see that the inner forces at work in his life are organic and therefore prophetic.

DISCIPLINE

So *interior discipline of an Ideal* thus set up in the citizen will go to work. Undreamed of potentialities show in the work of the workman as he becomes responsible to *himself* for himself. He is the only *safe* man because he is the man now disciplined not by government (the police) but from within by himself! Herein lies the great social potential worthy of the greatest of human works of art and science. Democracy itself.

So free men will soon walk abroad in modern times, nobler men among nobler-minded manhood—more than ever potent in making a fairer-minded world. A better sense of proportion now to go with his sense of humor and his true sense of himself.

As world citizen the Usonian's power no longer lies in peddling or meddling or borrowing or lending or becoming stupidly mischievous with

money "abroad." Power no longer in the control of vicarious officialism at public expense. Individual aspiration would never consist in or subsist on imitating anything. First of all—for all—quality. Only because of well-founded confidence in his own strength will man be eager to *share* in the work of the world. The world will be invigorated by his happiness because it will have the vitality of good sense. His actual practice of the democracy we preach will be no less inspiring. Were the world to see this citizen, results would become ideal for all the world. Exemplar in his own life in his own home, feet on his own ground! See a man free, alive.

"WHERE THERE IS NO VISION THE PEOPLE PERISH"

Here, then, a vision? I give you the ideal *practical* democrat: he the Usonian citizen of the great free city of this book. No longer impotent robot: he the potent citizen of the new natural city that is taking place among us already. Then comes a nation as example to free the whole world, to prove that freedom is not several but ever one and indivisible! Practical become integral.

THE WAGE SLAVE

Tillers of the fields, owing to universal electrification and mobility, today may enjoy anything the big city offered the wage-slave of yesterday as reward. White-collarites and industrialists, parasites immured, restless, longing to go from here to there where establishment insures full measure of occupation at work they like. Widening margins of leisure everywhere the machine now insures: a margin that does not mean more or less unemployment for anyone but more time to spend as the independent workman may like to spend time. The workman citizen of our nation must see his native birthright as green: the green of the ground. Once there free on his own, by his own character, skill and voluntary labor he is bound to succeed in "the pursuit of happiness." No other secure basis for happiness is as intelligent as good *use* of good ground. Then, why not go there and learn how—or learn how and go there?

Industrial occupations may then grow to mean to him so much more that no official guaranty of urban "employment" is good enough for him. His own initiative and consciousness of manhood *protected,* here at home! There is no longer reason for a man of good conscience to doubt that all that he is or may become should not work in full harmony *with* other men according to nature and each man be secure in the nature of himself. Therefore all mankind secure. His own nature may be so attuned to the nature of the cosmos that he in himself would be a new, more vital, kind of success. Only through such interior organic process is he (or are we) going to be able to build the city of democracy.

Do you question this Fundamental direction for American citizens of the future? Then first learn the meaning of these words.

"Organic."

"Decentralization."

"Integration."

"Democracy."

Words never properly identified by the American citizen because never properly interpreted to him in action. Then how could the words be applied by him or to his work or his life in this or any culture, ancient or modern? They were misunderstood or misapplied terms by civilization after civilization—civilizations now dead.

The significance of these words (watchwords) may now belong to the awakened American citizen. Qualifications at last for his "vote." An understanding opens to the significance of the law of change— what is insignificant in life fades, falls away as the inner meaning of the words comes clear. Inevitably he will come face to face with *this* new reality in the words of Laotze: *"The reality of the building does not consist in the four walls and roof but in the space within to be lived in."* The significance of this lies where his life is now concerned—with these words.

Former practices of the vicarious power that once meant fortune will leave the twentieth century industrialist all but useless. He was a worker immured in government, in housing or some form of conscription. A conscript to be cast aside. But in the free city homemaking for manhood can mean spiritual stagnation no more nor strangulation of his finer sensitivities. Work, and his home, must be the honor of his own better self. "Home" only then

having all the meaning and privileges it must have in genuine Democracy. New spirit forces are now going to work upon our vast material resources in this new direction—material resources worked upon by whatever spiritual force the free man has left to him. All this force opens to the citizen if he should so decide. No man need be a kept or "Yes" man; if he goes intelligently to his birthright in nature he is now independently a "No" man, if he so chooses. Here now we have the broad base of capital where it belongs—on the ground—the base of the pyramid no longer up in the air.

Only the democratic citizen liberated can put to work forces that make the machine no longer a destructive imposition upon human life, elevating instead of exhausting man's innate spiritual power. Spiritual force in a way of life wherein man feels, thinks, and learns to live anew as a *natural aristocrat.* The ideal Usonian aristocrat, the American citizen could, if he would, use the word "aristocracy" honestly in describing the great new city. A great integrity.

Now here at last, we have capitalism for genuine Democracy. The capitalist himself his own impregnable defense!

NIGHT IS BUT A SHADOW CAST BY THE SUN

Looking back over this book I see it was not written to *please* anyone, not even myself. The same urge impelling me to build has impelled me to write. The book began, 1932, as *The Disappearing City.* 1945, it was expanded into *When Democracy Builds.* Now here entirely rewritten as *The Living City.*

This matter (a direct continuous study beginning 1921) was first presented as "The City" in a lecture at Princeton University. Subsequently that lecture was published with five others by the Princeton University Press. While in Arizona, pushed there by the national breakdown of 1929, the Broadacre City model—12 feet by 12 feet—was made by the Taliesin Fellowship. It was first exhibited at the Industrial Arts Exposition, Radio City, New York, April 15, 1935. This modeling is now a feature of Taliesin.

Does "The Art and Craft of the Machine," the paper first read at Hull House, 1903 [sic] (since translated into seven languages), seem to suffer contradiction here?

No. I then dreaded the machine *unless well in the hand of the creative artist*. Saying so then, I say so now. I knew then that this power we call the Machine was, otherwise, socially malevolent. The creative artist (culture his consideration), I believed, would be in the place where he belongs in a civilization ready to accept the machine but only as a new tool: a new facility capable of improving or destroying man on earth. Well . . . he is not there where he belongs. "The machine" is cutting him off on the ground! He must begin at the beginning again at the root—a radical.

But today the Machine is running away. I find it hard to believe that the machine would go into the creative artist's hand even were that magic hand in true place. It has been too far exploited by industrialism and science at expense to art and true religion.

Machine facilities have increased inordinate quantity production beyond consumption until total mechanization is trying to control distribution and the market. By total industrialism war, more war is always in sight, paid for in advance—all but the bloodshed. The machine is now become more the engine of destruction, and propaganda for increasing our national insecurity by wage-slavery is everywhere in the social fabric of the news. Higher human faculties, which the machine should serve to release in our Democracy, are officially and academically emasculated, the humane interest fast disappearing. That is why the belated rewriting of this—seeming to me now—more timely, more important than ever book, original advocate of organic architecture; again to take the stand for the consumer (the people) as against the ubiquitous, thoughtless producer for profit. The "consumer" now must take what "production" decides to make. Whatever production decides to make, for profit, is all the consumer can get in any line. This antithesis of the democratic process is a menace, a drift toward deadly conformity. For the sake of conformity, we the people get quantity defying quality.

Owing largely to facility beyond our means, since time immemorial no blacker time for Principle has existed than our own "present." Of course, our "present" is no exception to all the "present"

there ever was in time, as history is written.

If the advertising we see spread by the "big-production boys" is indicative of our commercial activity, no lasting benefit of our bomb-throwing extravaganzas on foreign soil will ever get over to us as we live here. Must we of this nation—free—wait for the vitality and depth of a right-minded inevitable free city? The pattern is not to come from "over there." We, if square with the ideal of Democracy, must make a new city. Must we wait for our big-production boys to "cash in" and go to spend their hard-gained profits in heaven or hell, maybe? Of course, *à la mode*—but what mode?

Plainer to me every day that not only our professional streamliners—experts (hired for the backrooms of our big-production boys)—see nothing yet of the citizen's first needs first. The big boys have yet seen nothing at all of *interior* nature on their own.

Production is trying too hard to manufacture the same old things, in a reversion of the same old ignorance of good design that built creatures of the hand, and to manufacture them by *negation of that hand*. Now in a dead house for dead men. And trying, too, to make themselves believe it is a brand new way! How can anyone with half a mind tolerate eventual negation such as this not only of the man who makes the house but of any man who gets the house to live in? And by house I mean also the city and the nation. Negation of Democracy itself is—and therefore—inevitable: a mere matter of time. Education seems to know little or worse. The old steel post and girder framing of the nineteenth century bridge engineer is still a rigid concept to the "expert" in twentieth century architecture. Not one but builds from outside inward instead of from inside outward. Yet the talk is "modern."

Probably our many big city survivals (yes, feudal—plus gadgetry) will escape destruction from inside if not overhead only to find their originals (European cities devastated by us) replanned and built more nearly as a modern city should be than ours. We have had no benefit from the devastating bomb ourselves except to make the bomb, market it and drop it ourselves over "on the other side." So we are likely, as things are, to find ourselves far outmoded by any standard of comparison when the smoke of destruction clears away in the light of reconstruction and V for Victory may look more like V for Vanquished.

Finally, then, this long discourse, hard to write or read, is a sincere attempt to take apart and show (from the inside) the radical simplicities of fate to which our own machine skills have now laid us wide open and try to show how radical eliminations are now essential to our spiritual health, and to the culture, if not the countenance, of democratic civilization itself. These are all changes valid by now if we are to have indigenous culture at all and are not to remain a bastardized civilization with no culture of our own, going all the way down the backstairs of time to the usual untimely end civilizations have hitherto met.

Wholesome destruction may eventually *compel* an open change for improvement that our young architects must accept as a challenge. They can be equal (I think so) to the tremendous task only by seizing upon urban obsolescence to destroy these rubbish-heaps that are with us here at home. Do this by learning how to help the inevitable natural city to go on building itself: the right kind of buildings, built the right way in the right place for the right people—this, and the right kind of city will grow for us. But I see a studied avoidance of such interference by mediocre professional meddlers as a feature of the new "planning" we do not need.

"The Living City" then is nothing less than inspiration, or better, than restraint upon the effects of ill planning by the trustees whose responsibility it is—our young architects.

I hope this architect's book is at least an exhortation for them, a warning for the farmer, a caution and encouragement for the small manufacturer and for national colleges of architecture and agriculture, or such cultural nurseries in this nation as the machine age has raised or razed or carelessly left standing. We cannot achieve our democratic destiny by mere industrialism, however great. We are by nature gifted as a vast agronomy. In the humane proportion of those two—industrialism and agronomy—we will produce the culture that belongs to Democracy organic. And in the word "organic" lies the meaning of

this discourse. So this book is all the more for that great invisible but potent "in-between"—that new *reality* we call, here, his majesty the American citizen.

Democracy! Can we in these United States of America make it work? Or will we in honesty change the name of the politics of our Republic? THE PRESENT IS THE EVER MOVING SHADOW THAT DIVIDES YESTERDAY FROM TOMORROW.

IN THAT LIES HOPE.

APPENDIX
FROM RALPH WALDO EMERSON'S ESSAY ON FARMING

The glory of the farmer is that, in the division of labors, it is his part to create. All trade rests at last on his primitive activity. He stands close to Nature; he obtains from the earth the bread and the meat. The food which was not, he causes to be. The first farmer was the first man, and all historic nobility rests on possession and use of land. Men do not like hard work, but every man has an exceptional respect for tillage, and a feeling that this is the original calling of his race, that he himself is only excused from it by some circumstance which made him delegate it for a time to other hands. If he have not some skill which recommends him to the farmer, some product for which the farmer will give him corn, he must himself return into his due place among the planters. And the profession has in all eyes its ancient charm, as standing nearest to God, the first cause. . . .

Poisoned by town life and town vices, the sufferer resolves: "Well, my children, whom I have injured, shall go back to the land, to be recruited and cured by that which should have been my nursery, and now shall be their hospital." . . .

The farmer times himself to Nature, and acquires that live-long patience which belongs to her. . . .

In the great household of Nature, the farmer stands at the door of the bread-room, and weighs to each his loaf. . . .

The city is always recruited from the country. The men in cities who are the centers of energy, the driving-wheels of trade, politics or practical arts, and the women of beauty and genius, are the children or grandchildren of farmers, and are spending the energies which their fathers' hardy, silent life accumulated in frosty furrows, in poverty, necessity, and darkness.

He is the continuous benefactor. He who digs a well, constructs a stone fountain, plants a grove of trees by the roadside, plants an orchard, builds a durable house, reclaims a swamp, or so much as puts a stone seat by the wayside, makes the land so far lovely and desirable, makes a fortune which he cannot carry away with him, but which is useful to his country long afterwards. The man that works at home helps society at large with somewhat more of certainty than he who devotes himself to charities. If it be true that, not by votes of political parties but by the eternal laws of political economy, slaves are driven out of a slave State as fast as it is surrounded by free States, then the true abolitionist is the farmer, who, heedless of laws and constitutions, stands all day in the field, investing his labor in the land, and making a product with which no forced labor can compete.

We commonly say that the rich man can speak the truth, can afford honesty, can afford independence of opinion and action—and that is the theory of nobility. But it is the rich man in a true sense, that is to say, not the man of large income and large expenditure, but solely the man whose outlay is less than his income and is steadily kept so. . . .

Who are the farmer's servants? Not the Irish, nor the coolies, but Geology and Chemistry, the quarry of the air, the water of the brook, the lightning of the cloud, the castings of the worm, the plough of the frost. Long before he was born, the sun of ages decomposed the rocks, mellowed his land, soaked it with light and heat, covered it with vegetable film, then with forests, and accumulated the sphagnum whose decays made the peat of his meadow.

Science has shown the great circles in which Nature works; the manner in which marine plants balance the marine animals, as the land plants supply the oxygen which the animals consume, and the animals the carbon which the plants absorb. These activities are incessant. Nature works on a method of *all for each and each for all*. The strain that is made on one point bears on every arch and foundation of the structure. There is a perfect solidarity. . . .

Nature is as subtle as she is strong. . . .

Nature suggests every economical expedient somewhere on a great scale. Set out a pine tree, and it dies in the first year, or lives a poor spindle. But Nature drops a pine-cone in Mariposa, and it lives fifteen centuries, grows three or four hundred feet high, and thirty in diameter—grows in a grove of giants, like a colonnade of Thebes. Ask the tree how it was done. It did not grow on a ridge, but in a basin, where it found deep soil, cold enough and dry enough for the pine; defended itself from the sun by growing in groves, and from the wind by the walls of the mountain. The roots that shot deepest, and the stems of happiest exposure, drew the nourishment from the rest, until the less thrifty perished and manured the soil for the stronger, and the mammoth Sequoias rose to their enormous proportions. The traveler who saw them remembered his orchard at home, where every year, in the destroying wind, his forlorn trees pined like suffering virtue. In September, when the pears hang heaviest and are taking from the sun their gay colors, comes usually a gusty day which shakes the whole garden and throws down the heaviest fruit in bruised heaps. The planter took the hint of the Sequoias, built a high wall, or—better—surrounded the orchard with a nursery of birches and evergreens. Thus he had the mountain basin in miniature; and his pears grew to the size of melons, and the vines beneath them ran an eighth of a mile. But this shelter creates a new climate. The wall that keeps off the strong wind keeps off the cold wind. The high wall reflecting the heat back on the soil gives that acre a quadruple share of sunshine—

Enclosing in the garden square
A dead and standing pool of air,

and makes a little Cuba within it, whilst all without is Labrador. . . .

See what the farmer accomplishes by a cart-load of tiles: he alters the climate by letting off water which kept the land cold through constant evaporation, and allows the warm rain to bring down into the roots the temperature of the air and of the surface soil; and he deepens the soil, since the discharge of this standing water allows the roots of his plants to penetrate below the surface to the subsoil, and accelerates the ripening of the crop. . . .

There has been a nightmare bred in England of indigestion and spleen among landlords and loomlords, namely, the dogma that men breed too fast for the powers of the soil; that men multiply in a geometrical ratio, whilst corn multiplies only in an arithmetical; and hence that, the more prosperous we are, the faster we approach these frightful limits: nay, the plight of every new generation is worse than of the foregoing, because the first comers take up the best lands; the next, the second best; and each succeeding wave of population is driven to poorer, so that the land is ever yielding less returns to enlarging hosts of eaters. Henry Carey of Philadelphia replied: "Not so, Mr. Malthus, but just the opposite of so is the fact."

The first planter, the savage, without helpers, without tools, looking chiefly to safety from his enemy—man or beast—takes poor land. The better lands are loaded with timber, which he cannot clear; they need drainage, which he cannot attempt. . . .

Meantime we cannot enumerate the incidents and agents of the farm without reverting to their influence on the farmer. He carries out this cumulative preparation of means to their last effect. This crust of soil which ages have refined he refines again for the feeding of a civil and instructed people. The great elements with which he deals cannot leave him unaffected, or unconscious of his ministry; but their influence somewhat resembles that which the same Nature has on the child—of subduing and silencing him. We see the farmer with pleasure and respect when we think what powers and utilities are so meekly worn. He knows every secret of labor; he changes the face of the landscape. Put him on a new planet and he would know where to begin; yet there is no arrogance in his bearing, but a perfect gentleness. The farmer stands well on the world.

Plain in manners as in dress, he would not shine in palaces; he is absolutely unknown and inadmissible therein; living or dying, he never shall be heard of in them; yet the drawing-room heroes put down beside him would shrivel in his presence; he solid and unexpressive, they expressed to gold-leaf. But he stands well on the world—as Adam did, as an Indian does, or Homer's heroes, Agamemnon or Achilles, do. He is a person whom a poet of any clime—Milton, Firdusi, or Cervantes—would appreciate as being really a piece of the old Nature, comparable to sun and moon, rainbow and flood; because he is, as all natural persons are, representative of Nature as much as these.

That uncorrupted behavior which we admire in animals and in young children belongs to him, to the hunter, the sailor—the man who lives in the presence of Nature. Cities force growth and make men talkative and entertaining, but they make them artificial. What possesses interest for us is the *naturel* of each, his constitutional excellence. This is forever a surprise, engaging and lovely; we cannot be satiated with knowing it, and about it; and it is this which the conversation with Nature cherishes and guards.

1. See *Frank Lloyd Wright Collected Writings Volume 3*, pp. 70–112.

2. University of Chicago Press.

3. *The Living City*, pp. 343.

4. FLLW note from original text: Samuel Butler's suggestion of a name for our nameless nation (see his *Erewhon*).

5. St. Marks-in-the-Bouwerie, 1929, for William Norman Guthrie. Unbuilt project. See *The Story of the Tower* in this volume.

6. Arizona Biltmore Hotel, Phoenix, Arizona, opened 1929. San Marcos in the Desert for Alexander Chandler, Chandler, Arizona, 1928. Unbuilt project.

7. Charles H., Warren, Jr., and Albert Chase McArthur. Charles and Warren were active in building tourism in Arizona in the early years of statehood. Promoters of a number of hotels in the state, they invited brother Albert to design the Arizona Biltmore Hotel. See Robert L. Sweeney, *Wright in Hollywood: Visions of a New Architecture*, The Architectural History Foundation (MIT Press), 1994.

8. Design for summer colony at Lake Tahoe, California, 1922. It included barges and teepee-like cabins. Unbuilt project.

CUT RUG TO
FIT FIXTURES

A CULTURE OF OUR OWN

Of all that Wright had written up to the time this article was published, three months before his death, perhaps this text best sums up his ideas. He defines his vision of culture in the United States, of architecture, of the necessity for beauty. As his architectural forms simultaneously became both stronger and simpler toward the end of his life, his writing became clearer and more precise. In this article he wove together a splendid totality of his thoughts; his criticisms are less harsh, his salient ideas more succinct, his solutions more apparent—and hope is ever present. [Progressive, January 1959]

I WOULD LIKE TO SAY A WORD FOR CULTURE—INDIGENOUS, American culture—as distinguished from American education, education not being on speaking terms with culture at the present time. There is a great difference. I do not think that we, as a people, are sufficiently aware of that difference.

For instance, in the garden is the little larkspur; charming little flower, lovely pattern. Dutchmen saw it, admired it, and gave it "culture." They found, by going over to the root, what the little plant loved best, tried it—and it flourished. They took the more promising ones, gave them more of what they liked, and kept this up until now, owing to patience and skill in culture, we have the queen of the garden: we call it delphinium.

I imagine that if you want an architect, a painter, a teacher, a sculptor, if you want any expression of our life which you can say is directly and intimately related to culture, that is the proper process. I can't see how we are going to get true culture out of the trampling of the herd. Probably that is why we of Taliesin are now way off in the western countryside with a group of students who come from all over the world to sit and work and live in an atmosphere and have the doors and windows open through which they see something which they love and learn to practice. But in American life today, culture such as we have is not indigenous—not our own.

We have lived a long time as an independent civilization—more than 175 years—and have done little in that time to make life something beautiful of our own. There is no true culture that is not indigenous. Even the Gothic atmosphere in which we so often sit was, in its day, an integral expression of the human soul. We have it with us today chiefly because there were in it elements of the beautiful. Nothing, I believe, that we have in American thought or enterprise can be a great success and bear fruit unless it is in some respects beautiful. The beautiful always "pays off." So far as an architect's human experience goes, it is the only pay-off.

Today, what is "beautiful" in American life? We have what we call modern architecture. But most of it is not new. Modern is not necessarily new—as new would be necessarily modern. We have novelty, we have the old steel frames with the new glass effects—but in structure or form, no change of thought.

Architecture is out of the ground into the light—by its nature a great integrity. Without that in-

Max Hoffman House Carpet Design (executed for Taliesin, Spring Green, Wisconsin). 1957. Plan. Pencil and color pencil on tracing paper, 36x34". FLLW Fdn#5707.002

tegrity, what hope is there for a future life for the building or its makers? There is no joy possible to us in the culture of our country until we too recognize the integrity of the indigenous in whatever we call culture. Taste is not sufficient. Taste is a matter of ignorance. You taste; you like. You taste again because it pleases you, but you will "taste" because you don't know. If you knew you wouldn't have to taste, so knowledge is what we need for culture. Can't we in some manner treat the youth of our country so that they are not merely educated, but developed and cultivated according to the nature of our own life, our circumstances, our new opportunities?

Science has so far outrun what we call civilization. Nearly everything we have, including the city we live in, is dated. There is no more unfortunate instance of a survival of ancient customs than our present great city of today. It is still the medieval plan. Old. The Middle Ages developed it, and there it was genuine and useful, because only by way of the city could culture be had. But now, quite differently, it is difficult to get culture by way of the city. You have to get away from it to find out where culture lies and to share it. It is quite impossible to create a culture where people are so crowded as in the city—elbows in each others' ribs, trampling on each others' feet, everybody crowding to prepare for more crowds. The crowd becomes the ideal, and the crowd, of course, is the common man.

Somebody asked me the other day, "You've been talking a lot about the common man, what do you mean?" The common man is a man who believes in only what he sees and sees only what he can put his hand on. He may be a truck driver, a college president, or a preacher. He is not on speaking terms with progress; progress must come in spite of him, even though it is for him.

In these many years of practicing architecture I have come to regard the common man as the enemy of culture. That should be the other way around. But the common man is becoming more and more the prevailing American: more and more powerful because he is numerical, and politics depends on numbers. If a man wants to be President of the United States, or if he would be a success along almost any line, he must cater to this common man. So the common man may have brought our democracy, but not the feeling our ancestors had. They were sick of a phony aristocracy—an aristocracy that was handed down as a privilege or handed out by self-interests.

They thought that if all men were free and equal, we would eventually have the greatest and the best in mankind as a natural consequence. They felt that if human nature were only once able to toe the mark equally, and self-improvement was available to all, out of it we would get a new—an innate—aristocracy. Thomas Jefferson said as much. And out of that new aristocracy we would probably become the most fruitful, happy, creative, productive nation on earth.

Well, there is something the matter. There seems to have been something wrong with that ideal of an integral aristocracy—not an aristocracy conferred but won from within the man by his character, by his own effort. Had we followed those precepts, those hopes, of our ancestors, we would have today an architecture and an art of our own. Because architecture is the basic endeavor of mankind, the mother art, architecture *presents* man. Literature tells you about him; painting will picture him to you; you can listen and hear him. But if you want to realize him and experience him, go into his buildings. That is where you will find him *as he is*. He can't hide from you there. He can't hide from himself. So until we have indigenous architecture and understand what it means to live in it, until we know the difference between a good building and a bad one, and know what makes the one good and the other inferior, or merely superficial, how can we claim to have a culture?

Why and where have we missed the thing so essential to our future happiness and the very life of our democracy?

Most of us have gone somewhere to be educated. Liebermeister's definition of a high-brow is a man educated far beyond his capacity, and I believe that is what is happening to most of us: we are being educated far beyond our capacity and are missing native, natural culture. Now, of course, it is hard to "culture" the trampling of the herd. It is difficult, if not impossible, to take 20,000 students in a single university and give them anything at all commensurate with what is known as culture, or ought to be known as culture. Is that why we are not trying it?

Out of our efforts we get specimens, we get fragments, but only shallow characteristics. We get traits, but we don't get a developed individual. If American democracy means anything at all, it means "the sovereignty of the individual." That is the dignity and the beauty of the faith we live under and live for. If we do not develop and use our own best and bravest; if this numerical affair of politics is to wipe out all thought and feeling of our ancestors, I think, as Lord Acton said, we will probably be the shortest-lived civilization in history and the lowest form of socialism in existence. It looks now as though we were headed in that direction, and I believe that unless we wake up and do something definite, to rescue ourselves from this trend toward equalitarianism, toward the idea that every man is as good as every other other man, that we will find ourselves settled in it.

The uncommon man is extremely unpopular; as H. I. Phillips said, he "is now unconstitutional." There is one place at least where we can see our failure, one place where we put our finger on something wrong. Why should we always calculate, arrange, and conduct ourselves by way of numbers? What democracy means is quality, not quantity. And when quantity lacks quality, don't talk about democracy. Quantity and quality are enemies. To me the stigma of communism lies in the fact that the individual signs away his sovereignty as an individual to a government. I think that is the man's degradation.

Our universities? Look at them from the standpoint of architecture—a heterogeneous collection of inept antiquities, life gone out of them long ago. The young go there and form hallowed associations with unworthy things, unworthy atmospheres, and they come away with that association. The first thing education should do if it were on speaking terms with culture would be to teach boys and girls how to live beautifully in a beautiful environment, to know what it is not to have a taste-built culture, such as we have had, which will fall apart at any time, and which is falling apart now. (I wish it might fall apart even more quickly—we might then have something

we could call our own. We might have something worthy of Thomas Jefferson and his aristocracy.)

I never go to Washington that I don't go to the foot of the stair in the Capitol with the big picture of Washington crossing the Delaware to look at the effigy—I won't call it sculpture—of Thomas Jefferson. He is the only one of the whole series whose clothes fit him. Of course it isn't Thomas Jefferson, but even his effigy is worthy of a bended knee from every living American. He didn't live long enough to become aware of organic architecture, but he prophesied it when he built a little four-inch wall on a curve so that the four-inch-thick wall would stand. Davy Crockett showed something of it when he tied the tail of a coon to the back of his coonskin cap.

You see, perhaps, what we have missed in our educational development: culture. Culture lies in *the nature of things; it is of* the nature of the thing, *for* the nature of the thing. It is only by way of a nature study intimate, persistent, relentless, that young men or women can inform themselves of what constitutes reality in this life. I don't believe they can get it just by going to any university or to any educational institution.

The thing we need most in our nation today is a *culture of our own!* And we cannot get it out of books. We cannot get it by bending the knee to the past too much. Victor Hugo has pointed out to us in a memorable chapter of *The Hunchback of Notre Dame* that the Renaissance, which we have copied (and there has been a renaissance in Gothic, of our own colonial, a renaissance in all ways), was the restatement of restatements, and he saw that art could be no restatement, that "the one will kill the other." So he declared that the Renaissance was the setting sun all Europe mistook for the dawn.

Architecture had died, and has been dead 500 years, so far as any true vitality is concerned. It is now coming alive again as Hugo prophesied it would. It was his thought, I believe, knowing now so well that art can be no restatement, that by now no new meanings, new ways would enable us to think straight, act with courage again, and provide ourselves with a living culture worthy of our freedom.

PREAMBLE TO *THE WONDERFUL WORLD OF ARCHITECTURE*

This opening message, in Wright's handwriting, was found on his desk the morning he died. It was to preface a book about architecture for young people as part of a British publisher's series entitled "The Wonderful World Of . . . ." Other titles in the series included books on mathematics, theater, and music.[1] In 1957, when Wright was on his way back to the United States from Iraq, he was invited to stop in London to confer with the publisher at Rathbone Press, about this history of architecture from ancient times to the present. He accepted the task and looked forward to writing the book. After speaking with his apprentices about the task, he spent long hours creating lists and charts pertaining to the architecture of ancient cultures as well as more recent ones. But other, more pressing work in the studio at Taliesin—buildings to design, works going into construction (the Guggenheim Museum had started construction at this time)—kept him away from the text for this series. He was also working on the book The Living City.

He was not able to write more than this short foreword, but in it is to be found one of the most moving and reverential treatises—however brief—on the meaning of architecture: "where space is embodied in the world of form we call architecture. This is the greatest consequence of the life of art by mankind as man comes from his aboriginal cave on the way from his gods to God." [Preamble to The Wonderful World of Architecture, *in* Architecture: Man in Possession of His Earth, *Doubleday & Company, Garden City, New York, 1962]*

BUILDING IS A CIRCUMSTANCE MAN SHARES WITH ANIMALS, birds, the fish and the insect. But architecture—great mother-art—begins where such creature-building leaves off and man's sovereignty—his spirit—reigns. Lower orders of life build by hereditary instinct: sea shells, bird-nests, the honeycomb of the bee, the citadel of the ant. All such creature-building is a gift by nature. In bewildering variety we find in lives of the creatures basis of earthly building long before man's civilization of himself began or ever could begin to appear, as architecture.

So, although architecture is building, this vast world of creature-building is not architecture. Well informed by heredity, its beauty is natural—for instance, the tortoise-shell fashioned by the awkward turtle. All creature-building is elemental and its beauty inevitable. We see this in the little sea-houses picked up on the seashore or found miraculously on the bottom of the sea. This creature-world builds with an elementary sense of unity circumscribed by the actual circumstances of its own life and environment. Beauty, then, is the consequence of innate gift. So we see the unity of being, with the forces that measure, determine and mature this gift of nature-building by heredity.

The plant also builds; growing from seed to root, stem and branch, in order to carry the exquisite flower and consequent fruit. The tree itself rises to majesty. Congruity, continuity and plasticity we see as qualities throughout all natural building. Beauty is due to some mystic innate-power elemental as life is to life itself. Harmony is organic and comes forth to the human eye. Everywhere creature-life is so lived and it appeals to our sense of the appropriate. We call this concordance beauty and we see it as a great gift of nature.

Man, though himself originally a nature-pattern like the antelope and the horse, seems to have had no such in-born building instruction. Man seems to be dependent upon inspiration from a higher source. Neither by heredity nor by instinct does man succeed in the life-beautiful. He seems to have missed much of this accord, concord and simplicity and instead left a trail of ugliness in his wake, instead of what we call this reality of nature—beauty. In all of man's attempted civilizations this natural right to beauty seems left to man's vision of himself and the affair seems to rest not so much in his education as in the culture of his spirit.

Not until the spirit of man becomes conscious of *need* for the benison of beauty *in his way of being* in order to sustain his soul and uplift his spirit as well as comfort and protect his body, does man himself seem to share the instinct for beauty with subordinate orders and forms of life. So man's building is largely the mere craft of the carpenter with his square. By using his multifarious sciences man is furnished and circumscribed until he awakens; to the vision of the intrinsic truth of form. Then beauty comes to his rescue and we have architecture—the mother-art of human-kind. As a consequence we also see sculpture, painting and music.

Science may produce a civilization but not a culture. Man's life under science alone stays sterile. These crafts in essence are similar to that of the carpenter's square. Due to this, recourse in building is that of "the rectilinear frame of reference," his intellectual deduction by way of the carpenter. The engineer is a scientist, but however ingenious and inventive he may be, he is not a creative artist. He is without true reference to the form of organic harmonics to be found as the determining circumstance of man's creative life. Qualities that should characterize man and enable him to rise above his protoplasmic associates on earth seem rare—hard to come by. But man's great gift lies in his vision. Owing to

over-reliance on science, too seldom is this vision turned inward toward the beauty of himself: man's own spiritual-haven. When vision does come into his being and as the mind of man takes hold of his destiny, beauty becomes a vital experience of great consequence to him. There and then, beyond the instincts of the lower orders of life on lower levels of being, we have man's creative architecture: the greatest proof of his immortal soul. To qualify his life on earth his art has more and more consciously grown out of his own spirit overcoming the obstructions by science of the circumstances of his earthly life. Man's necessities include the spiritual life and out of this his buildings as architecture grew, the very flower and fruit of human vision. Architecture lies deep as the basic culture of all civilizations, serving and served by the arts of sculpture, painting and music.

Through his architecture we shall see how man has triumphed over mere building during the past ages: see how ethnic eccentricities varied his vision and molded "style." Finally, we shall see how great changes in his life have developed his architecture as recorded by and for posterity.

In the animal kingdom we may see form always following function. But man sees form and function as one of the imaginative realm, where space is embodied in the world of form we call architecture. This is the greatest consequence of the life of art by mankind as man comes from his aboriginal cave on the way from his gods to God.

As man—the savage—emerges from the natural cave to build one of his own, origins of the history of architecture are lost in perspective. As he civilized himself he adorned these artificial caves as he set them upon the ground out under the sun. Soon after came buildings from the mind of man himself. He created space in which to live; not only protected from the elements but protected from his fellow man as well. But that was not enough—to live content, now civilized, he *meant* to make these cave-buildings beautiful. Then was architecture born.

1. J. B. Priestley, *The Wonderful World of Theatre,* and Lord Bertrand Russell, *The Wonderful World of Mathematics,* edited by James Fisher and Wolfgang Foges, Doubleday & Company, Garden City, New York, 1962.

INDEX

Page numbers in *italics* refer to illustrations.